A detailed history of
BRITISH RAILWAYS STANDARD STEAM LOCOMOTIVES

Volume Two: The 4-6-0 and 2-6-0 Classes

THE RAILWAY CORRESPONDENCE AND TRAVEL SOCIETY
2003

Cover photo: 73089 *Maid of Astolat* awaits departure from Nine Elms Shed on a fine cool winter day, 15th December 1962.
(R.C. Riley)

A SECTION OF COLOUR ILLUSTRATIONS IS PRESENTED ON PAGES 132-139

ISBN 090 1115 93 2

Published by the Railway Correspondence and Travel Society,
Foxwood House, 7 Cherry Fields, Peterborough, PE2 5XD, England

COVER DESIGN by
JOHN HOLROYD

Printed by The Amadeus Press, Cleckheaton
Page Layout by Highlight Type Bureau Ltd, Bradford

Double chimney 75070 leaves Southampton Terminus en route to Fareham and Gosport with the RCTS 'Solent Limited' rail tour of 20th March 1966; details of this working are given in the text.

(P.J. Russell)

CONTENTS

INDEX OF TABLES, APPENDICES AND DIAGRAMS

Appendices

Diagrams

PREFACE

This book is the third to appear in a series of four volumes which the Railway Correspondence and Travel Society is producing to cover the British Railways Standard Steam Locomotives. They were designed, following Nationalisation of Britain's railways on 1st January 1948, with a life expectancy of forty years. The plan envisaged twelve locomotive classes but a change in policy in the middle fifties dictated a rapid change to diesel and later electric traction. Nine hundred and ninety nine engines were actually constructed but they all had a short life because of this policy change.

John Walford, the author, has described in this book the history of five classes which cover the 4-6-0 and 2-6-0 locomotives. He has been supported by a number of RCTS members and others with a keen interest including some railwaymen who had working experience with these engines. Others have been generous with photographs which have been used to illustrate the text and also to aid research into liveries and detail features of locomotive design. The names are recorded of those who have assisted with the contents of this book.

There is quite a lot of missing information, however, as British Railways during the fifties and sixties did not keep records as conscientiously as in earlier years probably due to the rapid demise of steam traction. Locomotives were also transferred frequently between sheds as steam was being eliminated completely from whole districts. Some reallocations, although planned, did not actually occur due to the speed of the change. Any additional information which comes to light will be included in volume four of the series. I shall be very grateful on behalf of the RCTS to hear from readers with regard to new information.

R.K. Taylor,
(Hon. Editor, British Railways Standard Steam Locomotive series)
'The Meadows',
Bardon Mill,
Hexham
Northumberland
NE47 7AA

SUMMARY OF BRITISH RAILWAYS
STANDARD 4-6-0 AND 2-6-0 CLASSES

WHEEL ARRANGEMENT	POWER CLASS	NUMBERS	PARENT DESIGN WORKS	BUILDING WORKS	PERIOD OF BUILDING	NO. IN CLASS
4-6-0	5	73000-171	DONCASTER	DERBY, DONCASTER	1951-7	172
4-6-0	4	75000-79	BRIGHTON	SWINDON	1951-7	80
2-6-0	4	76000-114	DONCASTER	DONCASTER, HORWICH	1952-7	115
2-6-0	3	77000-19	SWINDON	SWINDON	1954	20
2-6-0	2	78000-64	DERBY	DARLINGTON	1952-6	65
					TOTAL	452

BUILDING WORKSHOPS	CLASSES					TOTAL NO. OF ENGINES
	73000	75000	76000	77000	78000	
DARLINGTON	–	–	–	–	65	65
DERBY	130	–	–	–	–	130
DONCASTER	42	–	70	–	–	112
HORWICH	–	–	45	–	–	45
SWINDON	–	80	–	20	–	100
TOTALS	172	80	115	20	65	452

ABBREVIATIONS USED IN THIS BOOK

Companies and Organisations

BR	British Railways
	British Rail (from 1.1965)
CLC	Cheshire Lines Committee
CR	Caledonian Railway
ER	Eastern Region
FA	Football Association
GC/GCR	Great Central Railway
GE/GER	Great Eastern Railway
GNR	Great Northern Railway
GNSR	Great North of Scotland Railway
GSWR	Glasgow & South Western Railway
GWR	Great Western Railway
HBR	Hull & Barnsley Railway
ICI	Imperial Chemical Industries
LCGB	Locomotive Club of Great Britain
LMR	London Midland Region
LMS	London Midland & Scottish Railway
LNER	London & North Eastern Railway
LNWR	London & North Western Railway
LSWR	London & South Western Railway
LTE	London Transport Executive
LYR/L&YR	Lancashire & Yorkshire Railway
M&GN	Midland & Great Northern Railway
MR	Midland Railway
MSWJR	Midland & South Western Junction Railway
NBR	North British Railway
NBL	North British Locomotive Company
NER	North Eastern Railway (pre-1923)
	North Eastern Region (1948-1967)
P&O	Peninsular & Oriental Steam Navigation Company
RCTS	Railway Correspondence & Travel Society
ROD	Railway Operating Division (Royal Engineers)
ScR	Scottish Region
S&DJR	Somerset & Dorset Joint Railway
SECR	South Eastern & Chatham Railway
SKF	SKEFCO (a global bearing manufacturer)
SMJR	Stratford on Avon & Midland Junction Railway
SR	Southern Railway (pre-1948)
	Southern Region (from 1.1.1948)
WD	War Department
WR	Western Region

Other Abbreviations

ATC	Automatic Train Control
AWS	Automatic Warning System
BT	British Thermal
BSS	British Standards Specification
Cl.	Class
CME	Chief Mechanical Engineer
CM&EE	Chief Mechanical and Electrical Engineer
cu. ft.	cubic feet
cwt	Hundredweight
DMU	Diesel Multiple Unit
ECML	East Coast Main Line
Fig.	Figure
Galls	Gallons
FO	Fridays Only
HP	High Pressure
lb	Pounds (weight)
LP	Low Pressure
Max	Maximum
Min	Minimum
mph	miles per hour
MPD	Motive Power Depot
MT	Mixed Traffic
N/A	Not Available/Not Applicable
p.s.i.	Pounds per square inch
p.w.	Permanent Way
p.w.s.	Permanent Way Slack (Speed restriction)
RA	Route Availability
Ref.	Reference
RT	Recovery Time
Sch	Schedule
Sec	Seconds
Sigs.	Signals
SO	Saturdays Only
sq. ft.	Square feet
SX	Saturdays Excepted
SuX	Sundays Excepted
T	Tank Engine
TIA	Traitement Intégral Armand (French Water Treatment System)
TOPS	Total Operations Processing System
WCML	West Coast Main Line

Notes

This volume makes frequent reference to locomotive sheds and depots. Some of their names may be unfamiliar to some readers. Appendix 6 provides a selected list of depots to which the Standard 4-6-0 and 2-6-0 classes were allocated or were regular visitors. Although not devised until well after the withdrawal of steam traction from British Railways, the widely recognised TOPS classification system is used in this book as a simplified means for the identification of non-steam locomotive classes.

THE 4-6-0 AND 2-6-0 CLASSES

John Walford

1. INTRODUCTION

The Standard locomotive classes introduced after the formation of British Railways on the first of January 1948 represented the final attempt to produce a comprehensive range of steam designs suitable for the requirements of both main line and secondary duties for the rail network in Great Britain. The decision to go for steam traction was the only realistic option at the time. The United Kingdom was still in a period of recovery after World War II. The finance required for the electrification of the major routes was simply not available at a time of austerity and materials rationing. Although the LMS with H.G.Ivatt as Chief Mechanical Engineer had rolled out the first main line diesel electric locomotive, number 10000, in the last few weeks of 1947, diesel traction in Europe was still at the early stages of development. Much more progress on dieselisation had been made in the 1940s in the USA and although some novel steam designs were emerging, many major rail networks there were rapidly converting to diesel traction to the extent that there was little or no spare capacity for manufacturers to consider supplying European markets. In any case the latter would have required extensive redesign work to conform to their more restricted loading gauges. Lack of foreign exchange in the UK, both for overseas capital purchases and the ongoing imports of fuel oil were also a significant factor; as a side issue the latter constraint also affected the extent to which steam locomotives in the UK could be converted from coal to oil burning.

On the positive side, the wealth of expertise in steam locomotive design and operation within Great Britain meant that a large number of engines could be manufactured and put to work quickly, cheaply and efficiently. Ample supplies of domestic coal production, albeit of varying quality, were also available. Thus, the first Standard classes designed for British Railways were based on steam power. Long before the completion of the manufacturing programme for the Standard designs in 1960 however, it was clear that with the continuing rapid development of powerful and robust diesel units and the obvious economic advantages of electrification, the days of steam locomotive operation on British Railways would be numbered in years rather than in decades.

The post war situation of Britain's railways was not good. The infrastructure had inevitably been run down through intensive use and lack of both capital and opportunity for modernisation. Working conditions were dirty and uncomfortable, both for footplate crew and maintenance personnel, which did little to attract skilled staff already in short supply. Any new steam locomotive designs would have to take these factors into account. The situation also clearly called for as small a number of classes with as many interchangeable parts as possible. This would minimise the amount of working capital tied up in spares and reduce the time and cost of the training required for shed staff to provide a first class maintenance service. The locomotives would need to be simple to construct, robust in service and easy to maintain. They should be capable of high mileages between overhauls and sustained high quality performance under all conditions especially bearing in mind the varying quality of available coal supplies.

Of the four major companies taken into nationalisation in 1948, ie. the GWR, LMS, LNER and SR, the first two named had gone further with the standardisation concept than the others. Under successive Locomotive Superintendents and Chief Mechnical Engineers from G.J.Churchward, C.B.Collett and F.W.Hawksworth on the GWR and W.A.Stanier, C.E.Fairburn and H.G.Ivatt on the LMS robust standard types had been developed for most requirements.

After the end of World War II, the LMS had taken locomotive design a stage further with the adoption in new designs of hopper ashpans, rocking grates and self cleaning smokeboxes for ease of preparation and maintenance. The LMS was thus regarded as in the vanguard of locomotive development in Great Britain at that time. By 1946 further refinement of the standardisation concept resulted in the designation of eight classes of locomotive as sufficient for the company's needs for all main and secondary line duties. These types together with the standard LMS 0-6-0 diesel shunter and a few small specialised classes of steam tank locomotives mainly used for shunting in dockland areas were to be built to replace all other classes.

Given this background, it was perhaps no surprise when a former LMS engineer, R.A.Riddles was appointed to the new Railway Executive to take charge of all mechanical and electrical matters. He had held several senior positions within the LMS including principal assistant to Stanier from 1935-7. Later, in 1941 Riddles had been seconded to the Ministry of Supply and was responsible for the design of the WD 2-8-0s and 2-10-0s produced during World War II. In 1943 he returned to the LMS and in due course was made vice president for all engineering matters. In this capacity he was the most senior locomotive engineer in any of the Groups at the end of 1947 and an obvious candidate to take the mechanical and electrical engineering portfolio in the new nationalised concern. Not unnaturally, Riddles chose former colleagues, key members of Stanier's locomotive development team, to assist him in the new enterprise. R.C.Bond became Chief Officer for locomotive construction and maintenance and E.S.Cox was made the Executive Officer responsible for design. The latter was no stranger to the concept of standard locomotive design as he had assisted George Hughes, the first CME of the LMS, in the preparation of proposals for some dozen new standard classes put before the board of the newly-formed LMS in April 1924.

These moves inevitably resulted in a considerable, although by no means exclusive, LMS influence over the new Standard designs. After much discussion it was eventually concluded that twelve locomotive classes would be necessary to fulfil the requirements of the new British Railways. A comparison between this and Ivatt's scheme for standardising the LMS locomotive fleet in 1946 is given in Table 1.

Of the five classes which are the subject of this volume, three were directly derived from former LMS designs; these were:

Class 5 4-6-0 (73XXX): essentially the next stage in the development of the tried and tested LMS mixed traffic Cl. 5 4-6-0, the famous 'Black Five' as introduced by Stanier in 1934 and later developed by Ivatt. Class size: 172.

TABLE 1

Comparison of Standard Locomotive Schemes
British Railways 1951 and LMS 1946

Traffic Requirement	British Railways 1951 Scheme	LMS 1946 Scheme
Class 8 Express Passenger	71XXX Pacific 'Duke of Gloucester'	Coronation Pacific
Class 7 Express Passenger	70XXX Pacific 'Britannia'	Rebuilt Royal Scot 4-6-0
Class 6 Express Passenger	72XXX Pacific 'Clan'	Not required
Class 5 Mixed Traffic	73XXX 4-6-0	Stanier Class 5 4-6-0
Class 4 Mixed Traffic	75XXX 4-6-0	Not required
Class 4 Mixed Traffic (reduced axle load)	76XXX 2-6-0	Ivatt Class 4 2-6-0
Class 3 Mixed Traffic	77XXX 2-6-0	Not required
Class 2 Mixed Traffic	78XXX 2-6-0	Ivatt Class 2 2-6-0
Class 4 Tank Engine	80XXX 2-6-4T	Fairburn Class 4 2-6-4T
Class 3 Tank Engine	82XXX 2-6-2T	Not required
Class 2 Tank Engine	84XXX 2-6-2T	Ivatt Class 2 2-6-2T
Class Heavy Freight	92XXX Class 9F 2-10-0	Stanier Class 8F 2-8-0

Note: Of the four BR Standard classes considered superfluous in the LMS 1946 scheme, two of them, the Clan Pacifics (72XXX) and the Class 3 2-6-0s (77XXX) had the fewest individual class members (apart from the solitary 71000, *Duke of Gloucester*), ten in the case of the Clans and twenty for the Class 3s. The other two designs, the Class 4 4-6-0s (75XXX) and the Class 3 2-6-2 tank engines (82XXX) were introduced specifically in response to the WR's perceived requirements. It is perhaps ironic that allocations of the Class 4 4-6-0s to the WR were relatively few, the engines probably performing their best work on the SR. The class eventually achieved distinction towards the end of steam on the section for which they were probably designed, the former GWR Cambrian lines from Shrewsbury to the Welsh coast; by this time however, the route was under the control of the LMR.

Class 4 2-6-0 (76XXX): derived from the LMS Ivatt Cl. 4 2-6-0 (43XXX) which had been developed as a replacement for the standard LMS Cl. 4F 0-6-0 freight engine; the 2-6-0s were also at home on secondary passenger duties to which they were more suited than the 0-6-0s. Class size: 115.

Class 2 2-6-0 (78XXX): virtually identical to the LMS Ivatt Cl. 2 2-6-0 (464XX-465XX) for light mixed traffic branch line work. Class size: 65.

The two remaining Standard designs were regarded as unnecessary in Ivatt's LMS scheme, their duties being considered to fall within the remit of a Cl. 4 2-6-4 tank engine or the Cl. 2 2-6-0; these designs were:

Class 4 4-6-0 (75XXX): a tender version of the LMS Cl. 4 2-6-4 tank engine originally designed with the WR in mind for longer distance running on lines where a Cl. 5 4-6-0 would be too heavy. Class size: 80.

Class 3 2-6-0 (77XXX): development based on a GWR Swindon designed boiler for mixed traffic duties on branch lines where an engine more powerful than a Cl. 2 2-6-0 was required but where the track could not stand the weight of a Cl. 4 2-6-0. Class size: 20.

The above five mixed traffic tender classes, totalling 452 engines, added up to approaching half the total of 999 examples built to the twelve Standard designs. It had always been the intention throughout the exercise to strengthen the medium size mixed traffic fleet as many of the types performing branch line and secondary duties up to Nationalisation were there because they had been displaced from main line work by newer classes. Over the whole system almost half of this secondary fleet was over-age and some were very elderly indeed. Keeping such an ageing and diverse fleet operational was inevitably a costly business and the new designs were welcomed as a means of significantly reducing overall operating costs. Apart from the Cl. 5 4-6-0s, the four other classes were thus unusual in British railway practice in that they were sent brand new to replace much older secondary duty types.

Design of the new classes was much influenced by experience with the S160 Cl. 2-8-0s built by Alco, Baldwin and Lima in the USA and sent to the UK in 1943/4 for the war effort in Europe. These locomotives were regularly noted at work on the British system prior to their being shipped over to northern France after the June 1944 D-Day landings. Some 50 examples had been received by the LMS between May and October 1943 and were based mainly at Toton, Crewe South and Mold Junction (Chester). The authorities had over a year to study their design and assess their operating capabilities before the engines began transferring to Continental Europe. H.G.Ivatt, CME of the LMS from 1945 until Nationalisation had been impressed by the accessibilty of the working parts of the locomotives. The higher position of the running plate on the S160s was a feature adopted by Ivatt both for his new Cl. 4 2-6-0s (43XXX) introduced in 1947 and for the last of the modified Stanier Cl. 5 4-6-0s, 44686/7 turned out in 1951. A departure from previous British practice was the use of the strong rigid structure of the boiler rather than the frames to attach components such as the cab, running plate and injectors, and this was used for the new Standard designs also. In contrast to the somewhat 'unfinished' look of the Ivatt designs, the appearance of the new Standard classes was improved by extending the high running plate sharply downwards at the front end to join up with the buffer beam. At the other end, the running plate, now with a deep valance for all designs except the Cl. 2 2-6-0, was extended to the middle of the cab front. Except in the case of the Pacifics the underside of the cab sheet then sloped downwards at an angle to achieve a pleasing sense of balance. These features bestowed on the Standard classes a distinct family 'marque'.

The valance attached to the running plate was used to tuck away much of the pipework, usually exposed on similar designs at work in the USA and Europe. This resulted in a tidier look to the locomotives without compromising accessibility for maintenance and repair work. The 'stovepipe'

chimney, traditionally a feature of designs in other countries was also not allowed to spoil the looks of the new Standards. With the possible exception of the design for the double blastpipe for the Cl. 4 4-6-0s, the chimney designs for the Standards in general contributed to the new locomotives' overall attractive appearance.

Opinions vary over the wisdom of allocating the quite considerable resources to the Standard steam locomotive project. Some argue, with the benefit of hindsight that, in what turned out to be a shorter period than envisaged between Nationalisation and the phasing out of steam power, it would have been sounder to have perpetuated the designs, with modifications, developed by the former railway companies. In the event, some 1,550 locomotives built to several of these companies' designs, continued to appear until 1954. It was claimed that expansion of this policy would have saved much engineering effort which could have been devoted to developing newer forms of traction.

This view ignores three important aspects of the exercise:
(1) the need to evaluate systematically and adopt where practicable, the latest ideas worldwide, for maximising the efficiency of motive power operation in Britain during the difficult post World War II years.
(2) the value of generating a cohesive engineering management team in the Railway Executive by focusing key personnel on joint projects based on shared experience. The development of cooperation with a free exchange of ideas could be expected to foster good working relationships when embarking on future engineering projects.
(3) the requirement to keep the pool of British expertise in design and operation of steam locomotives up to world class levels to take advantage of the many opportunities in the still important export market.

Regarding the level of success of the project, performance data shows that the subjects of this volume, the Standard 4-6-0s and 2-6-0s were generally competent machines when crews took the trouble to establish driving techniques to get the best out of them. During day to day operation, they were also much easier to service and maintain than the locomotives they were designed to replace. All in all, it is fair to say that the Standard classes provided a fitting finale rather than an embarrassing footnote to the end of steam power operation on British Railways.

2. Class 5 4-6-0 73000-73171

2.1 Purpose

The classic two cylinder 4-6-0 locomotive had been a stalwart of the British railway scene for many years. Examples operating at the time of Nationalisation in 1948 included the LMS Stanier Cl. 5; the LNER Cl. B1, itself said to have been inspired by the Stanier 5; the GWR Halls and the SR's King Arthur Cl. N15s. With these four classes totalling over 1,500 examples, it was clear that the requirement for a locomotive in this power bracket still existed and a new design capable of replacing them in due course would be required. A comparison of the leading dimensions of these locomotive classes is given in Table 2.

2.1.1 Design Development

All but the SR N15s had taken part in the locomotive exchange trials of 1948, the Bulleid light Pacifics being chosen in preference to the N15s. The Stanier 5s and the B1s emerged with approximately equal honours, the former performing less well and the latter rather better than anticipated. The Bulleids turned in remarkably good results on the GCR and Highland main lines with respect to drawbar horse power figures. Members of the Riddles team were impressed to the extent that they actively considered the possibility of designing the Cl. 5 as a Pacific. R.C.Bond, Chief Officer for Construction and Maintenance in Riddles' team wrote a memo entitled 'Notes on the Design of the Proposed New Standards' which discusses this subject amongst others; it is reproduced here as Appendix 4.

On the plus side the scope for a larger boiler on the Pacific should allow higher continuous steam production particularly when abnormal demands were being made. At normal rates of evaporation, a larger boiler would give improved economic performance as a result of the lower combustion rates. In addition, a Pacific with its trailing wheel might be expected to give a smoother ride. The benefits from this would be a reduction in mechanical wear and tear and increased confidence in the crew that their machine was stable, up to the job and capable of being safely pushed to a special effort if required.

On the other hand, a 4-6-0 should cost less to build, a rough estimate indicating that twelve 4-6-0s could be built for the cost of ten Pacifics; maintenance costs for the Pacific would also be higher. Due to its inherently lower adhesion factor, the Pacific would show a greater tendency to slipping when starting from rest compared with the 4-6-0. A comparison of the two types in day to day service could be made on the undulating route of the S&DJR between Bath and Bournemouth where Stanier Cl. 5 4-6-0s and Bulleid Light Pacifics worked regularly alongside each other on both inter-regional holiday expresses and ordinary services. Experience suggested that due to their slipping tendency and inability to develop high tractive effort at low speeds with heavy loads, the Bulleids were not star performers in conditions of heavy uphill slogging work. Hence maximum loads were restricted to not much more than the those for the 4-6-0s. Bearing the cost and adhesion factors in mind and also the availability of modern 4-6-0 designs such as the Stanier Cl. 5 and Thompson Cl. B1 as a basis for the new Standard Cl. 5, the decision was finally made in favour of the 4-6-0 type.

It was probably inevitable that Riddles' team, consisting as it did mainly of former LMS engineers, would choose the Stanier 4-6-0 as its model for the new Cl. 5. The largest component, the boiler, was almost identical to the LMS 3B design introduced in 1949 for the final batches of Stanier Cl.

TABLE 2
Standard Cl. 5 4-6-0s 73000-73171
Comparison of Leading Dimensions of Some Mixed Traffic 4-6-0s

Class	Date of Introduction	Cylinders Diameter x Stroke	Coupled Wheel Diameter	Boiler Pressure p.s.i.	Total Heating Surfaces sq. ft.	Superheater sq. ft.	Grate Area sq. ft.	Tractive Effort at 85% boiler pressure lb	Engine Weight in Working Order
BR Standard 5	1951	19" x 28"	6' 2"	225	2008	358	28.7	26,120	76 tons 0 cwt
LMS Stanier 5 (Type 3B Boiler)	1934 (1949)	18½" x 28"	6' 0"	225	1998	348	28.7	25,455	72 tons 12 cwt
LNER B1	1942	20" x 26"	6' 2"	225	2005	344	27.9	26,878	71 tons 3 cwt
GWR Hall	1924	18½" x 30"	6' 0"	225	2104	263	27.1	27,275	72 tons 10 cwt* 75 tons 0 cwt
GWR Modified Hall	1944	18½" x 30"	6' 0"	225	2052	315	27.1	27,275	75 tons 16 cwt
SR Maunsell N15 King Arthur	1925	20½" x 28"	6' 7"	200	2215	337	30.0	25,320	80 tons 19 cwt
*Prototype 4900 only									

5s. Compared with the B1's boiler which was fitted with the traditional LNER round topped firebox, the LMS boiler had the edge in steam production by using the square topped Belpaire firebox which concentrated the greatest depth of water at the position of greatest heat. A chronic fault in the original Stanier Cl. 5 4-6-0s was the frequent occurrence of cracked frames where the thickness was initially only 1", later increased to 1⅛" in stages for subsequent batches. For the Standard Cl. 5 4-6-0, frame thickness was set at 1¼", virtually eliminating the problem. The 5% increase in total weight did not result in significantly reduced route availability as many lines had been upgraded since the appearance of the first Stanier Cl. 5s in 1934 whilst other lines had been closed. Features from the Cl. B1 design were incorporated however. Driving wheels were increased to the B1 diameter of 6' 2" and valve gear operation incorporated the LNER minimum weight crosshead arrangement adopted for all the larger of the Standard designs from the Cl. 5 upwards. The new Cl. 5 would be expected to fulfil the role of a medium size express engine when called upon and the higher diameter wheels would result in lower maintenance costs where continuous high speeds were involved. In common with the Pacific designs, the Cl. 5 was required to conform to the L2 loading gauge. This, the larger of the two standard gauges, covered all routes where nine feet wide corridor stock was permitted; the lower L1 gauge restricted the dimensions of the smaller classes but enabled them to operate almost anywhere on the system.

The only significant variation from the original Standard Cl. 5 4-6-0 design was the adoption of British-Caprotti valve gear for a batch of thirty locomotives, 73125-54 which Derby turned out in 1956/7. H.G.Ivatt, CME of the LMS from 1945 until Nationalisation had undertaken development work on Caprotti valve gear by fitting it to Stanier Cl. 5 4-6-0s introduced in 1948 (twenty engines, 44738-57) and 1951 (two engines, 44686/7). Despite the reputation for fast and free-running at speed, the 1948 batch had suffered from complaints of slow starting and sluggishness at speeds below 40mph. In the two 1951 locomotives, the valve events were altered resulting in a marked improvement in performance; this success led to the adoption of the modified gear for the Standard Caprottis. The incentive for the move was an anticipated mileage increase between piston and valve examinations from between 30,000-36,000 for the Walschaerts piston valve locomotives to 40,000-48,000 for the Caprottis. Even at the higher mileage it was found that less work was required compared with the Walschaerts type to restore the mechanism to specification; the reduced wear was attributed to the by-pass action of the valves during coasting. Although the Caprottis incurred higher construction costs of around 20%, overall maintenance savings for the projected 45 year life-span of the locomotives indicated the extra capital expenditure would be recovered many times over. In the event, all the Caprottis had been withdrawn by the end of summer 1968 along with the rest of British Railways steam fleet, after an average life-span of little more than ten years.

Another form of valve gear, the Stephenson link motion, had been fitted to Stanier Cl. 5 4-6-0, 4767 in 1947. The results of trials with this locomotive on service trains against both a Caprotti version (4752) and a Walschaerts type (4766) were not published but it is known the Stephenson gear was

Fig.1   73000 is about to leave Bristol Temple Meads with an express for the Midlands and North on 10th May 1951 a few weeks after delivery to Derby shed. The engine is in mixed traffic black livery with full lining, paired to the BR1 type tender.   *(G. Wheeler)*

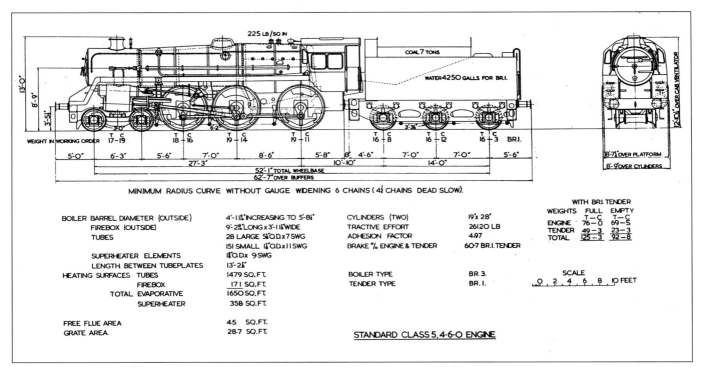

Diagram 1. Standard Class 5 4-6-0: Locomotive diagram for Walschaerts valve gear engines.

less mechanically robust than the Walschaerts type. Anecdotal evidence from experienced observers at the time however suggested 4767 was an excellent machine, powerful and free-running and it is perhaps surprising that there were no proposals to fit a Standard Cl. 5 4-6-0 with the Stephenson gear. A summary of the annual building programme for the Standard Cl. 5 4-6-0s is given in Table 3. Appendix 1 details year end totals for the class from 1951–1968.

2.2 Dimensions and Data

The main design office for the Standard Cl. 5 4-6-0s was Doncaster with certain components designed at Brighton, Derby and Swindon. Principal dimensions and axle loads are given in Diagram 1 for the Walschaerts valve gear engines and Diagram 2 for those fitted with British-Caprotti valve gear.

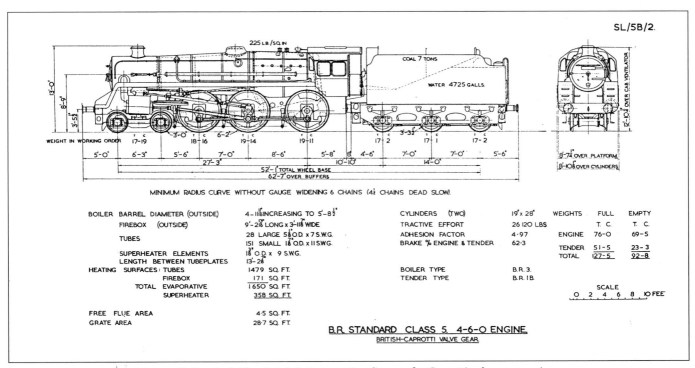

Diagram 2. Standard Class 5 4-6-0: Locomotive diagram for Caprotti valve gear engines.

<table>
</table>

TABLE 3

Standard Cl. 5 4-6-0s 73000-73171: Annual Building Programme

Programmme Year	Works	Lot Numbers	Engine Numbers	Total	Delivery Date	Initial Allocated Region
1951	Derby	5122	73000-04	5	04.51-06.51	London Midland
			73005-09	5	06.51-07.51	Scottish
			73010-29	20	08.51-01.52	London Midland
1952	Derby	6230	73030-39	10	06.53-09.53	Scottish
			73040-49	10	10.53-12.53	London Midland
1953	Derby	6735	73050-52	3	06.54	Southern
			73053-54	2	06.54	London Midland
			73055-59	5	06.54-08.54	Scottish
	Derby	8035	73060-64	5	08.54-10.54	Scottish
	Derby	8025	73065-74	10	10.54-12.54	London Midland
1954	Derby	8241	73075-79	5	04.55-05.55	Scottish
			73080-89	10	06.55-09.55	Southern
1955	Derby	8845	73090-99	10	10.55-12.55	London Midland
	Doncaster	402	73100-04	5	08.55-09.55	Scottish
	Doncaster	403	73110-19	10	10.55-12.55	Southern
	Doncaster	404	73105-09	5	12.55-01.56	Scottish
			73120-24	5	01.56-02.56	Scottish
1956	Derby	9247	73125-34★	10	07.56-10.56	Western
			73135-44★	10	10.56-12.56	London Midland
			73145-54★	10	01.57-06.57	Scottish
1957	Doncaster	406	73155-59	5	12.56-01.57	Eastern
			73160-64	5	01.57-03.57	North Eastern
	Doncaster	407	73165-71	7	03.57-05.57	North Eastern

★ Fitted with British-Caprotti valve gear.

Boiler

The boiler was essentially the LMS 3B design adopted in 1949 for the last batches of the Stanier Cl. 5 4-6-0; full details are given in section 2.3 and Appendices 2 and 2A.

Firebox

The firebox was of the square topped Belpaire type; dimensional details are given in Appendices 2 and 2A. The firebox had a forward sloping throatplate, the tube plate being 1" thick. All firebox water space stays were of Monel metal, fitted with steel nuts inside the firebox; the roof, longitudinal and transverse stays were of steel. Both the firebox and the boiler were lagged with lightweight fibreglass; a manually operated blowdown valve was fitted.

Grate and Ashpan

A rocking grate was adopted, consisting of eight rocking sections, each section carrying 14 renewable firebar units, making a total of 112 units for the whole grate. The grate was divided into two parts, front and back, which could be rocked separately, the mechanism being operated from the footplate. The operating gear was so arranged that two different travels

Fig. 2   Busy scene at Oxford as 73000 wanders through with an up freight on 30th October 1965. The engine carries a non-standard front numberplate, possibly made of wood, as substitute for the original, likely to have been removed by souvenir hunters.

(Courtney Haydon)

Fig. 3   A special braking-test vacuum-fitted express coal train from Finedon Sidings, north of Wellingborough to Brent Yard in north London, is seen passing Harpenden Common at a controlled speed of 40mph. The rake of steel bodied BR mineral wagons specially 'fitted' for the series of trial runs is doubleheaded by 73000/1 on October 26th 1952.

(E.D. Bruton)

Fig. 4   On March 15th 1952, 73002 approaches Elstree at about 45mph with the 12.05pm Derby-St Pancras express loaded to ten coaches; the rake is in the livery of carmine and cream, affectionately re-named 'blood and custard' by contemporary railway enthusiasts. 73002 was one of four Standard Cl. 5 4-6-0s selected for the fitting of double chimneys in early 1958. The project was cancelled when development resources were re-directed from steam to diesel and electric traction in the 1958 BR modernisation plan.

(E.D. Bruton)

could be employed, full travel for dropping the fire when the locomotive was over an ashpit and a shorter travel for agitating the fire to eliminate ash and break up clinker while the engine was on the road. The ashpan had three hoppers and was of the self-emptying type, having bottom flap doors on the hoppers, which were operated by a hand lever from ground level. The front and back damper doors were opened and closed separately by screw gear, worked by handwheels.

Smokebox
The smokebox was of the cylindrical type resting on a fabricated saddle. The blastpipe had a plain circular cap which incorporated the blower ring. The smokebox was of the self-cleaning type with diaphragm plates and a wire mesh grid so arranged as to prevent accumulation of ash in the bottom of the smokebox when the engine was working. The diaphragm plates were placed in front of the tubeplate and the superheater elements, so that the gases emerging from the flues and tubeplates were led to the bottom of the smokebox. After passing to the blast, the gases were baffled by deflector plates, carried on the end of the table plates forming a constriction. This enabled the char to be lifted up by the suction of the exhaust steam from the blastpipe and as the char came into contact with the netting frames, the large pieces

were broken up and the resulting small pieces ejected via the chimney. The self cleaning device was not always well received by operating staff as it was alleged to inhibit steaming if distorted by wear and tear. So much so, that certain depots would remove the screens when engines reappeared from works overhaul and refit them for their return. It is likely that the pristine appearance of the returned screens would not have puzzled the Works authorities for very long.

Main Frames
These were of 1¼" thick plates spaced 4' 1½" apart, braced by horizontal and vertical stretchers and by pin-jointed cross stays attached to the axlebox guides. The dragbox at the back end was fabricated and a single drawbar transmitted the power to the tender through rubber springs. The boiler was supported at the back end of the firebox on brackets which were integral with the dragbox. Side footplating was carried by brackets fixed to the smokebox and boiler.

Axleboxes and Bearings
The engine and tender were fitted throughout on Timken roller bearing axleboxes; those for the bogie and coupled axles were of the non-split cannon type. The faces of the axleboxes in contact with the guides were provided with manganese

steel liners welded to the body of the axlebox. All springs for both the engine and tender were of the laminated type with plates of carbon steel. Underhung spring brackets with rubber damping pads and links in tension were provided for the coupled axle springs, which had a span of 4 feet when loaded. The links were solid with cotters at top and bottom ends; adjustment was obtained by fitting cotters of suitable depths.

Cylinders and Valve Gear

Valve gear was of the conventional Walschaerts type for the majority of the class. The exception was the group of thirty locomotives, 73125-54, referred to earlier, introduced in 1956 and fitted with British-Caprotti valve gear. Cylinder and valve gear dimensions are given in Appendices 3 and 3A.

Walschaerts Valve Gear Locomotives

Lubrication of motion pins was by grease nipple and gun; those for the reversing shaft and expansion link were grouped together on the motion bracket. The eccentric rod big end ran on a Skefco self-aligning ball bearing. Valve and cylinder lubrication was by atomised oil delivered by mechanical lubricators. Steam operated cylinder cocks of large diameter were fitted for quick draining of the cylinders of any water which may have accumulated. The same kind of reversing gear was used as on the Standard Cl. 7 Britannia Pacifics. It consisted of a reversing screw and nut acting directly on the reversing shaft arm, actuated by means of a tubular shaft from a handwheel which occupied an end-on position in the cab. A drum type steam cut-off indicator was provided.

Caprotti Valve Gear Locomotives

Apart from the incorporation of British-Caprotti valve gear in place of the Walschaerts type, the locomotives were basically the same as the other class members. The British-Caprotti valve gear included separate inlet and exhaust poppet valves at each end of the cylinder, actuated by cams. Each valve was a self-contained unit within a cage in which valves work vertically and are pushed down by cam action to open. The main locomotive dome-type regulator incorporated a special valve which automatically admitted saturated steam through an actuation pipe to the bottom of the valve spindles. This action lifted the valves into their working position before the main steam supply was admitted and also provided the closing force during running.

The camboxes, situated on top of each cylinder to control the valve movements, incorporated the improvements developed as a result of the experience gained from the Stanier Cl. 5 4-6-0s fitted with this form of valve gear in 1948 and 1951. The drive for the camboxes was taken from the intermediate coupled wheels through a worm gearbox mounted on each return crank. Tubular shafts transmitted the drive from the gearboxes to the camboxes. The reversing wheel in the cab was connected by a transmission tube to a self-locking worm reversing box on the left-hand side of the locomotive. A reversing shaft with flexible couplings connected across the the locomotive to the right-hand worm reversing gearbox. From each reversing gearbox a transmission tube with flange coupling at the rear and spline coupling at the front connected to the respective camboxes. Reversing was done by advancing or retarding the angular position of the cams relative to the camshafts, any desired steam cut-off being obtained by the angular adjustment of the inlet cams in relation to each other.

Wheels

The coupled wheels were 6' 2" in diameter on tread. The tyres were shrunk on and secured by two small lips, one each side of the wheel centre; there were no separate rings, studs or rivets. Built-up weights in the wheels balanced the revolving weight and fifty per cent of the reciprocating weight. Timken roller bearings were fitted to all class members except 73090-9 which instead had the SKF parallel roller variety. Sanding was by steam using the Downs system and was fitted to the front and rear of the driving wheels. The bogie was identical to that fitted to the Standard Pacific locomotives and had wheels of three feet diameter on tread, with Timken roller bearings of the non-split cannon type. The locomotive was carried by side bolsters and laminated springs fitted in compensating beams. Side play control of the bogie was by means of double coil springs.

Cab and Tender

The cab layout was the same as that approved for all the Standard locomotives. The structure was carried by brackets from the main frames with a cantilever extension backwards to the tender front plate, dispensing with the usual hinged fall plate. The exhaust and live steam injectors were both carried on the right hand side of the engine under the cab and all steam and water controls for both injectors were operated from the fireman's side of the locomotive.

Different types of tender were fitted to different production batches of the locomotives, depending on traffic requirements. Details of tender types and their allocation to individual locomotives are given in section 2.4.

Brakes

Both locomotive and tender had steam brakes which could be worked independently or in conjunction with the vacuum brake by a separate driver's valve. Brake blocks of the single type supplied the brake power to the six-coupled engine wheels and all tender wheels.

Variations from Standard

There were several variations from the original design. Beginning with 73050, the cab layout and tender were modified to combat excessive draughtiness; gangway doors were fitted to the tenders and the rear hand-rail from the cab roof to the floor was discarded in favour of a grab rail on the front of the tender. Further detail on tender design is given in section 2.4. Again from 73050 onwards, coupling rods were of rectangular cross-section rather than fluted. The side of the running plate was cut away to give improved access to the lubricator starting with 73006; the earlier engines were also modified within a short time. The Smith-Stone speedometer activated from the rear driving wheel was introduced from 73030 onwards and many of the earlier batch, 73000-29, were so fitted at a later stage.

The original tri-tone chime whistle, mounted vertically on the smokebox behind the chimney and operated from the cab by a cable running down the right hand side boiler hand rail, had an unfortunate tendency to stick open in use and eventually to disintegrate. One instance of this problem occurred with 73000 whilst working the 8.28am Nottingham-St. Pancras on 31st January 1957. On entering

Ampthill tunnel, the whistle jammed and sounded continuously almost to Flitwick, a distance of some two miles. As a result of this tendency, many of the class, particularly those based on the SR, had their chime whistles replaced from the late 1950s onward by what was known as the 'bell' type. Beginning with 73100, the first of the Doncaster built batches, an ordinary monotone whistle was fitted horizontally on top of the firebox; another minor modification for this and subsequent batches was that the cab front windows were now hinged instead of fixed.

The Doncaster batches had detail variations compared with those produced at Derby. On Doncaster engines, the chequer plating on the footplate had a different pattern stamped on it. Handles for pulling up the two flaps set in the cab floor, to expose the rocking grate control gear, were in a different position and the tender shovelling plate was level and not of the lipped edge type. Also the eccentric cranks were secured by four nuts instead of the pressed-on fixing whilst firehole doors were of a thinner design having less internal air space. Finally, on the Walschaerts valve gear engines, there was a difference in the placing of the steps bolted to the running plate angle at the front. The top step was in line with the top of the frame on the Doncaster-built examples whereas on the Derby engines it was lower. The Caprotti valve gear engines, 73125-54 all built at Derby, were similar to the Doncaster batches in this respect. Engines sometimes re-appeared after Works visits with the Derby-style steps on one side of the engine and the Doncaster type on the other; known examples were 73052/7. Poultney reversing gear was installed on 73105-9 and 73120-4 in place of the normal BR hand screw type. The BR AWS apparatus was fitted from new to some of the early Derby engines including the pioneer 73000 and also to several of the later deliveries from Doncaster among which were 73160/6. The equipment was later fitted to a large number of the class; details are given in section 2.9.2.

Two members of the class, 73030/1, emerged from Derby in May and June 1953 fitted with both the standard vacuum braking system and the Westinghouse air brake equipment similar to that carried by Britannia Cl. 7 Pacifics 70043/4. The engines were to be involved in comparative trials of air and vacuum brake systems on coal trains on the Midland main line. The objective of the trials was to establish the feasibility and cost effectiveness of running express block coal trains on certain routes. 73030/1 had compressors attached to their offside front ends and large reservoir tanks located each side under the running plate near the cab. Originally intended for the ScR, 73030/1 were on loan to Derby for the duration of the trials. 73030 was then almost immediately transferred to Rugby Testing Station for a series of steaming trials before returning to Derby in November 1953; after this both engines spent some four years officially allocated to Derby. From 22nd-25th September 1953, 73031 was observed testing the fitted coal train between Trowell and Ilkeston Junction, north of Toton, before commencement of long distance workings from Toton to Brent in October. The trains, known as the 'Flying Colliers' were run to a modified class C freight schedule. Time from Toton to Brent was around 3 hours 40 minutes with a fifteen minute pause at Wellingborough reducing the normal journey time to much less than half. The route was via Loughborough, Syston North Junction and Melton Mowbray, rejoining the main line at Kettering.

Another itinerary was from Toton to Bedford Junction via Loughborough, Leicester and Kettering and return, journey time being of the order of 2½ hours each way. The trains typically consisted of between 50 and 70 coal wagons, a recording car and a brake van all fittted with the Westinghouse equipment. All vehicles had a large area of the top left hand side painted yellow and lettered: 'Westinghouse-Return to Toton'. Apart from 73030/1 and Britannia Pacifics 70043/4, LNER Cl. L1 2-6-4 tank engines 67729/37, on loan from Stratford and already fitted with air brake equipment for the Liverpool Street suburban passenger services, also took part in the trials. In some tests the two braking systems were compared by working the trains up to around 40mph, after which the brakes were fully applied and the stopping distance measured. Further tests continued from time to time until the spring of 1955, latterly mainly with the Britannia Pacifics. Following completion of the trials, both 73030/1 were relieved of their air brake equipment during routine intermediate overhauls at Derby, 73030 in November 1955 having run 88,635 miles and 73031 in March 1956 with 101,261 miles on the clock. The trials were not followed up by mass conversion of the coal wagon fleet to either the standard vacuum or the Westinghouse air brake system mainly because of the difficulties of assembling and making up the train into a fitted freight and dispersing the coal wagons at the end of the run; the high cost of wagon conversion was also a factor. It was left until much later for the concept of the 'merry-go-round' system to be introduced to solve the logistical problems. 73031 was later nominally allocated to Rugby Testing Station for three years from January 1958 for further steaming trials, see section 2.9.1, although it spent much of its time operating from Bristol Barrow Road, albeit without its depot shedplate. 73030/1 were also reported as having been fitted from new with the Transom Tablet Catching Apparatus for a short period, although photographic evidence is lacking.

Two other modifications, the installation of Franco-Crosti boilers and the fitting of double chimneys, were considered for the Standard Cl. 5 4-6-0s but ultimately not implemented. The Franco-Crosti boiler sought to increase boiler efficiency by directing flue gases from the main boiler back from the smokebox through a secondary drum situated, in the case of the proposed Standard designs, directly under the main boiler. Here the gases were used to pre-heat incoming boiler feed water thus utilising heat normally lost through the conventional chimney; the flue gases were then discharged through a chimney placed alongside the main boiler near the cab, the normal chimney being closed off except when used for lighting-up purposes. The system was installed on ten Standard Cl. 2-10-0s, 92020-9 in the 1953 building programme at Crewe; the boilers were necessarily smaller than on the rest of the class and the fitted engines were unofficially downrated from Cl. 9F to Cl. 8F. The results were not encouraging, anticipated savings being marginal and at the expense of considerable smokebox and side chimney corrosion by dilute sulphuric acid condensed from the flue gases as a result of their temperature now being below the dew point of the acid. The problem of drifting smoke was also never satisfactorily resolved. The proposal to apply the system to some of the Standard Cl. 5 4-6-0s, which would also have been fitted with Caprotti valve gear, was thus abandoned, although not before a drawing had been prepared, see Diagram 3.

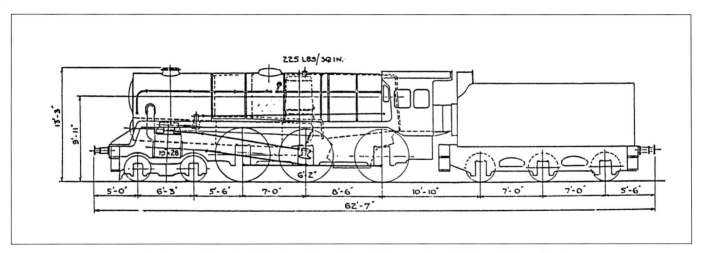

Diagram 3. Proposed Standard Class 5 4-6-0 engine with Franco Crosti boiler and Caprotti valve gear.

Fig. 5   73003 starts out from Southampton Central on Whit-Sunday 1953 with the thirteen coach relief to the 10.30am Waterloo-
Bournemouth. 73003, allocated to Leicester Midland at the time, was one of several engines loaned to the SR's Nine Elms depot
as substitutes for the Merchant Navy Pacific class, temporarily withdrawn for driving axle examination.   (G. Wheeler)

Fig. 6   73004 threads Harper Lane Bridge north of Radlett on August 18th 1951 with train M32, the 7.15am Saturdays Only Leicester
London Road-St Pancras. Later, when allocated to Sheffield Millhouses depot, 73004 managed to accrue a mileage of nearly 50,000
during 1959.   *(E.D Bruton)*

In October 1957, with the reported improvement in steaming capacity of a Standard Cl. 4 4-6-0 75029 fitted with double blast pipe and chimney on the WR, Doncaster was asked to prepare drawings for a similar modification to the Standard Cl. 5 4-6-0s. Chosen for the application were locomotives on the WR and LMR normally used on demanding express passenger and freight duties. On the WR, 73019 allocated to Bristol St Philip's Marsh and 73038 (Chester West), were put forward whilst the LMR offered 73002 (Nottingham) and 73046 (Leicester); locomotives on the SR allocation were to be included in the programme later. The smokebox self cleaning apparatus was to be retained initially, although design work was put in hand for the subsequent fitting of basket type spark arrestors. Another initiative not pursued was the production by Doncaster of a design to use the Cl. B1 4-6-0 chimney for experimental fitting to one or more of the class to improve steaming characteristics. Interest in these initiatives diminished in the summer of 1958 when work on steam locomotive modification was phased out in order to focus resources on the new BR modernisation plan directed towards the development of diesel and electric traction.

2.3 Boilers

The boiler adopted for the Standard Cl. 5 4-6-0s was designated BR3 with a working pressure of 225 psi. It was essentially the ultimate version of the LMS 3B boiler designed for the Stanier Cl. 5 4-6-0 incorporating the 28-element 4-row superheater and sloping throatplate; the existing flange plates were utilised during construction. The shell was of high tensile carbon manganese steel, as opposed to the nickel steel of the LMS boiler, with the barrel consisting of two rings, the second tapered. The smokebox tube plate was of the drumhead type ¾" thick; dimension details are given in Appendices 2 and 2A. The regulator in the dome was of the vertical grid type, operated by an external pullrod connected to a transverse shaft which worked through a stuffing box on the second barrel plate. The boiler was fed with water through two separate clack valves placed at approximately 30 degrees on each side of the vertical centre line of the front barrel. The clack valves delivered the water on to two inclined trays, which deflected the liquid round the inside of the barrel clear of the tubes to minimise potential corrosion problems. A steam manifold was fitted on the top of the firebox in front of the cab. It was provided with separate shut-off cocks to each steam supply pipe as well as a main shut-off valve, operated from inside the cab. Two direct loaded safety valves were mounted on the top of the firebox, immediately in front of the manifold.

For the 130 Standard Cl. 5 4-6-0 built at Derby, boilers were supplied by Crewe whilst for the 42 Doncaster-built engines, ten boilers were also constructed there, the

TABLE 4

Standard Cl. 5 4-6-0s 73000-73171: Initial Boiler Allocation

Locomotive Number	Boiler Number Nominal Allocation	Date of Boiler Construction	Boiler Built at
73000-29	836-865	12.50-06.51	Crewe
73030-49	993-1012	04.53-10.53	Crewe
73050-74	1168-1192	01.54-11.54	Crewe
73075-99	1492-1506	03.55-08.55	Crewe
	1609-1618	09.55-11.55	Crewe
73100-24	1619-1628	06.55-11.55	Darlington
	1629-1638	10.55-12.55	Doncaster
	1639-1643	04.55-06.55	Darlington
73125-54	1750-1779	12.55-01.56	Crewe
73155-71	1780-1796	10.56-04.57	Darlington
Spare	965-966	01.54-02.54	Crewe
Boilers	1367	02.54	Crewe
	1606	03.55	Crewe
	1871	03.57	Crewe
	1897-1898	03.59	Crewe
	1905-1906	12.58	Darlington
	1909-1911	04.59-07.59	Crewe

Note: Boilers were not installed in numerical sequence (see Table 5). In at least three cases, new boilers 1498, 1617, 1618 were not used in new locomotives but were fitted as replacements for those previously carried by 73010/03/04 respectively during their first general overhaul. Three spare or reconditioned boilers were used as substitutes for new boilers nominally allocated to locomotives in the 73075-99 range.

remaining 32 being supplied by Darlington. There were 12 spare boilers manufactured for the class, ten at Crewe and two at Darlington. Details are given in Table 4. The record of which boilers were carried by individual locomotives is far from complete, especially for the ScR. Information available from traceable engine record cards is given in Table 5. As a rule, boiler changes were made at each general overhaul.

2.4 Tenders

The Standard Cl. 5 4-6-0s were not all delivered into service with tenders of the same pattern. Six different types were used dependent on the region to which the locomotives were allocated and also on their anticipated duties. Each type had standardised coupling and connecting arrangements and could be readily exchanged as and when necessary. In the vast majority of cases, tenders were manufactured at the same works as the engine although it is known that several of the Doncaster built engines had tenders supplied by Darlington. Details of tenders and the original engine-tender pairings are given in Table 6; all were allocated in sequence as far as is known.

Much thought went into the design of the cab and tender to enable the crew to work efficiently. In particular, to assist the fireman in his task of transferring several tons of coal from the tender to the firebox during the average trip, the cab floor was extended from the engine to terminate under the tender shovelling plate. The resulting platform had the excellent stability normally associated with a tank engine and made the fireman's task much easier. The traditional tender fall plate which normally rested on the rear of the cab floor was thus considered unnecessary and omitted. Gangway doors were fitted to the cab and a rear handrail extended from the corner of the cab roof to the floor.

Experience in service soon showed that the absence of the tender fall plate had an unanticipated consequence. The design allowed air to run up the front of the tender and round the sides of the rear of the engine directly into the cab itself, resulting in excessively draughty conditions for the crew. The tenders affected were the BR1, BR1A and BR2 types. The problem was only partially overcome by fitting flexible screens between the rear of the cab and the front of the tender. For all subsequent designs, the extended cab floor was retained but a short full-width fall plate was fitted to the front of the tender and rested on the cab floor. Rather than being attached to the cab, gangway doors were now fitted to the tenders and incorporated anti-draught flaps beneath them. The cab hand rails were discarded in favour of grab rails fitted

TABLE 5

Standard Cl. 5 4-6-0s 73000-73171: Record of Boilers Fitted

Engine Number	Boiler Number and Fitting Date		Engine Number	Boiler Number and Fitting Date		Engine Number	Boiler Number and Fitting Date	
73000	836	12.04.51 N		1001	16.12.61		1185	17.07.59
	859	16.11.56	73025	861	19.11.51 N	73054	1170	09.06.54 N
	849	29.12.61		847	03.01.57		1001	01.08.58
73001	837	09.05.51 N	73026	865	27.11.51 N		1795	08.12.61
	846	15.05.55		857	21.03.57		836	02.11.63
73002	838	18.05.51 N		1909	07.04.60	73055-64	No information	
	839	15.06.56		1506	24.08.62	73065	1181	13.10.54 N
	1505	17.09.60	73027	863	18.12.51 N		1613	06.05.61
73003	839	31.05.51 N		857	21.12.56	73066	1182	15.10.54 N
	1617	27.03.56	73028	862	20.12.51 N		861	19.02.59
	1003	11.01.62		853	20.09.57	73067	1183	22.10.54 N
73004	840	08.06.51 N		854	11.08.62		1169	01.08.59
	1618	12.04.56	73029	864	17.01.52 N		1795	01.12.64
	1635	27.10.61		994	02.05.58	73068	1184	29.10.54 N
73005-9	No information			1761	27.07.63		998	07.05.60
73010	846	14.08.51 N	73030	993	20.06.53 N	73069	1185	05.11.54 N
	1498	07.07.55		865	22.01.58		1189	07.05.59
	1757	19.10.61	73031	994	03.07.53 N	73070	1186	12.11.54 N
73011	847	17.08.51 N		862	23.12.57		1995	26.02.60
	850	26.10.56	73032	995	10.07.53 N	73071	1187	19.11.54 N
	1911	16.10.64		1007	15.05.59		1751	06.10.61
73012	848	24.08 51 N	73033	999	07.08.53 N	73072	1188	08.12.54 N
	856	26.04.56		1000	02.07.59	73073	1189	16.12.54 N
73013	850	31.08.51 N	73034	996	14.08.53 N		1182	03.04.59
	848	29.06.56		1184	05.05.62	73074	1190	22.12.54 N
73014	853	06.09.51 N	73035	No information			839	17.01.61
	855	05.07.57	73036	1184	01.09.53 N		846	29.07.64
	1861	14.03.64		1617	03.03.62	73075-9	No information	
73015	856	12.09.51 N	73037	851	08.09.53 N	73080	1495	10.06.55 N
	837	16.03.56	73038	1000	12.09.53 N		1500	04.02.61
	1996	19.05.62		1005	17.02.59	73081-2	No information	
73016	851	21.09.51 N	73039	1001	25.09.53 N	73083	1606	01.07.55 N
	861	30.01.57		860	28.11.57		1168	10.10.59
	1905	13.02.59	73040	1005	05.10.53 N	73084	1499	29.07.55 N
73017	849	28.09.51 N		993	01.10.58		1012	31.10.59
	858	26.04.57	73041	1006	14.10.53 N	73085	No information	
	1502	09.09.61		1871	08.11.58	73086	1501	16.08.55 N
73018	852	04.10.51 N	73042	1002	22.10.53 N		1499	12.12.59
	840	31.05.56		1606	14.11.59	73087	1502	26.08.55 N
	858	30.12.61	73043	1008	30.10.53 N		1630	27.05.61
73019	854	10.10.51 N		1181	18.08.61	73088	1503	01.09.55 N
	863	25.01.57	73044	1007	09.11.53 N		863	06.05.61
	1495	11.03.61	73045	1009	18.11.53 N	73089	1504	09.09.55 N
73020	855	10.10.51 N	73046	1010	25.11.53 N		997	04.06.60
	854	06.03.57		1780	15.02.61	73090	1505	07.10.55 N
	1497	25.11.61	73047	997	08.12.53 N		1612	13.08.60
73021	857	22.10.51 N		1623	28.05.60	73091	1506	14.10.55 N
	852	05.09.56	73048	1011	17.12.53 N		838	27.05.60
73022	858	26.10.51 N	73049	1012	30.12.53 N	73092	1609	21.10.55 N
	836	08.02.57		1006	20.12.58	73093	1610	04.11.55 N
	1626	22.09.62	73050	No information.			1760	27.04.65
73023	859	05.11.51 N	73051	1168	10.05.54 N	73094	1611	10.11.55 N
	838	14.09.56		1906	09.05.59	73095	1612	17.11.55 N
	1183	13.05.60	73052	965	20.05.54 N		1506	14.07.60
73024	860	15.11.51 N		1621	25.06.60		1793	18.07.62
	849	18.06.57	73053	1169	04.06.54 N			

TABLE 5 continued

Standard Cl. 5 4-6-0s 73000-73171: Record of Boilers Fitted

Engine Number	Boiler Number and Fitting Date		Engine Number	Boiler Number and Fitting Date		Engine Number	BoilerNumber and Fitting Date	
73096	1613	25.11.55 N		999	05.05.61		1190	25.01.61
	1610	24.03.61	73127	1752	09.08.56 N	73156	1781	19.12.56 N
73097	1614	06.12.55 N	73128	1753	28.08.56 N	73157	1782	28.12.56 N
73098	1615	15.12.55 N	73129	1754	31.08.56 N		1762	08.01.65
73099	1616	30.12.55 N		1775	01.10.61	73158	1783	28.12.56 N
73100-9	No information		73130	1756	12.09.56 N	73159	1784	11.01.57 N
73110	1619	24.09.55 N	73131	1755	24.09.56 N		1766	20.10.64
	1501	23.01.60	73132	1757	04.10.56 N	73160	1785	23.01.57 N
73111	1620	15.10.55 N		1186	09.06.61	73161	1786	27.01.57
	1624	23.11.60	73133	1758	11.10.56 N	73162	1787	15.02.57 N
73112	No information			1187	18.01.62	73163	1788	22.02.57 N
73113	1622	29.10.55 N	73134	1759	18.10.56 N	73164	1789	05.03.57 N
73114	1623	02.11.55 N		1754	10.11.61	73165	1790	16.03.57 N
	1629	19.03.60	73135	1760	26.10.56 N		1453	26.02.65
73115	1629	15.11.55 N	73136	1761	31.10.56 N	73166	1791	29.03.57 N
	1502	30.01.60	73137	1762	09.11.56 N	73167	1792	11.04.57 N
73116	1624	15.11.55 N	73138	1763	15.11.56 N	73168	1793	12.04.57 N
	965	01.10.60	73139	1764	22.11.56 N		1170	06.07.62
73117	1630	22.11.55 N	73140	1765	29.11.56 N	73169	1794	26.04.57 N
73118	1631	02.12.55 N		1758	19.05.62	73170	1795	17.05.57 N
	853	02.02.63	73141	1766	06.12.56 N		1796	27.10.61
73119	1626	09.12.55 N	73142	1767	13.12.56 N	73171	1796	24.05.59 N
	840	16.03.62	73143	1768	20.12.56 N		1008	22.09.61
73120-4	No information		73144	1769	23.12.56 N			
73125	1750	06.07.56 N	73145-54	No information				
73126	1751	13.07.56 N	73155	1780	19.12.56 N	N: fitted from new.		

TABLE 6

STANDARD CL. 5 4-6-0 73000-73171: INITIAL TENDER ALLOCATION

Tender Type	Tender Side	Water Capacity gallons	Coal Capacity tons	Weight in Working Order tons	Allocated to Engine Numbers	Tender Serial Numbers	Tender Notes
BR1	Inset at top	4250	7	49.15	73000-29 73030-49	794-823 864-883	No fall plate fitted. Modified with draught excluders after service experience.
BR1B	Flush	4725	7	51.25	73080-89 73100-09 73120-24 73125-34 73145-71	1206-15 1282-91 1302-06 1413-22 1433-59	Increased water capacity. Fall plate and gangway doors fitted. Tenders for 73080-9 allocated to SR (no water troughs) were not fitted with water pick-up gear.
BR1C	Flush	4725	9	53.25	73065-74 73075-79 73090-99 73135-44	1004-13 1201-05 1272-81 1423-32	Increased capacity for both coal and water. Fall plate and gangway doors fitted.
BR1F	Flush	5625	7	55.25	73110-19	1292-1301	Highest Standard tender water capacity. Fall plate and gangway doors fitted. Locomotives allocated to the SR; hence tenders not fitted with water pick-up gear.
BR1G	Inset at top	5000	7	52.50	73050-52	989-991	Identical to BR1A (the modified form of BR1 with higher water capacity) but fitted with fall plate and gangway doors.
BR1H	Inset at top	4250	7	49.15	73053-64	992-1003	Identical to BR1 but fitted with fall plate and gangway doors

Fig. 7
Perth-based 73005 storms through the northern suburbs of Glasgow in the summer of 1952 with 'The Granite City', the 10.00am Glasgow Buchanan Street to Aberdeen, reached in just under four hours; the title 'Granite City' refers to the popular name for Aberdeen. For the group of five engines, 73005-9, allocated new to Perth in 1951, maintenance responsibility was originally assigned to the LMR at Derby. This policy was later changed and the role taken over initially by St Rollox and then by Cowlairs. *(E.R. Wethersett)*

Fig. 8
73007 leaves Perth on 18th September 1954 with the 9.35am Aberdeen-Glasgow Buchanan Street, which carried the title 'The Saint Mungo', named after the patron saint of Glasgow. The class was still seen on the accelerated Glasgow-Aberdeen three-hour service in the 1960s, occasionally deputising when the usual power in the shape of one of the legendary LNER Cl. A4 Pacifics was unavailable.

(E.V. Fry)

Fig. 9
Perth based 73007 waits at Forres on a local train to Elgin and Keith in the mid-1950s. The engine remained at Perth for thirteen years before transfer to Grangemouth in June 1964.
(David Tyreman Collection).

to the tenders. The BR1, BR1A and BR2 tenders were not modified and continued in service with their partially effective draught excluders until withdrawal. The water capacity of the tender was controlled by slots in the water pick-up pipe at the water-line. As soon as the tank was filled to nominal capacity, the excess water flowed out of the tender through the pick-up pipe. To increase tank capacity, all that was necessary was to position the slots higher up on the pipe. The BR1 tender was altered in this way to carry a further 750 gallons, the modified design being classified BR1A. None of this type was ever carried by any of the Standard Cl. 5 4-6-0s as far as is known but a further modification was made to the BR1A type by the addition of a fall plate and gangway doors. This was designated BR1G and examples were attached to 73050-2, giving improved operating flexibility when the engines were allocated to Bath Green Park for use on the S&DJR route which did not have the provision of water troughs.

Of the tenders carried by the Standard Cl. 5 4-6-0s, the BR1, BR1G and BR1H had inset coal bunkers and spectacle plates, allowing the crew an unrestricted view when running in reverse. All were modified in service to include a horizontal footstep on the rear of the tender to enable the fireman to stand safely whilst filling the tank. When increased water capacity was required, particularly on the SR which had no water troughs, several batches of the class were fitted with BR1B, BR1C and BR1F tenders, the first two types having water capacities of 4725 gallons each whilst the last filled up to 5625 gallons, the highest water capacity of any of the BR Standard tenders. These tenders were designed to the full loading gauge width with flush sides incurved at the top similar to the Stanier LMS tenders; the marginal advantage of the unrestricted view afforded by the earlier tenders when running in reverse was thus sacrificed. In the absence of water troughs on the SR, none of the tenders of its initial allocation of Standard Cl. 5 4-6-0s 73080-9, 73110-9 had water pick-up apparatus fitted. This could lead to potentially embarrassing situations during summer seasons when class members were loaned to Bath Green Park for holiday workings over the S&DJR. On one occasion, 73116 was booked to work through to Sheffield Midland by a Green Park crew. The first scheduled stop was Gloucester where the driver was unable to take water having slightly misjudged the stopping distance to come to a stand just out of reach of the water column. The 5625 gallon tender still had well over 4000 gallons remaining and the crew resolved to push on and pick up water at Haselour troughs between Tamworth and Burton-upon-Trent. Only after passing Tamworth was the absence of pick-up apparatus on this particular locomotive recalled. At the booked Derby stop, the tender still had some 2000 gallons remaining, quite enough for the 36 mile run to Sheffield and no water was taken. On arrival at Sheffield Midland, 73116 had covered the 171 miles from Bath without replenishing the tender which still had around 1000 gallons left for the trip to Millhouses for servicing.

According to available record cards, all but a few of the Standard Cl. 5 4-6-0s retained the same tender for the whole of their working lives. Towards the end of steam some changes did occur. Usually this involved the acquisition of a tender of the same type but in better condition, cannibalised from a withdrawn locomotive. There were instances of changes of type however; 73115, for example, was noted at work on the Waterloo-Bournemouth line in the summer of 1965 with a BR1B tender in exchange for its original BR1F type. Following the scrapping of Standard Cl. 6 Clan Pacific 72002 at Darlington in February 1964, 73005 was noted in the same month coupled to the Clan's green-painted tender. Later several Standard Cl. 5 4-6-0s were believed to have exchanged their tenders for the higher nine ton coal capacity BR1D types, fitted with steam coal pushers, obtained from withdrawn Standard Cl. 7 Britannia Pacifics in the 70045-54 group.

In June 1956, a leading axle taken from a BR Standard tender was found with cracks possibly caused by corrosion fatigue; on the BR1 and BR2 tender types, the shovelling plate drain and brake cylinder drain discharged over the leading axle. After due deliberation, the LMR authorised a programme of work to install a protection shield to be fitted when the leading axle was removed during overhaul. Several Standard classes were affected including the Cl. 5 4-6-0s in the range 73000-99. By October 1964, with an unrecorded number of tenders still to be modified, the programme was discontinued in view of the accelerating rate of steam locomotive withdrawals. Another potential problem with the BR tenders was the tendency of the external water sieves, designed to remove rust particles and other debris before water entered the boiler, to freeze in winter weather, causing the engine to be failed until a replacement was fitted.

2.5 Construction Costs

A comparison of estimated, record card and official construction costs for the Standard Cl. 5 4-6-0s is given in Table 7. The final batch of Walschaerts valve gear locomotives delivered in 1957 at £22,606 per locomotive shows a 28% increase in official final cost compared with the 1951 batch and an almost 38% increase compared with the last two Walschaerts gear Stanier Cl. 5 4-6-0s 44696/7 turned out by Horwich in December 1950. Much of this increase was attributed to general wage and raw material inflation over the period; later batches of the Standard Cl. 5 4-6-0s were fitted from new with additional equipment such as BR type AWS and Smith-Stone speedometers which also added to the delivery cost. The Caprotti geared batches at £28,075 each cost some 24-30% more than the contemporary Walschaerts gear locomotives and 36% more than the final LMS Caprotti Stanier Cl. 5 4-6-0s 44686/7 delivered from Horwich in the spring of 1951. It will be noted that all final costs were significantly higher than the estimated costs. It is clear that the age-old problem of accurate cost estimation, the bane of many otherwise well-managed engineering projects, also applied to the Standard locomotive manufacturing programme, the under-estimate in the case of the Cl. 5 4-6-0s ranging from 20% to 35%.

2.6 Liveries

The BR standard mixed traffic livery of gloss black with grey, cream and red lining on the running plate, cab and tender sides was applied to the Standard Cl. 5 4-6-0s. The grey lining was situated nearest to the edge of the painted item and was nominally ⅝" wide; it was abutted by a cream line of ⅛" width. There was then a 1⅝" gap before the final ¼" wide red line. The boiler had ¼" red linings on each side of the casing bands whilst the cylinder casings had similar linings somewhat inset from their edges. Initially it had been planned to paint the inner edges of the running plates with a simple red line to form a panel similar to the orange panel on the standard green

TABLE 7

Standard Cl. 5 4-6-0s 73000-73171
Manufacturing Cost Comparisons
Standard Cl. 5 4-6-0s 73000-73171 & Final Batch of LMS Stanier Cl. 5 4-6-0s

Programme Year	Locomotive Number	Delivery Year	Estimated Cost (£)	Record Card Final Cost (£)	Official Final Cost (£)
BR Standard					
1951	73000-17	1951	14,750	17,345	17,603
	73018-29	1951/2	14,750	17,359	17,617
1952	73030-49	1953	16,000	19,085	19,974
1953	73050-52	1954	16,900	N/A	20,682
	73053/4	1954	16,900	20,164	20,164
	73055-64	1954	16,900	20,165	21,004
	73065-74	1954	16,900	20,165	21,171
1954	73075-79	1955	18,600	20,165	21,909
	73080-89	1955	18,600	20,165	21,750
1955	73090-99	1955	20,900	21,369	22,490
	73100-04	1955	20,900	21,370	22,490
	73105-09	1955/6	20,900	21,370	21,560
	73110-19	1955	20,900	21,370	21,183
	73120-24	1956	20,900	21,370	21,560
1956	73125-34★	1956	20,750	26,690	28,075
	73135-38★	1956	20,750	26,619	28,075
	73139-54★	1956/7	20,750	26,615	28,075
	73155-58	1956	20,750	23,947	22,606
	73159-71	1957	20,750	23,945	22,606
LMS Stanier					
1947	44696/7	1950	14,175	N/A	16,424
	44686/7★	1951	14,175	N/A	20,642

★ Fitted with British-Caprotti valve gear.   N/A: Not Available.

Note: the final batch of LNER Thompson B1 4-6-0s delivered during 1950-2 from the North British Locomotive Company's Queens Park Works in Glasgow was officially costed at £16,190 per locomotive.

livery of the Pacifics. At least one locomotive, 73000, was so treated but the policy was soon changed to the grey, cream and red lines along the lower edge only.

The majority of the Works used BR standard 8" size numerals for the cabsides. A curious feature of some the Standard locomotives repainted at Swindon was the use of thicker 8" numerals without the usual black edging, often mixed together with 9" numerals on the same locomotive. Darlington, Cowlairs and St. Rollox continued with their normal 10" size figures; it was reported that Doncaster also used 10" numerals for all the Standard Cl. 5 4-6-0s built there. The Doncaster linings on the cabside and tender were different from those applied at Derby in that they were positioned much closer to the edges. In the early 1960s, both Doncaster and Darlington adopted the 8" size numerals for some of the class passing through for overhaul.

The Caprotti valve gear locomotives, 73125-54 had minor lining variations compared with other members of the class. The cylinders were unlined and the running plate lining was positioned higher up from the edge to clear the cut-out

in the plate above the top of the Caprotti cylinder casing. This variation was also applied to some of the Walschaerts geared engines during repaints on works visits. Later this variation was discontinued on both types of locomotive and lining reverted to the lower position, resulting in a break in the grey/cream base line on the running plates of the Caprottis; in other cases as an economy measure the running plate lining was omitted completely.

On the ScR, in common with many locomotives used on express passenger duties, the front numberplate and shed plate of several of the class were repainted with a light blue or maroon background; the numberplate was in some cases edged in white. Consistent with normal practice at Cowlairs, the Standard Cl. 5 4-6-0s repaired there had their depot name painted on the front buffer beam. On the SR, the whole of the original allocation, 73080-9, 73110-9, carried either the yellow spot or, later, the yellow triangle, beneath the cabside number which signified the engine had been fitted with water softening treatment apparatus. The yellow spot referred to the French T.I.A. system whilst the triangle denoted the BR

Fig. 10   73010 pilots rebuilt Royal Scot 4-6-0 46133 *The Green Howards* between Smardale and Kirkby Stephen on the 1 in 100 climb to Ais Gill summit with 'The Thames Clyde Express', the 9.15am Glasgow St Enoch–London St Pancras on 3rd June 1952. 73010 lasted almost until the end of steam operation on BR, being withdrawn in June 1968.   *(E.D. Bruton)*

Fig. 11   73016 from the local Millhouses depot pilots LMS Caprotti valve gear Cl.5 4-6-0 44745 as they accelerate a Newcastle–Bristol train away from Sheffield Midland on 6th June 1953. Later, in 1956/7, thirty Caprotti valve gear Standard Cl. 5 4-6-0s, 73125-54 were built at Derby Works, using experience gained from operating the LMS Caprottis introduced in 1948.   *(E.D. Bruton)*

TABLE 8

Standard Cl. 5 4-6-0s 73000-171: Locomotives Acquiring BR Green Livery

Engine Number	BR Green Livery Date	Applied at	Engine Number	BR Green Livery Date	Applied at
73001★	11.58	Swindon	73034	2.59	Swindon
	3.61	Doncaster		4.60	Doncaster
73003	11.59	Swindon		5.62	Doncaster
	1.62	Doncaster	73035★	6.59	Swindon
73012	12.58	Swindon		1.62	Doncaster
	5.61	Doncaster		8.64	Darlington
	5.65	Cowlairs★★		9.65	Cowlairs★★
73014	3.64	Eastleigh	73036	4.59	Swindon
73015	1.60	Swindon		3.62	Doncaster
	5.62	Doncaster	73037	3.60	Wolverhampton
73018	12.58	Swindon	73040	12.65	Eastleigh
73021	2.60	Swindon	73049	8.63	Eastleigh
73023	3.60	Doncaster	73051	9.63	Eastleigh
73024	2.60	Swindon	73054★	9.59	Swindon
	11.60	Doncaster		12.61	Doncaster
73026	4.60	Swindon		10.63	Eastleigh
	8.62	Doncaster	73068★	10.58	Swindon
	8.64	Darlington		5.60	Doncaster
	5.65	Cowlairs★★	73090	8.60	Doncaster
73027	8.60	Swindon	73091	5.60	Doncaster
73029	7.63	Eastleigh	73092	5.60	Doncaster
73031★	7.60	Swindon		2.64	Darlington
73032	11.64	Darlington	73093	5.60	Wolverhampton
			73094	11.60	Doncaster
			73095	7.60	Doncaster
				7.62	Doncaster
			73096	12.59	Swindon
				3.61	Doncaster
				11.65	Cowlairs★★
			73097	10.59	Wolverhampton
				1.61	Doncaster
				9.62	Doncaster
				4.64	Darlington
			73098	11.60	Doncaster

★73001/31/5/54/68 carried the WR 'Red Spot' route restriction indicator below the cab numerals; there may have been others.

★★73012/26/35/96 were overhauled at Cowlairs in 1965 and emerged in green livery but it is not clear whether green repaints were applied during the visits.

briquette system adopted from early 1957. Some of the class on the SR also carried a brass test number plate, see section 2.9.2, fixed to the nearside cabside at the bottom right, superimposed over the lining.

In April 1955, Swindon began applying BR standard lined Brunswick green livery to former GWR locomotives previously turned out in lined black. Apart from the narrow gauge Vale of Rheidol's No. 7, *Owain Glyndwr* (actually turned out in unlined green), the first class to be so treated were members of the County Cl. 4-6-0s beginning in June, closely followed in September by the 'Modified' Hall Cl. 4-6-0s. It was not until over three years later, towards the end of 1958, that the first Standard Cl. 5 4-6-0s, 73001/68, received lined green livery; details of locomotives known to have carried green livery together with the date of application and Works where it was applied are given in Table 8; there may have been others which have gone unrecorded. Working from the outside edge, the linings for the tender and cabside consisted of a ⅛" wide orange line then a "½" green gap followed by a 1" wide black line, completed by a symmetrical repeat of the green gap and orange line. The boiler casing bands were similarly treated whilst the cylinder casings had orange lines of ⅛" width inset from the edges. The treatment of the running plate was different to that on the Standard Pacifics. The latter had an orange line round the inner edges of the plate to form a panel whereas the Standard Cl. 5 4-6-0s had a single yellow line along its lower edge. The earlier Swindon repaints also included the application of a 'red spot' route restriction indicator below the cabside numerals, 73001/31/5/54/68 being noted in traffic with this adornment; 'red spot' engines were limited to the main lines and lines capable of carrying the heaviest locomotives. Swindon, in common with other WR Works was accustomed to include 'paint dates' usually applied to the bottom right hand corner of the left hand side of the tender, just beyond the outer lining edge. One such example was 73027 which was noted with the legend '21/8-60/W' thus applied. The 'W' represented the code of the leader of the paint team responsible for the work.

Fig. 12
73018, with non-standard numberplate, pauses at Basingstoke with the 11.15am Waterloo-Weymouth on 27th August 1966. Based at Weymouth and Guildford, the engine had operated on the SR's Western Section from September 1958 until withdrawal at the end of SR steam operation in July 1967.

(J. Walford Collection)

Fig. 13
73020 passes Brewham Signal Box near Bruton, Somerset on the WR West of England main line with train 1V32, the 10.45am Wolverhampton-Weymouth on 24th July 1965. 73020 received general overhauls at both Derby, in January 1957 and at Eastleigh, in November 1961.

(Hugh Ballantyne)

Fig. 14
Gloucester based 73021 drifts down the Lickey Incline towards Bromsgrove with the 4.40pm Birmingham New Street-Worcester Shrub Hill local on 6th June 1964. 73021 had received lined green livery during a visit to Swindon Works in February 1960.

(Courtney Haydon)

Fig. 15   73022 glides through Crystal Palace on 26th April 1965 with a rail tour bound for the South Coast. The engine has a rather elegantly fashioned non-standard front numberplate.   (Rodney Lissenden)

Fig. 16   Green-liveried 73029 with a non-standard front numberplate pilots Bulleid light Pacific 34023 *Blackmore Vale* with the Farewell to Southern Steam RCTS tour held on 18th June 1967 in aid of the Southern Railwaymen's Home for Children at Woking; the sum of £1,400 was raised (said to be enough in those days to run the home for a week!). The tour, beginning at Waterloo, took in Southampton, Bournemouth and Salisbury inclusive of a trip on the Swanage branch. The train is pictured here passing Petersfield on the Waterloo-Portsmouth line and is climbing the 1 in 100 towards the 485 yard Buriton Tunnel. The two locomotives were replaced by 34089 *602 Squadron* at Fareham for the next leg of the tour. 73029 survived another month before withdrawal, whilst 34023 is currently preserved on the Bluebell Railway in East Sussex.   (Rodney Lissenden)

The figures were applied by hand in very small characters about 5 mm high. Later, Doncaster and Darlington Works dealt with repairs for WR members of the class and reapplied the green livery to engines already carrying it.

The Eastleigh application of the green livery was different from that of Swindon in one small detail. The running plate was painted in the same way as the rebuilt Bulleid Pacifics in that an orange line was applied around the inner edges of the plate to form a panel. Eastleigh used a thicker orange line and positioned it further away from the edges of the running plate compared with the Crewe treatment of the Standard Pacifics.

None of the original SR allocation of Standard Cl. 5 4-6-0s, 73080-9, 73110-9, which had acquired the names of the withdrawn Urie King Arthur Cl. N15 4-6-0s by the summer of 1961, were repainted in green; even 73086 *The Green Knight* carried mixed traffic black for the whole of its career. This may have been the result of a rather luke-warm reception to the idea by officialdom in May 1956. A letter from the CM&EE Brighton to the Chief Operating Superintendent at Waterloo suggested that, considering Maunsell's Schools Cl. V 4-4-0s were to be repainted green during their next overhauls, the same policy should be applied to the Standard Cl. 5 4-6-0s. After all they were a direct replacement for the King Arthur Cl. N15 4-6-0s, always in green livery, and were mainly to be used on passenger services. The reply was that the Schools 4-4-0s were exclusively used on passenger services, whereas the Standard Cl. 5 4-6-0s were mixed traffic engines. Hence the justification for painting them green, although acceptable, was 'not so important'. The reasoning may have been theoretically sound but did not reflect contemporary practice; nevertheless, the initiative seems to have been dropped. From early 1964, however, it was reported that the new livery policy at Eastleigh was to apply green livery to all Standard Cl. 5 4-6-0s undergoing heavy repairs there. Again, this initiative was not carried through and the SR's 'Standard Arthurs' as they came to be known remained in black. Inter-regional transfers meant that some green liveried members of the class operated on the SR, 73018/29/92/3 being observed on routes from Waterloo towards the end of steam. A minor change in some of the class overhauled at Eastleigh was the provision of smaller front number plates; 73029 and Caprotti 73133 were among those noted. A few engines on most Regions carried non-standard front numberplates towards the end of steam, the victims usually of souvenir hunters.

The locomotive classification insignia carried by the Standard Cl. 5 4-6-0s varied depending on where they were manufactured and to which region they were allocated. Derby and Horwich applied '5' above the cabside number whereas Doncaster omitted the cabside classification mark completely, favouring the application of the legend 'BR5' to the fireman's side of the front buffer beam. The usual Doncaster treatment for engines painted at the Works was to apply the appropriate 'Route Availability' or 'R.A.' number, usually offset towards the tender, under the cabside running number; in general a locomotive was not permitted to work over a line of lower R.A. number than it carried. Standard Cl. 5 4-6-0s were classified 'R.A.7' but there is no evidence that this marking was applied to any of the class constructed or repaired at Doncaster. Swindon applied the figure '5' plus the 'red spot' route restriction on some of the green repaints referred to earlier. It is not clear whether the 'red spot' was applied to Standard Cl. 5 4-6-0s repainted there in black livery. Some of the SR allocation may have had their original '5' classification on the cabside elaborated to '5P5FA' by means of a stencil. 'P' and 'F' referred to 'Passenger' and 'Freight' confirming the mixed traffic status whilst 'A' referred back to the SR's Western Section system whereby locomotives were classified under letters A-K, according to haulage power, 'A' being the most powerful and 'K' the least. The elaboration policy was abandoned later, with reversion to the figure '5' for the cabside. Other variations by Eastleigh noted at various times were '5P5F', 5P 5F and 5P/5F.

Locomotives passing through Cowlairs works in Scotland emerged with the figures '5MT.' above the cabside number and in most cases the engine's home depot painted in full on the buffer beam. St Rollox, on the other hand, applied '5MT' above the cabside numerals and also the legend 'B.R.5' to the fireman's side of the front buffer beam but omitted the depot allocation.

From the early part of 1964, economies were beginning to be made on livery application to steam locomotives. As far as is known, only one member of the class reverted from green to black livery, 73037 being so noted in February 1964. In other cases, the linings on cylinders, boilers and tenders were sometimes omitted whilst the cabside panel linings were retained. Later, at least one Standard Cl. 5 4-6-0 was turned out in unlined black, 73069 from Crewe in September 1966; this was probably the last repaint of any of the class.

2.7 Allocation and Duties

2.7.1 Delivery period, 1951–1957

The first batch of thirty engines, 73000-29, was delivered from Derby Works over the period April 1951 to January 1952 to the LMR and the ScR; they were distributed as follows:

LMR	(25)	73000-4/10-29
ScR	(5)	73005-9

Initially 73000-4 were earmarked for Scotland, with 73005-9 for the LMR but Derby obviously chose to keep an eye on the first few engines as they were allocated to Derby and Leicester, within easy reach of the Works.

73000 was exhibited privately at Marylebone station on 26th April 1951 and the same evening worked the 7.22pm Cricklewood-Derby freight. Next day it was observed on the 4.10pm Derby-Manchester Central passenger train, returning during the late evening with a parcels train, a regular running-in turn for ex-Works engines. The 4.10pm was a fairly easy assignment, as it had nearly three hours to complete the sixty three miles to Manchester Central via Marple and Stockport Tiviot Dale, calling at virtually all stations. On the following day 73000 made a return trip to Sheffield. All the new engines usually spent a week or two working such duties in the Derby area before despatch to their allocated depots.

The twenty five engines allocated to the LMR, were distributed as shown:

Derby	(3)	73000-2
Leicester Midland	(2)	73003/4
Holbeck	(3)	73010-2
Millhouses	(3)	73013-5
Grimesthorpe	(1)	73016
Nottingham	(3)	73017-9
Chester Midland	(3)	73020-2
Patricroft	(2)	73023/4
Blackpool Central	(5)	73025-9

73000/1/2 joined a stud of Stanier Cl. 5 and Jubilee Cl. 4-6-0s at Derby in May 1951. Their early workings involved visits to Nottingham, Sheffield, York, Manchester, Crewe, Bristol, Bath Green Park and St Pancras turn and turn about with the other 4-6-0s. On 26th May, 73000 and 73001 worked to St Pancras from Nottingham on excursions organised by the Raleigh Cycle Works for the Festival of Britain. The new engines were also regular visitors to Newcastle upon Tyne and Scarborough on excursion trains.

During the temporary withdrawal of the Standard Cl. 7 Britannia Pacifics in October 1951, as a result of broken connecting rods caused by the coupled wheels shifting on their axles, 73000/2 were among several engines loaned to the ER's London Stratford depot as substitutes. At first the new arrivals were not well received but the situation improved on acquaintance by the crews. One engine regularly worked the 8.30am Liverpool Street-Norwich and the 'East Anglian' (6.30pm ex-Liverpool Street), whilst the other was often observed on the down 'Norfolkman' (9.30am ex-Liverpool Street) and the 2.45pm up from Norwich. By many accounts they had the edge in performance compared with B1 4-6-0s similarly employed.

The Leicester engines 73003/4 began work in June 1951 on duties which had normally been performed by LMS Compound 4-4-0s 41006/11 before their withdrawal earlier the same year. The work covered locals to Birmingham New Street, Peterborough and Northampton as well as semi-fasts to London St Pancras.

It was one of the Leicester engines, 73003, which was involved in an accident in February 1954 at Birmingham New Street, when it over-ran a signal and hit Gloucester LMS Compound 4-4-0 41047, causing extensive damage to the latter's cab and right hand footplate. The incident proved fatal for the Compound which was withdrawn the same month after examination at Derby Works.

All three Leeds Holbeck engines 73010-2 were at work on through London expresses in September 1951 including the down 'Thames-Clyde Express' (10.00am St Pancras-Glasgow St Enoch). During the following winter, they regularly appeared at Birmingham New Street and Bristol on through services to the West of England, including 'The Devonian' (Bradford Forster Square-Kingswear), together with occasional visits to Carlisle and Scotland.

Millhouses depot in Sheffield used their engines 73013-5 on the Hope Valley line to Manchester Central from September 1951. In common with the Holbeck examples, they were also regularly observed at York, Birmingham, Bristol and St Pancras. A Millhouses engine often appeared on the 10.10am York-Manchester Victoria express via the Calder Valley main line through Todmorden, running light to Agecroft for servicing and returning on the 5.10pm Manchester Exchange-York via the same route. The latter train was to be a regular steam working well into the diesel era in the mid-1960s.

The other Sheffield depot to receive a member of the class was Grimesthorpe. 73016 shared workings on the Sheffield, Nottingham and Derby routes with that depot's Stanier Cl. 5 4-6-0s. Following a rearrangement of duties in the Sheffield area in the early part of 1952, however, most of the 4-6-0s at Grimesthorpe were reallocated, 73016 going to join the three other Standard Cl. 5s at Millhouses.

Nottingham's new engines 73017-9 began work on semi-fast services to London, the Sunday 7.50am Nottingham-St Pancras becoming their almost exclusive preserve. They began to appear on the 9.05am Nottingham-Manchester Central, returning on the 3.22pm Liverpool Central-Nottingham, taking over at Manchester. Excursion traffic on the Lincoln line was also regularly powered by these engines.

In November 1951, to establish whether faster freight running was an option on the crowded Midland main line, 73019 was involved in a series of braking tests between the Brent (London) and Toton freight yards. A train made up of a dynamometer car, fifty-two sixteen-ton vacuum-fitted wagons plus a 20 ton brake van was assembled. The first of the trials was made between Radlett and St Albans. At milepost 17 at a speed of 45 mph, the brakes were applied and the train came to a stand within its own length, the brake van opposite the milepost. Further tests were carried out near Millbrook, Desborough and Syston. 73000/1 also featured in similar trials, sometimes appearing double-headed.

The Chester allocation 73020-2 began work in October 1951 on the North Wales coast line. The engines were frequently observed on the 5.45am Chester-Bangor, returning on the 12.45pm Bangor-Euston as far as Chester. Regular visits to the Manchester area occurred, especially in the busy summer holiday season of 1952. One working involved the 10.00am Holyhead-Manchester Victoria which ran via Broadheath, Stockport and Droylesden, a somewhat roundabout route.

Patricroft already had a large stud of over thirty Stanier Cl. 5 4-6-0s and the new engines 73023/4 were quickly put to work alongside the rest on regular duties to North Wales and across the Pennines to Leeds and York.

Blackpool received its allocation 73025-9 over the three month period from November 1951. The new arrivals became regular visitors to Manchester Victoria during December, two occasionally being seen together, one on the 3.44pm arrival from Blackpool Central and one on the 3.55pm departure. A frequent turn was the 4.35pm(SO) Rochdale-Blackpool through train. They were also used on another regular Blackpool duty, the 9.43am Liverpool Exchange-Glagow Central as far as Preston. Before reaching its new depot, 73027 was borrowed by other Central Division depots. It was observed working an Agecroft turn, the 10.10am Manchester Victoria-York and 1.55pm York-Liverpool Exchange during Christmas week 1951. In early January 1952, 73027 was working from Bank Hall on, for example, the 5.45pm Liverpool Exchange-Whitehaven. Once installed at its home depot, 73027 was then used on a return trip to Euston with an FA Cup special. From February 1952, the whole stud became frequent visitors to London, displacing Blackpool's LMS Jubilee Cl. 4-6-0s from a regular return duty, the 12.00 noon Euston-Crewe via Birmingham New Street.

Five of the first batch of thirty Cl. 5 4-6-0s, 73005-9, were destined for the Scottish Region and allocated to Perth, arriving during July and August 1951; 73008 did not stay long as it was selected for steaming trials and sent to the Rugby Test Plant from July 1951 to March 1952. Typical of their early duties were those recorded below on Friday 17th August 1951; the Glasgow station is Buchanan Street.

73005   11.55am Perth-Glasgow
         5.00pm Glasgow-Perth
         7.55pm Perth-Glasgow

Fig. 17
Green-liveried 73029 passes Yeovil South Junction with the 2.00pm Weymouth-Yeovil Pen Mill local on 18th April 1964. 73029's last general overhaul had been carried out at Eastleigh in July 1963 after an accrued mileage of 337,003.

(Courtney Haydon)

Fig. 18
Complete with a Willesden shedplate, a depot to which it was never allocated in BR service, the preserved 73050 is now in lined green livery, named *City of Peterborough* and the subject of admiration by a large crowd on the Nene Valley Railway on 28th August 1972.

(P.H. Wells)

Fig. 19
Bath Green Park's most senior driver, Mr. Dick Every, has the winter sun shining straight into his eyes as he slows 73051 for the first stop, at Midford, whilst working the 1.10pm Green Park-Templecombe local on 1st February 1964. 73051 was reported as having received lined green livery on its visit to Eastleigh Works in September 1963.

(Hugh Ballantyne)

Fig. 20
Scene at Bath on 1st February 1964 as lined green 73051 runs in from Bath Junction towards Green Park station with the 9.05am local from Templecombe. On the right, LMS Jinty Cl. 3F 0-6-0 tank engine 47544 waits for the single-line section to be free before heading light engine to Radstock sub-shed after wash-out at Bath. *(Hugh Ballantyne)*

Fig. 21
73054 of Bristol Barrow Road shed heads the 12.43pm Newcastle-Bristol Temple Meads at Pontefract Baghill on 30th July 1958. The engine was recorded as having received attention at no fewer than six Works during its eleven year lifespan, namely Crewe, Derby, Swindon, Caerphilly, Doncaster and Eastleigh. *(Peter Cookson)*

Fig. 22
Polmadie's 73063 pauses at Gleneagles on a southbound local from Perth on 1st July 1964. Note the vaccuum pipe extended above the buffer beam designed to accommodate a medium-size snow-plough. The engine was one of six of the class to spend their whole working lives allocated to Polmadie; the others were 73055/9/64/75/6. *(Rodney Lissenden)*

36

	11.15pm Glasgow-Perth
73006	8.25am Perth-Glasgow
	1.45pm Glasgow-Perth
	5.30pm (Postal) Perth-Law Junction
	Light engine, Law Junction-Carstairs
	10.17pm Carstairs-Perth
	(8.30pm ex-Carlisle)
73007	8.45am Perth-Glasgow
	1.35pm Glasgow-Aberdeen
	7.45pm Aberdeen-Perth (fish train)
73009	4.46am Perth-Glasgow
	10.00am Glasgow-Aberdeen
	5.30pm Aberdeen-Perth

Early reports suggested the engines did not distinguish themselves on hill climbing. Despite this, 73005/6 were entrusted with the Royal Train from Perth to Aberdeen on 3rd August 1951, handing over to two B1 4-6-0s to work forward to Ballater, the station for Balmoral Castle.

73007 appeared on the Highland main line in late July when it piloted a Stanier Cl. 5 4-6-0 to Inverness returning to Perth on the 4.45pm to Euston.

The missing 73008 had entered the test plant at Rugby on 31 July 1951 and spent several months there under static test. During November, it was observed equipped with dynamometer car on trials on the Settle and Carlisle line, visiting the ex-Midland Railway depot at Carlisle Durran Hill for servicing. After a further spell at Rugby, more trials were carried out on the same route during early March 1952, the engine later proceeding to Derby Works for attention. To remedy enginemen's complaints about draughts, 73008 was experimentally fitted with tarpaulin covers linking the cab and tender, the same device later being applied to other members of the class.

Meanwhile the crews were settling down with the new engines and obtaining good performances even on the hardest workings such as the 10.00am Glasgow-Aberdeen, 'Granite City'. For example, on 15th April 1952, this train, loaded to 272 tons tare, attained a speed of 80.5 mph at Dunning between Stirling and Perth with 73006 in charge; timekeeping and hill climbing were good throughout the journey.

The Highland section continued to have regular visits from the new engines during the summer of 1952, with 73009 sporting a tablet exchange catcher for use on the single line routes. Members of the class were also seen at Edinburgh Waverley on Perth semi-fasts.

In May 1953, the entire stud of Merchant Navy Class Pacifics operating on the SR was temporarily withdrawn for examination after 35020 had suffered driving axle failure at speed. To take over their duties and those of the Bulleid light Pacifics similarly withdrawn, 73003/15/7 from the LMR were loaned to Nine Elms along with Standard Cl. 7 Britannia Pacifics, LNER V2 2-6-2s, B1 4-6-0s, and Stanier Cl. 5 4-6-0s. The Standard Cl. 5s worked mainly Salisbury semi-fasts and Bournemouth reliefs. They were not as popular with crews as the Stanier Cl. 5s and appeared to lose time on most of their assignments, 73003, for example, causing some considerable disruption to the flow of Waterloo bound trains on Whit Monday evening whilst struggling with a heavy up Bournemouth express. 73003/15/7 had returned home by the end of June.

The second batch of twenty engines built at Derby, 73030-73049, delivered between June and December 1953,

was originally intended for the ScR and the LMR; allocations were as follows:

ScR	Carlisle Kingmoor	(5)	73030/2/4/6/8
	Polmadie	(5)	73031/3/5/7/9
LMR	Chester Midland	(3)	73040-2
	Patricroft	(2)	73043/4
	Leeds Holbeck	(1)	73045
	Millhouses	(2)	73047/8
	Leicester Midland	(2)	73046/9

The Scottish engines spent very little time at their new depots before being transferred to the WR with the exception of 73030/1 which were almost immediately loaned to Derby. 73030/1 were fitted with Westinghouse air brake equipment on delivery, in addition to the normal vacuum brake. 73030 was loaned to Rugby Test Plant for further steaming trials from July to November 1953 whilst 73031 was used in braking trials near Trowell on the Erewash Valley main line between Nottingham and Chesterfield; 73030 was similarly employed on return from testing at Rugby. When not on air brake testing work, 73031 was usually engaged on Northeast-Southwest route duties regularly being observed taking over the 12.40pm Newcastle-Bristol express at Derby; 73031 was also observed on the monthly Sunday Derby-Newcastle excursion on 19th September 1953. Braking trials continued in January 1954 when 73030/1 teamed up on several return Toton-Brent fitted coal trains. The engines eventually had their Westinghouse gear removed, 73030 in November 1955 and 73031 in March 1956; further details of the air brake tests are given in section 2.2.

In the short time they were in Scotland, the engines were noted on Glasgow Central-Edinburgh Princes Street trains, the Ayrshire coast route to Stranraer and both the Carlisle-Glasgow St Enoch and Carlisle-Glasgow Central routes with occasional forays to Leeds on the Settle and Carlisle line. The last three engines originally destined for Scotland, 73037/8/9, did not cross the border, their allocation being changed, before delivery, to the WR's Shrewsbury, Chester West and St Philip's Marsh depots respectively.

The LMR engines were allocated to depots already familiar with the type. 73042 broke new ground in August 1954 when it worked a public excursion from Euston to Crewe Works, conveying passengers right into the Works to the loading dock adjacent to the paint shop. The Leicester engines were noted for their use on long distance excursion traffic, 73046 visiting Norwich with a football Cup Tie special in February 1954 and taking Midland revellers through to Brighton on Whit Sunday 1956. Later, in the summer of the same year, the Leicester engines featured in a roster which took them as far as London Willesden on the 12.35pm(SO) to Hastings. The engine returned on the following weekend on the 10.51am(SO) Hastings-Leicester, after being used by Willesden during the week on workings such as the Euston-Tring locals. A Willesden engine, usually a Stanier Cl. 5 4-6-0, alternated on this duty, spending a week in the Midlands operating from Leicester depot. Another Leicester engine had an unusual through working to Immingham Docks on 1st May 1956 when it powered a train of specially treated ash from a Leicestershire firm for the Olympic athletic track at Melbourne, Australia, the venue for the games of that year.

During August and September 1953, the Scottish contingent and many of the Standard Cl. 5s still operating on the LMR were transferred to the WR which now had the full

Fig. 23   73067 rattles a Nine Elms-Southampton Docks fitted freight through Deepcut near Brookwood on 12th March 1965. The engine
was equipped with the high coal capacity (nine tons) BR1C tender. Allocated to the LMR's Oxley depot, Wolverhampton, 73067
was probably operating on the SR in connection with a visit to Eastleigh Works.   *(Rodney Lissenden)*

Fig. 24   Green-liveried 73068 passes Pontefract Baghill with the 8.05am Birmingham New Street-Newcastle on the 4th June 1960. The
engine was the first of the class to receive green livery, applied at Swindon Works in October 1958.   *(Peter Cookson)*

allocation as shown:

Shrewsbury	(13)	73012-5/7/8 73025/6/33-7
Chester West	(5)	73020/1/3/4/38
St Philip's Marsh	(7)	73019/22/7-9/32/9

The Shrewsbury engines took over duties on the so-called North to West route from Manchester and Liverpool to South Wales via Hereford, displacing Standard Cl. 4 4-6-0s 75000-9 not deemed powerful enough for the role. Early rosters also included the 12.45pm and 6.35pm Crewe-Manchester London Road (present-day Piccadilly) expresses. They also made an appearance on the Central Wales line trains to Swansea as well as helping to relieve a severe shortage of freight power at Shrewsbury. During the next few years, the Shrewsbury engines gained a reputation for roaming far and wide. Examples included a pigeon special at Ripon, excursions to Aintree for the Grand National horse race, a fitted freight at Cambridge and in October 1956, on Manchester (Victoria) to Barrow and Windermere workings

Bristol engines became frequent visitors to Newton Abbot on goods trains and in 1954 were noted on Southampton freights as far as Salisbury on several occasions. The Chester contingent was also employed mainly on freight work. The reason for their initial lack of use on passenger trains on the WR was the fact that they were not fitted with Automatic Train Control (ATC) equipment until much later, in 1956 at Derby Works. A few of the class, 73014/24/5/6, operated from Cardiff Canton on Northwest-South Wales expresses as well as on parcels and freight work in the mid-1950s.

The third batch of twenty five engines, 73050-74, delivered from Derby were for the SR, ScR and LMR; delivery was over the six months from June 1954 with allocations as follows:

SR	Bath Green Park	(3)	73050-2
ScR	Polmadie	(10)	73055-64
LMR	Leeds Holbeck	(3)	73053/4/66
	Millhouses	(1)	73065
	Nottingham	(1)	73067
	Derby	(2)	73068/9
	Chester Midland	(3)	73070-2
	Patricroft	(2)	73073/4

The Bath engines were acquired for use over the Somerset and Dorset line (S&DJR) to Bournemouth West, displacing Bulleid light Pacifics which were not ideally suited to the undulating nature of that line. These were the first Standard engines allocated to the S&DJR which had lost out when the second batch of Standard Cl. 6 Clan light Pacifics, 72010-24, had been cancelled; rumour had it that the first five engines of the second batch of Clans had been earmarked for the line.

Before delivery, 73050, together with selected diesel, electric and other standard steam engines had taken part in the International Railway Congress Exhibition at Willesden in June 1954. The engines had been given special 'exhibition' finishes and were immaculate. All three Bath engines were paired with BR1G tenders having an inset coal bunker and no water pick-up apparatus.

The new engines were soon at work between Bath and Bournemouth on 'The Pines Express', the 10.25am Manchester London Road-Bournemouth West and the 9.45am return. They also appeared regularly on the 7.43am(SO) and 9.18am(SO) Birmingham New Street-Bournemouth and 2-45pm Bournemouth-Bristol as well as

several other summer Saturday services. Initially, they were not considered the equal of the Stanier Cl. 5 4-6-0s, of which two, 44917 and 45440 remained on the S&DJR line for a time. Nevertheless, during July, 73052 was recorded as reaching 74 mph on the descent to Evercreech Junction with the 12 coach 10.08am Bath-Bournemouth, followed by 80 mph at Baileygate; it was reported that the engine gave a rougher ride compared with the Stanier type.

The engines did not spend all their time on the S&DJR as they were employed on workings to the Midlands, one roster in the summer of 1954 being as follows:

1.58pm	Bath-Gloucester semi-fast
4.17pm	Gloucester-Birmingham New St semi-fast
7.45pm	Birmingham New St-Leicester local
12.40am	Leicester-Bath parcels

During the same period, they also operated on the 12.01pm(FO) Bath-Birmingham returning next day with the 10.38am Manchester London Road-Bournemouth from Birmingham New Street to Bath. Occasionally appearances further afield were noted such as when 73050 was observed at Castleford, Yorks. in the summer of 1957 having worked a holiday relief via the LMR Western Division main line through Stafford and Stockport.

For the summer traffic of 1955, four more of the type 73047/9/73/4 were operating from Bath at various times, the first two remaining for several years. In subsequent summers, Standard Cl. 5s from SR depots were loaned to Bath. The same two engines, 73087, 73116 were used each year, the former from 1956-61 and the latter from 1956-59. As with virtually all the Standard Cl. 5 4-6-0s which spent time on the S&DJR, the engines were fitted with the Whitaker automatic tablet exchange apparatus which was affixed to the driver's side of the tender for working on the single line stretches. Both 73087 and 73116 retained their tablet catcher brackets after summer stints at Bath and although 73116 did not return for the 1960 summer season, it was occasionally appropriated during visits to Bournemouth Central depot for one of the latter's rostered turns on the S&DJR.

73055-64 were delivered to Polmadie in the period June to October 1954, displacing several 4-6-0s of the LMS Jubilee and Stanier 5 classes to neighbouring Corkerhill. The new engines were first noted on the Glasgow Central-Edinburgh Princes Street service, regularly appearing on the 6.35am from Glasgow and the 6.12pm return. They were also frequently observed on the Glasgow Central-Manchester/Liverpool trains, normally rostered for the Standard Cl. 6 Clan light Pacifics. During their stopover in Lancashire, engines from these workings were often employed by Newton Heath on local and excursion trains and the sight of a Polmadie Standard Cl. 5 was not unusual either at Blackpool or along the North Wales coast. 73057 was also noted at Morecambe Euston Road with the summer Saturday 11-50am from Glasgow Central on 17th July 1954. Towards the end of that year the Polmadie engines began working to Aberdeen, regularly appearing on the 6.55pm fish train for Manchester. In October 1955, 73060-2 were transferred to Motherwell from where they were regularly noted on fitted freights to Carlisle, Perth and Aberdeen.

The rest of the third batch, 73053/4/65-74 were allocated to the LMR and joined other members of the class at their respective depots, sharing the workings. A Leeds Holbeck engine was regularly observed at this time on the Friday and

Fig. 25
Bletchley based 73070 leaves Bletchley with a partially fitted freight in early 1964. The engine acquired the BR AWS apparatus, as confirmed by the guard plate behind the front coupling hook, during a general overhaul at Derby Works in February 1960.   (P.H. Wells)

Fig. 26
73073 leaves Stamford Town with one of two special trains for the local Blackstone Works outing to Swindon Works on 1st June 1957. The other train was also powered by a Standard Cl. 5 4-6-0, 73046; both engines were allocated to Leicester Midland shed at the time. 73073 had a short spell working on the S&DJR from Bath Green Park in 1955.   (P.H. Wells)

Fig. 27
Newly allocated to the SR, 73080 heads an express from Dover to Victoria via Maidstone East past Folkestone Warren Halt on 1st August 1955. The engine carries the high water capacity (4725 gal.) BR1B type tender useful for engines based on the SR which had no water troughs. 73080 was named *Merlin* in February 1961 and remained on the SR for the whole of its working life; it was maintained throughout by Eastleigh Works apart from a non-classified repair at Ashford Works in June 1956.   (L.Hanson)

Saturday 8.46 am Bradford Forster Square-Scarborough, returning on the 12.24pm Scarborough-York and the 3.10pm York-Leeds City services. The class also appeared from time to time deputising for LMS Compound 4-4-0s, Hughes-Fowler Cl. 6P/5F Crab 2-6-0s and Fowler Patriot Cl. 4-6-0s on the Leeds City-Morecambe Promenade services. The Millhouses engines were used on Sheffield Midland-St Pancras expresses, particularly 73065/74 with the larger capacity tenders.

In February 1956, 73071, together with Stanier Cl. 5 44911, was transferred on loan to London Kings Cross in connection with tests on Automatic Train Control (ATC) on the East Coast route. The equipment was not fitted until April at Doncaster Works. Meanwhile the pair were put to work on the Kings Cross-Cambridge Buffet Car service although 73071 was quickly out of action with broken rocker bars and spent several weeks at Cambridge awaiting replacements. Both engines continued on the Cambridge trains with occasional visits to Hull on a lodging turn as well as the duty involving the 6.18pm Kings Cross-Cleethorpes, returning next day on the 8.35pm Grimsby-Kings Cross freight. 73071 returned to Chester Midland in May 1957.

At the same time, the LMR depot at Bristol Barrow Road received its first allocation of the type, 73015/54/68 from Derby in exchange for Stanier Caprotti valve Cl. 5 4-6-0s; they were used on the main line to Birmingham New Street, Sheffield and Leeds. It was one of these engines, 73054, which earlier in its career had taken part in an unusual test of prototype line detonators of safer design. On 15th April 1956, between mileposts 14¾ and 15½ on the Tamworth to Burton-on-Trent sector, a train was run at high speed over some 200 such detonators in succession, the driver being requested to attain a speed of as near 80 mph as possible. 73054 duly appeared with a train of five coaches and, passing over the detonators, produced a sound like that of rapid

gunfire, resulting in a considerable cloud of smoke. As soon as the train had passed, a group of permanent way staff collected the remains to be taken away for close scrutiny of the fragmentation characteristics.

The fourth batch of twenty five Derby built locomotives, 73075-99, was despatched from the Works during the period April to December 1955, five for the ScR, ten for the SR and ten for the LMR; the engines were allocated as shown:

ScR	Polmadie	(2)	73075/6
	Eastfield	(2)	73077/8
	Corkerhill	(1)	73079
SR	Stewarts Lane	(10)	73080-9
LMR	Patricroft	(10)	73090-9

During April and May 1955, 73075/6 took their places alongside 73055-64 already at Polmadie, sharing their duties which now included occasional visits to the Glasgow Central-Gourock line, normally the preserve of Cl. 4 2-6-4 tank engines. In July 73075 was noted working the initial stage of the new express freight service, the 'Hielan Piper'. This train left Renfrew South at 5.00pm running to Aberdeen, thence to Inverness, arriving about 6.00am next day. Major areas served were Rutherglen, Larbert, Dubton, Keith, Elgin and Forres. Later, Polmadie engines had a regular freight turn on the North Leith branch, probably filling-in between Glasgow-Edinburgh passenger duties.

73077/8 arrived at Eastfield during May 1955. 73077 was used on Glasgow Queen Street-Edinburgh Waverley trains. Later both engines spent virtually all their time on the West Highland line between Glasgow Queen Street and Fort William. A regular duty was the 5.45am ex-Glasgow and the 2.56pm return. In May 1955, 73079 was the lone representative of its class at Corkerhill but was later joined by five Doncaster-built engines, 73100-4 in August and September. 73079 was employed on both passenger and freight duties on the undulating Stranraer Road alongside

Fig. 29
73082 is seen at Dover on 2nd August 1955 with a Victoria express. 73080-9 were initially allocated to Stewarts Lane, the majority remaining there until displacement by electrification in 1959. In the hands of several of the depot's footplate artists, notably Driver Sam Gingell, the class gained a reputation for fast running on the London-Chatham-Kent Coast service.
(L. Hanson)

Fig. 30   73082, now carrying the name *Camelot*, leaves Fratton with a train for Portsmouth on 8th October 1961. The engine was withdrawn in June 1966 and is now preserved in full working order on the Bluebell Railway at Sheffield Park. The triangle (in yellow) observable below the cabside numerals indicates the engine has been fitted with the standard BR briquette water softening system.
(P.H. Wells)

Fig. 31
The now restored 73082, *Camelot*, is about to depart from Sheffield Park with a train for Horsted Keynes in the late 1990s. *(J.B. Arnold)*

Fig. 32
73084, later named *Tintagel*, powers the 11.35am Victoria-Ramsgate under Downs Bridge up the 1 in 100 from Beckenham Junction towards Shortlands on 16th May 1959; the train formation still includes several Pullman cars. The 11.35am was formerly an all-Pullman train introduced in May 1948 and named 'The Thanet Belle', linking Victoria with Whitstable, Herne Bay, Margate, Broadstairs and Ramsgate. The train was renamed 'The Kentish Belle' in June 1951 and the all-Pullman service discontinued in September 1958. *(Rodney Lissenden)*

Fig. 33
Operating from Eastleigh depot, 73087 later named *Linette*, approaches Allbrook Junction with a Nine Elms-Southampton Docks goods on 5th May 1957. 73087 was regularly loaned to Bath Green Park depot to assist with the summer holiday traffic over the S&DJR from 1956 to 1961. *(L. Elsey)*

Stanier Cl. 5 and Jubilee Cl. 4-6-0s.

Apart from 73050-2 at work on the Somerset and Dorset line (S&DJR) the SR saw little of the Standard Cl. 5s until 73080-9 were allocated to Stewarts Lane during June-September 1955. The new engines displaced a similar number of Maunsell King Arthur Cl. N15 4-6-0s to the Waterloo-Bournemouth line. By early July, the Standard Cl. 5s were engaged on Victoria-Ramsgate and Folkestone trains and later in the summer assisted on the heavy Continental boat traffic. By autumn, virtually all Stewarts Lane's Ramsgate line duties were worked by the class.

In early August, 73081 made the class debut on the Oxted line powering the 10.56am Brighton-Victoria and 3.52pm return, both via Uckfield. By the end of the year, however, the engines were officially barred from the Uckfield line due to clearance problems. In the summer of 1956, they were regularly appearing on Ramsgate-Cannon Street and Charing Cross-Ramsgate via Tonbridge duties, later including Charing Cross-Dover line workings.

73080-9 were mainly confined to the London-Kent Coast route until displaced after the various stages of electrification in the late 1950s and early 1960s. Occasional excursion duties took them further afield such as when 73088/9 worked to Bournemouth with Tottenham Hotspur Cup Tie specials via Kensington Olympia on 16th February 1957. Stewarts Lane also usually loaned one of the class, 73087, to Bath Green Park during the summer months for summer Saturday workings over the S&DJR line. Generally speaking, the engines were welcomed on the SR's Eastern Section. Their performance was regarded as almost equal to that of the Bulleid light Pacifics on the difficult Kent Coast route, speeds in excess of 85 mph being regularly recorded on the Bromley South-Chatham section through Farningham Road; several runs on this route are described in section 2.11.1.

The new Patricroft contingent 73090-9 arrived from October to December 1955, displacing a similar number of Stanier Cl. 5 4-6-0s mainly to LMR Western Division depots. In addition to North Wales coast line duties, the engines began appearing regularly to and from Leeds on the 5.00pm Liverpool Lime Street-Newcastle returning on the 8.55am Newcastle-Liverpool; during 1957, they also displaced Patricroft Jubilee Cl. 4-6-0s from some of their regular Manchester Victoria-Glasgow Central workings. The class also shared with Stanier Cl. 5 4-6-0s the working of the regular monthly Sunday Manchester Exchange-Newcastle excursions which ran in the 1950/60s. These excursions could prove interesting to passengers as a number of different routes would be used through County Durham depending on where the East Coast Main Line would be blocked with permanent way operations.

The first batch of twenty five Doncaster-built engines, 73100-24 were delivered between August 1955 and February 1956, fifteen to the ScR and ten to the SR; allocations were as follows:

ScR	Corkerhill	(9)	73100-4/21-4
	Eastfield	(5)	73105-9
	Perth	(1)	73120
SR	Nine Elms	(10)	73110-9

Running-in turns were mainly Cl. B1 4-6-0 passenger workings to Hull, Sheffield Victoria, and Cleethorpes, with freights to Wakefield, Boston and Cambridge, although at least one (73105 on 28th December) made an appearance at Kings Cross depot. During delivery, the ScR allocation usually worked north on the East Coast main line with Edinburgh-bound freights.

73100-4 arrived at Corkerhill during September/October with 73121-4 appearing six months later. Together with 73079, allocated earlier in the year, the new engines began to monopolise Corkerhill's Stranraer line duties, including the 8.55am, 12.30pm and 9.00pm 'Irishman' boat train ex-Glasgow St Enoch and the 7.25am, 4.25pm and 9.15pm 'Irishman' returns from Stranraer. Also included were freight workings, notably the 1.00am 'College' goods to Stranraer and the return 'Milk' which despite its name carried mainly sundries off the Irish boat.

The Eastfield engines, 73105-9, although scheduled for production in numerical sequence, were deferred whilst 73110-9 were turned out for the urgent requirements of the SR. Eastfield eventually took delivery over two months from early December 1955. The new engines were used principally on the Fife Coast line and Glasgow Queen Street-Edinburgh Waverley passenger service. They also regularly worked as far as Edinburgh with the 'Queen of Scots' Pullman for Kings Cross via Newcastle, Harrogate and Leeds Central. In June 1957, 73106/7 left Eastfield for Inverness where they were observed working on the Kyle of Lochalsh and Perth routes respectively. It has not been confirmed that either of the engines was tried out on the 'Far North' Wick and Thurso line. Both engines then joined the Perth contingent in October 1957 to bring the class strength there up to eight which now included 73120, delivered in January 1956.

Nine Elms took delivery of 73110-9 between October and December 1955. The new engines took over the duties of a number of elderly 4-6-0s of the N15 Urie King Arthur and N15X Remembrance classes which were soon withdrawn. 73111 was reported to be the first in use on 29th October when it took charge of the 9.30am Waterloo-Bournemouth. Other Bournemouth line workings included the Sunday duty No. 22, a Waterloo-Southampton turn as far as Eastleigh; by New Year 1956, several of the class had been noted working into Southampton Docks on boat trains for the Far East and the still regular sailings across the North Atlantic to New York. On 10th January 1956 73112 worked the 1.00pm Waterloo-Exeter throughout; rostered workings to Exeter Central on both stopping trains and expresses were established early in 1956. Regular turns included the 5.40am Waterloo-Templecombe and a duty incorporating the 10.45am Basingstoke-Salisbury going forward with the 12.36pm to Exeter as far as Yeovil, thence taking over the 1.10pm Exeter-Salisbury all stations.

At this time, due to the occasional shortage of Bulleid Pacifics, the Standard Cl. 5s found themselves deputising on such workings as the 'Bournemouth Belle' Pullman. On 9th January, 73118 with a nine coach train reached Bournemouth two minutes early. On the return trip, 73118 appeared to find time-keeping more difficult even before several permanent way slacks and signal checks; these delays contributed to a seven minute late arrival at Waterloo. On another occasion, however, a Standard Cl. 5 took over from an ailing Bulleid Pacific at Southampton, again on the down Pullman, and was used by choice of the driver on the up train, managing to keep time with nine Pullmans plus van.

Another working on which these engines showed good performances was the 5.39pm Waterloo-Salisbury, 73116 completing the 29¼ miles to Woking in 29 minutes on 4th May with an eleven coach train. There had been several cases of over-running the platform end at Woking with this train, which led to speculation that the braking power was not as good as it might be.

By the summer of 1956, the weekend scene on the Waterloo line had shown changes from previous years. The influx of Standard Cl. 5 4-6-0s and Cl. 4 4-6-0s (75XXX) plus the Maunsell King Arthur Cl. N15 4-6-0s displaced from the Kent Coast lines caused much reduced dependence on the S15 and H15 Cl. 4-6-0s for summer Saturday traffic. Regular workings by the Standard Cl. 5s also included the daily Brighton-Plymouth Friary service as far as Salisbury and the Brighton-Bournemouth trains. They were also regular visitors to Willesden LMR to take over workings from the North and Midlands to the South Coast. Examples included 73111/5 picking up football Cup Tie specials for Bournemouth from Manchester on 2nd March 1957, whilst on 15th May, a train of impressive dimensions, a 19-coach troop special from Liverpool Edge Hill to Basingstoke was double-headed out of Willesden by a pair of Standard Cl. 5s.

Earlier, in February 1956, 73001/10/45 from the LMR together with 73085/8 and 73110/4/7 were loaned to the WR for a few weeks to assist in the substitution programme for the King Cl. 4-6-0s temporarily withdrawn for bogie examination following discovery of frame fractures on certain engines. The Standard Cl. 5s undertook secondary duties in the London and Bristol areas with occasional appearances on the Birmingham line thus releasing Castle Class 4-6-0s to fulfil the Kings' duties. 73119 was also noted near Swindon on these workings, although it was not officially recorded as having been loaned to the WR.

The fifth batch of Standard Cl. 5 4-6-0s to be delivered from Derby Works consisted of thirty engines, 73125-54. They differed from other members of the class in that they were fitted with British Caprotti valve gear as opposed to the Walschaerts variety carried by the rest. They were allocated equally between the WR, LMR and ScR as shown:

WR	Shrewsbury	(10)	73125-34
LMR	Holyhead	(5)	73135-9
	Leicester Midland	(5)	73140-4
ScR	St Rollox	(10)	73145-54

The Shrewsbury engines 73125-34 were delivered between July and October 1956 replacing an equal number of Walschaerts valve gear members of the same class and taking over their duties on expresses, parcels and fast freights on the Manchester and Liverpool to South Wales route via Hereford. The displaced engines, 73001/12/7/8/20/33-7 went to three other WR depots, Oxley, Swindon and Tyseley. 73036/7 began operation from Tyseley mainly on freight duties previously handled by ex-ROD 2-8-0s 3017/44 recently withdrawn. 73033/4/5 performed similar duties from Oxley whilst the remainder were allocated to Swindon. Here they were not too well received and spent much of their time on freight work.

The LMR engines, 73135-44 were turned out in the period October to December 1956. The Holyhead allocation was used on both passenger and freight duties along the North Wales coast, with frequent visits to Manchester.

Regular rosters for the Leicester contingent took them mainly on St Pancras line work. During the early part of 1957 the new engines were kept busy on football excursion duties.

For example, on 5th January 73141-3 were in charge of three specials for the Tottenham Hotspur-Leicester City Cup Tie, travelling to Northumberland Park via Peterborough East, Cambridge and Broxbourne. Later, on 26th January, 73138/41 were part of a cavalcade of some twenty specials run for the Huddersfield-Peterborough Cup Tie, the other motive power being mainly B1 4-6-0s; in the period between the above dates, 73138 and 73140 had exchanged depots.

During 1957, the class made frequent appearances on the heavily-loading 5.30pm St Pancras-Nottingham. Another regular duty involved returning north as pilot on the 12.46pm Worcester-Birmingham New Street local. On 7th November, 73144 worked the Royal train to Edmonthorpe and Wymondham station on the occasion of the Duke of Edinburgh's visit to Rutland the following day.

The Scottish allocation was based at St Rollox which at the time had been short of Cl. 5 engines to fulfil its diagrammed work. 73145-54 arrived between January and June 1957 displacing about half their number of Stanier Cl. 5 4-6-0s to other ScR and some LMR Lancashire depots. 73154 was the last steam locomotive to be built at Derby and one of the first to receive the large new 'British Railways' tender crest. The new engines were soon on main line work from Glasgow Buchanan Street, notably the 7.15am, 9.15am and 6.15pm to Dundee and 2.00pm return, and the 8.15am to Aberdeen and 6.10pm return. They proved equal to the task on the heavily graded tightly timed Aberdeen road and excellent performances were recorded with eight coach three hundred ton trains. Together with 73005-9 and 73106/7/20 of Perth depot, the Standard Cl. 5s were well represented on the Glasgow to Dundee and Aberdeen line.

The final batch of seventeen engines, 73155-71, for the ER and the NER was delivered from Doncaster between December 1956 and May 1957, allocated as shown:

ER	Neasden	(5)	73155-9
NER	Blaydon	(2)	73160/1
	York	(10)	73162-71

73155-9 arrived at Neasden during January, displacing B1 4-6-0s to other ER depots. At the same time, the last Cl. 7P A3 Pacific at Neasden, 60108, was reallocated to Kings Cross. The new engines began working on Great Central main line services, 73155 being noted on the 'Master Cutler', the 6.45pm Marylebone-Sheffield Victoria on 19th January. The class did not win favour at Neasden, reportedly being heavy on coal and not master of their duties. This was not surprising perhaps as not long previously, their jobs had been handled by Cl. 7P A3 Pacifics and V2 2-6-2s. During the summer of 1957, the engines were noted at York on the famous 'Starlight Specials', well known at the time for offering cheap overnight travel during peak holiday periods. York regularly used the engines on Hull, Scarborough and Harrogate line duties during their weekend stopovers.

The complaints at Neasden of the relative lack of power of the Standard Cl. 5 4-6-0s persisted and in September 1957 three of the allocation, 73157-9 were exchanged for Cl. V2 2-6-2s 60855/76/7 from Kings Cross. 73157-9 were found employment on the Great Northern main line outer suburban services with occasional visits to Hull and Cleethorpes on express freights.

The first two NER engines 73160/1 were allocated initially to Blaydon in early 1957 and used on passenger and parcels services between Newcastle and Carlisle. They were

Fig. 34   73088, later named *Joyous Gard*, starts an afternoon boat train out of Victoria for either Folkestone Harbour or Dover Marine via Tonbridge and Ashford on 15th June 1956. 73088 was loaned to the WR's Oxford depot for several weeks from February 1956 to assist in substituting for the King Class 4-6-0s temporarily withdrawn for bogie examination.

(Alan Bowman)

Fig. 35   73093 heads an up breakdown train near Earlsfield between Wimbledon and Clapham Junction on 30th April 1966. The engine was one of ten of the class, 73090-9, fitted with SKF roller bearings rather than the standard Timken variety and carried the BR1C tender with higher coal and water capacity.

(Peter Groom)

also tried on various freight diagrams including Blaydon-Shildon and Addison-Carlisle turns. The turntable at the ex-North Eastern Railway yard at Carlisle London Road proved too tight a fit for the new engines and workings very quickly reverted to K1 2-6-0 power. Within a few weeks, 73160/1 were reallocated to Gateshead in exchange for B1 4-6-0s. Here the Standard Cl. 5 4-6-0s were used on freights from Park Lane to the South and parcels trains between Newcastle and York, although by early March, their appearances were becoming rare on the fitted freights. The engines were no match for the Cl. V2 2-6-2s normally used on these duties, it being necessary to reduce either the classification or the load of the freights they were turned out to work. A regular passenger turn was the 12.05 pm Newcastle-Colchester via Sunderland as far as York, returning with the 4.30 pm York-Newcastle parcels via the ECML. In September they were on the move again, this time to Normanton to work the 12.05am express freight to Birmingham Lawley Street when it was upgraded from class 'D' to class 'C'. The normal return working was either the 2.20pm or 9.45pm fast freight from Birmingham.

73162-71 arrived at York between February and June 1957 taking over some B1 and B16 4-6-0 duties. During the last week in February 73162 went into service on the 10.15am York-Yarmouth as far as Lincoln, returning at 2.38pm on the 9.00am Lowestoft-York. In March they became consistent performers as far as Sheffield Victoria on the 10.23am York-Bournemouth. Later, in May, the 10.10am York-Manchester Victoria and 5.10pm return both via the Calder Valley line became a regular duty. The new engines also featured on York-Bristol expresses as far as Sheffield Midland with occasional visits further south to the Midlands on specials. They were also to be seen on passenger and parcels services to Wakefield Kirkgate, Scarborough and Hull via Selby and Market Weighton. The class also worked north to Darlington, Newcastle, Low Fell, Park Lane and Heaton on passenger, parcels and freight turns. Their duties on the York-Harrogate-Leeds circuit included for a time the up 'Yorkshire Pullman' between Harrogate and Leeds Central. The engines were rare visitors on the Great Northern main line to Kings Cross. By the end of September 1957, 73171 had been transferred to Leeds Holbeck.

2.7.2 From 1957 to Withdrawal

North Eastern Region
In November 1958, 73162-6 of the York allocation were displaced to Huddersfield by Cl. V2 2-6-2's 60828/55/76/7/8 from the Great Central main line. In February 1959, the remainder of the York contingent, 73167-70 went to Scarborough where they were reportedly warmly welcomed by the crews who had depended for so long on the D49 4-4-0s. The regular York Standard Cl. 5 turn to Lincoln now reverted to B16 haulage. Much to the chagrin of the maintenance staff at Scarborough, who had worked hard to get the engines into tip-top condition, 73167-70 were reallocated to Normanton and Holbeck after only a few months, to be replaced at Scarborough by B1 4-6-0s from Hull Botanic Gardens.

73162-6 at Huddersfield were employed on freight and passenger workings across the Pennines to Stockport, Manchester and Liverpool. It was 73164 which had the sad task of working one of the last Huddersfield top link steam duties on 3rd March 1962 when it powered the 7.34am to Stockport, the service subsequently being given over to diesel multiple units.

The Normanton engines at this time, 73160/1/7, were still on the Birmingham freights and were regularly seen on York line freights. 73161, after transfer to Neville Hill, was involved in one of the few accidents to befall the class during their stay on the NER. The engine was working the 5.45pm Scarborough-York fitted freight on 10th July 1962 when it was derailed by trap points to the west of Malton station, toppling over on its left hand side; 73161 was re-railed the following day.

In December 1962, the NER allocation was twelve engines:

Normanton	(2)	73160/7
Neville Hill	(4)	73161/2/8/9
Huddersfield	(3)	73163-5
Royston	(3)	73166/70/1

The Neville Hill engines were employed on freight traffic in the Leeds area and on mail or weekend excursion traffic, mainly on the Scarborough line; the Royston group performed duties similar to those of the Normanton allocation.

In the twelve months from October 1963, the whole of the remaining NER allocation, displaced by dieselisation, migrated to the SR's Western Section (73161/2/6-71) the LMR (73160/3/5) and the WR (73164). No further members of the class were subsequently allocated to the NER.

Eastern Region
At the end of 1957, the five Standard Cl. 5 4-6-0s on the ER were still at Neasden, (73155/6 for the Great Central line services), and Kings Cross, (73157/8/9 for express freights to Humberside and outer suburban services to Baldock and Cambridge). The engines were never popular at Kings Cross, home grown B1 4-6-0s being preferred. The depot must have found it difficult to provide suitable work for its Standard Cl. 5s as they departed for Darnall for a short period in October 1958 before eventually reverting to Neasden for a further stint on the Great Central line, by now under the control of the LMR.

The LMR had taken over the Great Central line services in February 1958; at the same time the former LMR depots at Grimesthorpe, Millhouses and Canklow came under the control of the ER. By May 1958, Standard Cl. 5s from several LMR sheds had been drafted into these depots in exchange for Stanier Cl. 5 4-6-0s. After the reorganisation, the ER allocation was:

Grimesthorpe	(2)	73000/43
Canklow	(1)	73002
Millhouses	(11)	73004/11/6/46/8
		73065/7/73/4
		73155/6

The class operated on the York-Bristol and Leeds-St Pancras routes until gradually displaced by more powerful steam classes made redundant in other areas by diesels. The Millhouses engines were also to be seen on football excursion traffic to Newcastle, Sunderland and Middlesbrough. In 1962 the eight engines remaining on the ER 73000/2/16/43/6/65/74 and 73155 were reallocated, 73000 to Derby in January and the rest to Eastleigh and Nine Elms on the the SR's

Fig. 36
73099 stands at Wigan North Western on 11th August 1956 with the stock of the 4.18pm stopping train to Leeds City via Manchester Exchange and Huddersfield. This service took almost three and a half hours for the 60 mile journey to Leeds, calling at virtually all stations. *(Russell Leitch)*

Fig. 37
73099 awaits departure from Birmingham New Street with the Stephenson Locomotive Society's SMJR rail tour on Sunday 29th April 1956. The special was run from Kings Cross with LNER Cl. D16/3 62605 as far as Hitchin. There MR Cl. 3 0-6-0 43222 took charge for the ride over the Stratford-on-Avon and Midland Junction line. The 0-6-0 continued with the train to Birmingham where it was replaced by 73099 for the return to Euston via Rugby.
(Philip J. Kelley)

Fig. 38
73105 from the first batch of Doncaster-built engines heads the up 'Queen of Scots' Pullman, the 10.55am Glasgow Queen St-Kings Cross, near Greenhill Upper between Castlecary and Bonnybridge on 30th July 1960. Stops on this service were limited to Edinburgh Waverley, Newcastle upon Tyne, Darlington, Harrogate and Leeds Central. The train ran for the last time on 12th January 1963. Note the Doncaster trademark 'Class 5' on 73105's buffer beam.
(W.T. Stubbs)

Western Section in the following November. No further Standard Cl. 5s were allocated to the ER from that time.

Scottish Region

The arrival of Caprotti engines 73145-54 at St Rollox by June 1957 brought the allocation of Standard Cl. 5 4-6-0s in Scotland to forty five, distributed as shown:

Perth	(6)	73005-9, 73120
Polmadie	(9)	73055-9/63/4/75/6
Motherwell	(3)	73060-2
Eastfield	(5)	73077/8, 73105/8/9
Corkerhill	(10)	73079, 73100-4/21-4
Inverness	(2)	73106/7
St Rollox	(10)	73145-54

In October 1957, the two Inverness engines 73106/7 were exchanged for two Stanier Cl. 5 4-6-0s from Perth. Together with the St Rollox Standard Caprotti Cl. 5s, the Perth stud was now well established on the Glasgow Buchanan Street-Dundee and Aberdeen services. On 2nd August 1958, a combination of the Bank Holiday and return Glasgow Fair holiday traffic produced an exceptionally busy day on the Perth-Glasgow line. Observers at Bonnybridge noted all the Perth and St Rollox Standard Cl. 5s in action. On a regular basis, the latter depot had the lion's share of the Glasgow-Dundee workings including the 7.15am, 9.15am, 1.15pm, 3.15pm and 6.15pm to Dundee, returning respectively on the 12 noon, 2.00pm, 6.00pm, and 8.00pm departures from Dundee; the engine off the 6.15pm returned on a fish train to Glasgow Central.

Workings from Polmadie and Corkerhill depots continued much as before including occasional visits of the latter's engines to Leeds on through services from Glasgow St Enoch. Towards the end of 1958, the Corkerhill stud was being used in preference to the depot's Stanier Jubilee Cl. 4-6-0s as they were considered more economical to maintain.

Polmadie gained three more Standard Cl. 5s, 73072/98/9 on loan from England in November 1958 and these engines became permanently allocated a few months later. Regular workings for the class were the Glasgow Central-Manchester Victoria sevices as well as excursions and holiday services from Scotland to the Fylde Coast. The Polmadie engines occasionally strayed further afield when for example 73072 was noted at Oban together with Eastfield's 73108 double-heading a return television train excursion for Glasgow.

At the turn of the year, the first Type 2 diesels, the Cl. 26s, were being tried out on the Highland main line Inverness-Perth-Glasgow services, although it was not until 1961 that the new diesel power, now both Cl. 26 and Cl. 27, made significant inroads into the work of the Standard Cl. 5s on this route. By then the Glasgow-Dundee services were largely in the hands of the Type 2 Cl. 21 diesels, whilst the Cl. 26/27s had virtually ousted steam on the Inverness line. Diesel failures were a regular occurrence however, especially with the Cl. 21s and the Standard Cl. 5s were frequently called on to help out. The Cl. 21s proved so unreliable, until twenty of them were re-engined and became Cl. 29, that steam power, including several of the legendary LNER A4 Pacifics, continued to appear on the majority of Glasgow-Aberdeen services until 1966. The Perth-Edinburgh Waverley route via Glenfarg still featured the Standard Cl. 5s frequently until 1962 when rostered steam haulage on these services was virtually eliminated.

Although the Standard Cl. 5s had a relatively incident free time in Scotland, an unusual accident did occur on the main line from Glasgow St Enoch to Kilmarnock in the early hours of 27th January 1962. The line was blocked when a down freight from Carlisle ran into a landslip between Nitshill and Kennishead. The engine, 73098, appears to have 'climbed' the obstruction and landed on the other side of the debris leaving its train in some disarray. Trains to Kilmarnock were diverted via Paisley and Dalry for the following two days.

In December 1962, five more Standard Cl. 5s were displaced by diesels to Corkerhill, 73005/6/9 and 73120 arriving from Perth, whilst Eastfield supplied 73077, one of the former regulars on the West Highland line. This enabled several Hughes-Fowler Crab Cl. 2-6-0s to be retired from the Ayrshire district. The years 1963/4 saw a gradual dieselisation of many services in Scotland, although by June 1965, forty Standard Cl. 5s were still operating in the region, mainly at their old haunts; allocation was as follows:

Corkerhill	(13)	73005/9/57/79 73100-4/20-2/4
Grangemouth	(2)	73007, 73105
Aberdeen Ferryhill	(2)	73008/56
Polmadie	(10)	73055/9 73060/2-4/72/5/98/9
Eastfield	(2)	73078, 73108
Motherwell	(1)	73107
St Rollox	(10)	73145-54

The St Rollox stud, albeit in poor external condition, was still extensively used on the Glasgow-Dundee services. 73149, reckoned to be the pick of the bunch, was observed several times operating the 8.25am Glasgow-Aberdeen and the 5.15pm return during the latter part of August 1965 when the roster temporarily reverted to steam power. Also observed at this time was a high speed exploit by 73008 on the four coach 10.10am Aberdeen-Perth when it touched 91 mph on the level between Forfar and Stanley Junction, the 25.3 miles of which were covered in twenty minutes after a standing start.

By August 1965, the Corkerhill engines were still regularly seen in strength on the former Glasgow and South Western lines from Glasgow St Enoch to Ayr, Stranraer and Carlisle; duties included both freight and passenger work although the latter had been extensively dieselised by this time.

In early 1966, the Polmadie stud was still featuring on Glasgow Central-Edinburgh Waverley trains, the 5.16pm ex-Glasgow often being worked by either 73059 or 73072. The Polmadie and Corkerhill engines also found regular employment during the 1966 summer season working through on Glasgow-Blackpool holiday trains and Illuminations excursions.

By July 1966, the Glasgow-Aberdeen passenger service had been almost completely dieselised, initially by the re-engined Type 2 Cl. 21 locomotives, reclassified Cl. 29, but later by Type 4 Cl. 40s and Cl. 47s. 73146 was destined to be the last active Caprotti Standard Cl. 5 working on Glasgow Buchanan St-Fife Coast and Perth-Carlisle lines. As a sad comment on the extent of neglect which had overtaken the remaining steam power operating at this time, 73146 put up a rather poor performance on the Carlisle-Symington leg of the 12.05pm Euston-Perth on Christmas Eve 1966 when it took one and a half hours to cover the distance of 66.8 miles.

By January 1967, the number of Standard Cl. 5s operating

from Scottish depots was down to six, allocated thus:

Polmadie	(3)	73059/60/4
Corkerhill	(2)	73079, 73100
Motherwell	(1)	73146

With the exception of 73100, withdrawn later that month, the other engines were taken out of service on 1st May 1967 when Scottish based steam workings ceased.

Western Region

By the end of 1957, with all the Standard Cl. 5 4-6-0s in service, the WR had thirty five engines allocated as shown:

Swindon	(8)	73001/12/7/8
		73020/2/7/9
Chester West	(4)	73013/21/3/38
Cardiff Canton	(4)	73014/24-6
St Philip's Marsh	(4)	73019/28/32/9
Oxley	(3)	73033-5
Tyseley	(2)	73036/7
Shrewsbury	(10)	73125-34

On 23rd February 1958, the WR took over responsibility for the Somerset and Dorset (S&DJR) line from the SR. At the start of that summer, Bath Green Park gained 73019/28 from St Philip's Marsh and 73088 from Stewarts Lane, in addition to the SR based regulars 73087 and 73116 for the summer holiday traffic. At the same time, the SR took over Weymouth depot from the WR and in September 1958, a group of Standard Cl. 5s, 73017/8/20/2/9 was moved there from Swindon in exchange for GWR Hall Cl. 4-6-0s 5964/78/81/3/97. The Standard Cl. 5s were permitted to run between Basingstoke and Waterloo whereas the Hall class was prohibited for clearance reasons. A few months earlier, St Philip's Marsh had lost its remaining allocation of Standard Cl. 5s to Birkenhead in exchange for GWR Grange Cl. 4-6-0s. The Bath Standard Cl. 5s, in addition to S&DJR line duties, continued regular workings to the Midlands still occasionally being observed in Lancashire and Yorkshire on through summer Saturday holiday trains. For the 1961 summer traffic however only one of the regular SR visitors, 73087, appeared on the S&DJR line and was accompanied for the first time by the temporary transfer of three Standard Cl. 9F 2-10-0s, 92000/1 from Newport Ebbw Junction and 92212 from Banbury. This was the start of the short-lived but successful deployment of the 9Fs on the S&D line.

In 1962, the beginning of the end of the S&DJR line as a through route was signalled by the proposal to divert the all year round 'Pines Express' from Manchester Piccadilly to Bournemouth West away from the route. From Crewe, instead of going via Birmingham New Street through Gloucester to Bath Green Park, the service would instead go via the Market Drayton line to Birmingham Snow Hill thence to Bournemouth via Oxford, Reading and Basingstoke, thus enabling a substantial train mileage saving. The year 1963 saw the last summer of scheduled long distance through workings on the S&DJR and by the end of January 1964, only six Standard Cl. 5s, 73047/9/50-2/4 remained at Bath. They were used on Bath-Bournemouth semi-fasts and freights and the occasional through excursions to Bournemouth from the Midlands and Bristol areas. By August 1965 the Bath 'Old Faithfuls', 73050-2 were no longer at the depot, 73050 now working from Shrewsbury and 73051/2 having been withdrawn. The two remaining Standard Cl. 5s at Bath, 73001/68 shared workings with Standard Cl. 4 2-6-4 tanks

until withdrawn in December 1965. On 5th March 1966, the route closed completely, thus effectively eliminating steam from the WR.

In 1957, the Shrewsbury allocation of Caprotti Standard Cl. 5 4-6-0s, 73125-34 was still engaged mainly on Northwest-South Wales route services via Hereford. In the summer of 1958, they also had a regular daily visit to the Nuneaton area. This involved powering the 8.20pm local from Stafford to Nuneaton, followed early next morning by a turn to Coventry on a workman's train. The Shrewsbury stud still clung to their reputation as 'wanderers', being noted during the spring and summer of 1958 variously at Ripon (more pigeon specials), Paddington (73126 on a Cup Final excursion from Wrexham), Newton Abbot (73133 performing pilot duties on the South Devon banks) and Euston (73132 as pilot to an up 'Ulster Express'). In August 1958 however this group's meanderings came to an end as all were exchanged for Walschaerts gear engines 73090-7 from Patricroft. Here they remained for the rest of their working lives apart from 73128 which had a two month spell at Rowsley from February 1964 before returning to Patricroft. 73131 did manage a final fling in the process of transferring to Patricroft during August however, when it was observed as follows:

4th Morecambe-Crewe parcels.
5th 6.10pm Manchester Victoria-Southport.
8th 8.00am Blackpool-Euston (at Preston).
11th Out of action at Ayr (via Wakefield) with 'big-end' trouble.
16th 8.25am Ayr-Newcastle as far as Carlisle
18th Back at Ayr.

In September 1961, Shrewsbury began hosting a 4-6-0 class new to its books, the Stanier Jubilee Class 4-6-0s; six of the class arrived from Bristol Barrow Road, 45572/7, 45651/60/2/99 having been displaced by dieselisation of the Birmingham-Bristol main line expresses. Four of Shrewsbury's Standard Cl. 5s, 73091-4 were assigned to the Gloucester/Bristol area where they were noted on Bristol-Birmingham semi-fasts. The Shrewsbury Standard Cl. 5s lost some of their work on the Manchester and Liverpool to South Wales route via Hereford, the Chester-Wolverhampton line and the Shrewsbury-Stafford services. They were still the regular power on the Central Wales line to Swansea, whilst the corresponding Swansea rosters on the same route also featured occasional appearances by the Llanelly-based class members which by now included 73021/3.

At the time of the transfer of the Shrewsbury district depots from the WR to the LMR in January 1963, eight of the class, were on the books, 73025/6/34-6/90/5/7, their duties being unaffected by the change. In the spring of 1964, one of the few remaining steam hauled trains on the Wolverhampton line was the 8.42am parcels ex Shrewsbury, the engine returning from Wolverhampton on the 3.10pm (SX) Paddington-Shrewsbury; Standard Cl. 5s were regularly noted on the working. In September, with the dieselisation of the routes to Wales and the withdrawal of the Shrewsbury-Stafford passenger service, the class began to appear more frequently on freights in the West Midlands area.

By April 1965, Shrewsbury had fifteen Standard Cl. 5s on its books, 73000/25/34-6/50/3/67/70/1/90/4/5/7, 73167. Even at this time, almost all the Paddington-Birkenhead passenger trains were worked northward from Shrewsbury by

Fig. 39
73105 piloting an unidentified Stanier Cl. 5 4-6-0 leaves Crianlarich Upper with the 4.30am Edinburgh Waverley to Fort William and Mallaig on 19th August 1961. The train includes through coaches plus sleeping car from Kings Cross. The classification 'BR5' is just discernable on the fireman's side of 73105's buffer beam. There is no sign of the name of its depot, Eastfield, having been painted on the driver's side; this would have been normal practice for engines passing through Cowlairs Works and suggests 73105's last Works visit was to St Rollox.
(Courtney Haydon)

Fig. 40
Having just crossed the Forth Bridge, 73108 heads south with a freight through Dalmeny on 4th July 1964. The view illustrates one of the minor differences between the Derby- and Doncaster-built examples of the class. The placing of the top step bolted to the running plate angle above the buffer beam was in line with the top of the frame on Doncaster-built engines whereas on the Derby-built examples it was lower.   *(Rodney Lissenden)*

Fig. 41
73109 pilots Stanier Cl. 5 4-6-0 44996 out of Crianlarich Upper with the 10.15am Glasgow Queen St to Fort William and Mallaig on 5th September 1960. 73109 was allocated to Eastfield for the whole of its working life and was withdrawn in 1964 after less than nine years service. Note the large 10" cabside numerals applied by both St Rollox and Cowlairs to engines passing through their paint shops.   *(Courtney Haydon)*

Fig. 42
73112, now named *Morgan le Fay*, passes Vauxhall with the 9.30am Waterloo-Bournemouth on 7th August 1963. 73110-9 were the only Standard Cl. 5 4-6-0s to be equipped with the high water capacity (5625 gal.) BR1F type tender fitted to allow for greater flexibility when operating on the water trough-less SR. *(Peter Groom)*

Fig. 43
73114, now named *Etarre*, passes Brockenhurst with a Waterloo-Bournemouth express on 14th October 1961. The engine had two major overhauls at Eastleigh, the first in March 1960 and again in May 1964. Other visits were made to Brighton and Ashford Works for non-classified repairs in November 1956 and July 1959 respectively. *(L. Elsey)*

Fig. 44
73117, formerly named *Vivien* but now lacking at least one nameplate, heads for Poole through Bramley between Reading and Basingstoke with a heavy holiday train from the North in 31st July 1965. Note the guard plate fitted behind the front coupling to protect the AWS apparatus installed in February 1959.

(Rodney Lissenden)

Cl. 5 4-6-0s both Standard and Stanier types. The engines also found employment on summer Saturday holiday services for Devon, Cornwall and the South Coast, although rarely penetrating south of Wolverhampton. A few locals and semi-fasts on this route were also steam powered. At the start of the winter 1965/6 timetable, the 3.10pm(SX) and 7.10pm(SO) Paddington-Shrewsbury were still diagrammed for steam haulage from Wolverhampton and the Standard Cl. 5s were still frequent performers.

By May 1966, although many trains on the Shrewsbury-Chester line were still in the hands of steam, the Standard Cl. 5s had been moved away to the Manchester area leaving the Stanier Cl. 5 4-6-0s with the lion's share of the work. In the closing weeks of the Birkenhead-Paddington through services in 1967 however, Patricroft-based Standard Cl. 5s were still in evidence and provided some thrilling runs despite the relatively poor condition of the engines. On 18th February, for example, 73159 attained 77 mph on the Gobowen-Shrewsbury section with the seven coach 9.33am ex-Chester. On 5th March, the very last day of through Paddington workings, 73097 made one of the finest runs known with steam over the Shrewsbury-Chester section. The engine was on the 4.37pm ex Shrewsbury, the 1.10pm(SO) ex-Paddington, covering the 18 miles to Gobowen in 18¼ minutes net with a six coach load, only a severe signal check preventing a 'mile a minute' arrival time. 73097 cleared the summit of the four mile climb at 1 in 150/180 out of Shrewsbury at 60 mph reaching 82 mph at Baschurch, truly a spectacular finale; a full log is detailed in Table 20.

On other parts of the WR, at the end of 1964, only nineteen Standard Cl. 5s remained, the rest having left for the scrapyard or been transferred to other regions. The former SR Western Section depots of Exmouth Junction and Yeovil Town were by now part of the WR's responsibility; allocation was as shown:

Bristol Barrow Road	(4)	73001/3/15/30
Gloucester Horton Road	(4)	73021/31/91/3
Oxford	(4)	73023/37/49
		73164
Exmouth Junction	(2)	73044/162
Bath Green Park	(4)	73051/4/68/92
Yeovil Town	(1)	73166

The Exmouth Junction allocation was used on the former SR main line to Salisbury and the SR's so-called 'Withered Arm' line to Plymouth. Earlier limits on the use of Standard Cl. 5 4-6-0s on the latter route were by now rescinded. These restrictions, which had effectively barred the class from the line, had been similar to those applied to the N15, S15, and H15 Cl. 4-6-0s, confining the engines to a maximum speed of 40 mph and never allowing them to be run coupled together.

With the gradual thinning of the numbers of GWR 2-6-0 and 2-8-0 classes, the Standard Cl. 5s spent much of their time, when operational, on freight workings in the Bristol and Oxford areas. The last members of the class on the WR, 73001/3/68, were withdrawn in December 1965, leaving only a few more weeks of steam operation on the region which terminated, as noted earlier, with the closure of the S&DJR line on 5th March 1966.

Southern Region

In June 1957, the SR had an allocation of twenty five Standard Cl. 5 4-6-0s, 73047/9-52/80-9 and 73110-9 distributed as follows:

Bath Green Park	(5)	73047/9-52
Stewarts Lane	(9)	73080-6/8/9
Eastleigh	(2)	73087, 73116
Nine Elms	(9)	73110-5/7-9

In the early part of 1958, Bath Green Park came under the control of the WR, although the SR continued to loan the usual two engines to Bath, 73087 for four more summer seasons and 73116 for two more. Meanwhile, the Nine Elms allocation handled much of the Western Section holiday traffic on summer Saturdays and Bank Holiday weekends. By the summer of 1958, they had displaced some of the older 4-6-0s such as the S15s from these duties, thus making a great contribution to improved punctuality. In June 1958, 73041/2 joined the Stewarts Lane stud from the LMR in exchange for Standard Cl. 7 Britannia Pacifics 70004/14 sent to support the accelerated St Pancras-Manchester Central timings. It was 73042 which was involved in one of the worst accidents to befall a member of the class. On 25th August, the engine ploughed into the rear of the 7.27am Eastbourne-London Bridge electric service in Eastbourne station whilst working the southbound Glasgow-Eastbourne car sleeper. The twelve car electric set was severely damaged, the two leading vehicles of 6-PUL 3014 being a total loss with heavy casualties. 73042 was derailed and badly damaged at the front end, repairs being undertaken at Eastleigh; 73042 was returned to traffic in November.

In February 1958, the SR took over responsibility for Weymouth depot from the WR and in September exchanged five GWR Hall Cl. 4-6-0s for Standard Cl. 5s, 73017/8/20/2/9; the latter were permitted to run between Basingstoke and Waterloo, a route from which the Halls were barred.

June 1959 saw the introduction of Stage One of the Kent Coast Electrification scheme. This resulted in the displacement of Eastern section Standard Cl. 5s 73041/2/80-6 from Stewarts Lane to Nine Elms, although nearly all worked out the summer at Stewarts Lane before transfer; also moved to the Western section were a number of Schools Cl. V 4-4-0s and Maunsell King Arthur Cl. N15 4-6-0s. The new arrivals, operating from Nine Elms, allowed for the almost complete retirement of the ageing S15 Cl. 4-6-0s from passenger work even on the intensive summer Saturday programme. The Glasgow-Eastbourne car sleeper service recommenced on 22nd June and for the first three weeks was handled exclusively by Nine Elms Standard Cl. 5s, 73041/2/81/3 being noted. The Weymouth engines continued to be used intensively on Waterloo workings but several were seen rather further afield on Saturdays in the early summer heading the 8.35am Liverpool Lime Street-Penzance from Shrewsbury to Bristol. The new Weymouth Quay-Waterloo Channel Islands boat train which commenced on 2nd November was also diagrammed for Standard Cl. 5s, 73041/2/80 transferring from Nine Elms to assist with this traffic. Weymouth members of the class were also observed in Paddington at this time on through workings via the WR route through Westbury.

Several of the class including 73083 and 73117 were borrowed for a short period by the Eastern Section in January 1960 to ease a difficult situation caused by successive Cl. 71 electric locomotive failures. They appeared on a few passenger trains into Charing Cross but were mainly observed on freight workings. During the summer of 1960, the class continued regular appearances on Southampton and Weymouth line boat trains. Subject to speed restrictions, the engines were also allowed onto the Ringwood line between Southampton and Bournemouth, a route normally barred to them.

During the 1961 and 1962 summer seasons, the Standard Cl. 5s continued to take a large share of the Western Section's Saturday traffic and with the trend to reduced loads and fewer restaurant cars, most trains were within their capabilities. They also made regular visits west of Exeter as far as Okehampton, occasionally working through to Plymouth in an emergency. In 1962, Schools Cl. V 4-4-0s, Maunsell King Arthur Cl. N15 4-6-0s and Lord Nelson Cl. 4-6-0s were virtually all displaced from their last remaining Waterloo services and by the year end had all been withdrawn.

In November and December 1962 a further group of Standard Cl. 5s was ousted by diesels from the ER's Sheffield area and were assigned to the SR Western Section. 73002/16/43/65 and 73155 went to Eastleigh and 73046/74 to Nine Elms. Despite the increase in number, the class lost one of its duties at Waterloo about this time when Standard Cl. 3 2-6-2 tanks (82XXX) took over the terminus' empty stock workings. During 1963, the Bulleid Pacifics and Standard Cl. 5s worked virtually all the steam-hauled passenger services on the Western Section, including the Bournemouth-Oxford leg of through services to the north. The Eastleigh contingent could still be seen on Portsmouth-Cardiff trains as far as Salisbury, although this duty was rostered for Cl. U and Standard Cl. 4 2-6-0s (76XXX).

During September 1963, further refugees arrived from the north in the shape of 73167-71 from the NER's Leeds district. They were allocated to Feltham and deployed on freight work. In October 1963, 73030/44 and 73166 were allocated to Exmouth Junction which by now was in the hands of the WR. They worked to Plymouth via the Okehampton line on both passenger and freight diagrams previously handled by Bulleid light Pacifics and Maunsell Cl. N 2-6-0s. Early 1964 saw the addition of 73016/43/65 and 73155 to the Feltham stud. Together with the Bulleid Austerity Q1 0-6-0s, they worked SR-LMR/ER cross-London freights for a period.

At the end of January 1964, the SR allocation of Standard Cl. 5s was thirty nine engines distributed as shown:

Nine Elms	(21)	73046/74/81-9, 73110-9
Feltham	(9)	73016/43/65, 73155/67-71
Weymouth	(9)	73002/17/8/20/2/9/41/2/80

With Stewarts Lane now closed to steam, Nine Elms was being called on to cover Central Section steam commitments such as relief boat traffic on the Newhaven line. Regular duties also included working inter regional services and reliefs for Brighton and Eastbourne to and from Mitre Bridge Junction Willesden, 73082/8 and 73113/4 being noted. Additionally, LMR examples 73032/67 and 73159 worked in, mainly on the Glasgow-Newhaven sleeper and the Manchester-Eastbourne through train. Also in 1964, Nine Elms Standard Cl. 5s made frequent appearances on stopping trains between Reading and Redhill. By the autumn, Redhill had acquired several of the class on unofficial loan, including 73112-4. All were used on the Reading line jobs as well as main line goods duties to Norwood Junction, Bricklayers Arms and Brighton due to a shortage of Type 3 Cl. 33 diesels.

For several months, the 4.45pm Portsmouth-Waterloo van train produced members of the class, 73074/81/4 being noted.

The bulk of the 1964 summer traffic on the West of England and Bournemouth main lines was in the hands of the Bulleid Pacifics and Standard Cl. 5s, Type 3 Cl. 33 diesels appearing when available. On 7th September, the Exeter-Waterloo line passenger service was scheduled to be taken over by Type 4 Warship Cl. 42 and 43 diesels operating from Laira depot on the WR, but failures were a regular occurrence and steam was commonplace for several months. Sixteen Standard Cl. 5s, 73022/9/41/3/87/9, 73110-9 were moved to Eastleigh in the August-October period. Along with Type 3 Cl. 33 diesels, they continued operating on the Bournemouth line and on the through South Wales trains on the Salisbury route including the Brighton-Plymouth service to and from Salisbury. The engines provided power regularly for the 8.35am and 9.30am Waterloo-Bournemouth services which were covered by Eastleigh diagrams as well as acting as substitutes for Pacific failures on other Bournemouth line trains.

On 1st January 1965, the SR allocation of thirty four engines was distributed as follows:

Weymouth	(6)	73002/18/20/42/80/3
Nine Elms	(9)	73016/65/81/2/4-6/8, 73112
Eastleigh	(19)	73022/9/41/3/87/9
		73110/1/3-5/7-9/55/68-71

Early in 1965, the Standard Cl. 5s were employed on several freight workings as a result of diesel shortages. Apart from services from Feltham, they were regularly noted on Snodland-Poole cement trains and worked to New Malden on block oil trains. In the first week of January, a new coal concentration depot began operations at Tolworth. Two trains from Wimbledon West Yard served the new depot departing at 5.48am and 12.18pm, returning from Tolworth at 6.40am and 1.32pm. These workings formed part of Nine Elms duty 81, rostered for a Standard Cl. 5; passenger train work continued as before.

In April 1965, 73037/92/3 were transferred to Eastleigh and within a few weeks, Guildford received 73022/9/37/41/3/65/81/2/7, its first Standard Cl. 5 allocation. The Guildford engines often worked to Redhill on parcels and ballast trains as well as appearing frequently on the 5.08pm Reading-Redhill passenger service; they were also noted on some Basingstoke-Waterloo trains. Regular workings to the WR still occurred, Weymouth engines reaching Westbury on freight and parcels trains, whilst several through holiday trains from Bournemouth and Portsmouth to the Midlands and North were in their charge as far as Oxford. The daily Plymouth-Brighton train was still regularly powered by a Standard Cl. 5 from Salisbury onward.

On 28th August 1965, steam working on the Salisbury-Exeter line came to an end and the Standard Cl. 5s featured on some fast runs. The 8.00am ex-Waterloo had 73089 with 315 tons which provided a superb run for the 61.1 miles from Salisbury to Axminster in 59 minutes 33 seconds, passing Yeovil Junction within the 39 minute timing of the old 'Atlantic Coast Express', 11.00am Waterloo-Devon/Cornwall (by then discontinued). Maximum speed was 83mph at Templecombe and 81mph at Sherborne; similar fast running took place on a return journey.

In January 1966, there were thirty one Standard Cl. 5s on

Fig. 45
73118, formerly named *King Leodegrance*, powers a Basingstoke-Waterloo semi-fast through Deepcut near Brookwood on 12th March 1965. 73118 achieved almost 300,000 miles before its first general overhaul at Eastleigh in February 1963.

(*Rodney Lissenden*)

Fig. 46
73119, now named *Elaine*, passes Lymington Junction with a Waterloo-Bournemouth express on St George's Day, 23rd April 1962. The engine had been outshopped from Eastleigh Works a few weeks previously following its first general overhaul after over 265,000 miles service, representing an average annual mileage of around 43,000.

(*Rodney Lissenden*)

Fig. 47
73125, the first of the class to be fitted with Caprotti valve gear, heads the 8.05am Birmingham New Street-Newcastle at Pontefract Baghill. Initially allocated to Shrewsbury, 73125 is probably on a running-in turn from Derby Works which would suggest a date sometime in July 1956 or shortly afterwards.

(*Peter Cookson*)

Fig. 48
Caprotti valve gear 73136 contemplates an array of signals as it awaits departure from Derby Midland with an northbound express on 25th February 1960. 73136 was one of several of the class at Rowsley in the early 1960s; this depot's Standard Cl. 5 4-6-0s could regularly be observed heading heavy summer Saturday holiday trains on the Sheffield-Bristol Temple Meads route at that time. *(P.H. Wells)*

Fig. 49
Caprotti valve gear 73137 pauses for water at Stamford Town with a train for Peterborough on 23rd July 1960. The engine is equipped with the high coal capacity (nine tons) BR1C tender. It was reported that the economic case for the adoption of the Caprotti valve gear arrangement assumed the locomotives would not be withdrawn until the year 2000!
(P.H.Wells)

Fig. 50
Caprotti valve gear 73138 heads eastward out of Stamford Town with the Kings Norton-Yarmouth Beach holiday train on 23rd August 1959. For some years at least, in the 1950s, this service, which also served Birmingham New St, operated over the M&GN route via South Lynn and Melton Constable.
(P.H. Wells)

the SR, allocated as shown:

Weymouth	(8)	73002/16/8/20/80/3, 73113/4
Guildford	(13)	73022/9/37/43/65/81/2/7-9 73092/3, 73110
Eastleigh	(9)	73085, 73115/7-9/55/69-71
Nine Elms	(1)	73086

In the January-April period, the engines were active on ballast trains from Woking to New Cross Gate and also still engaged on the Plymouth-Brighton service, sharing the duty with Bulleid light Pacifics. The latter train reverted to Type 3 Cl. 33 diesel haulage after cessation of train heating requirements at the end of April. At the same time, the Cl. 33s took over the through trains to the North as far as Oxford with only occasional substitution by a Standard Cl. 5.

In September 1966, three Type 4 Cl. 47 diesels were loaned to the Bournemouth line until completion of electrification. The diesels took over the 8.30am and 5.30pm Waterloo-Bournemouth and 4.35pm Waterloo-Weymouth returning on the 12.35pm and 12.59pm ex-Bournemouth and the 10.13pm ex-Weymouth. With many Merchant Navy Cl. Pacifics stored out of action, the Standard Cl. 5s were well to the fore on Bournemouth line trains. They were sometimes called on to haul huge loads such as on 1st November when 73092 set off from Bournemouth with an eleven coach train as far as Southampton. Here a boat train portion of three more carriages was added making fourteen vehicles in all for Waterloo. 73020 powered the up 'Bournemouth Belle' Pullman on 11th December whilst on the 19th, 73043 and 73018 were responsible for the 8.30am and 8.35am departures from Waterloo. During the same month, a further three Cl. 47 diesels arrived so that the only remaining steam powered Bournemouth line departures from Waterloo were as shown, rostered mainly for Bulleid Pacifics but occasionally featuring Standard Cl. 5s:
5.30am(SX), 8.35am, 11.30am, 1.30pm, 3.30pm(SX), 3.35pm(SO), 6.30pm, 9.20pm and 10.35pm.

By January 1967, the Standard Cl. 5s still featured at the same depots on the SR but had been reduced by withdrawals to eighteen.

Weymouth	(4)	73002/18/20, 73113
Nine Elms	(6)	73022/9/37/43/65/85
Guildford	(6)	73092/3, 73110/5/7/8
Eastleigh	(2)	73119/55

In April 1967, Eastleigh and Weymouth depot lost their remaining allocation of Standard Cl. 5s by withdrawals or transfers to Guildford where they replaced withdrawn engines. By 3rd April, some electric workings had begun between Waterloo and Bournemouth leaving only a few passenger services, mainly Channel Islands boat trains, booked for steam haulage. These were:
8.10am, 8.35am Waterloo-Weymouth and 11.18am, 4.00pm, 5.30pm, 6.15pm return.

The last official day of steam working on the SR was 9th July 1967, when 73029 powered a Fratton to Clapham Junction empty coaching stock train. On the same day, 73092 worked a perishables special from Weymouth to Westbury, having the previous day headed the 12.12am Weymouth-Bournemouth.

During the last steam week, the remaining engines made their way in ones and twos to Salisbury and Weymouth depots for storage pending disposal. Towards the end of July, Salisbury had assembled nine Standard Cl. 5s,

73029/43/65/85/93, 73115/7/8/55, whilst Weymouth had 73018/20/92. These engines were all forwarded to J.Cashmore's scrapyard at Newport (Monmouthshire) over the next few months to join other members of the class awaiting the breaker's torch.

London Midland Region

By the end of June 1957, with all the Standard Cl. 5 4-6-0s in service, the LMR had forty five members allocated as follows:

Nottingham	(3)	73000/2/67
Leicester Midland	(9)	73003/4/46/73, 73138/41-4
Millhouses	(5)	73011/6/48/65/74
Bristol Barrow Road	(4)	73015/31/54/68
Derby	(1)	73030
Chester Midland	(4)	73040/70-2
Holyhead	(7)	73041/2, 73135-7/9/40
Patricroft	(12)	73043/4/90-9

During the early part of 1958, there took place one of the periodic bouts of regional reorganisation. The LMR took responsibility for the ex-Great Central route between Marylebone and Manchester Central, whilst relinquishing its Sheffield district depots, Grimesthorpe, Millhouses and Canklow to the ER. The LMR gained two Standard Cl. 5s 73155/6 from the ER through acquisition of Neasden depot, but lost seven others, 73000/2/4/43/6/67/73 in exchange for the Sheffield area Stanier Cl. 5 4-6-0s. This move relieved the ER of the need to carry out overhauls of the latter type unfamiliar to both Doncaster and Stratford Works. Five of the incoming Stanier Cl. 5s were sent to Holyhead, its Standard Cl. Caprotti 5s moving thence to Leicester to give the latter depot an allocation of eight of these engines, 73135-42; Holyhead had lost 73143/4 to Nottingham two months earlier. The Caprottis, already a familiar sight on the main line to St Pancras and on summer Saturday traffic to the East Coast, now made occasional appearances at Bath Green Park handing over holiday trains to the S&DJR for Bournemouth. Other work included visits to South Coast resorts such as Brighton, Bognor Regis and Portsmouth on excursions from the Midlands.

In June 1958, 73041/2 left Holyhead for Stewarts Lane SR. Here they replaced Standard Cl. 7 Britannia Pacifics 70004/14 reallocated to Kentish Town on the LMR's Midland Division, to support the struggling Stanier Jubilee Cl. 4-6-0s on the accelerated Midland main line service introduced in the June 1957 timetable. During August 1958, the WR depot at Chester West came under control of the LMR. The remaining GWR express engines still at Chester West, mainly Hall Cl. 4-6-0s, were exchanged for 73014/24-6 from Cardiff Canton; 73098/9 also arrived from Patricroft in the same month. Just over a year later, several Standard Caprotti Cl. 5s, 73135-44, moved to Rowsley to replace Hughes-Fowler Cl. 6P/5F Crab 2-6-0s on mixed traffic duties on the Peak Forest line between Derby and Manchester Central. At about the same time, in preparation for the down-grading of the Great Central line by withdrawal of through services between Marylebone and Manchester scheduled for early 1960, several Standard Cl. 5s, 73010/45/53/66/9, from Holbeck moved to Leicester Central, displacing the latter depot's remaining Cl. V2 2-6-2s 60831/42/79, 60911/5 to

Fig. 51
Caprotti valve gear 73139, a rare visitor to Southampton, leaves the Old (now Eastern) Docks with the return working of an educational excursion from St Albans on 26th April 1961. 73139 is allocated to Rowsley whose Caprotti Cl. 5 4-6-0s were developing a 'wanderlust' reputation by this time, apparently borne out by the working depicted here. *(Courtney Haydon)*

Fig. 52
Leicester Midland based Caprotti valve gear 73142 passes Pontefract Baghill in charge of a return excursion from the East Coast on 30th June 1958. 73142 achieved the creditable annual mileage of nearly 50,000 in 1957. *(Peter Cookson)*

Fig. 53
73156 pilots Stanier Jubilee 4-6-0 45577 *Bengal* on the 8.05am Birmingham New Street–Newcastle at Pontefract Baghill on 13th June 1958. 73156 is attached to a BR1B type tender with the higher water capacity (4725 gal.). The engine is now preserved and undergoing restoration on the East Lancashire Railway at Bury. As the only Doncaster-built example of the class in preservation, it is hoped that the engine will be able to take part in the Doncaster Works 150 celebration in 2003.
(Peter Cookson)

York and Thornaby. Later, in May 1960, the same group of Standard Cl. 5s was moved to Neasden, together with 73157-9 fom Derby in exchange for Stanier Cl. 5 4-6-0s. A similar move occurred on the LMR Western Division at that time, 73004/13/4/32/3/9 transferring to Willesden. The reason given for the exchange was that the SR objected on clearance grounds to the use of the Stanier 5s on through workings via Herne Hill and Tulse Hill to the South Coast.

In December 1959, the distribution of the thirty nine Standard Cl. 5s on the LMR was as shown:

Leicester Central	(5)	73010/45/53/66/9
Chester Midland	(5)	73013/33/40/70/1
Chester West	(2)	73014/38
Patricroft	(12)	73030/44, 73125-34
Birkenhead	(2)	73032/9
Rowsley	(10)	73135-44
Derby	(3)	73157-9

The Chester Midland stud was still in use on the North Wales Coast line on parcels and semi-fasts whilst the Chester West and Birkenhead engines continued work mainly between Shrewsbury and Merseyside. From Patricroft, the engines were regularly employed on services to Liverpool Lime Street, Yorkshire and on North Wales services with occasional forays to the Fylde Coast.

From 4th January 1960, the Great Central line finally ceased to be a through route, the passenger service from then on being mainly semi-fasts between Marylebone and Nottingham. Standard Cl. 5s played a large part in their operation, 73032 and 73156 being further additions to the Neasden allocation by October 1960. In June 1962, Neasden depot closed, the remaining steam visitors to London then being serviced by Cricklewood. The ten Standard Cl. 5s on Neasden's books were moved to three depots, Woodford Halse, 73010/32/45/53; Leicester Central, 73066/9, 73156/9 and Cricklewood, 73157/8. By March 1963, 73069 and 73156/9 were also at Woodford Halse. The class was now the depot's first choice for mixed traffic work, the faithful B1 4-6-0s having disappeared through withdrawals and transfers. Earlier in the year 73000 itself had been the first Standard Cl. 5 to be considered a candidate for withdrawal and had spent some time at Doncaster Works awaiting reprieve; the engine was spared, finally being withdrawn in March 1968. A Woodford Halse roster typical of the period was:
Light Engine to Rugby
5.20pm Rugby-Nottingham semi-fast.
Late evening parcels to Banbury
Light Engine to Woodford Halse

By the summer of 1963, most of the line's passenger workings had been taken over by the LMS Cl. 7P rebuilt Royal Scot 4-6-0s based on Annesley depot near Nottingham; they had been displaced there by the influx of Type 4 Cl. 40 diesels on to the LMR Western Division main line. The Standard Cl. 5s still continued to appear on passenger services during 1964, the 8.15am Nottingham-Marylebone being rostered for a Woodford Halse-based engine, for example. By early 1965, however, the remaining Standard Cl. 5s had moved to the Birmingham and Manchester areas. From then on Stanier Cl. 5s predominated and in spring 1965 they were almost exclusively in charge of the passenger workings until the end of the Great Central line semi-fasts in September 1966.

In May 1961, the LMR distribution of forty five engines was as follows:

Willesden	(5)	73004/13/4/33/9
Neasden	(10)	73010/32/45/53/66/9 73156-9
Holyhead	(3)	73011/67/73
Patricroft	(12)	73030/44, 73125-34
Chester Midland	(5)	73038/40/8/70/1
Rowsley	(10)	73135-44

By the summer of 1961 on the Midland Division main line from St Pancras the new 'Peak' Type 4 Cl. 45 diesels were dominating the passenger services. Standard Cl. 5s from Rowsley still appeared in the London area along with Stanier Cl. 5 and Jubilee Cl. 4-6-0s on mixed traffic duties and Saturday reliefs. This pattern continued well into 1964 with the night fitted freights, especially, producing a variety of steam power. By the end of October 1964, all the Standard Cl. 5s had left the Midland Division for Patricroft and Leamington Spa.

On the Western Division, the stud of Standard Cl. 5s at Willesden during the early 1960s was mainly engaged on fast fitted freights to Crewe and the North Wales area as well as making the usual regular visits to South Coast resorts on specials. In January 1964, Willesden had ten examples on its books, 73004/13/4/33/8-40/8/67/70, although by the end of March they had all transferred to Bletchley to be replaced by Stanier 5s. Services into the SR were now handled mainly by diesels so the clearance restrictions applying to the Staniers no longer appeared to be an issue.

In October 1964, the LMR allocation of fifty seven engines, including those of Shrewsbury depot by now transferred from WR to LMR control, was distributed as shown:

Woodford Halse	(5)	73000/10/1/71, 73157
Bletchley	(10)	73004/13/4/33/8-40/8 73067, 73160
Patricroft	(22)	73006, 73125-44/58
Shrewsbury	(14)	73025/6/34-6/47/50/3 73070/90/4/5/7, 73167
Nuneaton	(4)	73032/45/73, 73159
Cricklewood	(2)	73069, 73156

Within a few months however, the Standard Cl. 5s from Bletchley, Woodford Halse and Cricklewood were transferred to the Birmingham area in exchange for Stanier 5s. This move was made in an attempt to standardise spares stocks at particular depots. As a result, Oxley had some twenty of the class on its books for a few months, these engines taking over from GWR 4-6-0 types. Also at this time, 73066/9 and 73156 moved from the Great Central line to Leamington Spa to work the stone and cement traffic from Greaves sidings near Harbury. The loadings of these trains had been increased and, following the withdrawal of two GWR Grange Cl. 4-6-0s, 6842/5, from Tyseley, no other suitable power had been available. The Standard Cl. 5s were not in good shape and spent some time under repair at Bescot and Saltley depots before taking up their duties. Another role for the Leamington Standard Cl. 5s, now joined by 73026, was providing assistance on Hatton bank for diverted Banbury-South Wales iron ore trains which formerly ran via the ex-Stratford on Avon and Midland Joint line but were now routed to Stratford via Hatton. When Leamington depot closed in June 1965, the engines transferred to Tyseley. Several Standard Cl. 5s were moved to Nuneaton at this time, displacing the Stanier Cl. 5s which had less headroom under the new 25kV electric wires then being installed on this part of the West Coast main line. By April 1965, Nuneaton had some eleven of the class on its books, 73004/32/3/8-40/5/8/73/96 and 73159. From 3rd May, an experimental working of 21-ton mineral wagons had been brought into operation from Coventry colliery to the local Hams Hall power station in readiness for full working of the briquette fuel plant expected by the end of the year. By June, as many as four or five such trains were run daily; all were rostered for Nuneaton Standard Cl. 5s. Another Nuneaton duty involved working some of the steel traffic from the NER, now diverted from the Great Central line and running from Middlesbrough via Burton-on-Trent to Nuneaton and Banbury. These workings were dieselised with Type 2 Cl. 25s early in 1966, whilst about the same time, Bescot Type 4 Cl. 47s began replacing the Standard Cl. 5s on the Coventry-Hams Hall mineral trains. In general, during the autumn of 1965, Standard Cl. 5s and 9F 2-10-0s together with Stanier 5s and 8F 2-8-0s were in charge of most of the remaining steam hauled freights in the West Midlands. This was the situation until May 1966, when steam was virtually eliminated from the area, the remaining Standard Cl. 5s transferring to Bolton, one of the last bastions of steam on the BR system.

In the North West in the mid-1960s, Standard Cl. 5s could still be seen along the North Wales and Fylde Coast areas as well as on both main Manchester-Leeds routes across the Pennines. Patricroft engines were employed from time to time as the Manchester Exchange pilot and also on banking duties, mainly for freights, up the one mile at 1 in 59/47 to Miles Platting, eastbound from Manchester Victoria. By the beginning of 1964, the North Wales allocation had been replaced by Stanier Cl. 5s, although Patricroft engines continued to appear regularly. By April 1965, the latter depot's allocation had increased to twenty eight, the majority of the additions having been ousted from the Midlands area by diesels. A further influx occurred during July when several more of the class were received from Croes Newydd, Nuneaton and Shrewsbury. The new arrivals strongly featured on North Wales and trans-Pennine summer reliefs.

It was one of the Patricroft engines which was involved in an accident at Holyhead on 9th September 1965. The incident occurred at 3.25pm when the 2.30pm local passenger service from Bangor with 73165 in charge of eight coaches and two vans was running under the authority of the 'calling-on' signal into platform one. This was partly occupied by a parcels van and the stock of the 4.00pm Holyhead-Euston in which some passengers were already entrained. The collision force of about 7-8 mph pushed the standing train with brakes applied into the terminus stop blocks. Two coaches of the 2.30pm were telescoped with one fatality and several injuries. The accident inspector stated that a dull day with drizzle and poor visibility aggravated by smoke and steam from the station pilot blowing across the field of vision were contributory causes to the accident.

In April 1966, there were still four passenger trains rostered for Patricroft Standard Cl. 5s on the North Wales Coast line the 7.40am Llandudno-Manchester Exchange and 3.10pm, 4.30pm and 5.30pm (SO) return. During the summer, Manchester Exchange became a veritable stronghold for the class, two or three frequently being on view simultaneously. By the last holiday weekend, 29th August,

only four North Wales trains were hauled by Patricroft Standard Cl. 5s, 73073 and 73141 each making a return trip. Towards September, steam haulage on the route was rapidly diminishing and 1st October saw the last day of steam at Llandudno Junction depot, 73073 and 73096 featuring on the 10.45am Manchester Exchange-Llandudno and 11.40am return respectively. Even after this date, there were still several steam passenger workings on a regular basis, the 7.40am and 4.30pm(SX) Llandudno-Manchester Exchange and 5.35pm (SO) return often being in the charge of a Standard Cl. 5.

On the trans-Pennine routes, the Standard Cl. 5s continued to appear on freights, reliefs and parcels trains. In May 1966, a further batch arrived in the North West from the Shrewsbury and Birmingham areas. They were allocated to Agecroft and Bolton and were also used, when serviceable, on the Pennine routes. By November 1966, the whole of the remaining LMR allocation of Standard Cl. 5s, fifty two in total, was at either Patricroft or Bolton, although many were in store:

Patricroft	(42)	73000/6/10/1/25/33-5/9/45
		73050/3/67/71/3/94/6/7
		73125-44/57-60
Bolton	(10)	73004/14/9/26/40/8/66/9/70
		73156

Operation of the Christmas reliefs on the Leeds-Manchester section showed an approximately equal number of Standard Cl. 5 and Stanier 5 workings, 73073, 73157/9 featuring strongly. Later, on 21st January 1967, 73006 gave an excellent performance on the 11.00am Liverpool Lime St-Newcastle as far as Leeds, losing only 2½ minutes on the Type 4 Cl. 40 diesel schedule with a nine coach train. A speed of 77 mph was attained across Barton Moss between Liverpool and Manchester; 73006 was withdrawn less than two months later. The following Easter, around twenty reliefs were run on the Leeds-Manchester section, of which sixteen were rostered for steam haulage, Standard Cl. 5s 73011/53/96 being noted. The Patricroft engines occasionally appeared on Manchester to Blackpool and Barrow-in-Furness services as well on the Preston-Liverpool Exchange line. One Furness line working involved the 5.14pm Manchester-Barrow parcels and the following day's 8.35am Barrow-London Euston as far as Lancaster. Another regular appearance was the 5.34pm (FO) Manchester Victoria-York which after retiming to 5.47pm and routing through Hebden Bridge was allowed 80 minutes for the journey to Leeds with one stop at Rochdale. This working remained regularly steam hauled until January 1968.

In the summer of 1967, both Standard and Stanier Cl. 5s from Patricroft were frequently seen on the 9.30am Manchester Victoria-Newcastle as far as Leeds, arriving at 10.48am and returning at 12.30pm from Leeds. This working produced 73053, 73135/57/9 during July and August. Patricroft Standard Cl. 5s were also noted on summer Saturday services from Leeds/Bradford to the East Coast resorts of Scarborough, Bridlington and Filey as well as to Blackpool and North Wales. During August, 73039/45/50 and 73135/57 were observed on these workings.

By October 1967, a large number of Standard Cl. 5s was in store at Patricroft, prior to despatch to breaker's yards. At the beginning of January 1968, Patricroft and Bolton were the only two depots on the rail system to have an allocation of the class:

Patricroft	(21)	73000/10/33-5/50/3/67
		73125/6/8/31-6/8/42/3/57
Bolton	(2)	73040/69

Rostered steam passenger workings in the North West were down to single figures by the beginning of March 1968, with Standard Cl. 5s making regular appearances. The class also deputised for failed diesels on the Leeds-Manchester routes usually to provide warmth for passengers in the event of diesel train heating boiler failure. By mid-April 73040/69 had left Bolton to join the remainder of the class at Patricroft which hence became the sole depot for Standard Cl. 5s on the BR network with thirteen of the class in total, 73010/40/50/69 and 73125/6/8/33/4/8/42/3/57. Many 'Farewell to Steam' tours took place in the spring and summer of 1968. On 20th April 73134 and 73069 traversed the Bradley Wood branch between Huddersfield and Halifax on a rail tour from Birmingham, with a repeat appearance a week later on another tour. On 18th May, 73069 and Stanier 5 44949 double-headed a tour over Copy Pit incline, running from Manchester Victoria to Preston via Blackburn and Bolton West, later picking up the same train at Morecambe for the return to Manchester.

On 1st July, both Patricroft and Bolton depots were closed leaving 73069 as the only active Standard Cl. 5 survivor. It was reallocated to Carnforth, where by 3rd August, the remaining seventeen active steam engines were gathered. Apart from 73069, these included twelve Stanier Cl. 5s, three Stanier Cl. 8F 2-8-0s and Standard Cl. 7P Britannia Pacific 70013. 73069 was not in steam that day but was resuscitated for an RCTS railtour the following day. It was reported in excellent condition and together with Cl. 8F 2-8-0 48476 as pilot, made a spectacular ascent between Manchester Victoria and Oldham, 73069's crew adamant that they were pushing the ailing Cl. 8F 2-8-0 as well as pulling the thirteen coach train. After this final moment of glory, 73069 was dumped at the closed Lostock Hall depot later in the month and moved to J. Cashmore's yard at Newport for breaking up during February 1969.

Fig. 54
On 21st July 1962, 73157 approaches Wolverton past the Carriage Works with a down freight whilst English Electric Cl. 40 Type 4 diesel D232 (later 40 032) now carrying the name *Empress of Canada* heads an up express. 73157 was initially allocated to the ER Great Central section and later to the Great Northern line. In 1957, the engine was recorded as having run nearly 64,000 miles during the year.

(Courtney Haydon)

Fig. 55
73157 heads a semi-fast on GCR metals near Rugby on 17th October 1964. The engine is adorned with electric warning flashes on the front of the frame alerting enginemen to the presence of overhead power lines when operating on electrified sections of the BR network.

(P.H. Wells)

Fig. 56
73160 of Normanton shed rolls into Preston on a Blackpool Central-Barnsley holiday extra on 22nd August 1959. Southport based Standard Cl. 4 4-6-0 75015 awaits signals in the adjacent platform. Within two weeks, 73160 would enter Doncaster Works for a heavy intermediate overhaul, having run a recorded 93,060 miles in service by that date. *(Russell Leitch)*

Fig. 57
73163 leaves Pontefract Baghill with the 10.00am York-Bournemouth West on 19th June 1957. The Doncaster Works-applied 'BR5' power classification mark is barely visible on the fireman's side of the buffer beam. For the majority of its short life, 73163 was an NER engine allocated to Yorkshire depots.
(Peter Cookson)

Fig. 58
Another view of the 10.00am York-Bournemouth West as it leaves Pontefract Baghill with 73166 in charge in the summer of 1956. The 'BR5' power classification mark applied to the buffer beam of this Doncaster-built engine is clearly visible. It is estimated that 73166 accrued over 250,000 miles in traffic during its short life. *(Peter Cookson)*

2.7.3 Allocation Summary

No	Motive Power Depot Allocation and Date
73000	4.51 Perth; 4.51 Derby; 11.51 Stratford; 3.52 Derby; 1.53 Millhouses; 2.53 Derby 10.53 Nottingham; 5.58 Grimesthorpe; 1.61 Canklow; 1.62 Derby; 9.62 Woodford Halse; 1.65 Oxley; 4.65 Shrewsbury; 4.66 Agecroft; 10.66 Patricroft; 3.68 Withdrawn.
73001	5.51 Derby; 2.56 St Philip's Marsh 3.56 Shrewsbury; 11.56 Swindon; 1.64 Bristol Barrow Road; 1.65 Gloucester Horton Road; 2.65 Bath Green Park; 12.65 Withdrawn.
73002	5.51 Derby; 11.51 Stratford; 1.52 Derby; 10.53 Nottingham; 5.58 Canklow; 1.60 Millhouses; 4.61 Canklow; 11.62 Eastleigh; 9.63 Weymouth; 3.67 Withdrawn.
73003	6.51 Leicester Midland; 5.53 Nine Elms; 6.53 Leicester Midland; 1.58 Bristol Barrow Road; 3.63 Shrewsbury; 9.63 Bristol Barrow Road; 6.65 Oxford; 12.65 Withdrawn.
73004	6.51 Leicester Midland; 12.51 Derby; 1.52 Leicester Midland; 1.57 Heaton Mersey; 3.57 Leicester Midland; 5.58 Millhouses; 2.60 Chester Midland; 5.60 Willesden; 3.64 Bletchley; 1.65 Nuneaton; 6.65 Croes Newydd; 4.66 Bolton; 10.67 Withdrawn.
73005	6.51 Perth; 1.63 Corkerhill; 6.66 Withdrawn.
73006	7.51 Perth; 1.63 Corkerhill; 7.64 Patricroft; 3.67 Withdrawn
73007	7.51 Perth; 6.64 Grangemouth; 10.65 Stirling; 3.66 Withdrawn.
73008	7.51 Perth; 7.51 Rugby Testing Station; 4.52 Perth; 7.64 Aberdeen Ferryhill; 9.65 Withdrawn.
73009	7.51 Perth; 1.63 Corkerhill; 7.66 Withdrawn.
73010	8.51 Holbeck; 2.56 St Philip's Marsh; 3.56 Holbeck; 9.59 Leicester Central; 6.60 Neasden; 6.62 Woodford Halse; 1.65 Oxley; 4.65 Patricroft; 6.68 Withdrawn.
73011	8.51 Holbeck; 10.53 Millhouses; 2.60 Holyhead; 2.63 Llandudno Junction; 11.63 Woodford Halse; 1.65 Oxley; 4.65 Patricroft. 11.67 Withdrawn.
73012	8.51 Holbeck; 9.53 Millhouses; 9.53 Shrewsbury; 11.56 Swindon; 1.64 Llanelly; 6.64 Bristol Barrow Road; 11.64 Withdrawn.
73013	8.51 Millhouses; 9.53 Shrewsbury; 7.55 Chester West; 9.59 Chester Midland; 5.60 Willesden; 3.64 Bletchley; 1.65 Oxley; 6.65 Banbury; 4.66 Bolton; 5.66 Withdrawn.
73014	9.51 Millhouses; 9.53 Shrewsbury: 8.55 Cardiff Canton; 8.58 Chester West; 4.60 Chester Midland; 5.60 Willesden; 3.64 Bletchley; 2.65 Oxley; 6.65 Banbury; 4.66 Bolton; 7.67 Withdrawn.
73015	9.51 Millhouses; 5.53 Nine Elms; 5.53 Millhouses; 9.53 Shrewsbury; 3.56 Derby; 5.57 Bristol Barrow Road; 6.65 Bath Green Park; 8.65 Withdrawn.
73016	9.51 Grimesthorpe; 3.52 Millhouses; 1.53 Derby; 2.53 Millhouses; 1.62 Canklow; 11.62 Eastleigh; 12.63 Feltham; 11.64 Nine Elms; 10.65 Feltham; 11.65 Weymouth; 12.66 Withdrawn.
73017	9.51 Nottingham; 5.53 Nine Elms; 5.53 Nottingham; 9.53 Shrewsbury; 6.56 Cardiff Canton; 7.56 Shrewsbury; 11.56 Swindon; 9.58 Weymouth; 10.64 Withdrawn.
73018	10.51 Nottingham; 9.53 Shrewsbury; 11.56 Swindon; 9.58 Weymouth; 4.67 Guildford; 7.67 Withdrawn.
73019	10.51 Nottingham; 9.53 St. Philip's Marsh; 6.58 Bath Green Park; 7.60 Bristol Barrow Road; 10.60 Bath Green Park; 4.62 Gloucester Barnwood; 4.64 Gloucester Horton Road; 11.64 Oxley; 4.66 Bolton; 1.67 Withdrawn.
73020	10.51 Chester Midland; 9.52 Willesden; 10.52 Chester Midland; 9.53 Chester West; 9.54 Shrewsbury; 11.56 Swindon; 9.58 Weymouth; 4.67 Guildford; 7.67 Withdrawn

73021 10.51 Chester Midland; 9.53 Chester West; 4.59 Cardiff Canton; 4.60 Shrewsbury; 5.60 Llanelly; 7.62 Bristol Barrow Road; 9.62 Gloucester Barnwood; 4.64 Gloucester Horton Road; 6.65 Oxford; 8.65 Withdrawn.

73022 10.51 Chester Midland; 9.53 St Philip's Marsh; 12.53 Landore; 1.54 St. Philip's Marsh; 7.54 Swindon; 9.58 Weymouth; 9.64 Eastleigh; 5.65 Guildford; 6.66 Nine Elms; 4.67 Withdrawn.

73023 11.51 Patricroft; 9.53 Chester West; 4.59 Cardiff Canton; 5.60 Llanelly; 6.64 Bath Green Park; 9.64 Oxford; 8.65 Withdrawn

73024 11.51 Patricroft; 9.53 Chester West; 9.54 Shrewsbury; 7.56 Cardiff Canton; 8.58 Chester West; 4.59 Cardiff Canton; 4.60 Shrewsbury; 7.62 Bristol Barrow Road; 10.62 Gloucester Barnwood; 3.63 Shrewsbury; 9.63 Llanelly; 6.64 Bristol Barrow Road; 9.64 Oxford; 11.64 Withdrawn.

73025 11.51 Blackpool; 9.53 Shrewsbury; 7.54 Cardiff Canton; 8.58 Chester West; 4.59 Shrewsbury; 1.65 Oxley; 3.65 Shrewsbury; 4.66 Agecroft; 10.66 Patricroft; 10.67 Withdrawn.

73026 11.51 Blackpool; 9.53 Shrewsbury; 7.54 Cardiff Canton; 8.58 Chester West; 4.59 Shrewsbury; 10.64 Leamington Spa; 6.65 Tyseley; 4.66 Bolton; 4.67 Withdrawn.

73027 12.51 Blackpool; 9.53 St. Philip's Marsh; 7.54 Swindon; 2.64 Withdrawn.

73028 12.51 Blackpool; 9.53 St. Philip's Marsh; 5.58 Bath Green Park; 7.60 Bristol Barrow Road; 10.60 Bath Green Park; 5.61 Bristol Barrow Road; 11.63 Swindon; 1.64 Gloucester Barnwood; 4.64 Gloucester Horton Road; 11.64 Oxley; 4.66 Bolton; 12.66 Withdrawn.

73029 1.52 Blackpool; 9.53 St. Philip's Marsh; 12.53 Carmarthen; 1.54 St. Philip's Marsh; 9.57 Swindon; 9.58 Weymouth; 8.64 Eastleigh; 5.65 Guildford; 6.66 Nine Elms; 7.67 Withdrawn.

73030 6.53 Carlisle Kingmoor; 6.53 Derby; 6.53 Rugby Testing Station; 11.53 Derby; 7.57 Bristol Barrow Road; 1.58 Leicester Midland; 5.58 Patricroft; 10.63 Exmouth Junction; 9.64 Bristol Barrow Road; 1.65 Bath Green Park; 2.65 Bristol Barrow Road; 6.65 Oxford; 8.65 Withdrawn.

73031 7.53 Polmadie; 7.53 Derby; 6.57 Bristol Barrow Road; 1.58 Rugby Testing Station (operating from Bristol Barrow Road when not undergoing tests at Rugby); 2.61 Bristol Barrow Road; 11.61 Bath Green Park; 4.62 Gloucester Barnwood; 4.64 Gloucester Horton Road; 6.65 Oxford; 9.65 Withdrawn.

73032 7.53 Carlisle Kingmoor; 9.53 St. Philip's Marsh; 6.58 Birkenhead; 5.60 Willesden; 10.60 Neasden; 6.62 Woodford Halse; 8.64 Nuneaton; 5.65 Croes Newydd; 8.65 Withdrawn.

73033 8.53 Polmadie, 9.53 Shrewsbury; 10.56 Oxley; 6.58 Chester West; 9.59 Chester Midland; 5.60 Willesden; 7.62 Chester Midland; 8.62 Willesden; 3.64 Bletchley; 1.65 Oxley; 3.65 Nuneaton; 7.65 Patricroft; 1.68 Withdrawn.

73034 8.53 Carlisle Kingmoor; 9.53 Shrewsbury; 10.56 Oxley; 6.58 Shrewsbury; 4.66 Agecroft; 10.66 Patricroft; 3.68 Withdrawn.

73035 8.53 Polmadie; 9.53 Shrewsbury; 10.56 Oxley; 6.58 Shrewsbury; 7.65 Patricroft; 1.68 Withdrawn.

73036 9.53 Carlisle Kingmoor; 9.53 Shrewsbury; 10.56 Tyseley; 1.58 Shrewsbury; 9.65 Withdrawn.

73037 9.53 Polmadie; 9.53 Shrewsbury; 10.56 Tyseley; 1.58 Shrewsbury; 4.62 Llanelly; 6.64 Bristol Barrow Road; 9.64 Oxford; 4.65 Eastleigh; 5.65 Guildford; 6.66 Nine Elms; 7.67 Withdrawn.

73038 9.53 Carlisle Kingmoor; 9.53 Chester West; 4.60 Chester Midland; 11.62 Llandudno Junction; 11.63 Willesden; 3.64 Bletchley; 1.65 Oxley; 3.65 Nuneaton; 7.65 Shrewsbury; 10.65 Withdrawn.

73039 9.53 Polmadie; 9.53 St. Philip's Marsh; 5.58 Birkenhead; 5.60 Willesden; 3.64 Bletchley; 1.65 Nuneaton; 7.65 Patricroft; 9.67 Withdrawn.

73040 10.53 Chester Midland; 11.63 Willesden; 3.64 Bletchley; 1.65 Nuneaton; 7.65 Croes Newydd; 4.66 Bolton; 4.68 Patricroft; 5.68 Withdrawn.

73041   10.53 Chester Midland; 7.57 Holyhead; 6.58 Stewarts Lane; 5.59 Nine Elms; 11.59 Weymouth; 2.61 Eastleigh; 4.61 Weymouth; 8.64 Eastleigh; 5.65 Guildford; 6.65 Withdrawn.

73042   10.53 Chester Midland; 7.57 Holyhead; 6.58 Stewarts Lane; 5.59 Nine Elms; 11.59 Weymouth; 2.61 Eastleigh; 4.61 Weymouth; 8.65 Withdrawn

73043   10.53 Patricroft; 5.58 Grimesthorpe; 4.61 Canklow; 11.62 Eastleigh; 12.63 Feltham; 8.64 Eastleigh; 5.65 Guildford; 6.66 Nine Elms; 7.67 Withdrawn.

73044   11.53 Patricroft; 10.63 Exmouth Junction; 1.65 Oxford; 3.65 Withdrawn.

73045   11.53 Holbeck; 2.56 Shrewsbury; 3.56 Holbeck; 9.59 Leicester Central; 6.60 Neasden; 6.62 Woodford Halse; 6.64 Shrewsbury; 9.64 Nuneaton; 5.65 Croes Newydd; 7.65 Patricroft; 8.67 Withdrawn.

73046   11.53 Leicester Midland; 5.58 Millhouses; 4.61 Canklow; 11.62 Nine Elms; 9.64 Withdrawn.

73047   12.53 Millhouses; 8.55 Bath Green Park; 7.64 Shrewsbury; 12.64 Withdrawn.

73048   12.53 Millhouses; 2.60 Chester Midland; 11.63 Willesden; 3.64 Bletchley; 1.65 Nuneaton; 6.65 Banbury; 4.66 Bolton; 10.67 Withdrawn.

73049   12.53 Leicester Midland; 8.55 Bath Green Park; 4.60 Shrewsbury; 6.62 Bristol Barrow Road; 7.62 Bath Green Park; 9.64 Oxford; 3.65 Withdrawn.

73050   6.54 Bath Green Park; 8.62 Gloucester Barnwood; 11.62 Bath Green Park; 3.64 Llanelly; 4.64 Shrewsbury; 4.66 Agecroft; 10.66 Patricroft; 6.68 Withdrawn. Preserved at Nene Valley Railway, Wansford.

73051   6.54 Bath Green Park; 8.65 Withdrawn.

73052   6.54 Bath Green Park; 12.64 Withdrawn.

73053   6.54 Holbeck; 9.59 Leicester Central; 6.60 Neasden; 6.62 Woodford Halse; 5.63 Cricklewood; 7.63 Bedford; 8.63 Woodford Halse; 7.64 Shrewsbury; 7.65 Patricroft; 3.68 Withdrawn.

73054   6.54 Holbeck; 8.55 Derby; 5.57 Bristol Barrow Road; 4.61 Bath Green Park; 8.65 Withdrawn.

73055   6.54 Polmadie; 5.66 Withdrawn.

73056   7.54 Polmadie; 7.64 Aberdeen Ferryhill; 6.65 Withdrawn.

73057   7.54 Polmadie; 6.64 Corkerhill; 3.66 Withdrawn.

73058   7.54 Polmadie; 7.64 Aberdeen Ferryhill; 11.64 Withdrawn.

73059   8.54 Polmadie; 5.67 Withdrawn.

73060   8.54 Polmadie; 10.55 Motherwell; 9.57 Polmadie; 5.67 Withdrawn.

73061   9.54 Polmadie; 10.55 Motherwell; 6.57 Polmadie; 12.64 Withdrawn.

73062   9.54 Polmadie; 10.55 Motherwell; 6.57 Polmadie; 6.65 Withdrawn.

73063   9.54 Polmadie; 6.66 Withdrawn.

73064   10.54 Polmadie; 5.67 Withdrawn.

73065   10.54 Millhouses; 1.62 Canklow; 11.62 Eastleigh; 12.63 Feltham; 11.64 Nine Elms; 5.65 Guildford; 6.66 Nine Elms; 7.67 Withdrawn.

73066   10.54 Holbeck; 9.59 Leicester Central; 6.60 Neasden; 6.62 Leicester Central; 1.63 Woodford Halse; 5.63 Cricklewood; 10.64 Leamington Spa; 6.65 Tyseley; 4.66 Bolton; 4.67 Withdrawn.

73067	10.54 Nottingham; 2.58 Leicester Midland; 5.58 Millhouses; 1.60 Holyhead; 2.63 Chester Midland; 11.63 Willesden; 3.64 Bletchley; 1.65 Oxley; 4.65 Shrewsbury; 4.66 Agecroft; 10.66 Patricroft; 3.68 Withdrawn.
73068	10.54 Derby; 5.57 Bristol Barrow Road; 9.62 Gloucester Barnwood; 4.64 Bath Green Park; 1.65 Gloucester Horton Road; 4.65 Bath Green Park; 12.65 Withdrawn.
73069	11.54 Derby; 8.55 Holbeck; 9.59 Leicester Central; 6.60 Neasden; 6.62 Leicester Central; 2.63 Woodford Halse; 5.63 Cricklewood; 10.64 Leamington Spa; 6.65 Tyseley; 4.66 Bolton; 4.68 Patricroft; 7.68 Carnforth; 8.68 Withdrawn.
73070	11.54 Chester Midland; 11.63 Willesden; 3.64 Bletchley; 6.64 Shrewsbury; 4.66 Bolton; 4.67 Withdrawn.
73071	11.54 Chester Midland; 2.56 Kings Cross; 5.57 Chester Midland; 5.63 Cricklewood; 7.63 Bedford; 8.63 Woodford Halse; 1.65 Oxley; 4.65 Shrewsbury; 7.65 Patricroft; 9.67 Withdrawn.
73072	12.54 Chester Midland; 11.58 Polmadie; 10.66 Withdrawn.
73073	12.54 Patricroft; 3.55 Bath Green Park; 8.55 Leicester Midland; 5.58 Millhouses; 2.60 Holyhead; 2.63 Llandudno Junction; 11.63 Woodford Halse; 7.64 Nuneaton; 7.65 Patricroft; 11.67 Withdrawn.
73074	12.54 Patricroft; 3.55 Bath Green Park; 8.55 Millhouses; 2.56 Holbeck; 3.56 Millhouses; 1.59 Grimesthorpe; 4.61 Canklow; 11.62 Nine Elms; 9.64 Withdrawn.
73075	4.55 Polmadie; 12.65 Withdrawn.
73076	4.55 Polmadie; 7.64 Withdrawn.
73077	5.55 Eastfield; 1.63 Corkerhill; 12.64 Withdrawn.
73078	5.55 Eastfield; 1.66 Carstairs; 7.66 Withdrawn.
73079	5.55 Corkerhill; 4.67 Polmadie; 5.67 Withdrawn.
73080	6.55 Stewarts Lane; 5.59 Nine Elms; 11.59 Weymouth; 2.61 Eastleigh; 4.61 Weymouth; 12.66 Withdrawn.
73081	6.55 Stewarts Lane; 5.59 Nine Elms; 5.65 Guildford; 7.66 Withdrawn.
73082	6.55 Stewarts Lane; 5.59 Nine Elms; 5.65 Guildford; 6.66 Withdrawn. Preserved on the Bluebell Railway, Sheffield Park.
73083	7.55 Stewarts Lane; 5.59 Nine Elms; 8.64 Feltham; 11.64 Weymouth; 9.66 Withdrawn.
73084	7.55 Stewarts Lane; 5.59 Nine Elms; 10.65 Feltham; 11.65 Eastleigh; 12.65 Withdrawn.
73085	8.55 Stewarts Lane; 2.56 Oxford; 4.56 Stewarts Lane; 5.59 Nine Elms; 10.65 Feltham; 11.65 Eastleigh; 6.66 Nine Elms; 7.67 Withdrawn.
73086	8.55 Stewarts Lane; 5.59 Nine Elms; 10.66 Withdrawn.
73087	8.55 Stewarts Lane; 8.56 Bath Green Park; 10.56 Eastleigh; 7.57 Bath Green Park; 10.57 Stewarts Lane; 5.58 Bath Green Park; 9.58 Nine Elms; 5.59 Bath Green Park; 10.59 Nine Elms; 6.60 Bath Green Park; 9.60 Nine Elms; 6.61 Bath Green Park; 9.61 Nine Elms; 8.64 Feltham; 9.64 Eastleigh; 5.65 Guildford; 10.66 Withdrawn.
73088	9.55 Stewarts Lane; 2.56 Oxford: 4.56 Stewarts Lane; 5.58 Bath Green Park; 6.58 Stewarts Lane; 9.58 Nine Elms; 10.65 Guildford; 10.66 Withdrawn.
73089	9.55 Stewarts Lane; 5.58 Nine Elms; 9.64 Eastleigh; 10.65 Guildford; 9.66 Withdrawn.
73090	10.55 Patricroft; 8.58 Shrewsbury; 1.65 Oxley; 3.65 Shrewsbury; 10.65 Withdrawn.
73091	10.55 Patricroft; 8.58 Shrewsbury; 9.61 Gloucester Barnwood; 4.64 Gloucester Horton Road; 5.65 Withdrawn.

73092	10.55 Patricroft; 8.58 Shrewsbury; 9.61 Gloucester Barnwood; 4.64 Gloucester Horton Road; 7.64 Bath Green Park; 4.65 Eastleigh; 10.65 Guildford; 7.67 Withdrawn.

73092   10.55 Patricroft; 8.58 Shrewsbury; 9.61 Gloucester Barnwood; 4.64 Gloucester Horton Road; 7.64 Bath Green Park; 4.65 Eastleigh; 10.65 Guildford; 7.67 Withdrawn.

73093   11.55 Patricroft; 8.58 Shrewsbury; 9.61 Gloucester Barnwood; 4.64 Gloucester Horton Road; 2.65 Bath Green Park; 4.65 Eastleigh; 10.65 Guildford; 7.67 Withdrawn.

73094   11.55 Patricroft; 8.58 Shrewsbury; 9.61 Bristol Barrow Road; 11.61 Gloucester Barnwood; 2.64 Withdrawn; 5.64 Reinstated Shrewsbury; 7.65 Patricroft; 5.67 Withdrawn.

73095   11.55 Patricroft; 8.58 Shrewsbury; 8.65 Croes Newydd; 4.66 Agecroft; 8.66 Withdrawn.

73096   11.55 Patricroft; 8.58 Shrewsbury; 7.62 Gloucester Barnwood; 4.64 Gloucester Horton Road; 11.64 Oxley; 3.65 Nuneaton; 6.65 Croes Newydd; 7.65 Patricroft; 11.67 Withdrawn. Preserved on the Mid Hants Railway, Alresford.

73097   12.55 Patricroft; 8.58 Shrewsbury; 7.65 Patricroft; 5.67 Withdrawn.

73098   12.55 Patricroft; 9.58 Chester West; 11.58 Polmadie; 3.66 Withdrawn.

73099   12.55 Patricroft; 9.58 Chester West; 11.58 Polmadie; 7.60 Hamilton; 9.61 Polmadie; 10.66 Withdrawn.

73100   8.55 Corkerhill; 1.67 Withdrawn.

73101   8.55 Corkerhill; 8.66 Withdrawn.

73102   9.55 Corkerhill; 12.66 Withdrawn.

73103   9.55 Corkerhill; 10.65 Withdrawn.

73104   9.55 Corkerhill; 10.65 Withdrawn.

73105   12.55 Eastfield; 12.64 Grangemouth; 10.65 Stirling; 6.66 Corkerhill; 9.66 Withdrawn.

73106   12.55 Eastfield; 6.57 Inverness; 10.57 Perth; 6.64 Corkerhill; 6.65 Withdrawn.

73107   12.55 Eastfield; 6.57 Inverness; 10.57 Perth; 6.64 Motherwell; 9.66 Withdrawn.

73108   12.55 Eastfield; 1.66 Carstairs; 12.66 Withdrawn.

73109   1.56 Eastfield; 10.64 Withdrawn.

73110   10.55 Nine Elms; 2.56 Old Oak Common; 4.56 Nine Elms; 8.64 Eastleigh; 10.65 Guildford; 1.67 Withdrawn.

73111   10.55 Nine Elms; 8.64 Eastleigh; 9.65 Withdrawn.

73112   10.55 Nine Elms; 8.64 Eastleigh; 9.64 Nine Elms; 6.65 Withdrawn.

73113   10.55 Nine Elms; 8.64 Eastleigh; 10.65 Weymouth; 1.67 Withdrawn.

73114   11.55 Nine Elms; 2.56 Reading; 4.56 Nine Elms; 8.64 Eastleigh; 10.65 Weymouth; 6.66 Withdrawn.

73115   11.55 Nine Elms; 8.64 Eastleigh; 6.66 Nine Elms; 10.66 Guildford; 3.67 Withdrawn.

73116   11.55 Nine Elms; 8.56 Bath Green Park; 10.56 Eastleigh; 7.57 Bath Green Park; 9.57 Nine Elms; 5.58 Bath Green Park; 9.58 Nine Elms; 5.59 Bath Green Park; 10.59 Nine Elms; 8.64 Eastleigh; 11.64 Withdrawn.

73117   11.55 Nine Elms; 2.56 Reading; 4.56 Nine Elms; 8.64 Eastleigh; 6.66 Nine Elms; 10.66 Guildford; 3.67 Withdrawn

73118   12.55 Nine Elms; 8.64 Eastleigh; 6.66 Nine Elms; 10.66 Guildford; 7.67 Withdrawn

73119   12.55 Nine Elms; 8.64 Eastleigh; 3.67 Withdrawn.

73120	1.56 Perth; 1.63 Corkerhill; 12.66 Withdrawn.
73121	1.56 Corkerhill; 2.66 Withdrawn.
73122	1.56 Corkerhill; 9.65 Withdrawn.
73123	2.56 Corkerhill; 5.65 Withdrawn.
73124	2.56 Corkerhill; 12.65 Withdrawn.
73125	7.56 Shrewsbury; 8.58 Patricroft; 6.68 Withdrawn.
73126	7.56 Shrewsbury; 8.58 Patricroft; 4.68 Withdrawn.
73127	8.56 Shrewsbury; 8.58 Patricroft; 11.67 Withdrawn.
73128	8.56 Shrewsbury; 8.58 Patricroft; 2.64 Rowsley; 4.64 Patricroft; 5.68 Withdrawn.
73129	8.56 Shrewsbury; 8.58 Patricroft; 11.67 Withdrawn. Preserved at the Midland Railway Centre, Butterley.
73130	9.56 Shrewsbury; 8.58 Patricroft; 1.67 Withdrawn.
73131	9.56 Shrewsbury; 8.58 Patricroft; 1.68 Withdrawn.
73132	10.56 Shrewsbury; 8.58 Patricroft; 3.68 Withdrawn.
73133	10.56 Shrewsbury; 8.58 Patricroft; 6.68 Withdrawn.
73134	10.56 Shrewsbury; 8.58 Patricroft; 6.68 Withdrawn.
73135	10.56 Holyhead; 5.58 Leicester Midland; 1.59 Derby; 11.59 Rowsley; 2.61 Derby; 4.62 Rowsley; 4.64 Derby; 9.64 Patricroft; 3.68 Withdrawn.
73136	11.56 Holyhead; 5.58 Leicester Midland; 1.59 Derby; 11.59 Rowsley; 2.61 Derby; 4.62 Rowsley; 4.64 Derby; 5.64 Patricroft; 3.68 Withdrawn.
73137	11.56 Holyhead; 5.58 Leicester Midland; 5.58 Nottingham; 6.58 Leicester Midland; 1.59 Derby; 11.59 Rowsley; 2.61 Derby; 4.62 Rowsley; 5.62 Leicester Midland; 6.62 Rowsley; 4.64 Derby; 6.64 Patricroft; 6.67 Withdrawn
73138	11.56 Holyhead; 1.57 Leicester Midland; 1.59 Derby; 11.59 Rowsley; 2.61 Derby; 4.64 Derby; 4.62 Rowsley; 5.64 Patricroft; 4.68 Withdrawn.
73139	11.56 Holyhead; 5.58 Leicester Midland; 1.59 Derby; 11.59 Rowsley; 4.64 Derby; 6.64 Patricroft; 5.67 Withdrawn.
73140	12.56 Leicester Midland; 1.57 Holyhead; 5.58 Leicester Midland; 9.58 Trafford Park; 10.58 Leicester Midland; 1.59 Derby; 11.59 Rowsley; 9.61 Derby; 3.62 Rowsley; 4.64 Derby; 5.64 Patricroft; 10.67 Withdrawn.
73141	12.56 Leicester Midland; 1.59 Derby; 11.59 Rowsley; 4.64 Derby; 5.64 Patricroft; 7.67 Withdrawn.
73142	12.56 Leicester Midland; 1.59 Derby; 11.59 Rowsley; 4.64 Derby; 5.64 Patricroft; 4.68 Withdrawn.
73143	12.56 Leicester Midland; 3.58 Nottingham; 1.59 Derby; 1.59 Nottingham; 1.59 Derby; 11.59 Rowsley; 2.64 Patricroft; 6.68 Withdrawn.
73144	12.56 Leicester Midland; 3.58 Nottingham; 1.59 Derby; 1.59 Nottingham; 1.59 Derby; 11.59 Rowsley; 9.61 Derby; 2.62 Rowsley; 4.64 Derby; 5.64 Patricroft; 8.67 Withdrawn.
73145	1.57 St Rollox; 1.66 Eastfield; 9.66 Ayr; 9.66 Withdrawn.
73146	2.57 St Rollox; 1.66 Eastfield; 11.66 Motherwell; 5.67 Withdrawn.

73147	2.57 St Rollox; 8.65 Withdrawn.

73147   2.57 St Rollox; 8.65 Withdrawn.

73148   3.57 St Rollox; 9.65 Withdrawn.

73149   3.57 St Rollox; 11.66 Stirling; 12.66 Withdrawn.

73150   4.57 St Rollox; 11.66 Stirling; 12.66 Withdrawn.

73151   4.57 St Rollox; 8.66 Withdrawn.

73152   5.57 St Rollox; 12.65 Withdrawn.

73153   5.57 St Rollox; 11.66 Stirling; 12.66 Withdrawn.

73154   6.57 St Rollox; 12.65 Stirling; 6.66 Motherwell; 12.66 Withdrawn.

73155   12.56 Neasden; 5.58 Millhouses; 1.62 Canklow; 11.62 Eastleigh; 12.63 Feltham; 11.64 Eastleigh; 4.67 Guildford; 7.67 Withdrawn.

73156   12.56 Neasden; 5.58 Millhouses; 1.59 Grimesthorpe; 8.60 Derby; 9.60 Neasden; 6.62 Leicester Central; 3.63 Woodford Halse; 5.63 Cricklewood; 10.64 Leamington Spa; 6.65 Tyseley; 4.66 Bolton; 11.67 Withdrawn; Preserved on the East Lancashire Railway at Bury.

73157   12.56 Neasden; 9.57 Kings Cross; 10.58 Darnall; 12.58 Neasden; 2.59 Derby; 6.60 Neasden; 6.62 Cricklewood; 5.63 Chester Midland; 11.63 Woodford Halse; 1.65 Oxley; 4.65 Patricroft; 5.68 Withdrawn.

73158   12.56 Neasden; 9.57 Kings Cross; 10.58 Darnall; 12.58 Neasden; 2.59 Derby; 6.60 Neasden; 6.62 Cricklewood; 7.63 Bedford; 8.63 Cricklewood; 4.64 Patricroft; 10.67 Withdrawn.

73159   1.57 Neasden; 9.57 Kings Cross; 10.58 Darnall; 12.58 Neasden; 2.59 Derby; 6.60 Neasden; 6.62 Leicester Central; 1.63 Woodford Halse; 9.64 Nuneaton; 7.65 Patricroft; 10.67 Withdrawn.

73160   1.57 Blaydon; 2.57 Gateshead; 9.57 Normanton; 4.64 Bletchley; 1.65 Oxley; 4.65 Patricroft; 11.67 Withdrawn.

73161   2.57 Blaydon; 2.57 Gateshead; 9.57 Normanton; 6.62 Neville Hill; 6.63 Wakefield; 9.63 Exmouth Junction; 12.64 Withdrawn.

73162   2.57 York; 10.58 Huddersfield; 6.61 Neville Hill; 6.63 Wakefield; 9.63 Exmouth Junction; 1.65 Oxford; 5.65 Withdrawn.

73163   2.57 York; 10.58 Huddersfield; 8.64 Wakefield; 11.64 Oxley; 4.65 Patricroft; 11.65 Withdrawn.

73164   3.57 York; 10.58 Huddersfield; 9.63 Bath Green Park; 11.63 Bristol Barrow Road; 9.64 Oxford; 12.64 Withdrawn.

73165   3.57 York; 10.58 Huddersfield; 8.64 Wakefield; 11.64 Oxley; 4.65 Patricroft; 10.65 Withdrawn.

73166   3.57 York; 10.58 Huddersfield; 4.59 Holbeck; 9.60 Huddersfield; 4.62 Holbeck; 9.62 Royston; 6.63 Patricroft; 10.63 Exmouth Junction; 9.64 Yeovil Town; 6.65 Oxford; 12.65 Withdrawn.

73167   4.57 York; 2.59 Scarborough; 6.59 Normanton; 6.63 Holbeck; 9.63 Feltham; 8.64 Shrewsbury; 8.65 Withdrawn.

73168   4.57 York; 2.59 Scarborough; 6.59 Holbeck; 10.61 Neville Hill; 6.63 Wakefield; 9.63 Feltham; 11.64 Eastleigh; 12.65 Withdrawn.

73169   4.57 York; 2.59 Scarborough; 6.59 Holbeck; 6.61 Neville Hill; 6.63 Wakefield; 9.63 Feltham; 11.64 Eastleigh; 10.66 Withdrawn.

73170   5.57 York; 2.59 Scarborough; 6.59 Holbeck; 9.62 Royston; 9.63 Feltham; 11.64 Eastleigh; 6.66 Withdrawn.

73171   5.57 York; 9.57 Holbeck; 9.62 Royston; 9.63 Feltham; 11.64 Eastleigh; 10.66 Withdrawn.

Fig. 59
73168 pulls into Lincoln Central with a train from York to Norwich, Yarmouth and Lowestoft about 1957/8. The engine entered Doncaster Works in May 1962 having achieved an average annual mileage of around 40,000, a figure typical for NER based class members at this time.
(David Tyreman Collection)

Fig. 60
Feltham based 73169 passes the SECR signal box at Ash on the Reading-Redhill line with an express from the North to the Kent Coast on 3rd October 1964. A few weeks later, 73169 was transferred to Eastleigh from where it was withdrawn in October 1966 after accruing an estimated 300,000 miles in service. *(Rodney Lissenden)*

Fig. 61
73170 heads the 12.15pm Sundays York-Bristol Temple Meads near Pontefract Baghill in the winter of 1957/8. The engine was one of a group of ten of the class, 73162-71, delivered new to York shed in the Spring of 1957. The class does not appear to have found favour there and all had been transferred to other NER depots by the end of February 1959. *(Peter Cookson)*

Fig. 62
73170 leaves Scarborough on a return holiday express for the LMR in the early 1960s. Four of the class, 73167-70, were allocated to Scarborough shed from February 1959 but the stay was short-lived and the engines were replaced by LNER B1 4-6-0s from Hull Botanic Gardens four months later.

(David Tyreman Collection)

Fig. 63
73171 heads the Saturdays Only Scarborough-Bristol Temple Meads holiday train near Pontefract Baghill on 4th July 1959. Although nominally the last of the class, it was not the last to be delivered; Caprotti valve gear 73154 emerged from Derby Works in June 1957, one month later than 73171's completion at Doncaster.

(Peter Cookson)

Fig. 64
Fresh from Works, 73003 stands at Derby shed on 27th March 1956 after its first general overhaul, having accrued a mileage of 172,218 in traffic. The engine had received an intermediate overhaul in December 1953 but was involved in a collision at Birmingham New Street in February 1954 and spent a further few weeks at Derby Works undergoing repair.

(Peter Groom)

Fig. 65
73003, allocated to Oxford, is on shed at Bristol Barrow Road on 9th October 1965. Obviously in a rather sorry state, 73003 was withdrawn at the end of the year. (*Courtney Haydon*)

Fig. 66
73006 awaits its next turn at Perth shed in the early 1960s; the first style BR tender crest, known to enthusiasts as the 'cycling lion' is prominent. The chime whistle of the type fitted to the first one hundred examples of the class is mounted behind the chimney. The engine spent much of its working life on the ScR but moved to Patricroft in July 1964 from where it was withdrawn in March 1967. (*E.V. Fry*)

Fig. 67
73008 is at rest on Aberdeen Ferryhill shed on 14th August 1965. Note the large 10" numerals on the cabside of the type applied by both Cowlairs and St Rollox Works. The boiler and running plate lining appear to have been omitted at the last repaint. Between July 1951 and April 1952, 73008 was allocated to Rugby Testing Station for steaming trials.

(*Courtney Haydon*)

2.8 Maintenance

For the Standard Cl. 5 4-6-0s, Works visits for major overhaul achieved the design rate of between 15 and 30 months. This normally equated to a mileage of the order of 70,000- 90,000; other periods in Works to deal with, for example, accident damage or major component failure were infrequent. A typical schedule for repairs to the class is as follows.

Piston and Valve Examination.

This would occur between 24,000 and 36,000 miles although the Caprotti valve gear members of the class could achieve anything up to 25% more. The work involved clearing of carbon deposits and the renewal of piston rings and was usually carried out at sheds.

Intermediate Overhaul

As mileage accumulated, the locomotive tended to develop poor riding characteristics due to wear in the axleboxes and on the tread and flanges of tyres. Depots were not equipped to deal with this problem and deterioration was sufficient at around 90,000 miles (24-30 months) to require a Works visit. This was termed the 'intermediate overhaul' and could be described as 'Heavy Intermediate' or 'Light Intermediate' depending on the extent of the work carried out. At the same time, other parts of the chassis including valve gear, piston rods and brakes would be examined and any faults rectified. Boilers did not usually require major repairs at this stage although they were always thoroughly examined; tubes, superheater elements and firebox stays were serviced as required with the boiler remaining in place.

General Overhaul

At the next intermediate overhaul, the boiler usually required greater attention and more often than not would be lifted for re-tubing and replacement of tube plates. This was termed a 'general overhaul' and for the Standard Cl. 5 4-6-0s typically occurred after around 180,000 to 200,000 running miles equating to about five years' service. Repairs to a boiler took longer than those to a chassis and a previously refurbished boiler was usually substituted to return the locomotive to traffic as quickly as possible. On some regions, particularly on the ER in the early days after Nationalisation, Doncaster continued its practice of lifting the boiler at some nominally intermediate overhauls, this occurring for example in the case of Cl. B1 4-6-0s at around 85,000 miles. One Standard Cl. 5 4-6-0 known to have been dealt with in this way was 73016 in February 1959 after an estimated mileage of around only 80,000 since the previous general overhaul. On the other hand some SR members of the class achieved well over 200,000 miles between general overhauls. Examples were:

No.	Date of General Overhaul	Accumulated Mileage ('000s)
73089	13.04.60	206.6
73111	20.10.60	236.1
73113	21.11.61	266.4
73118	12.12.62	296.4
73119	01.02.62	265.8

This high mileage between boiler lifts on these SR locomotives was attributed to reduced corrosion resulting from the fitting of the French T.I.A. water softening treatment apparatus, later replaced by the standard BR briquette method. The average mileage achieved between overhauls by Standard Cl. 5 4-6-0s compared with that of other classes engaged in broadly similar work is given in Table 9; also shown is a comparison of representative repair costs. The low cost figures achieved in 1953 when the class was relatively new had increased by 1957 as a result of the higher

Table 9

Standard Cl. 5 4-6-0s 73000-73171

Comparison with Selected Classes
Representative Repair Cost and Average Mileage to Overhaul

Class	Data For Year	Cost per Mile (New Pence)			Average Mileage ('000s) to:	
		Engine & Boiler	Tender	Total	Intermediate Overhaul	General Overhaul
4-6-0						
BR Standard Cl. 5 (1)	1953-6	2.22	0.22	2.44	98.3	207.2
	1957	3.83	0.42	4.25	95.1	189.0
LMS Stanier Cl. 5	1953-5	3.05	0.29	3.34	73.0	167.1
LNER B1	1953	3.17	0.19	3.36	75.9	168.0
GWR Hall	1953	3.19	0.28	3.47	86.2	174.5
GWR County	1953	3.95	0.30	4.25	92.7	189.0
SR King Arthur	1953-6	4.25	0.76	5.01	63.0	102.7
4-6-2						
SR Bulleid light Pacific	1953	3.46	0.51	3.97	79.7	245.3
	1957	4.63	0.51	5.14	82.5	249.5

Key: (1) Figures for LMR only.

proportion of general overhauls falling due; labour cost inflation was also a significant factor, a figure of 28% being reported over the 1953-7 period. In the case of the Standard Cl. 5 4-6-0s, the ultimate design objective was to achieve 100,000 miles to intermediate and 200,000 miles to general overhauls even after several years in service. This goal, although within reach in the early 1960s, was not achieved on a regular basis due to the decision to give steam locomotive maintenance lower priority as steam power was being phased out. Details of average annual mileage accumulated by region in the period 1952-60 are given in Table 10. Cumulative mileages for all class members at various dates, except those allocated to the ScR where data have not been traced, are listed in Table 10A. It should be noted that these are not the final mileages for these locomotives; they are the most recent figures traceable in each case. For the Caprotti valve gear fitted engines, it will be noted that after achieving initial higher annual mileage compared with the class average in 1957/8, lower figures were reported in later years for the LMR allocation which by now included the former WR engines. Little data is available for the Scottish allocation but anecdotal evidence suggests that the Caprottis were worked harder north of the border. Annual mileages in excess of 50,000 for individual class members are as follows; very high annual average values for the initial ScR allocation 73005-9, intensively used on the Glasgow-Aberdeen services, were reported for the years 1952-4 (Table 10) but individual engine mileages were not traced.

Table 10

Standard Cl. 5 4-6-0s 73000-73171
Annual Mileage by Region 1952-1960

Year End		Average Mileage per Locomotive ('000s)					
		LMR	ScR	WR	SR	ER	NER
1952		42.0	72.4	-	-	-	-
1953		35.2	65.2	ND	-	-	-
1954		41.4	67.9	32.0	-	-	-
1955		41.8	49.3	30.3	37.1	-	-
1956		40.4	49.2	25.3	42.1	19.8 (3)	-
1957	(1)	41.4	49.8	36.6 (4)	41.3	59.5 (5)	-
	(2)	45.2	ND	37.2	-	-	-
1958	(1)	30.8	47.3	30.8	41.0	37.9	39.0
	(2)	42.6 (6)	ND	-	-	-	-
1959	(1)	37.0	43.2	30.6	37.6	41.8	30.5
	(2)	32.2	ND	-	-	-	-
1960	(1)	36.0	39.1	30.7	35.9	36.4	36.1
	(2)	29.9	ND	-	-	-	-

Key:
- No allocation
ND No data traced.
(1) Class total including Caprotti valve gear locomotives where allocated.
(2) Caprotti valve gear locomotives only.
(3) Refers to 73071 only; allocated to Kings Cross for ATC testing; lengthy downtime awaiting repairs.
(4) Data available for only about half WR allocation but including all WR Caprotti locomotives.
(5) Average for three locomotives, 73157-9, half the total ER allocation of 73071(to LMR in May) & 73155-9.
(6) Includes total annual mileage for WR allocation transferred to LMR in August.

Engine	Miles	Year	Engine	Miles	Year
73010	50,085	1959	73054	56,910	1957
73011	53,650	1952	73065	52,066	1957
	50,070	1959	73066	52,457	1955
73027	54,575	1952	73068	56,912	1957
73028	50,334	1952	73069	51,838	1955
73045	51,924	1954	73157	63,703	1957
73048	52,569	1954	73158	62,078	1957
73053	51,656	1959	73159	52,826	1957

At the other end of the scale, several engines recorded annual mileages of less than 20,000.

Engine	Miles	Year	Engine	Miles	Year
73019	19,458	1954	73125	15,009	1961
73020	17,809	1955		15,821	1963
73025	16,566	1958	73127	11,931	1961
73032	12,226	1958		14,054	1963

Works responsibility for all major overhauls of Standard Cl. 5 4-6-0s is given in Table 11. Also included is a list of Works in which the class was noted from time to time undergoing light and non-classified repairs. Although SR allocated 73086 was nominally maintained by Eastleigh from 1957, it is believed the engine was unique among the original SR allocation (73080-9,73110-9) in receiving a light

intermediate overhaul at Derby; this took place between March and June 1963. Caprotti-fitted locomotives received major overhauls at Cowlairs, Darlington, Derby and Eastleigh. Several LMR-based Standard Cl. 5 4-6-0s were given overhauls at Cowlairs Works in the 1960s; the following examples appeared on 'running-in' turns from either Corkerhill, Eastfield or St Rollox on the dates quoted.

Engine	Date	Engine	Date
73000	09.65	73125	07.65
73004	10.61	73129	11.61
73010	07.65	73134	11.61
73012	05.65	73141	11.65
73025	06.65	73142	11.64
73026	05.65	73144	04.65
73035	09.65	73158	03.66
73096	11.65		

Towards the end of steam operation, with several Works given over exclusively to diesel and electric traction repairs, the class was assigned to any Works still handling major steam overhauls; examples were noted at Eastleigh, Caerphilly and Crewe in addition to those at Cowlairs listed above.

2.9 Modifications in Service

Several of the features adopted in the Standard class designs were modified as a result of experience in service. These included the Hulson rocking grate bars, the system of cylinder

Table 10A

Standard Cl. 5 4-6-0s 73000-73171: Cumulative Mileage at Various Dates

Engine Number	Cumulative Mileage	Date	Engine Number	Cumulative Mileage	Date	Engine Number	Cumulative Mileage	Date
73000	387,340	12.61	73049	336,201	7.63	73116	248,569	4.63
73001	340,503	3.61	73050	146,702	3.58	73117	113,398	8.58
73002	354,002	9.60	73051	265,634	9.61	73118	296,421	12.62
73003	413,972	11.61	73052	220,509	5.60	73119	265,773	2.62
73004	378,180	12.60	73053	296,539	3.61	73120-4	No information	
73005-9	No information		73054	323,522	11.61	73125	193,245	12.63
73010	399,769	12.60	73055-64	No information		73126	211,655	12.63
73011	383,999	12.60	73065	265,536	3.61	73127	190,752	12.63
73012	326,588	5.61	73066	272,756	4.61	73128	189,871	12.63
73013	311,873	12.60	73067	258,571	6.61	73129	198,359	12.63
73014	329,442	6.61	73068	335,558	3.60	73130	194,681	12.63
73015	384,368	5.62	73069	271,952	12.60	73131	215,631	12.63
73016	381,823	11.62	73070	257,173	12.60	73132	210,598	12.63
73017	299,233	9.61	73071	249,491	7.61	73133	190,696	12.63
73018	312,397	12.62	73072	175,841	3.59	73134	188,948	12.63
73019	361,210	1.64	73073	267,870	9.61	73135	154,143	12.60
73020	311,259	10.61	73074	234,244	12.60	73136	160,975	12.60
73021	232,772	12.58	73075-9	No information		73137	161,786	12.60
73022	311,376	8.62	73080	213,641	1.60	73138	155,163	12.60
73023	304,975	3.60	73081	153,339	3.59	73139	171,921	12.60
73024	208,158	12.58	73082	236,978	8.61	73140	157,228	12.60
73025	234,525	12.58	73083	182,549	9.59	73141	163,901	12.60
73026	256,650	12.58	73084	171,214	10.59	73142	164,759	12.60
73027	166,061	11.56	73085	213,190	8.60	73143	152,534	12.60
73028	330,066	6.62	73086	191,066	11.59	73144	171,599	12.60
73029	337,003	5.63	73087	208,906	4.61	73145-54	No information	
73030	294,909	12.60	73088	212,622	4.61	73155	192,921	12.60
73031	183,279	12.57	73089	306,643	9.62	73156	166,734	12.61
73032	209,872	4.60	73090	161,129	6.60	73157	171,541	3.61
73033	256,016	4.61	73091	156,182	4.60	73158	152,893	9.61
73034	243,788	3.62	73092	164,902	4.60	73159	194,611	8.61
73035	256,308	11.61	73093	117,244	7.58	73160	93,060	9.59
73036	260,749	11.62	73094	171,920	9.60	73161	92,829	5.59
73037	93,985	3.56	73095	226,502	5.62	73162	85,093	4.59
73038	253,642	8.61	73096	175,279	2.61	73163	93,418	7.59
73039	205,554	3.61	73097	159,393	12.60	73164	91,274	6.59
73040	301,465	12.60	73098	132,221	3.59	73165	155,352	5.62
73041	211,089	10.58	73099	132,231	3.59	73166	201,288	6.63
73042	304,802	5.62	73100-9	No information		73167	177,811	1.64
73043	268,997	7.61	73110	308,501	2.64	73168	201,273	5.62
73044	240,834	12.60	73111	321,642	2.64	73169	210,837	12.63
73045	321,020	12.60	73112	199,973	3.60	73170	179,055	9.61
73046	337,580	12.62	73113	266,431	11.61	73171	204,402	8.61
73047	243,303	3.60	73114	301,966	11.62			
73048	281,641	12.60	73115	292,303	12.62			

lubrication, the Downs pattern sanding gear, the drawgear between engine and tender and the cab-tender arrangement.

The Hulson rocking grate was originally designed to use small size, relatively dusty high grade coal producing low levels of clinker residues. Such fuel was typically used on mechanical stoker-fired engines which ran with relatively thin fires evenly spread throughout the firebox. The air passages were cast within the bars to give a 'honeycomb' type structure and were turned through a right angle to diffuse the primary air sideways into the fuel bed. They were narrower than the firebars fitted to LMS Stanier Cl. 5 4-6-0s but had the disadvantage that the airspaces were more easily blocked than those of conventional types of firebar, especially with certain types of coal. This did not prove serious on 'top-link' locomotives such as Pacifics with better grade fuel and relatively large grates, or on engines engaged on short runs with plenty of opportunity to clean the fire. For the Standard Cl. 5 4-6-0s however, problems occurred during periods of

Table 11

Standard Cl. 5 4-6-0s 73000-73171
Works Repairs

Region	All Repairs including Intermediate and General Overhauls	Light Casual and Non-classified Repairs Only ★
LMR	Derby (to November 1963) Darlington (September 1963 to mid-1964) Eastleigh (from mid-1964)	Crewe, Horwich, Rugby, Nottingham depot
ScR	Derby (to mid-1952) St Rollox (1953 to mid-1958) Cowlairs (from early 1958)★★	Inverurie Inverness
WR	Swindon (to end 1962) Doncaster (January 1960-November 1963) Darlington (September 1963 to mid-1964)	Caerphilly, Oswestry, Shrewsbury, Worcester Wolverhampton★★★ Bristol Bath Road depot
SR	Crewe (to end 1956) Derby (to mid-1957) Eastleigh (from mid-1957)	Ashford, Brighton, Stewarts Lane depot
ER & NER	Doncaster (to November 1963) Darlington (September 1963 to mid-1964)	All repairs carried out at Doncaster or Darlington

Note: ★ Crewe and Caerphilly carried out a small number of major overhauls towards the end of steam operation.
★★ Cowlairs gave general overhauls to several LMR-based members of the class in the 1960s; see section 2.8.
★★★ Wolverhampton undertook heavy intermediate repairs on occasion, eg. 73037 (March 1960) and 73093 (May 1960).

continuous hard steaming with the typically high clinker coal normally supplied to the majority of depots. Once embedded in the bars, the clinker was almost impossible to remove and resulted in significantly reduced steaming performance. An adaptation of the LMS system was later fitted which increased the air space from 32.6% to 37.4% of grate area. This system was still capable of handling coal in the form of small 'nutty slack' but resulted in much improved combustion, reduced smoke production and an approximate increase of 5% in maximum water evaporation from 18,000lb to 19,000lb per hour; the two types of firebars were readily interchangeable.

The method of cylinder lubrication was an adaptation of the former GWR regulator controlled system. This required the regulator to be open by at least a small amount even when coasting, otherwise no atomiser steam would be available to break up the oil into small droplets and deliver it through to the valves and cylinders. The authorities considered that this method of working was not always appreciated by non-GWR crews brought up in the tradition of coasting with closed regulators and hence was the cause of excessive wear to the piston liners and rings such that the latter sometimes needed changing every 12,000 miles or up to three times more often than the planned rate. In response, many drivers were adamant that the root of the problem was not in their method of operating but in the design of the Standard regulator. Crews observed that when running with the regulator fractionally open as advised, normal footplate vibration caused

it to close of its own accord unless constantly monitored: this did not occur with the GWR regulator design. Despite continuing advice by the authorities on correct operation, the problem was solved only by re-adopting the LMS system whereby oil delivery was controlled via the operation of the cylinder cocks, atomised steam flowing only when the cocks were closed.

The Downs pattern steam coil sanding system had a tendency to clog due to ingress of water and condensed steam into the sand boxes and was replaced on several members of the class.

The drawgear between locomotive and tender was a modification of the LNER single screwed-drawbar type favoured by Doncaster, nutted at the back of the tender dragbox and without safety links. Corrosion fatigue at the drawbar threads caused at least two cases of breakage in the Standard Cl. 7 Britannia Pacifics when on both occasions the engine suddenly parted company with the tender and rest of the train. After these incidents, a programme of replacement with LMS solid link coupling, side buffers and additional safety links was authorised. The cab-tender arrangement led to excessive draughtiness on the footplate; the modifications carried out to deal with the problem are noted in section 2.4 dealing with tenders.

Another feature of the Standard designs was the recurrence of a shaking or 'fore and aft' oscillation transmitted from engine to train. Typically for two-cylinder locomotives, balancing the engine to reduce vertical hammer blow on the rail to levels acceptable to the Civil Engineer inevitably gives rise to this oscillatory motion unless the correct relationship between unbalanced reciprocating weight and overall locomotive weight is achieved. Even then careful attention must be given to the train coupling arrangement to ensure any remaining forces are not magnified. The problem was resolved by modification of the drawbar spring assembly on the tender. The initial compression during assembly was reduced thus enhancing its cushioning effect and reducing the 'fore and aft' problem to negligible proportions.

2.9.1 Steaming Characteristics

The initial reaction from engine crews accustomed to handling Stanier Cl. 5 and Thompson Cl. B1 4-6-0s was that the Standard Cl. 5 4-6-0s were much less free steaming. The application of a range of different firing techniques from 'little and often' to larger quantities less frequently did nothing to alleviate the problem. As a result, from August 1951 to March 1952, tests were carried out on the stationary testing plant at Rugby and on the road between Skipton and Carlisle using the LMR No. 1 Dynamometer Car. The locomotive selected was 73008, allocated to Perth on delivery and having run only 880 miles in traffic. A total of 9,120 test miles were run on the plant and 2,800 miles on the road in the course of the Dynamometer Car tests; the locomotive was still fitted with the original Hulson type firebars. Two types of coal were used during testing, South Kirkby Grade 1A Hard South Yorkshire and Blidworth Grade 2B Hard East Midlands; samples showed little variation in chemical analysis and calorific value at around 14,000 BT Units per lb. A satisfactory maximum water evaporation of 25,000 lb per hour was achieved with the higher grade South Kirkby coal but only 18,000 lb per

Fig. 68
Nottingham-based 73018 rests between excursion duties at Bridlington in the early 1950s. The engine was transferred to the WR in September 1953 and later to the SR's Western Section, surviving until the end of steam on the SR in July 1967. The appendage at the base of the front part of the tender is the sieve box, designed to filter adventitious impurites from the water before injection into the boiler.

(Real Photographs)

Fig. 69
73022 is at Eastleigh depot in mixed traffic lined black livery after a general overhaul on 6th October 1962 with an accumulated mileage of more than 310,000; the engine has a non-standard front number-plate. Also observable below the cabside numerals are the triangle indicating 73022 has been fitted with the standard BR water softening apparatus and the adjacent metal plate showing the engine is the subject of at least one experimental test procedure.

(Courtney Haydon)

Fig. 70
73030, fitted with Westinghouse airbrake equipment, is running at 55mph with a cut-off of 20% and full regulator on the rollers at Rugby Test Plant in August 1953. This engine and 73031 were reported to have been fitted with Transom Tablet Exchange Apparatus for a short period after delivery but there does not appear to be any photographic evidence to confirm this.

(John G. Click/L. Elsey Collection)

Fig. 71
73031, complete with Westing-house air brake equipment, is pictured on shed at Derby in the mid-1950s. The engine was allocated to Rugby Testing Station from January 1958 to February 1961; when not required for testing purposes, 73031 operated from Bristol Barrow Road depot.
(J.B. Arnold)

Fig. 72
73031, now relieved of its Westinghouse air brake equip-ment, awaits the go-ahead at Sheffield Midland with a North East-South West express in 1960. The engine, then operating from Bristol Barrow Road depot had recently acquired a lined green livery at Swindon Works. Note the 'red spot' route restriction indicator applied below the cabside numerals.
(David Tyreman Collection)

Fig. 73
73049 began life as an LMR engine at Leicester Midland but was transferred to Bath Green Park in August 1955 and never received a major overhaul at Derby Works. The engine is depicted here at Eastleigh during its Bath Green Park days in the late 1950s. 73049 visited Brighton Works on two occasions for light repairs, in November 1955 and July 1957 but was otherwise maintained at Eastleigh. Note the absence of power classification mark usually applied above the numerals on the cabside.
(L. Elsey)

Fig. 74
73049, in fully lined green livery, after a heavy intermediate overhaul at Eastleigh on 14th September 1963. Note the application by Eastleigh of the lining to both edges of the running plate; this was in contrast to Swindon practice where only the lower edge was lined. *(G. Wheeler)*

hour with the Blidworth fuel. Previous results with a Stanier Cl. 5 4-6-0 using Firbeck Grade 2B fuel similar to that from the Blidworth source gave a comparable figure of 22,000 lb per hour. On the road tests 73008, fired with South Kirkby coal, confirmed the plant test results managing a steady 23,100 lb per hour water evaporation rate with coaling rate at 3,360 lb per hour. Hauling 433 tons, increased to 560 tons by electric dynamic braking from two Mobile Test Units included in the train, the engine produced an excellent performance, achieving a pass to pass time of 26 minutes 55 seconds for the 17.5 miles from Appleby to Ais Gill summit, an average speed of 39 mph on a ruling gradient of 1 in 100. A train of this weight was considerably more than the engine would be expected to handle on such a route in day to day service.

Several more months experience with the lower grade coal typically supplied for day to day running confirmed the unsatisfactory steam producing performance and a further series of tests was arranged on the Rugby plant during the summer of 1953, this time using 73030, new from Derby in June. The engine incorporated the LMS grid type firebars instead of the Hulson type, which allowed an increase from 18,000 to 19,000 lb per hour for maximum water evaporation even before new tests were begun. Work carried out at Swindon on the improvement of locomotive front ends indicated that increasing the draught by reducing blastpipe diameter from 5½" to 5" or even 4⅞" might be more appropriate to the capacity of the locomotive. Results confirmed this view, the 19,000 lb per hour maximum water evaporation being raised to 22,000 lb per hour with a 5" blastpipe cap (15% increase) and 24,000 lb per hour with the 4⅞" size (26% increase). Caps of the latter dimensions were quickly applied to all members of the class. The much improved results were accompanied by no loss of boiler efficiency nor increase in steam consumption per indicated horse power throughout the range of working. The solution was in effect a vindication of the age-old practice of fitting 'Jimmies' or 'Snickles' usually in the form of a piece of thick wire, over the blastpipe of steam-shy locomotives on return to the running shed from Works overhaul. This remedy was regularly perpetrated by experienced 'old hands' on the shed staff, a practice strongly discouraged by the authorities over the years in the belief that it reduced boiler efficiency and increased fuel consumption. No comparable tests were carried out on any of the Caprotti valve gear members of the class. Neither does there appear to be a record of any official tests applying the reduced blastpipe modification to any of the Stanier Cl. 5 4-6-0s.

Between February and October 1958, 73031 was at Rugby Testing Station for a series of experiments on factors affecting cylinder efficiency. Steam temperature was increased by electrical means to make it independent of evaporation level in the boiler. Later, for a period of six weeks in the spring of 1959, 73031 was selected for a further series of cylinder efficiency tests at Rugby. The electrical power on this occasion was provided by two diesel shunters. The primary objective was to isolate the separate effects of running speed and inlet steam temperature on cylinder efficiency. Tests were carried out over a range of different steam 'cut-offs' (from 15% to 50%) and various speeds (20mph to 70mph). Results for a typical mixed traffic locomotive roster indicated potential savings in the region of £270 per locomotive per year after deduction of necessary expense. The report recommended that further tests with a Giesl oblong ejector type blastpipe and superheater damper control be made both at Rugby and in traffic. These tests were not commissioned due to the restricted availability of resources for steam traction development following a change in BR policy in favour of diesel and electric power.

One of the Caprotti valve gear members of the class, 73138, was selected for the testing of an alternative sanding gear system. The experiments were connected with a number of incidents where diesel multiple units (DMUs) had apparently 'vanished' from signalbox track circuit panels at certain times. Due to their light weight, the DMUs' wheels were not able to cut through any sand remaining on the track deposited there by steam locomotives for improved adhesion. The sand, being a very effective insulator, disrupted the continuity of the track circuit effectively causing the DMUs

Fig. 75
73050 proudly displays its 'exhibition finish' alongside Standard Cl. 3 2-6-0 77009 at the International Railway Congress Exhibition at Willesden depot's roundhouse in June 1954.

(G. Wheeler)

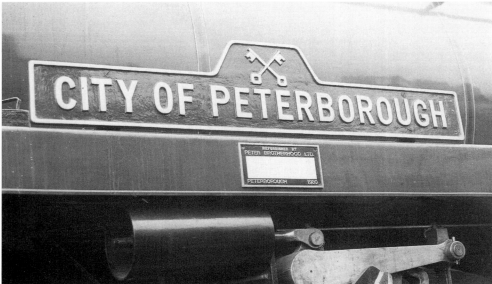

Fig. 76
Preserved 73050's *City of Peterborough* nameplate complete with the refurbishment plate supplied by Peter Brotherhood Ltd., the engineering establishment which carried out the restoration.

(R.R. Darsley)

Fig. 77
Preserved 73050's cabside numerals and *City of Peterborough* crest.

(R.R. Darsley)

Fig. 78
73052 at Bath Green Park depot on 7th September 1962. The engine has lost its cylinder and boiler linings at the last repaint. Note the different positioning of the access steps to the running plate from the buffer beam on the driver's side compared with that on the fireman's side. *(Peter Groom)*

Fig. 79
73057 on shed at Glasgow Corkerhill on 18th April 1965. Note the Cowlairs-applied depot name on the front buffer beam, the white edged front numberplate, the non-standard depot code plate at the base of the smokebox door, the different configuration of the running plate access steps on the left side of the engine compared with that on the right and the vacuum pipe extended above the buffer beam to accommodate a snowplough.
(Courtney Haydon)

Fig. 80
73059 is seen in company with another of the class at its home depot Polmadie on 16th August 1960. At this time, the Polmadie class members were regularly noted on holiday services to destinations south of the border such as Morecambe and the Fylde Coast.
(Peter Groom)

to 'disappear'. 73138 was fitted with 'pencil' type sanding gear which consisted of two small steam cylinders with pistons, one for forward running and one for reverse, each of which held a 'stick/pencil' of sand about 2" in diameter. The experiment was unsuccessful as test results confirmed that the quantity of sand deposited was insufficient to prevent slipping.

2.9.2 Detail Modifications

To accommodate the SR's white disc and lamp route codes, all locomotives permanently allocated to the region were fitted with four additional lamp brackets, two at mid-height either side of the smokebox door and two similarly positioned on the tender back plate. GWR pattern lamp brackets were fitted to all members of the class allocated to the WR; the GWR lamp was attached to its bracket on the side of the lamp whereas other companies used a rear fitment. Several of the class, 73012-5/7-29/32-9, received GWR type Automatic Train Control (ATC) equipment when transferred to the WR in 1956 as did the first Caprotti valve gear engines, 73125-34, on allocation when new to Shrewsbury in the same year. Details of known fitting dates are given in Table 12 under the reference WR01. From 1958 many members of the class acquired the BR Automatic Warning System apparatus and it is likely that virtually all of the class had been so equipped by the early 1960s. Details of fitting dates, where known, are given under reference 4983 in Table 12; where no date is quoted, confirmation has been by photographic evidence. WR engines transferred to other regions were reported to have had their Swindon type ATC gear replaced by the BR type AWS apparatus.

Several of the class allocated to the ScR had their frames drilled to accommodate the small cowcatcher type snow ploughs, 73005-9/77/8 being so fitted at various times. Manson type tablet exchange gear was also carried by some if not all of this group for operating on single line routes. The apparatus was also earmarked for a further group, 73055-64, but as the latter were allocated to Polmadie, the proposal was not pursued. Instead, 73055-64 were furnished with front vacuum pipes located higher on the buffer beam than normal to be clear of the larger snow plough attachments where fitted; photographic evidence confirms the earlier ScR batch, 73005-9, was similarly altered after delivery. Virtually all members of the class allocated to Bath Green Park for service on the S&DJR route to Bournemouth West were equipped with the Whitaker automatic tablet exchange apparatus which was affixed to the tender on the driver's side; engines known to have been so fitted were 73001/19/28/47/9/50-2/4/68/87 and 73116. A further minor modification noted on some of the class working on the LMR was the fitting of a bracket on the cabside just above the number to hold the driver's nametag; 73065/138, along with some of the LMR's Standard Cl. 7 Britannia Pacifics, were known to have carried this modification and there may have been a few others.

There were many other detail modifications made to various members of the class, particularly in the early years; a list is given in Table 12, together with details of which locomotives were so fitted and on which date. The information is incomplete as changes were not fully recorded from the early 1960s onwards. The modification reference numbers are given below with a brief description of the work and costs involved. Reference Numbers 3980 and 4175 appear to apply to the same modification ie. provision and fitting of cab draught shields and padded back to the fireman's seat. Engines modified are noted under the specific reference number. Three locomotives, 73018/22/6, are recorded as having received both modifications. It is not clear why two different reference numbers should be made for the same modification at the same cost.

Ref. No.	Work Involved
1871	Discharge of continuous blowdown into ashpan. Cost: £1.15s.10d (£1.79).
3329	Modified pistons for continuous blowdown valves. Cost £1.00.
3345	Atomiser and bogie lubrication. Cost £86.13s.0d (£86.65).
3400	Fitting manganese liners to intermediate rubbing plates and buffer faces. Cost £30.14s.0d (£30.70).
3622	Alteration to spring balancing arrangement and fitting stops to prevent reversing gear jamming. Cost £14.7s.0d (£14.35).
3698	Provision and fitting of new tank holding down bracket and packing. Cost £5.12s.0d (£5.60).
3980	Fitting of: (1) padded backs to fireman's seat. Cost £3.9s.0d (£3.45) and (2) cab draught shield. Cost £66.2s.0d (£66.10)
4147	Fitting of screwed type smokebox door hinge. Cost £9.13s.0d (£9.65).
4175	Fitting of: (1) padded backs to fireman's seat. Cost £3.9s.0d (£3.45) and (2) cab draught shield. Cost £66.2s.0d (£66.10).
4341	Removal of Downs sanding gear. Cost £33.4s.9d (£33.24).
4542	Additional cross-bracings to frame. Cost £27.14s.1d (£27.70).
4983	Fitting of BR type ATC equipment. Cost £383.0s.0d.
5173	Fitting of Smith-Stone speed indicator & recorder. Cost £140.0s.0d.
5548	Provision and fitting of hinged cab windows. Cost £76.0s.0d.
5731	Modification of grease lubricator for axlebox and spring bracket pin. No cost quoted.
5900	Fitting of safety links between engine and tender. Cost £21.15s.6d (£21.78).
6132	Fitting of protective shield over tender leading axle. Cost £11.17s.5d (£11.87)
8895	Piston rod modified packing. No cost quoted.
9089	Modification of briquette tube feeder, part of the standard BR water softening system. No cost quoted.
9129	Continuous blowdown apparatus. Cost £32.14s.0d (£32.70).
9216	Modification of manual blowdown gear. No cost quoted.

A list of LMR experimental fittings to Standard Cl. 5 4-6-0s, dated March 1959, is given as follows. In several cases, individual engines were recorded as 'deleted' with respect to certain modifications. This could mean that the planned modification was either not carried out or was subsequently terminated.

Table 12

Standard Cl. 5 4-6-0s 73000-73171: Detail Modifications

Mod.★	Locomotive Modified and Date of Modification				
1871	73024:29.12.51				
3329	73000:16.06.57	73002:16.06.57	73003:16.06.57	73004:16.06.57	73010:16.06.57
	73011:03.11.56	73014:08.07.57	73015:16.06.57	73016:16.06.57	73017:26.09.59
	73018:27.06.59	73020:05.09.59	73028:31.10.59	73030:16.06.57	73031:16.06.57
	73032:15.06.57	73033:15.06.57	73034:15.06.57	73035:15.06.57	73036:15.06.57
	73037:15.06.57	73038:15.06.57	73039:30.11.57	73041:08.11.58	73042:14.11.59
	73043:21.08.64	73045:16.06.57	73046:16.06.57	73047:03.05.58	73048:16.06.57
	73049:13.05.61	73050:no date	73051:09.05.59	73052:14.06.58	73054:18.05.57
	73065:16.06.57	73067:07.09.57	73068:16.06.57	73070:20.04.57	73071:13.07.57
	73083: ? 10.59	73084: ? 10.59	73086: ? 12.59	73087: ? 12.59	73088: ? 05.61
3345	73001:28.11.53	73002:no date	73003:02.01.54	73004:30.01.54	73010:28.11.53
	73011:09.10.54	73012:09.10.54	73013:14.09.56	73014:04.12.54	73017:16.07.55
	73018:04.12.54	73019:29.01.55	73020:05.11.55	73021:26.03.55	73023:22.05.54
	73024:18.06.55	73026:04.12.54	73027:26.12.53	73028:08.10.55	73029:31.12.55
3400	73002:22.02.58	73003:02.01.54	73004:28.11.53	73010:28.11.53	73011:09.10.54
	73012:19.05.56	73013:05.11.60	73014:04.12.54	73015:04.12.54	73016:19.06.54
	73017:16.02.55	73018:18.12.54	73019:29.01.55	73020:05.11.55	73021:26.03.55
	73022:01.01.55	73023:22.05.54	73025:28.11.53	73026:04.12.54	73027:26.12.53
	73028:08.10.55				
3622	73000:28.11.53	73001:28.11.53	73003:02.01.54	73004:28.11.53	73010:28.11.53
	73011:09.10.54	73012:09.10.54	73013:28.11.53	73014:28.11.53	73016:28.11.53
	73017:13.08.55	73018:04.12.54	73019:29.01.55	73020:30.01.54	73021:26.03.55
	73023:22.05.54	73024:30.01.54	73025:28.11.53	73026:04.12.54	73027:26.12.53
	73028:03.10.55	73029:31.12.55			
3698	73000:02.12.56	73002:16.06.56	73003:21.04.56	73004:21.04.56	73012:19.05.56
	73013:14.07.56	73019:27.01.57	73020:09.09.56	73023:06.10.56	
3980	73017:16.07.55	73018:04.12.54	73019:29.01.55	73022:01.01.55	73026:04.12.54
4147	73017:13.08.55	73018:01.01.55			
4175	73001:28.11.53	73002:28.11.53	73003:02.01.54	73004:28.11.53	73010:28.11.53
	73011:28.11.53	73012:28.11.53	73013:28.11.53	73014:28.11.53	73015:28.11.53
	73016:28.11.53	73018:04.12.54	73020:30.01.54	73021:15.10.53	73022:01.01.55
	73023:22.05.54	73024:30.01.54	73025:28.11.53	73026:04.12.54	73027:28.11.53
	73028:28.11.53	73081:11.04.59			
4341	73010:04.12.61	73016:23.02.57	73018:27.06.59		
4542	73012:19.05.56	73030:26.01.63			
4983	73002:no date	73010:13.08.59	73011:17.06.61	73013:06.10.62	73014:22.04.61
	73020:no date	73030:31.10.59	73033:17.06.61	73038:07.10.61	73039:20.05.61
	73040:28.11.59	73042:14.11.59	73043:22.08.64	73044:22.02.59	73055–64:no date
	73066:08.09.62	73067:15.07.61	73068:no date	73069:23.02.63	73070:27.02.60
	73071:27.02.60	73073:02.12.61	73077:no date	73078:no date	73080:12.04.58
	73081:11.02.59	73082:no date	73083:10.10.59	73084:31.10.59	73085:no date
	73086:11.01.58	73087:07.02.59	73088:07.08.59	73089:02.05.59	73100-9:no date
	73110:29.01.60	73111:no date	73112:08.05.59	73113:no date	73114:no date
	73115:no date	73116:no date	73117:11.02.59	73118 20.11.59	73119:11.06.59
	73120-4:no date	73125:22.03.59	73126:22.02.59	73127:26.12.59	73128:22.02.59
	73129:30.01.60	73130:22.03.59	73131:28.11.59	73132:30.01.60	73133:20.01.60
	73134:30.01.60	73140:19.05.62	73143:no date	73144:no date	73145-54:no date
	73156:23.03.63	73157:no date	73158:no date	73161:02.07.59	73162:23.05.59
	73164:25.07.59	73165:15.08.59	73166:no date	73167:no date	73168:no date
	73169:12.03.60	73170:no date	73171:03.06.59		
5173	73010:04.11.61	73011:17.06.61	73014:16.07.60	73018:30.12.61	73022:no date
5548	73017:26.09.59	73018:30.12.61	73019:no date	73020:05.09.59	73022:23.04.60
	73028:31.10.59	73041: ? 09.62	73042:14.11.59	73047:28.05.60	73049:13.05.61
	73050:no date	73051:14.10.61	73070:27.02.60	73071:07.10.61	73083:10.10.59
	73084: ? 03.62	73085: ? 09.60	73086:11.01.58	73087: ? 12.59	73089: ? 04.60
	73110: ? 01.63	73112: ? 01.63	73113: ? 12.59	73114: ? 03.60	73116: ? 10.60
	73118: ? 02.60				
5731	73030:no date				
5900	73000:02.12.58	73002:no date	73003:22.02.58	73010:04.11.61	73014:08.07.57
	73015:03.11.61	73016:23.02.57	73018:27.06.59	73023:01.11.58	73025:27.01.57
	73027:31.12.56	73028:31.10.59	73030:07.09.57	73031:28.12.57	73032:09.09.56
	73033:11.07.59	73038:07.10.61	73039:30.11.57	73040:01.11.58	73041:08.09.57
	73042:02.11.57	73044:24.01.59	73047:03.05.58	73049:13.05.61	73051:09.05.59

	73052:14.06.58	73054:18.05.57	73065:02.12.56	73066:28.11.59	73067:07.09.57
	73070:20.04.57	73071:13.07.57	73072:27.01.57	73073:31.12.56	73074:28.12.57
	73080:12.04.58	73081:09.11.57	73083:14.12.57	73084:12.10.57	73085:18.01.58
	73086:11.01.58	73087:26.10.57	73088:07.12.57	73090:28.12.57	73091:22.03.58
	73092:22.03.58	73093:28.12.57	73096:17.05.58	73097:25.01.58	73098:28.12.57
	73099:22.02.58	73125:16.05.59			
6132	73002:no date	73003:22.02.58	73011:29.12.62	73025:03.11.62	73031:28.12.57
	73039:30.11.57	73044:24.01.59	73074:28.12.57	73090:28.12.57	73093:28.12.57
	73097:25.01.58	73098:28.12.57	73099:22.02.58		
8895	See SR09.				
9089	73020:25.11.61	73080:12.04.58	73083:14.12.58	73085:18.01.58	73087:26.10.57
	73088:07.12.57				
9129	73125:30.01.60	73126:18.04.59	73127:26.12.59	73128:16.06.59	73129:no date
	73130:18.04.59	73131:28.11.59	73132:16.05.59	73133:20.01.60	73134:05.09.59
9216	73080:12.04.58	73081:09.11.57	73082:30.11.57	73083:10.10.59	73084:12.10.57
	73085:18.01.58	73087:26.10.57			
SR01	73017:26.09.59	73020:05.09.59	73022:23.04.60	73028:31.10.59	73042:14.11.59
	73047:28.05.60	73050:no date	73051:09.05.59	73081: ? 04.59	73082:15.08.59
	73083:10.10.59	73084:31.10.59	73085:08.08.59	73086:12.12.59	73087: ? 12.59
	73089: ? 04.60	73112: ? 01.63	73113: ? 12.59	73114: ? 03.60	73116: ? 10.60
	73118: ? 02.60	73119: ? 04.60			
SR02	73081:11.04.59	73083:10.10.59	73084:31.10.59	73086:12.12.59	73088:07.12.59
SR03	73020:05.09.59	73041:08.11.58	73042:04.11.59	73047:03.05.58	73049:13.05.61
	73050:no date	73051:no date	73052:no date	73080:12.04.58	73081:11.04.59
	73082:15.08.59	73083:10.10.59	73084:31.10.59	73085:08.08.59	73086:12.12.59
SR04	73017:26.09.59	73018:30.12.61	73020:25.11.61	73113: ? 01.62	73085:18.01.58
SR05	73047:28.05.60	73050:no date	73051:no date	73052:25.06.60	73083: ? 10.59
	73084: ? 10.59	73086: ? 12.59	73087:02.02.59	73088: ? 05.61	
SR06	73088:07.12.57	73089: ? 04.60	73116: ? 10.60		
SR07	73041:08.11.58	73047:03.05.58	73049:13.05.61	73051:09.05.61	73052:14.06.58
	73080:12.04.58	73110: ? 12.62	73111:no date	73112 ? 01.63	73114: ? 03.60
	73115: ? 01.60	73116: ? 10.60	73118: ? 02.60		
SR08	73049:13.05.61				
SR09	73017:26.04.59	73020:05.09.59	73028:31.10.59	73041:08.11.58	73042:14.11.59
	73047:28.05.60	73049:13.05.61	73050:no date	73051:09.05.59	73052:14.06.58
	73080:12.04.58	73081: ? 04.59	73082: ? 08.59	73083: ? 10.59	73084: ? 10.59
	73085:03.08.59	73086: ? 12.59	73087: ? 05.61	73088: ? 05.61	73089: ? 04.60
	73110: ? 01.60	73111:no date	73112:no date	73113: ? 12.59	73114: ? 03.60
	73115: ? 01.60	73116: ? 10.60	73117 ? 04.61	73118: ? 02.60	73119: ? 04.60
SR10	73019: ? 02.59	73049:13.05.61	73050:17.03.62	73052:25.06.60	73085:17.09.60
SR11	73017:26.09.59	73018:30.12.61	73020:25.11.61	73022:22.09.62	73082: ? 09.61
	73083: ? 10.59	73084: ? 03.62	73087: ? 05.61	73088: ? 05.61	73113: ? 01.62
	73117: ? 04.61				
SR13	73017:26.09.59	73018:27.06.59	73020:05.09.59	73022:30.05.59	73028:31.10.59
	73041 ? 11.58	73042:14.11.59	73082: ? 08.59	73083: ? 10.59	73084: ? 10.59
	73085: ? 09.60	73086: ? 12.59	73087: ? 05.61	73112: ? 01.63	73113: ? 12.59
	73114: ? 03.60	73115: ? 01.60	73118: ? 02.60		
SR19	73022:23.04.60	73028:31.10.59	73042:14.11.59	73047:28.05.60	73049:13.05.61
	73050:no date	73051:14.10.61	73052:25.06.60	73083: ? 10.59	73084: ? 10.59
	73086: ? 12.59	73087: ? 12.59	73089: ? 04.60	73112 ? 01.63	73113: ? 12.59
	73114: ? 03.60	73115: ? 01.60			
SR20	73088: ? 05.61	73114: ? 03.60			
SR21	73018:30.12.61	73116: ? 10.60			
SR22	73017: ? 09.61	73020:25.11.61	73029:27.07.63	73052:25.06.60	
SR23	73041: ? 05.61				
SR24	73029:27.07.63				
SR25	73110: ? 12.62				
SR26	73119 ? 04.60				
SR27	73017:26.09.59	73020:25.11.61	73022:23.04.60	73042:14.11.59	73047:28.05.60
	73081: ? 04.59	73088: ? 05.61	73089: ? 04.60	73110: ? 01.60	73112: ? 01.63
	73113: ? 12.59	73114: ? 03.60	73116: ? 10.60	73117: ? 04.61	73118: ? 02.60
WR01	73012:26.04.56	73013:29.06.56	73014:14.05.56	73015:16.03.56	73017:21.06.56
	73018:21.05.56	73019:30.05.56	73020:06.08.56	73021:11.06.56	73022:11.06.56
	73023:14.09.56	73024:23.08.56	73025:27.06.56	73026:02.10.56	73027:21.12.56
	73028:04.07.56	73029:12.11.56			

★ See text for key to work carried out under individual modification job numbers.

Mod No.	Modification Detail
MDL/1305	Specification not identified Engines: 73012/40
MDL/1308	Improved boiler insulation by fitting a lightweight asbestos mattress 1" thick in place of usual fibreglass mattress. Engines: 73040-4
MDL/1310	Rocksil boiler mattress. Engines: 73045/6
MDL/1318	Simplefix joints on lubricator and steam pipes to lubricator system Engines: 73070-3 (73072 deleted)
MDL/1320	Piston valve liners with increased number of ports Engines: 73030/70/1/3/91-4 (73072 deleted)
MDL/1321	Boiler fitted with 'Stallite' mattress Engines: 73070/1/3 (73072 deleted)
MDL/1329	Modified drainage cocks. Engine: 73074
MDL/1330	Specification not identified Engine: 73037
MDL/1337	Fitted with intermediate rubbing plates and plungers with hard surfacing deposit of OK Hardtop 8 Electrode on working surfaces. Engines: 73031/42/72
MDL/1338	Specification not identified Engine: 73096
MDL/1340	Specification not identified Engine 73041
MDL/1343	Specification not identified Engine: 73015
MDL/1346	Tender has axles treated with zinc rich primer and black enamel to reduce corrosion Engines: 73004/13/5/31/2/7 73040/2-6
MDL/1351	Specification not identified Engine: 73001
MDL/1352	Mattresses made by Wright's Insulations Ltd. to improve insulation Engines: 73135-9
MDL/1369	All axleboxes (engine and tender) packed with special grease. Engines: 73138/42/6
MDL/1377	Comparison of Bogie bolster pads made from Railko A.L.2. (73041/71) compared with those manufactured from Ferrobestos (73098) All deleted.
MDL/1380	Firebox mattress made of glass weave. Engines: 73032/8
MDL/1411	Specification not identified Engine: 73030
MDL/1414	Shot peened laminated springs on coupled wheels Engines: 73023/30/2/8/40/4/71 73159
MDL/1468	Specification not identified Engine: 73138

On the WR, three modifications were confirmed but no costs were quoted; there may have been others.

WR01	Fitting of WR ATC apparatus See Table 12 for engines fitted.
W/SW/L/157	Comparative test of Bestobell (RTM) packing sleeves and Klinger AB.18 sleeves in boiler water gauge and drain cocks to determine which gives the better service; the former are fitted to the Left Hand and the latter to the Right Hand mountings Engine:73020; the modification was cancelled on 23.04.60.
No Ref.	Fitting of GWR boiler water gauge and drain cock backing sleeves Engine: 73022: no date

On the ER/NER, a limited number of modifications was recorded as detailed below; work was carried out at Doncaster.

E/DN/L8	Details are not confirmed but the modification probably refers to the lubrication of cylinders with Silvertown lubricators to decrease cylinder and piston wear through reduced levels of carbon deposits. Engine: 73000 (22.01.59)
E/DN/L68	Modified clearance on firebox supports. Engine: 73160 (10.59)
E/DN/L76	Improved piston rod packing. Engines: 73167/8/9 (04.57) 73170/1 (05.57) Experiment terminated: 01.61
E/DN/L86	Firebox support brackets clearance modified to 1/16". 73068 (12.58); 73168 (09.59); 73170 (05.57)

All the Standard Cl. 5 4-6-0s originally allocated to the SR, 73080-9, 73110-9, had their cabs modified at Eastleigh to incorporate rear glazed draught screens similar to those fitted to Bulleid Pacifics. It was also reported that Eastleigh applied 'lifting brackets' to the cab roofs of all Standard locomotives visiting the works from around 1960 onwards to facilitate ease of handling by overhead cranes during overhauls. The whole of the original SR allocation was fitted with the French T.I.A. water softening apparatus in a successful attempt to reduce boiler corrosion. From early 1957, the T.I.A system was replaced by the simpler, cheaper and more robust standard BR method using briquettes. At least four other class members subsequently re-allocated to the SR, 73022/9/41/2, were fitted with the BR system. In addition to these modifications the SR made a number of other detail alterations to the majority of their allocation. These were associated with a specific 'Test Number' but it has been possible to link only a few of the numbers to particular modifications; these are given where known. For the purposes of reference in Table 12, arbitrary numbers for each alteration are assigned as shown; no cost information is available. It is likely that all the Standard Cl. 5 4-6-0s originally allocated new to the SR, 73080-9, 73110-9 had similar modification test histories; this has not been confirmed by record card information and only official data has been noted in Table 12.

Ref. No.	Work Involved
SR01	Fitting of injector overflow pipes and brackets.
SR02	Fitting of Gresham and Craven graduable brake valve (engine & train)
SR03	Modification to allow atomiser steam for lubrication to be controlled by cylinder cock gear.
SR04	Pipework modification for access to washout plugs.

SR05 Piston head modification: SR Test No. 2272.

SR06 Provision of tread plates.

SR07 Fitting of safety chains to smokebox door.

SR08 Reversing shaft modification.

SR09 Piston rod modified packing. SR Test No. 2263. Same as Ref. Mod. 8895.

SR10 Regulator valves and various boiler valves modified with 'special material'. SR Test No. 2081.

SR11 Modification of tender coal hole door plates for improved access. SR Test No. 2291.

SR13 Isolating cocks and pipe gear.

SR19 Provision of modified steam brake pipes. SR Test No. 2278.

SR20 Modification of BR Standard firebars to permit improved steaming by reducing clinker build-up. SR Test No. 2298.

SR21 Improved axlebox grease lubrication. SR Test No. 2303.

SR22 Modification of boiler fusible plug system. Front plug: SR type, back plug: BR type. SR Test No. 2338.

SR23 Additional cross-bracing on tender.

SR24 Modifications to axlebox horn liners.

SR25 Modification of boiler fusible plug system. Both front and back plugs are of the SR type.

SR26 Modification of tender lateral clearance as specified by job no.3/SL/DE/20162.

SR27 Fitting of SR-type cab draught screens.

The test numbers were shown on the engine record cards but several of these were subsequently crossed out. This could mean that the tests were either not carried out, were terminated, or were regarded as successful and hence became adopted as a permanent feature of the locomotive. Engines subjected to the tests usually carried details of the test number on a small brass plate attached to the cabside under the numerals. A copy of The Railway Executive's protocol for dealing with experimental modifications to locomotives entitled 'Proposals for Standard Procedure for Dealing with Experiments' is reproduced as Appendix 5.

2.10 Names and Nicknames

Early in 1959 it was announced that the original SR allocation of twenty Standard Cl. 5 4-6-0s, 73080-9 and 73110-9 were to be given the names from recently withdrawn Urie King Arthur Cl. N15 4-6-0s. New brass nameplates were cast with lettering all of one size but which, unlike the originals, did not incorporate the legend 'King Arthur Class.' at the base. The nameplates, measuring approximately 4¼" in depth with lettering raised ⅛", were attached to the valance with the centre line of the plate on the centre line of the dome. Although it was the normal practice to give nameplates a black background, several of the class appeared with this feature in red. On naming, the locomotives retained their existing style of lined black livery and received the second style BR emblem, popularly known as the 'ferret and dartboard', on the tender. Names, naming dates and a brief summary of how each name related to the Arthurian legend are given in Table 13. Reference sources for the legend are 'Le Morte de Arthur' by Sir Thomas Malory published by William Caxton in 1485 and 'Idylls of the King' by Alfred, Lord Tennyson, composed over two creative periods, 1856-9 and 1868-74. The two sources differ in several respects but an attempt has been made to summarise the main elements of the legend as they relate to the twenty names borne by the class. All naming dates were by observation as the locomotives left Eastleigh works for the running shed. These agreed closely with engine record card data except for 73116 which was noted as having been named some two years after nameplates were actually fitted. Also included in the table are details of which names were carried by individual members of the original Urie King Arthur Class together with their withdrawal dates. As far as is known no other Standard Cl. 5 4-6-0s were considered for official naming.

Towards the end of steam operation, many named engines had their nameplates removed, either officially or 'unofficially' and this class was no exception. On 23rd May 1965, a spot check at Eastleigh depot on the SR's Western Section where the remaining named class members were operating, revealed the nameplate status of six engines as follows:

Both nameplates intact   : 73086, 73119
One nameplate only   : 73113/5
No nameplates   : 73112/8

The class picked up several nicknames during their short life span. One of the first was 'Derby's Dilemma', referring to the difficulties noted earlier (section 2.9.1) in achieving satisfactory steam generation with some lower grade coals in the early days; this name fell from use after the problems had been resolved following the 1953 tests at Rugby. Footplate crews at Kentish Town on the LMR often termed the class 'Bronchitis Engines', described as 'all hot in front and cold behind' due to the draughtiness of the cabs of the earlier locomotives. One railway enthusiast in the medical profession, Dr. P. Ransome-Wallis, suggested that a more apt description, given the symptoms, would have been 'Lumbago Engines'! The same crews also used the term 'Town Halls' which, as far as is known referred to the steep 'Town Hall Steps' from the buffer beam to the top of the running plate. Enthusiasts in the East Midlands dubbed the class 'Poor Man's Streak'. This derived from the chime whistle carried by the first 100 members of the class. Apart from the Standard Pacifics, chime whistles were only normally to be heard in that area on former LNER Gresley Cl. A4 streamlined Pacifics, commonly known as 'Streaks'. Clearly the Standard Cl. 5 4-6-0s were not in the same league as the glamorous A4s as far as enthusiasts were concerned, hence the 'Poor Man' reference. As replacements for the King Arthur Cl. N15 4-6-0s on the SR, the class inevitably picked up the name 'Standard Arthurs' especially after they received the former N15 names. No doubt there were other nicknames bestowed in various parts of the network but it is probably true to say that there were no complimentary sobriquets used by WR enginemen for the members of the class allocated to their region.

2.11 Performance

In the early days on the LMR the Standard Cl. 5 4-6-0s were not well received, mainly as a result of the steaming problems and draughty cabs. So much so that the prevailing view among some crews was that they must have done something to offend higher authority to be deprived of their familiar and trusty Stanier Cl. 5 4-6-0s in favour of one of the new locomotives! Later with increasing experience, particularly after the resolution of the steaming problems, the class gained wider appreciation. Many crews judged the performance on the road to be similar to that of the Stanier Cl. 5 4-6-0s and,

Table 13

Standard Cl. 5 4-6-0s 73000-73171: Acquisition of Names from Withdrawn Urie King Arthur Class N15 4-6-0s

Engine No.	Name	Place in Arthurian legend taken from Sir Thomas Malory's 'Le Morte d'Arthur' and Tennyson's 'Idylls of the King'.	Date Named*	Former No.	Carrier Withdrawn
73080	Merlin	Enchanter, bard and soothsayer at King Arthur's court;supplied the Round Table which sat 150 knights, for Uther Pendragon, Arthur's father and King of Britain; insisted Arthur be raised by foster parents, Sir Ector and his wife.	11.02.61	30740	12.55
73081	Excalibur	Arthur's sword,given to him by Nimue, the Lady of the Lake and returned to her by Sir Bedivere on Arthur's death	08.02.61	30736	11.56
73082	Camelot	The place where King Arthur held court; said to be located at Winchester in Hampshire (or Caerleon in Gwent).	28.08.59	30742	02.57
73083	Pendragon	A title meaning 'War Leader' conferred on the elected chief British king in times of great danger when they were invested with supreme powers similar to those conferred by the title 'Dux Bellorum' on Roman war leaders.	24.10.59	30746	10.55
73084	Tintagel	A castle on the north coast of Cornwall, fabled as King Arthur's castle where some allege he was born.	07.11.59	30745	02.56
73085	Melisande	Unconnected with Arthurian legend, Mélisande, also known as Mélusina, was the most famous of all the 'feés', or fairies, of French legend. Also the name of the tragic heroine of French composer Claude Debussy's only opera, 'Pelléas et Mélisande'; this Pelléas was not the Sir Pelleas at King Arthur's Court.	08.08.59	30753	03.57
73086	The Green Knight	The title by which Sir Pertolepe was known; brother of Sir Perimones (The Red Knight), and Sir Persant of Inde (The Blue Knight); all three were defeated in battle by Sir Gareth who required them to pledge allegiance to King Arthur; also brother to Sir Percord (The Black Knight) who insulted and was slain by Sir Gareth in battle.	19.12.59	30754	01.53
73087	Linette	Also known as the 'Damosel Savage'; accompanied Sir Gareth, son of King Lot of Orkney, on the successful mission to rescue her sister Lyonesse (spelt with one 'n') who had been besieged for two years in the Castle Perilous by Sir Ironside, Red Knight of the Red Launds; later married Sir Gaheris, brother of Sir Gareth.	03.06.61	30752	12.55
73088	Joyous Gard	The estate given to Sir Launcelot by King Arthur for defending Queen Guinevere's honour against Sir Mador; said by some to be either Alnwick Castle or Bamburgh Castle in Northumberland.	13.05.61	30741	02.56
73089	Maid of Astolat	Also known as Elaine, daughter of Sir Bernard of Astolat; refusing both food and drink, she died of unrequited love for Sir Launcelot. Astolat is usually identified as Guildford in Surrey.	12.05.59	30744	01.56
73110	The Red Knight	The title by which Sir Perimones was known; brother of The Black, The Green and The Blue Knights.	30.01.60	30755	05.57
73111	King Uther	King of Britain; father of King Arthur by an adulterous amour with Igraine, (widow of Gorlois, Duke of Cornwall), whom he later married. King Uther was awarded the title 'Pendragon' during the Saxon invasions of England in the late Fifth Century AD. Later gave the famous Round Table to Leodegrance, King of Camelard.	17.12.60	30737	06.56
73112	Morgan le Fay	An enchantress, the jealous and scheming sister of King Arthur; alerted him to the intrigues of Queen Guinevere and Sir Launcelot whose adulterous liaison led to war, the dissolution of the Round Table and the death of Arthur.	16.04.60	30750	07.57
73113	Lyonnesse	1. A rich farmland country said to stretch between Land's End & the Scilly Isles, now submerged: Tristram's home. 2. 'Lyonesse' (one 'n') was sister to Linette; she later married her rescuer Sir Gareth. (see note on 'Linette').	26.12.59	30743	10.55
73114	Etarre	Unfaithful lover of Sir Pelleas,who married Nimue after she dissuaded him from suicide over the faithless Etarre.	02.04.60	30751	06.57
73115	King Pellinore	King of Listinoise; father of Sir Lamorack of Gales; some locate the kingdom of Listinoise in south west Wales.	14.02.60	30738	03.58
73116	Iseult	Also known as Isolde, daughter of Agwisance, King of Ireland; wife of the treacherous King Mark of Cornwall who lived at Tintagel; deeply in love with King Mark's nephew, Sir Tristram after they both mistakenly drank a love potion destined for King Mark. The story of their tragic romance is related in Wagner's opera 'Tristan und Isolde'.	15.10.60**	*30749	06.57
73117	Vivien	The chief Lady of the Lake, also known as Nimue; abducted Sir Launcelot, son of King Ban of Brittany, as a child (hence his full name, Sir Launcelot du Lac) and presented him to King Arthur on his coming of age; mistress of Merlin whom she later imprisoned under a stone, an event which ultimately led to his death.	22.04.61	30748	09.57
73118	King Leodegrance	King of Camelard which some identify as part of Cornwall; father of Queen Guinevere, wife of King Arthur; gave the Round Table to Arthur as a dowry on the occasion of their marriage.	28.02.60	30739	05.57
73119	Elaine	Apart from the Maid of Astolat, four other 'Elaine's featured in Arthurian legend; (1)wife of King Nentres of Garlot,a land said be part of northern France;(2) daughter of King Pellinore and the Lady of the Rule; (3) wife of King Ban of Brittany, mother of Sir Launcelot;(4) daughter of King Pelles of Listinoise, mother of Sir Galahad by Sir Launcelot.	13.06.59	30747	10.56

* 'Date Named'   ** Not 'officially' named for the running shed.

* All dates are by observation as locomotives left Eastleigh Works for the running shed.   ** Not 'officially' named until 15.09.62.

Fig. 81
73068 is at Swindon depot after a visit to the Works in October 1958, having acquired lined green livery complete with cabside 'red spot' route restriction indicator. Note the running plate lining as applied at Swindon is confined to the lower edge only, in contrast to that of Eastleigh where both upper and lower edges were lined, the linings joining at the buffer beam and cab to form a panel. The previous year the engine, based at Derby and Bristol Barrow Road depots, had run a total of almost 57,000 miles mainly on North East-South West route services.

(G. Wheeler)

Fig. 82
73075 is at Derby depot on 21st April 1955, having just emerged from the Works prior to delivery to Polmadie depot; the engine has the high coal capacity (9 tons) BR1C type tender to allow greater flexibility for its intended duty, through running on the Glasgow-Manchester and Liverpool services.   *(Peter Groom)*

Fig. 83
73078 on shed at Polmadie on 28th June 1964; the engine is equipped with the BR1C type tender. Note the '5MT.' classification mark above the cabside numerals and the electric warning flashes on the firebox and tender. 73078 sports the second style BR tender crest, known to enthusiasts as the 'ferret and dartboard'.

(Courtney Haydon)

Fig. 84
73082 poses at Eastleigh on 28th August 1959 after having had its *Camelot* nameplates fitted, following a light intemediate overhaul. On the cabside, note the 5P/5F classification mark and also the (yellow) spot under the numerals indicating the engine is fitted with the T.I.A. water softening apparatus; later the T.I.A. equipment was replaced by the standard BR briquette system.

(Rodney Lissenden)

Fig. 85
73086, now named *The Green Knight*, takes water at Nine Elms depot on 5th May 1960. 73086 had received its first general overhaul six months previously at Eastleigh Works after completing more than 190,000 miles. Although nominally maintained by Eastleigh, 73086 visited Derby for a light intermediate overhaul between March and June 1963. Note the so-called 'bell type' whistle behind the chimney which has been installed in place of the original chime whistle, prone to corrosion and disintegration. The SR Test Plate affixed to the cabside below the numerals indicates the engine is the subject of a test procedure.

(Peter Groom)

Fig. 86   The nameplate *Joyous Gard*, acquired by 73088 on 13th May 1961, is still attached on 9th May 1964.   *(P.H. Wells)*

with self cleaning smokeboxes, hopper ashpans and rocking grates, shed disposal time was quicker and much less hard work. The engines allocated to the S&DJR for Bath-Bournemouth duties, 73050-2, worked alongside Stanier Cl. 5 4-6-0s and Bulleid light Pacifics eventually becoming the engine of choice for this difficult hilly route.

An entertaining assessment of the class from an engineman's viewpoint was made by Driver Bert Hooker, one of the celebrated 'footplate artists' at the SR Western Section's Nine Elms depot in London and neatly sums up the good and bad points.

Standard Class 5 4-6-0s; a view by driver Bert Hooker, Nine Elms SR

''As a young driver I did not get many opportunities to savour the BR Cl. 5s on the main line, although on one memorable summer Saturday, I was 'caught' to work a non-stop train to Salisbury; my mate on this occasion was Bill Botten, later train crew supervisor at Victoria. We were having a good trip until I thought that, judging by the noise up the chimney, I was heedlessly thrashing the engine and consequently 'eased her'. Soon I noticed the boiler pressure dropping back so Bill shut off the exhaust steam injector for a few moments to rally the boiler. I, in turn, further eased the regulator and Bill was beginning to struggle, giving me an imploring look as he turned on the blower. We were down to 180 psi. in the boiler with water about half glass and the engine was 'dead'. I quickly realised this was my fault! I opened the regulator wide and advanced the cut-off a couple of kicks to 25%. The response from my mate was immediate. 'That's better!' he called and as he plied his shovel, the boiler soon 'came round' on to the red line. The injector was restarted and easily maintained half to two thirds of the glass. After the soft sounding beats of the Bulleid Pacifics, the Standard 5s were noisy and I felt ear muffs would be handy, or in Cockney language, just 'cock a defun'! Thereafter I took little notice of the exhaust beat and judged my driving on the amount of coal and water the locomotive was using. I must say they were fairly economical engines and so they should be, after all they were new engines with a good 'front end'.

After my long-awaited entry into No. 3B link in late 1958, rostered main line work became my right and privilege, so BR Cl. 5 work on various jobs became regular and my experience increased. Once established in the gang with a good fireman, Charlie Philpot, I began to have a turn on the shovel and I have to record that I was not impressed. In my humble opinion the tender shovelling plate was totally inadequate, in common with all LMS-bred tenders. A nine inch to one foot extension on the plate would have prevented most of the coal on the tender front being deposited on the cab floor, resulting in the fireman doing unavoidable work in picking it up in order to shovel it into the firebox, apart from the inevitable loss of fuel which fell off the footplate on to the track. I quickly discovered the engines were miserably cold during bad weather, at least for the driver. It wasn't uncommon to sit on the left side with an overcoat on and with one's feet in a cardboard box with straw therein in order to keep them warm! Under these conditions, I sighed for the warmth, comfort and excellent riding qualities of the Bulleid Pacifics. But here I must confess the visibility problems associated with the latter were absent on the BR 5s; at least you could see where you were going!

The sanding arrangements on the Standard 5s left a lot to be desired. Upon a driver booking 'sands not working', the fitters would clear the sand traps and remove damp sand from the boxes. Along would come the fireman to refill them on preparation. The sands would run nicely when tested but when the boiler blowdown man had done his job, the steam released during this operation condensed in the sand boxes and made the sand damp again, so we were back to square one! The problem may have been avoided if the sand boxes had been placed on the gangway framing; the sand boxes on the rebuilt Bulleid Pacifics gave very little trouble. On one occasion I was working an up Bournemouth train with a BR 5 and my fireman of the time, Alan Newman, later a traction inspector at St. Pancras. We were going well up the bank after leaving Winchester but as we emerged from Wallers Ash tunnel doing about 55 mph, the engine went into a terrific slip on leaves on the rails. The speedometer went round to 'stop'(!) and the sands were in the usual condition of 'non-operative'. No matter what I did with the reverser and the regulator, she would not 'stand'. By Micheldever, we were down to 10 mph. and I began to doubt we would surmount the summit at Roundwood. Then, suddenly, to our vast relief, she 'found her feet' and we were able to get going again. I guess the juice that had been squeezed from the leaves and had adhered to the tyres had at last worn off. If ever there was an occasion when sand was sorely needed, it was on that day.

In some ways the Standard 5s were a boon both to the shed staff and footplate crews. They were easy on maintenance, preparation and disposal work. They did not become rough riding as would the 'King Arthurs' (N15) and 'Remembrance' (N15X) class engines when they had done 40,000-50,000 miles after 'shops overhaul' but they always rode 'hard'. 73110 was in my opinion the best BR 5 we had at Nine Elms, being a lively bouyant engine. But previously one or two of the class had gouged out a goodly hollow in the main frames above the trailing coupled wheels where the inside of the wheel rims had come into contact with the frames; in locomotive parlance, 'she was wagging her tail'. There is no doubt that the BR 5s were master of the heavy stopping passenger trains and fast fitted freights but I'll conclude by remaining loyal to the old Southern by saying 'give me a King Arthur in preference to a Standard 5!"

2.11.1 Performance in Day to Day Service

Performance logs of the Standard Cl. 5 4-6-0s in revenue service were recorded by many experienced enthusiasts. Several examples are given below over routes which saw the class perform some of their finest work. The routes are:

SR	Chatham-Bromley South, (Kent Coast Line). Victoria-Folkestone Junction. Waterloo-Salisbury.
ScR	Glasgow Buchanan Street-Aberdeen.
LMR	St. Pancras-Leicester. Shrewsbury-Gobowen.

The SR's Kent Coast Line from Victoria to Margate and Ramsgate saw the arrival of Standard Cl. 5 4-6-0s in the summer of 1955. Excellent performances were soon being achieved by several footplate crews at Stewarts Lane. A log of the 8.02pm Margate-Victoria together with details of engine working is given in Table 14. Driver Sam Gingell and Fireman Williams, a team renowned for producing

Table 14

Standard Cl. 5 4-6-0s 73000-73171

SR Chatham-Bromley South
Engine: 73083 (Stewarts Lane). Train: 8.02 pm Margate-Victoria. Date: 9th July 1956.
Load: 11 coaches, 359 tons tare, 375 tons gross
Driver/Fireman: S. Gingell/J. Williams (Stewarts Lane). Recorder: Mr. N. Harvey.

Distance Miles		Schedule min.	Actual min.sec.	Speeds mph	Boiler Pressure p.s.i.	Regulator Opening	Cut-off %	Steam Chest Pressure p.s.i.
0.0	CHATHAM	0	0.00		220	$1/4$	55/25	–
1.4	Rochester Bridge	3	2.50	35/40	210	$2/3$	43	–
3.4	Caxton Road		6.26	39/43	–	full	35/41	190
7.4	Sole Street	16	12.30	40 minimum.	205	–	45/50	200
8.4	Meopham		13.45	42	195/192	–	–	180
10.9	Fawkham		16.10	–	–	shut	–	–
13.8	Farningham Road		18.25	82/70	190	$2/3$	35	–
16.9	Swanley	26	21.05	63	–	–	–	–
19.5	St. Mary Cray		23.25	78	–	–	–	–
				sigs.	–	shut	–	–
20.9	St. Mary Cray Junction	32	25.40	15	–	$1/3$	–	–
				severe sigs.	200	–	–	–
21.9	Bickley Junction	33	28.30	15				
23.4	BROMLEY SOUTH	36	33.09					

First published in *Railway World*, Vol. 17, No. 197, October 1956.

Table 15

Standard Cl. 5 4-6-0s 73000-73171

SR Chatham-Bromley South
Engine: 73088 (Stewarts Lane). Train: Margate-Victoria. Date: not recorded.
Load: 7 coaches, 228 tons tare, 240 tons gross.
Driver/Fireman: S. Gingell/J. Williams (Stewarts Lane). Recorder: Mr. N. Harvey

Distance Miles		Schedule min.	Actual min.sec.	Speeds mph
0.0	CHATHAM	0.0	0.00	
1.4	Rochester Bridge	2.5	3.05	38
3.4	Caxton Road		5.55	50/64
7.4	Sole Street	16.0	10.25	60
8.4	Meopham		11.20	76 max.
		15.51	sigs. stand	
10.9	Fawkham		20.55	
13.8	Farningham Road		24.45	80
16.9	Swanley	28.0	27.15	73
19.5	St. Mary Cray		29.20	82
21.9	Bickley Junction	35.0	31.05	sigs.
23.4	BROMLEY SOUTH	38.0	33.57	
	net time (mins.)	24		

First published in *Railway World*, Vol 20, No. 233, October 1959

Table 16

Standard Cl. 5 4-6-0s 73000-73171

SR Victoria-Folkestone Junction
Engine: 73088 (Stewarts Lane).   Train: Victoria-Folkestone Continental Boat.
Load: 14 coaches. 430 tons tare, 470 tons gross. Date: not recorded.
Driver: S. Gingell (Stewarts Lane).   Recorder: Mr. B. Byrom.

Distance Miles		Schedule min.	Actual min.sec.	Speeds mph
0.00	VICTORIA	0.0	0.00	–
3.20	Brixton		7.38	36
3.95	HERNE HILL	8.5	8.51	37
5.70	Sydenham Hill		11.53	26/44
			sigs.	20
8.65	Beckenham Junction	16.5	17.31	28/32
			p.w.s.	17★
10.85	BROMLEY SOUTH		22.26	24
12.30	Bickley Junction	22.0	26.35	29
14.90	ORPINGTON	27.0	30.23	42
16.40	Chelsfield		32.33	38
17.65	Knockholt		34.35	35
21.65	Dunton Green		39.11	71
23.20	SEVENOAKS	37.0	40.30	63
28.15	Hildenborough		45.06	74
30.65	TONBRIDGE	44.5	47.19	54★
35.95	Paddock Wood	50.0	52.45	63
40.50	Marden		57.18	55
43.00	Staplehurst		59.55	61
46.35	Headcorn		63.07	63/59
51.55	Pluckley		68.18	64
55.10	Chart		71.41	63
			sigs.	23★
57.20	ASHFORD	71.0	74.35	34
61.50	Smeeth		79.57	56
65.30	Westenhanger		84.05	54
70.35	Folkestone West		88.57	60
71.05	FOLKESTONE CENTRAL		89.56	55
72.45	FOLKESTONE JUNCTION★★	92.0	93.04	–

★ Speed restriction   ★★ Sidings east of station.

First published in Railway World, Volume 29, No. 339, August 1968.

outstanding performances with all types of locomotive, were the footplate crew. With eleven bogies weighing 375 tons gross, 73083 achieved a minimum speed of 40mph on the 5½ mile climb to the summit of the 1 in 100 ruling gradient on Sole Street bank with a maximum of 82mph in the dip at Farningham Road. Another run with the same team is given in Table 15. With a lesser load of 240 tons gross, 73088 climbed past Sole Street station at no less than 60mph. An anticipated speed in excess of 90mph at Farningham Road, a figure regularly achieved by Driver Gingell, with Standard Cl. 5 4-6-0s, was thwarted by a signal stand at Fawkham. On the re-start however, the 12.5 miles from Fawkham to Bromley South were run in an astonishing 13 minutes 2 seconds, with a lightning acceleration to 80mph at Farningham Road.

A log of a Victoria-Folkestone Harbour boat train service again with Driver Gingell at the regulator is detailed in Table 16. A crowded 14 coach load of some 480 tons gross made up the train. There is no mention in the log of assistance for 73088 on the 1 in 62 climb out of Victoria and as the speed approaching Grosvenor Bridge was no more than 12mph, doubtless due to the driver's determination to avoid slipping, it may be assumed no assistance was given. Up the 1 in 101 from Herne Hill to Sydenham Hill, with full regulator and 45% cut-off, speed fell from 37 to 26mph and at the end of the climb, the boiler pressure was down to 170 p.s.i. Then followed a bad signal check and a worse permanent way slack; these certainly allowed the pressure to rise to 200 p.s.i. but recovery from the 17mph slack was up the 1 in 95 through Bromley South and by Bickley Junction, speed had crept up only to 29mph, again with full regulator and 45% cut-off. The

92

Table 17

Standard Cl. 5 4-6-0s 73000-73171

SR Waterloo-Salisbury
Engine:73113 (Nine Elms).   Train: 8.35am Waterloo-Salisbury.
Load: 12 coaches. 398 tons tare, 430 tons gross. Date: August 1961.
Driver: not recorded.   Recorder: Mr. B.L. Smith

Distance Miles		Schedule min.	Actual min.sec.	Speeds mph
0.0	WATERLOO	0.0	0.00	–
1.3	Vauxhall		4.10	–
		–	sig. stop	–
3.9	Clapham Junction	7.0	10.30	39
7.3	Wimbledon		15.05	51
8.7	Raynes Park		16.45	56
9.8	Malden		18.00	59
12.0	SURBITON	18.0	21.16	–
1.3	Hampton Court Junction	3.0	3.12	38½
2.4	Esher		4.37	47
5.1	Walton		7.39	56½
7.1	Weybridge		9.50	57½/65½
9.7	West Byfleet		12.16	63
12.4	WOKING	15.0	15.02	–
		–	p.w.s.	18
16.0	Brookwood		21.17	45
19.0	Milepost 31		26.07	50
21.2	Farnborough		28.28	60
24.5	Fleet		31.31	69
27.7	Winchfield		34.25	67
30.2	Hook		36.42	68½/75
35.8	BASINGSTOKE	43.0	41.45	–
2.5	Worting Junction	5.5	5.37	39
4.6	Oakley		8.26	54
7.8	Overton		11.14	64½
11.4	Whitchurch		14.48	73
13.3	Hurstbourne		16.22	75
18.6	Andover		20.30	83
25.0	Grately		26.03	56
30.5	Porton		31.07	73/79
		–	sig. stop	–
34.9	Tunnel Junction	44.0	39.49	–
36.0	SALISBURY	47.0	43.09	–

First published in Railway Magazine, Vol. 108, No. 739, November 1962.

subsequent easing of the grade allowed Driver Gingell to bring his cut-off back to 40% but the final 1 in 120 to Knockholt meant a drop in speed to 35mph and pressure down to 170 p.s.i. once again. On the descent to Tonbridge, speed rose to 71mph at Dunton Green and when 74mph had been reached at Hildenborough, the regulator was closed; by Tonbridge, the pressure was up again to 195 p.s.i. Between Tonbridge and Ashford, 30% cut-off with full regulator sufficed for a sustained speed of just over 60mph, with pressure maintained at 195-200 p.s.i. To recover from the bad 23mph signal check on the approach to Ashford, 45-35-40% cut-off with full regulator was used. The 21 minutes allowed in the schedule for the final 15.25 miles to Folkestone

Junction sidings included a recovery margin; this booking was cut to 18 min 29 sec, and the arrival in 93 min 4 sec from Victoria, a net time of only 85 min, was a solid performance for a Cl. 5 hauling a load of this magnitude on a route with such severe gradients over the first 30 miles.

The Standard Cl. 5 4-6-0s also put up fine performances on the SR's South Western main line from Waterloo; a typical run, recorded in the summer of 1961, is detailed in Table 17. The train was the heavy 12 coach 8.35am (Saturdays Only) Waterloo to Salisbury. With two stops, at Surbiton and Basingstoke, the schedule was not particularly tight but on this occasion there were several delays which the enterprising crew of 73113 was keen to recover. Starting from Waterloo

Fig. 87
The *Maid of Astolat* nameplate is depicted attached to 73089 at Eastleigh on 24th May 1959; the engine had completed over 165,000 miles by this date.

(Courtney Haydon)

Fig. 88
73108 is on shed at Eastfield on 18th April 1965. The engine had spent most of its life working from Eastfield depot, transferring to Carstairs in January 1966, where it remained until its withdrawal at the end of the year.

(Courtney Haydon)

1¼ min. late, the train was stopped by signals no further out than Locomotive Junction, passing Clapham Junction 4¾ min. late as a result. After leaving Surbiton, however, the road was clear and some fine running was made on to Basingstoke. A maximum of 65½ mph was touched near Weybridge and was held as far as the first part of the long rise to Milepost 31, until it was necessary to slow for a bad permanent way check after Woking. On the continuous rise of 1 in 326/314/300, the recovery to 50mph at the summit was excellent and some fast running on the level from Farnborough was rounded off by a maximum of 75mph in the slight dip after Hook. The net time of 37½ min. from Surbiton to Basingstoke was a fine piece of work with a 430 ton train over a stretch of line with a consistently adverse gradient. After Basingstoke, although the start is a difficult one up the continuous 1 in 259 gradient to the parting of the West of England and Bournemouth lines at Battledown flyover, there is plenty of opportunity for fast running afterwards; speeds of 75mph and 83mph were reached at Hurstbourne and Andover respectively. The five miles at 1 in 264/165 from just beyond Red Post Junction to Milepost 73¼ past Grately were breasted at a minimum speed of 56mph. With time now well in hand 73113 was run less vigorously down the final descent into Salisbury. Even so the speed was close to 80mph below Porton when adverse signals twice brought the train to a dead stand; arrival at Salisbury was still 1½ min. early. The net time of 37¾ min. from Basingstoke was again an impressive commentary on the capacity of the engine.

The ScR had an allocation of Standard Cl. 5 4-6-0s at St. Rollox and Perth where they were frequently rostered for the interval service on the former Caledonian Railway main line from Glasgow Buchanan Street to Dundee West and Aberdeen. Perth received five of the Walschaerts valve gear types, 73005-9, in 1951, whilst St. Rollox took delivery of ten of the Caprotti-geared locomotives, 73145-54, during the first six months of 1957. An 'unofficial' comparison between one of the early allocations to Perth, 73009 and Stanier Cl. 5 4-6-0 45365 was made in 1951 on the 10.00 am Glasgow - Aberdeen and the 5-30pm return to Perth. Details are as follows the top average speed was taken between timing points.

10.00am Glasgow-Aberdeen

	73009	45365
Coal Consumption (lbs/mile)	49.3	52.0
Water Consumption (galls/mile)	42.7	41.8
Top Average Speed	63.4	63.4

5.30pm Aberdeen-Perth

Coal Consumption (lbs /mile)	47.2	53.2
Water Consumption (galls/mile)	30.4	34.5
Top Average Speed	60.0	60.0

Top average speed was identical in both comparisons although 73009 had the edge in coal and water consumption.

Two logs featuring 73120 (Walschaerts gear) and 73153 (Caprotti gear) on this route are given in Table 18. In a run timed in 1956 by Mr. O.J. Beilby, 73120 had to tackle a nine coach load of 315 tons gross on the 10.15am 'Granite City' out of Buchanan Street. The allowance to Perth was 78 min. and might be considered rather tight in view of the 3½ mile start at 1 in 79-98 up to Robroyston and the 6¼ mile climb at 1 in 100/88 from north of Stirling to Kinbuck. At Robroyston, 73120 achieved a minimum speed of 40mph. Speed was restrained down the 1 in 128/98 from Cumbernauld to beyond Larbert but a minimum of 52mph was reached up the 1¾ miles at 1 in 120 to Plean. By far the finest work, however, was that from Stirling up to Kinbuck. Some 2½ miles at 1 in 100 lowered the speed to 51mph at Dunblane whilst 2¼ miles at 1 in 88 were climbed at a minimum of 40mph. 73120 showed no small ability to gallop also, with an average of 82.4mph over the 11.4 miles from Gleneagles down to Forgandenny and a maximum of 88mph at Dunning; Perth was reached 4½ min. early.

The run with 73153, hauling a seven coach load of 270 tons gross, was timed by Mr. A.J.S. Paterson in 1963 on one of the three hour Buchanan Street-Aberdeen services where the locomotive was deputising for a failed Gresley Cl. A4 Pacific. True to form, the Caprotti-geared 73153 was somewhat weak on the banks and in getting away from rest. The ascent to Robroyston was laboured and the engine had just got into its stride when there came a dead slowing for permanent way work. In consequence nearly 3 min. were dropped to Stirling, the check probably accounting for 2 min. of this. On the ascent to Kinbuck, 73153 achieved a minimum of 42½ mph but was driven fast afterwards with a maximum of 88mph down the bank before the stop at Perth. The logging of this run continued on to Aberdeen with a different crew and more splendid running. Between Stanley Junction and Forfar, the engine averaged 81.2mph over the 15.5 miles from Cargill to Glamis on a road that is generally level. Further fast running followed on to Stonehaven with a maximum of 86½ mph down Farnell Road bank and a minimum of of 60mph up the three miles mostly at 1 in 100 past Marykirk. The average of 73mph maintained over the 31.6 miles on the undulating route from Guthrie to Dunnottar was remarkable and Stonehaven was reached 6½ min. early; the remainder of the run was equally lively and Aberdeen was reached in 174½ min. from Glasgow, 5½ min. early.

As a comparison with the efforts of 73153, a log of a run from Perth to Aberdeen with Stanier Cl. 5 4-6-0 45179 timed by Mr. D. Murray-Smith in September 1961 is also included in Table 18; the load was eight coaches weighing 280 tons gross. Due to injector problems with the rostered engine, 45179 took over the 12-15pm Buchanan Street-Aberdeen at Perth. Setting off some 18 minutes late, the Stanier Cl. 5 passed Stanley Junction at 54mph but a 78mph max. at Alyth Junction was soon reduced to 5mph by a severe p.w. restriction. This prevented an 'even time' (ie. mile-a-minute) arrival at Forfar. The restart was vigorous with 82½ mph down Farnell Road bank. Yet another p.w.s. slowing reduced speed to 20mph over Kinnaber Junction but a sustained minimum of 56mph was achieved up Maryhill bank. A 76½ mph max. at Fordoun and another miminum of 56mph on the rise to Drumlithie allowed for an arrival at Stonehaven of less than 40 minutes for the 41.2 miles from Forfar; net time was estimated at 37½ minutes indicating a net average speed of 65.8mph. The run to Aberdeen saw a 64mph minimum at Portlethen and a 75mph max. at Craiginches South was sufficient to reduce the lateness to 10 minutes on arrival.

A final run quoted in Table 18 concerns the 8-25am 'Grampian', Buchanan Street-Aberdeen service in diesel days; NBL Type 2 Bo-Bo diesel D6123 was timed in 1966 by Mr. D. Chamberlain. The locomotive had been rebuilt with a 1365hp Paxman Ventura engine and had a light load of 6

Table 18

ScR Glasgow Buchanan Street–Aberdeen

Engine	73153 (St Rollox). Date 1963
Train:	Glasgow-Aberdeen
Load:	7 coaches, 248 tons tare, 270 tons gross.

Engine	(1) Glasgow-Perth: 73120 (Perth). Date 1956. 10-15am 'Granite City', Glasgow-Aberdeen. 9 coaches, 297 tons tare, 315 tons gross.
	(2) Perth-Aberdeen: Stanier Class 5 4-6-0: 45179 (Perth). 12-15pm Glasgow-Aberdeen. Date 1961. 8 coaches, 269 tons tare, 280 tons gross.

Engine	NBL Type 2 Diesel D6123 (1365hp)
Train:	8.25am 'Grampian', Glasgow-Aberdeen
Load:	6 coaches, 213 tons tare, 220 tons gross. Date: 1966

Distance Miles	Station	(1963) Schedule min.	(1963) Actual min.sec.	(1963) Speeds mph	(1956/1961) Schedule min.	(1956/1961) Actual min.sec.	(1956/1961) Speeds mph	(1966) Schedule min.	(1966) Actual min.sec.	(1966) Speeds mph
0.0	BUCHANAN STREET	0	0.00	–	0	0.00	0	0	0.00	–
1.0	St. Rollox		4.37	23½		3.48	–		2.39	33
3.4	Robroyston		9.26	35½		–	40		–	–
4.5	Stepps		–	–		–	–		–	–
6.0	Garnkirk		–	–		9.50	–		9.07	64/66½
7.8	Gartcosh		13.47	63½		11.22	62		–	–
9.0	Glenboig		–	–	15	14.18	55	15	12.02	72
13.2	Cumbernauld		19.09	68/63½		sig.stop	–		15.46	64/*58
–			p.w.s.	5		–	–		–	–
16.7	Castle Cary		24.20	53		23.28	–		19.14	*60
18.5	Greenhill		26.18	65		28.12	68		21.02	*51½/56
22.1	LARBERT	28	30.10	*47	28	33.07	45	28	25.01	*40/59
24.3	Alloa Junction		32.35	60/53		p.w.s.	–		–	–
28.6	Polmaise		36.55	67		–	–		–	–
30.2	STIRLING	36	38.54	–	36	41.52	*45	36	35.50	–
2.9	Bridge of Allan		4.21	54		45.00	64		4.18	59
4.9	Dunblane	7	6.46	46	7	47.18	51/40	7	6.42	50/44
7.6	Kinbuck		10.22	42½		50.45	46		10.11	47
10.8	Greenloaning		13.37	75		54.08	71		13.26	66/72
15.0	Blackford		17.11	63½		57.57	61		17.09	61½
17.2	GLENEAGLES	20	19.18	71½	20	60.04	–	20	19.16	65/75
19.3	Auchterarder		20.57	76½		61.44	84		20.57	*72/77
23.4	Dunning		24.04	88		64.37	88		24.16	70
29.1	Forgandenny		29.00	eased		68.42	80		28.55	73½
31.0	Hilton Junction	32	30.46	–		70.22	–	32	–	–
33.0	PERTH	36	34.49	–	78	73.30	–	36	33.55	–

Distance Miles		Schedule min.	Actual min. sec.	Speeds mph	Schedule min.	Actual min. sec.	Speeds mph	Schedule min.	Actual min. sec.	Speeds mph
4.2	Luncarty		–	60		6.10	56		–	★57½/60
7.2	Stanley Junction	9	11.04	57½		9.28	54	9	5.59	57
11.3	Cargill		14.37	80½/76		13.24	69		9.07	–
15.8	COUPAR ANGUS	16	18.11	83½		17.37	65	16	–	73/75½
18.3	Ardler		19.55	88/83		19.41	72/68		16.20	71
20.5	ALYTH JUNCTION	20	21.35	85/82		21.38	78 max.	20	20.11	–
	p.w.s.					p.w.s.	5			
24.6	Eassie		24.29	88		25.01	–		23.26	76
26.8	Glamis		26.04	82		29.18	–		25.12	73/75½
32.5	FORFAR	31	30.58	–	35	35.09	–	31	30.33	–
2.4	Clocksbriggs		4.17	–		3.52	–		3.42	61
7.0	Guthrie		9.12	74		7.58	75		7.38	★64
12.3	Farnell Road		13.03	86½		12.11	82½		9.28	67½/70
15.4	BRIDGE OF DUN	16	15.22	75/85		14.38	73	16	12.33	★60/66½
18.1	Dubton		17.28	73		16.40	78		15.28	★61/70
	p.w.s.					p.w.s.	20			
19.3	Kinnaber Junction	20	18.25	69		17.50	63	20	17.48	64
21.4	Craigo		20.14	74		21.18	61		18.54	62
23.5	Marykirk		22.06	60 min.		23.21	–		20.52	69/71
26.7	Laurencekirk	28	25.12	70		26.42	76½	28	22.46	67/56½
30.0	Fordoun		27.49	80½		29.25	56		26.01	64
34.0	Drumlithie		31.08	60 min.		32.58	67 max.		28.50	71
38.6	Dunnottar Box		35.23	75 max.		37.18	–		32.27	60/73
41.2	STONEHAVEN	42	38.04	–	48	39.50	–	42	39.15	–
2.6	Milepost 227½		5.18	33½		4.17	47		4.28	45
4.5	Muchalls		7.38	67		6.15	73½		6.30	70
7.9	Portlethen		10.47	61½ min.		9.17	64 min.		9.28	64/69
11.3	Cove Bay	(+4 RT)	13.47	74 max.		12.14	72	(+4 RT)	12.30	★63/71
14.4	Craiginches South		sigs. 16.46	–		15.03	–		–	–
16.1	ABERDEEN	24	p.w.s. 22.48	–	21	18.38	75 max.	24	18.21	–

★ Speed reduced by brakes.   RT: Recovery Time.

First published in Railway Magazine, Vol 103, No. 669, January 1957; Vol 108, No. 733, May 1962;

Vol 110, No. 753, January 1964. Modern Railways, Vol 23, No. 220, January 1967.

Table 19

Standard Cl. 5 4-6-0s 73000-73171

LMR St Pancras-Leicester
Engine: 73001 (Derby).   Train: 6.33pm St Pancras-Derby.
Load: 9 coaches. 293 tons tare, 320 tons gross. Date: 1953.
Driver/Fireman: Green/Ridout (Kentish Town).
Recorder: Mr. M. G. Langdon.

Distance Miles		Schedule min.	Actual min.sec.	Speeds mph
0.0	ST PANCRAS	0	0.00	-
1.5	Kentish Town		4.57	-
3.9	West Hampstead		9.11	38
6.9	HENDON		13.20	56
9.3	Mill Hill		15.56	49
12.4	Elstree		19.47	47
15.2	Radlett		22.33	71½
19.9	ST ALBANS		26.48	57½
-			sig.stop	-
24.6	Harpenden		37.03	-
30.2	LUTON		42.15	71½
32.8	Leagrave		44.30	66
37.3	Harlington		48.10	83½/88½
41.8	Ampthill		51.13	75/92
49.9	Bedford North Junction		57.12	79
53.0	Oakley		59.27	75/77½
56.6	Sharnbrook		62.23	75
59.7	Milepost 59¾		65.30	54½
62.7	Irchester		68.00	76½
65.0	WELLINGBOROUGH		69.50	★66/71½
69.3	Burton Latimer		73.34	68
72.0	KETTERING		76.00	67
75.6	Glendon		79.50	53/54½
78.5	Desborough North		83.13	50/72½
-			sigs.	★30
82.9	MARKET HARBOROUGH		88.15	-
86.3	East Langton		92.30	62½
88.9	Kibworth		95.21	46½
91.6	Great Glen		98.14	66/74
-			sigs.	★35
95.4	Wigston Magna		102.25	-
-			sig. stop	-
99.1	LEICESTER London Road	108	111.30	-

★ Speed restriction

First published in Railway Magazine, Vol. 100, No. 640, August 1954.

kept on the next leg to Forfar with speeds again in the 70-75mph range. From Forfar, various speed restrictions were observed down to Bridge of Dun, followed by a 62mph minimum of up the 1 in 108/125 past Dubton and a further minimum of 56mph on Marykirk bank. Drumlithie was passed at a minimum of 60mph giving an arrival at Stonehaven almost 3 minutes early. From there, a max. 71mph at Cove Bay meant that with the help of a 4 minute recovery time, the Aberdeen arrival was 6 minutes early. Throughout the journey, the impression was gained that it had not been necessary to work D6123 to its full capacity and that the locomotive with such a light load would be capable of gaining considerably on the 'Grampian's' three hour schedule from Glasgow.

The LMR Midland main line from St. Pancras to Leicester was one of the routes over which the early Standard Cl. 5 4-6-0s were able to show their paces. Table 19 gives details of a run logged in 1953 with 73001 then allocated to Derby and having the reputation as one of the best engines stationed there. The engine was in charge of the nine coach (320 tons gross) 6.33pm departure from St. Pancras to Derby run as a relief to the 6-40pm for Manchester Central and allowed 108 min. to reach Leicester. A fair but not outstanding start was made and it was not until a dead stop for signals at Sandridge box preceded by a long slowing that things really started to happen. With any type of steam locomotive a time of 14 min. 57 sec. for the 19.7 miles from Luton to Bedford North Junction would attract attention with its average of 79.1mph.; but with a mixed traffic 4-6-0, the maxima of 88½ mph and 92mph were remarkable. Equally with an engine of this moderate boiler capacity, the minimum of 54½ mph up the four miles of 1 in 119 to Sharnbrook summit was excellent, as was the 50mph at Desborough North after a climb of 8½ miles from Milepost 70, three miles at 1 in 118/136 and another three miles at 1 in 200 or so. Arrival at Leicester was some 3½ min. behind schedule

Table 20

Standard Cl. 5 4-6-0s 73000-73171

LMR Shrewsbury-Gobowen
Engine: 73097 (Patricroft).   Train: 1.10pm Paddington-Birkenhead.
Load: 6 coaches, 204 tons tare, 215 tons gross. Date 4th March 1967.
Driver Webb (Shrewsbury).

Distance Miles		Schedule min.	Actual min.sec.	Speeds mph
0.0	SHREWSBURY	0	0.00	-
3.7	Leaton		5.46	60
-	Oldwoods		7.16	64
7.5	Baschurch		9.01	75/80/82
11.7	Haughton		12.19	76
13.2	Rednal		13.32	76
16.2	Whittington		16.00	68
-			sigs.	-
18.0	GOBOWEN	22	18.43	-

First published in Railway World, Vol 38, No. 443, March 1977

coaches weighing only 220 tons gross. After a 72mph max. at Glenboig, Stirling was reached in 35 minutes 50 seconds, over a minute early with net time estimated at 34 minutes. A strong start resulted in a speed of 59mph at Bridge of Allan, a minimum of 44mph up the four miles at 1 in 100/88/91 to Kinbuck, and a max. of 77mph through Auchterarder. Speed was constrained to the low 70s on the descent to Perth which was again reached one minute early. The schedule was easily

Fig. 89   73111, now named *King Uther,* rests alongside rebuilt Merchant Navy Pacific 35020 *Bibby Line* at Nine Elms depot on 11th April 1964. In September 1965, 73111 was withdrawn, having completed over 350,000 miles in its ten year life.   *(Rodney Lissenden)*

Fig. 90   The high water capacity (5625 gal.) BR1F type tender No. 1293 is pictured attached to 73111 at Nine Elms depot on 13th January 1957.   Apart from 73110-9, the only other BR Standard engines originally allocated BR1F tenders were some examples of the Cl. 9F 2-10-0s.   *(A.R. Goult)*

Fig. 91
73113, with *Lyonnesse* nameplates removed probably for safe-keeping, undergoes an intermediate overhaul at Eastleigh Works on 6th March 1965. Towards the end of steam Eastleigh overhauled a number of 'foreign' locomotives; behind 73113 is Stanier Cl. 8F 2-8-0 48671 (Wellingborough depot) together with 48061 (Woodford Halse) of the same class; Ivatt Cl. 4 2-6-0 43097 (York) is also present. *(Courtney Haydon)*

Fig. 92
73118 at Eastleigh on 4th March 1960 a few days after its *King Leodegrance* nameplates had been affixed. 73118 appears to have sustained a significant dent to its boiler casing. Note what appears to be a '5P5F' power classification mark above the cabside numerals in place of the normal '5P/5F'.
(L.Elsey)

Fig. 93
73121 is pictured at its home depot Corkerhill on 4th October 1964; note the name of the depot on the buffer beam, received during a visit to Cowlairs Works and a white edged numberplate. 73121 was one of nine members of the class which spent the whole of their working lives allocated to Corkerhill; the others were 73100-4 and 73122/3/4. *(Courtney Haydon)*

Table 21

Standard Cl. 5 4-6-0s 73000-73171: Dates when Stored Serviceable

Loco Number	Date of Storage	Loco Number	Date of Storage
73000	14.11.65 - 27.04.66	73066	11.11.65 - 14.04.66
	02.05.66 - 13.05.67	73067	17.11.65 - 23.04.66
73004	16.11.65 - 12.04.66		02.05.66 - 04.12.67
73010	01.11.65 - 20.11.67	73069	26.11.65 - 14.04.66
73013	10.10.65 - 18.04.66	73070	14.11.65 - 23.04.66
73014	10.11.65 - 18.04.66	73095	11.02.66 - 04.04.66
73019	14.11.65 - 23.04.66	73125	29.08.65 - 20.11.67
73025	14.11.65 - 23.04.66	73126	11.10.65
	09.05.66 - 13.05.67	73129	23.08.65
73026	17.11.65 - 14.04.66	73133	21.02.66
73028	20.11.65 - 23.04.66	73134	23.08.65
73033	01.11.65 - 30.11.67	73138	21.02.66
73035	11.10.65 - 11.02.66	73143	23.08.65
73040	13.11.65 - 12.04.66	73155	10.09.61 - 21.12.61
73045	11.10.65 - 11.02.66	73156	10.11.65 - 14.04.66
73048	10.11.65 - 18.04.66		

due to later signal checks but the net time for the run from London was no more than 101 min.

The final log, timed by Messrs. Chris Magner and Richard Thomson, is one made on the penultimate day of services from Paddington to Birkenhead, 4th March 1967; details are given in Table 20. 73097 was in charge of the 1.10pm from Paddington forward from Shrewsbury. The start is not the easiest with nearly two miles at 1 in 100 followed by an ascent to Baschurch at 1 in 130 and then a further climb at 1 in 132 past Haughton. 73097 accelerated rapidly with the six coach train, after slippng violently in the quick start. Storming away, Leaton was passed at 60mph and Oldwoods, summit of the climb, was passed at 64mph. There was no holding the engine back and Baschurch was passed at 75mph with 82mph below Haughton. Whittington, 16.2 miles from Shrewsbury was passed in 16 min. exactly and only the Gobowen distant signal prevented a near 'even time' (ie. mile-a-minute) arrival at Gobowen in 18 min. 43 sec. or 18¼ min. net. It is a sad comment that, despite this fine work, 73097 was withdrawn two months later and in the breaker's yard by October 1967.

Fig. 94
73133, fitted with Caprotti valve gear, is at Eastleigh shed on 11th September 1965 a few days before entering the Works for a heavy intermediate over-haul; the engine has a leaking tender and no front numberplate.
(Courtney Haydon)

Fig. 95
73150 reposes at St Rollox shed on 17th May 1964. 73150 was one of a batch of ten Caprotti valve gear class members, 73145-54, delivered new to St Rollox over the first half of 1957; of these, 73147/8/51/2 remained at the depot for the whole of their working lives. *(Peter Groom)*

Table 22

Standard Cl. 5 4-6-0s 73000-73171

Construction, Withdrawal and Disposal Information

Engine	Built	With-drawn	Disposal	
73000	4.51	3.68	6.68	J. Cashmore, Great Bridge
73001	5.51	12.65	5.66	J. Cashmore, Newport
73002	5.51	3.67	10.68	J. Cashmore, Newport
73003	6.51	12.65	6.66	J. Cashmore, Newport
73004	6.51	10.67	3.68	J. Cashmore, Newport
73005	6.51	6.66	10.66	Motherwell Machinery and Scrap Co., Wishaw
73006	7.51	3.67	9.67	J. Cashmore, Great Bridge
73007	7.51	3.66	6.66	Motherwell Machinery and Scrap Co., Wishaw
73008	7.51	9.65	12.65	Motherwell Machinery and Scrap Co., Wishaw
73009	7.51	7.66	9.66	G. H. Campbell, Airdrie
73010	8.51	6.68	9.68	J. Cashmore, Great Bridge
73011	8.51	11.67	3.68	J. Cashmore, Great Bridge
73012	8.51	11.64	2.65	J. Buttigieg, Newport
73013	8.51	5.66	8.66	J. Cashmore, Great Bridge
73014	9.51	7.67	1.68	J. Cashmore, Newport
73015	9.51	8.65	11.65	J. Cashmore, Newport
73016	9.51	12.66	10.68	J. Cashmore, Newport
73017	9.51	10.64	3.65	J. Cashmore, Newport
73018	10.51	7.67	1.68	J. Cashmore, Newport
73019	10.51	1.67	5.67	J. Cashmore, Newport
73020	10.51	7.67	1.68	J. Cashmore, Newport
73021	10.51	8.65	11.65	J. Cashmore, Newport
73022	10.51	4.67	9.67	J. Cashmore, Newport
73023	11.51	8.65	11.65	J. Cashmore, Newport
73024	11.51	11.64	3.65	J. Buttigieg, Newport
73025	11.51	10.67	2.68	J. Cashmore, Newport
73026	11.51	4.67	10.67	J. Cashmore, Newport
73027	12.51	2.64	4.64	Swindon Works
73028	12.51	12.66	4.67	J. Cashmore, Newport
73029	1.52	7.67	3.68	J. Cashmore, Newport
73030	6.53	8.65	11.65	J. Cashmore, Newport
73031	7.53	9.65	12.65	J. Cashmore, Newport
73032	7.53	8.65	11.65	J. Cashmore, Newport
73033	8.53	1.68	5.68	J. Cashmore, Newport
73034	8.53	3.68	6.68	J. Cashmore, Newport
73035	8.53	1.68	5.68	J. Cashmore, Newport
73036	9.53	9.65	12.65	T. W. Ward, Beighton, Sheffield
73037	9.53	7.67	3.68	J. Cashmore, Newport
73038	9.53	10.65	5.66	J. Cashmore, Great Bridge
73039	9.53	9.67	2.68	J. Buttigieg, Newport
73040	10.53	5.68	7.68	J. Cashmore, Great Bridge
73041	10.53	6.65	12.65	G. Cohen at Eastleigh Works
73042	10.53	8.65	1.66	J. Cashmore, Newport
73043	10.53	7.67	9.68	J. Cashmore, Newport
73044	11.53	3.65	8.65	Birds Commercial Motors, Risca
73045	11.53	8.67	2.68	J. Cashmore, Newport
73046	11.53	9.64	3.65	J. Cashmore, Newport
73047	12.53	12.64	4.65	J. Cashmore, Newport
73048	12.53	10.67	1.68	J. Cashmore, Newport
73049	12.53	3.65	6.65	Birds Commercial Motors, Risca
73050	6.54	6.68		Preserved on the Nene Valley Railway, Wansford
73051	6.54	8.65	11.65	J. Cashmore, Newport
73052	6.54	12.64	4.65	J. Buttigieg, Newport

Engine	Built	With-drawn	Disposal	
73053	6.54	3.68	5.68	J. Cashmore, Newport
73054	6.54	8.65	10.65	J. Cashmore, Newport
73055	6.54	5.66	1.67	P. & W. McLellan, Langloan
73056	7.54	6.65	9.65	Arnott Young, Old Kilpatrick
73057	7.54	3.66	6.66	P. & W. McLellan, Langloan
73058	7.54	11.64	3.65	Motherwell Machinery and Scrap Co., Wishaw
73059	8.54	5.67	8.67	G. H. Campbell, Airdrie
73060	8.54	5.67	9.67	G. H. Campbell, Airdrie
73061	9.54	12.64	3.65	Motherwell Machinery and Scrap Co., Wishaw
73062	9.54	6.65	9.65	Arnott Young, Old Kilpatrick
73063	9.54	6.66	10.66	Motherwell Machinery and Scrap Co., Wishaw
73064	10.54	5.67	9.67	G. H. Campbell, Airdrie
73065	10.54	7.67	3.68	J. Cashmore, Newport
73066	10.54	4.67	8.67	J. Cashmore, Great Bridge
73067	10.54	3.68	6.68	J. Cashmore, Great Bridge
73068	10.54	12.65	4.66	J. Cashmore, Newport
73069	11.54	8.68	3.69	J. Cashmore, Newport
73070	11.54	4.67	11.67	J. Cashmore, Great Bridge
73071	11.54	9.67	10.68	J. Cashmore, Newport
73072	12.54	10.66	5.67	Arnott Young, Carmyle
73073	12.54	11.67	2.68	J. Cashmore, Newport
73074	12.54	9.64	3.65	J. Cashmore, Newport
73075	4.55	12.65	3.66	J. McWilliam, Shettleston
73076	4.55	7.64	2.65	Motherwell Machinery and Scrap Co., Wishaw
73077	5.55	12.64	3.65	Shipbreaking Industries, Faslane
73078	5.55	7.66	10.66	J. McWilliam, Shettleston
73079	5.55	5.67	9.67	G. H. Campbell, Airdrie
73080	6.55	12.66	5.67	J. Cashmore, Newport
73081	6.55	7.66	10.66	J. Cashmore, Newport
73082	6.55	6.66		Preserved on the Bluebell Railway, Sheffield Park.
73083	7.55	9.66	2.67	J. Cashmore, Newport
73084	7.55	12.65	4.66	Birds Commercial Motors, Bridgend
73085	8.55	7.67	4.68	J. Cashmore, Newport
73086	8.55	10.66	3.67	J. Cashmore, Newport
73087	8.55	10.66	4.67	J. Cashmore, Newport
73088	9.55	10.66	6.67	J. Cashmore, Newport
73089	9.55	9.66	6.67	J. Cashmore, Newport
73090	10.55	10.65	1.66	J. Cashmore, Newport
73091	10.55	5.65	8.65	Birds Commercial Motors, Risca
73092	10.55	7.67	1.68	J. Cashmore, Newport
73093	11.55	7.67	3.68	J. Cashmore, Newport
73094	11.55	5.67	2.68	J. Cashmore, Newport
73095	11.55	8.66	1.67	Arnott Young, Carmyle
73096	11.55	11.67		Preserved on the Mid-Hants Railway, Alresford
73097	12.55	5.67	10.67	J. Cashmore, Great Bridge
73098	12.55	3.66	6.66	Motherwell Machinery and Scrap Co., Wishaw
73099	12.55	10.66	6.67	Motherwell Machinery and Scrap Co., Wishaw
73100	8.55	1.67	5.67	Motherwell Machinery and Scrap Co., Wishaw
73101	8.55	8.66	11.66	Motherwell Machinery and Scrap Co., Wishaw
73102	9.55	12.66	4.67	G. H. Campbell, Airdrie
73103	9.55	10.65	2.66	Arnott Young, Carmyle
73104	9.55	10.65	2.66	Arnott Young, Carmyle
73105	12.55	9.66	2.67	Motherwell Machinery and Scrap Co., Wishaw
73106	12.55	6.65	10.65	P. & W. McLellan, Langloan
73107	12.55	9.66	6.67	Arnott Young, Old Kilpatrick
73108	12.55	12.66	4.67	G. H. Campbell, Airdrie
73109	1.56	10.64	2.65	Motherwell Machinery and Scrap Co., Wishaw
73110	10.55	1.67	6.67	J. Cashmore, Newport
73111	10.55	9.65	2.66	J. Cashmore, Newport
73112	10.55	6.65	11.65	T. W. Ward, Beighton, Sheffield

Engine	Built	With-drawn	Disposal	
73113	10.55	1.67	5.67	J. Cashmore, Newport
73114	11.55	6.66	10.66	J. Cashmore, Newport
73115	11.55	3.67	11.67	J. Cashmore, Newport
73116	11.55	11.64	2.65	J. Cashmore, Newport
73117	11.55	3.67	8.67	J. Cashmore, Newport
73118	12.55	7.67	9.68	J. Cashmore, Newport
73119	12.55	3.67	9.67	J. Buttigieg, Newport
73120	1.56	12.66	4.67	G. H. Campbell, Airdrie
73121	1.56	2.66	3.66	P. & W. McLellan, Langloan
73122	1.56	9.65	1.66	Motherwell Machinery and Scrap Co., Wishaw
73123	2.56	5.65	7.65	Motherwell Machinery and Scrap Co., Wishaw
73124	2.56	12.65	3.66	J. McWilliam, Shettleston
73125	7.56	6.68	10.68	J. Cashmore, Great Bridge
73126	7.56	4.68	7.68	A. Draper, Kingston upon Hull
73127	8.56	11.67	7.68	J. Cashmore, Newport
72128	8.56	5.68	8.68	J. Cashmore, Great Bridge
73129	8.56	11.67		Preserved at the Midland Railway Centre, Butterley
73130	9.56	1.67	9.67	J. Cashmore, Great Bridge
73131	9.56	1.68	5.68	J. Cashmore, Newport
73132	10.56	3.68	7.68	J. Cashmore, Great Bridge
73133	10.56	6.68	10.68	J. Cashmore, Great Bridge
73134	10.56	6.68	10.68	J. Cashmore, Great Bridge
73135	10.56	3.68	9.68	J. Cashmore, Great Bridge
73136	11.56	3.68	6.68	J. Cashmore, Newport
73137	11.56	6.67	1.68	J. Cashmore, Great Bridge
73138	11.56	4.68	9.68	J. Cashmore, Great Bridge
73139	11.56	5.67	1.68	J. Cashmore, Newport
73140	12.56	10.67	2.68	J. Cashmore, Newport
73141	12.56	7.67	2.68	J. Cashmore, Newport
73142	12.56	4.68	9.68	J. Cashmore, Great Bridge
73143	12.56	6.68	11.68	J. Cashmore, Great Bridge
73144	12.56	8.67	2.68	J. Cashmore, Newport
73145	1.57	9.66	9.67	Arnott Young, Troon
73146	2.57	5.67	11.67	G. H. Campbell, Airdrie
73147	2.57	8.65	11.65	Motherwell Machinery and Scrap Co., Wishaw
73148	3.57	9.65	1.66	Motherwell Machinery and Scrap Co., Wishaw
73149	3.57	12.66	4.67	Shipbuilding Industries, Faslane
73150	4.57	12.66	4.67	Shipbuilding Industries, Faslane
73151	4.57	8.66	10.66	Motherwell Machinery and Scrap Co., Wishaw
73152	5.57	12.65	2.66	J. McWilliam, Shettleston
73153	5.57	12.66	4.67	Shipbreaking Industries, Faslane
73154	6.57	12.66	5.67	G. H. Campbell, Airdrie
73155	12.56	7.67	3.68	J. Cashmore, Newport
73156	12.56	11.67		Preserved on the East Lancashire Railway, Bury
73157	12.56	5.68	8.68	J. Cashmore, Great Bridge
73158	12.56	10.67	2.68	J. Cashmore, Newport
73159	1.57	10.67	3.68	J. Cashmore, Newport
73160	1.57	11.67	3.68	J. Cashmore, Great Bridge
73161	2.57	12.64	4.65	J. Buttigieg, Newport
73162	2.57	5.65	8.65	J. Cashmore, Newport
73163	2.57	11.65	2.66	T. W. Ward, Killamarsh
73164	3.57	12.64	4.65	J. Friswell, Banbury
73165	3.57	10.65	3.66	J. Cashmore, Great Bridge
73166	3.57	12.65	5.66	J. Cashmore, Newport
73167	4.57	8.65	10.65	J. Cashmore, Newport
73168	4.57	12.65	4.66	Birds Commercial Motors, Bridgend
73169	4.57	10.66	6.67	J. Cashmore, Newport
73170	5.57	6.66	1.67	J. Cashmore, Weymouth Goods Yard
73171	5.57	10.66	3.67	J. Cashmore, Newport

2.12 Storage, Withdrawal and Disposal

Towards the end of steam operation by BR, many locomotives were stored prior to withdrawal. A list of Standard Cl. 5 4-6-0s known to have been mothballed for a period are given in Table 21 together with approximate storage dates. Table 22 gives dates of withdrawal and place of disposal; reported cutting-up dates appear to be unreliable and have been omitted.

2.13 Preservation

Five Standard Cl. 5 4-6-0s survived into preservation, four of them having been rescued from the famous scrapyard of Woodham Brothers at Barry in South Wales.

73050

The only preserved member of the class to be purchased direct from BR, 73050 was acquired in October 1968 by the Peterborough Railway Society for use on the Nene Valley Railway. For a period the locomotive was stored at the British Sugar Corporation's factory at Peterborough where it was utilised in October 1972 to supply steam for essential services whilst the works boiler was out of commission. After a two year general overhaul at the Peterborough engineering works of Peter Brotherhood Ltd, 73050 was returned to the Nene Valley line on 16th July 1980. It carries the livery of BR lined green together with the *City of Peterborough* nameplate. The locomotive is now owned by Peterborough City Council.

73082 *Camelot*

Rescued from Barry scrapyard by the 73082 Camelot Locomotive Society in 1979, the locomotive was moved to the Bluebell Railway at Sheffield Park near Uckfield, East Sussex on 26th October. After lengthy restoration work, 73082 entered traffic on the Bluebell line almost exactly sixteen years later on October 28th 1995. 73082 is the only one of the SR's 'Standard Arthurs' to be preserved.

73096

The locomotive was retrieved from Barry in July 1985 for use on the Mid-Hants Railway. After restoration work at Ropley, 73096 was re-steamed in 1993. It was initially painted in lined black, later appearing as 'Standard Arthur' 73080 complete with red-backed *Merlin* nameplates but without the 'correct' BR1B tender. Later there was another change of identity to 73054 although 73096 now has its original number and a BR lined green livery. The engine has also been used on mainline rail tours.

73129

One of the last batch of steam locomotives built at Derby works, 73129 is the only Caprotti valve geared Standard Cl. 5 4-6-0 to be preserved. It was purchased from Woodham's by Derby Corporation and taken by rail from Barry to Derby Works on 6th January 1973. Two years later it was moved to the Midland Railway Trust's centre at Butterley, near Ripley in Derbyshire, where it is currently undergoing restoration.

73156

This locomotive left Barry in October 1986, the only Doncaster-built member of the class to be preserved. Following lengthy periods of outside storage, considerable work was clearly needed to achieve restoration; this is now being carried out on the East Lancashire Railway's site at Bury with the aim of having the engine ready to take part in the Doncaster Works '150' celebration in 2003.

Fig. 96   Caprotti valve gear 73154 awaits repair at Dundee shed on 5th August 1965. The engine has a non-standard front numberplate and has part of its valve gear tied up with rope.

(Courtney Haydon)

Fig. 97
73162 stands at Huddersfield shed where it was allocated from October 1958 until June 1961; the engine was one the class fitted with AWS apparatus from new. 73162 was withdrawn from Oxford shed in May 1965 after a working life of just over eight years.

(David Tyreman Collection)

Fig. 98
A study of the Standard Cl. 5 4-6-0 Caprotti valve gear at Crewe Works on 13th October 1963. The running plate lining has been positioned slightly higher than usual to avoid that portion of the cylinder protruding into the plate.

(L. Hanson)

Fig. 99
York based 73166 rests at Agecroft depot on 21st August 1958. The engine has probably worked into Manchester Victoria with the 10.10am from York via the Calder Valley main line through Todmorden and is due to return via the same route on the 5.10pm from Victoria, a regular duty for the York class members at this time.

(Peter Groom)

3. Class 4 4-6-0 75000-79

3.1 Purpose

The standard designs developed by the LMS in 1947 (see Table 1) did not envisage the need for a Cl. 4 4-6-0 locomotive. The duties of such a type were considered to be within the scope of a Cl. 4 2-6-4 tank engine or a Cl. 4 2-6-0, at least as far as the LMS system was concerned. At Nationalisation however, the WR had a perceived requirement for a Cl. 4 4-6-0 with a longer working range than would be conveniently fulfilled by a tank engine. It was envisaged that the engines would be based on Shrewsbury to be used on the former Cambrian lines to the coastal resorts of Aberystwyth and Pwllheli and also on the former LNWR Central Wales line to Swansea. The restricted axle loading in force on the Cambrian route at the time precluded the use of heavier Cl. 5 4-6-0 types and the passenger services were mainly in the hands of the GWR Manor 4-6-0s introduced in 1938. Other Regions also saw the value of a Cl. 4 4-6-0 type as potential replacements for some of their ageing fleets; amongst these were the SR's U and U1 Cl. 2-6-0s and the ER's B12, B17/1 and B17/4 Cl. 4 4-6-0s (see Table 23 for comparison of dimensional details). It was not possible to include an updated version of the GWR Manor design as one of the proposed new BR Standard classes since width over cylinders rendered it out-of-gauge over many other parts of the BR rail network.

In the event, the WR received only 20 of the 80 Standard Cl. 4 4-6-0s, 75000-9, 75020-9 and retained only a few of them on the intended Cambrian line services, regarding them as inferior performers to the GWR Manor 4-6-0s established on the route. It was not until after these lines became part of the LMR system in 1963 that the Cl. 4 4-6-0s returned to achieve distinction in the latter days of steam. The SR's need for replacements for their 2-6-0s was adequately met by the Standard Cl. 4 2-6-0s (76XXX), the Region's 15 Cl. 4 4-6-0s, 75065-79, being deployed on passenger and freight work on the Victoria and Waterloo main lines and later on the S&DJR between Bath and Bournemouth. The need for the class on the ER had been virtually eliminated as most of the early B17 4-6-0s had been upgraded during the 1950s by reboilering to B17/6 rated as Cl. 5; also most of the B12 4-6-0s had been withdrawn, their work taken over by the increasing number of Type 2 diesels then being delivered. No other suitable work was available and the final batch, 75080-9, held in abeyance since October 1954, was finally cancelled in September 1956.

It is ironic that although the LMS had not identified a need for a Cl. 4 4-6-0 on its system, the majority of the class, some 45 locomotives, 75010-9, 75030-64, found a home on the LMR. Here they handled semi-fasts and locals in West Lancashire, North Wales, the Midlands and on the Oxford-Cambridge line as well as outer suburban work on both the Midland main line from St. Pancras and the West Coast main line from Euston. Their advent displaced LMS Compound Cl. 4-4-0s and Cl. 2P 4-4-0s, directly to the scrapyard in many cases and also released LMS Cl. 4 2-6-4 tank engines and Stanier Cl. 5 4-6-0s for other duties.

3.1.1 Design Development

The Standard Cl. 4 4-6-0s were in effect a tender version of the successful LMS Cl. 4 2-6-4 tank engine, developed in the BR Standard designs as the 80XXX class; a dimension comparison is given in Table 23. The class satisfied the L1 loading gauge and had a 17 ton axle loading allowing it a greater route availability than, for example, the GWR Manor Cl. 4-6-0s. Modifications as a result of service experience, including tender re-design and the provision of double blastpipe and chimney to some members of the class, are dealt with in the appropriate sections. A summary of the annual building programme for the class is given in Table 24. Appendix 1 details year end totals from 1951-1968.

Fig. 100
75004 roars through Sonning Cutting heading for Paddington with an express from Swindon on 1st September 1951; the engine is in full mixed traffic lined black livery.
(K.W. Wightman)

Table 23

Standard Cl. 4 4-6-0s 75000–75079: Comparison of Leading Dimensions of Selected Classes Designed for Similar Duties

Class	Date Introduced	Cylinders Diameter x Stroke	Boiler Pressure p.s.i.	Total Heating Surfaces sq. ft.	Superheater sq. ft.	Grate Area sq. ft.	Tractive Effort at 85% boiler pressure lb.	Engine Weight in Working Order
BR Standard 4 4-6-0	1951	18" x 28"	225	1702	258	26.7	25,100	69 tons 0 cwt
BR Standard 4 2-6-4T	1951	18" x 28"	225	1606	240	26.7	25,515	86 tons 13 cwt
GWR Manor 4-6-0	1938	18" x 30"	225	1608	182	22.1	27,340	68 tons 18 cwt
LMS Compound 4 4-4-0	1924 (1)	LP :21" x 26" HP:19" x 26"	200	1589	272	28.4	22,650 (2)	61 tons 14 cwt
LMS 'Light' 4 4-6-0	1934 (3)	18" x 28"	200	(4)	(4)	21.0	23,400	63 tons 15 cwt
LMS 4 4-4-0	1941 (5)	18" x 28"	225	(4)	(4)	(4)	23,600	66 tons 13 cwt
LNER B12/3 4-6-0	1932 (6)	20" x 28"	180	1874	315	31.0	21,970	69 tons 10 cwt
LNER B17 4-6-0	1928	17" x 26" 3 cylinders	180 (7)	2020	344	27.5	22,842	76 tons 13 cwt
SR U 2-6-0	1928	19" x 28"	200	1729	203	25.0	23,865	(8) 63 tons 0 cwt
SR U1 2-6-0	1928	16" x 28" 3 cylinders	200	1729	203	25.0	25,385	65 tons 6 cwt

Notes (1) LP: two x low pressure cylinders; HP: one x high pressure cylinder.
(2) Tractive Effort refers to low pressure cylinders calculated at 80% of boiler pressure.
(3) Ten locomotives proposed in the 1934 building programme but cancelled in favour of ten Stanier Cl. 5 4-6-0s.
(4) Detail not specified.
(5) Design drawing prepared for this class as possible replacement for the LMS Compound 4-4-0; abandoned at an early stage.
(6) Class was rebuilt from B12/1 (introduced in 1911) with large round topped boiler and long travel valves.
(7) Reduced from 200 p.s.i. from August 1943.
(8) Class consisted of 50 engines; twenty were rebuilds of Maunsell's 'River' Cl. 2-6-4 tank engines introduced in 1917 and weighed 63 tons 0 cwt. The thirty engines built new to Class U design weighed 62 tons 6 cwt.

Table 24

Standard Cl. 4 4-6-0s 75000-75079: Annual Building Programme

Programme Year	Works	Lot Numbers	Engine Numbers	Total	Delivery Date	Initial Allocated Region
1951	Swindon	390	75000-09	10	05.51-10.51	Western
	Swindon	391	75010-19	10	11.51-03.52	London Midland
1952	Swindon	400	75020-29	10	11.53-05.54	Western
	Swindon	401	75030-49	20	06.53-10.53	London Midland
1953	Swindon	408	75050-64	15	11.56-06.57	London Midland
	Swindon	409	75065-79	15	08.55-01.56	Southern
1954	Swindon	413	75080-89	10	Cancelled 09.56	Intended for Eastern

3.2 Dimensions and Data

Brighton was the main design office for the Standard Cl. 4 4-6-0s with certain components designed at Swindon, Derby and Doncaster. Principal dimensions and axle loads are given in Diagram 4.

Full details of the BR 4 boiler fitted to the class are given in section 3.3. The rocking grate, ashpan, self-cleaning smokebox, frame design, piston, crosshead, slidebars, method of lubrication, sanding arrangements, reversing gear, bogie and cab design were similar to those described for the Standard Cl. 5 4-6-0s, see section 2.2. Valve gear was of the conventional Walschaerts type, also detailed in section 2.2.

The Standard Cl. 4 4-6-0s were provided with plain bearing axleboxes rather than the roller bearing type fitted to the Cl. 5 4-6-0s. All the firebox water space stays were made of Monel metal fitted with steel nuts inside the firebox whilst the roof, longitudinal and transverse stays were of steel. The lagging of both the boiler and firebox consisted of asbestos mattresses. Dimensional details of the firebox are given in Appendices 2 and 2A with cylinder and valve dimensions appearing in Appendices 3 and 3A. Apart from the provision of different tenders for later batches discussed in section 3.4, there were few significant variations between production batches. The main changes were the adoption of rectangular

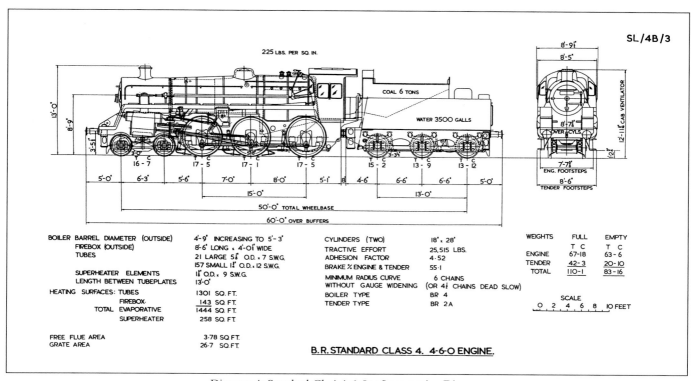

Diagram 4: Standard Cl. 4 4-6-0s : Locomotive Diagram

Table 25

Standard Cl. 4 4-6-0s 75000-75079: Initial Boiler Allocation

Locomotive Number	Boiler Number Nominal Allocation	Date of Boiler Construction	Boiler Built at
75000-19	866-885	04.51-01.52	Swindon
75020-49	1013-1022	10.53-03.54	Swindon
	1023-1042	03.53-09.53	Swindon
75050-79	1193-1207	04.56-04.57	Swindon
	1208-1222	05.55-12.55	Swindon
75080-89	1507-1516	Cancelled 09.56	
Spare Boilers	1370-1374	09.55-10.55	Swindon
	1595-1597	05.56	Swindon

Note: Boilers were not installed in numerical sequence, see Table 26

section coupling rods instead of the fluted type and the provision of Smith-Stone speedometers from 75020 onwards; also 75030/1 were delivered with manganese steel liners on the coupled wheel axleboxes only.

3.3 Boilers

The BR4 boiler adopted for the Standard Cl. 4 4-6-0 closely followed that designed for the Standard Cl. 4 2-6-4 tank engine (80XXX class) except that the barrel length was increased by 9". The same flanged plates were common to both but as the boiler pressure had been increased from 200 to 225 p.s.i., the staying had been re-designed. The boiler shell was manufactured from steel plate, the barrel consisting of two rings, the second of which was tapered; dimensional details are given in Appendices 2 and 2A. All boilers for the class, together with eight spares were constructed at Swindon; details are given in Table 25. The record of which boilers were carried by individual class members following general overhaul is incomplete; available information is given in Table 26.

Fig. 101
75005, allocated to Tyseley, canters through Solihull with an up parcels train on 9th October 1959. Note the 'blue spot' route restriction indicator under the cabside numerals.

(P.H. Wells)

Fig. 102
Busy scene at Buttington Junction on 5th March 1956 as 75005 hurries through off the Cambrian line with the 9.45am Whitchurch-Aberystwyth, watched by the driver of GWR 2251 Cl. 0-6-0 3207 working a p.w. train. 75005 entered Swindon Works for its first general overhaul in August 1956 having accrued a mileage of around 190,000. *(Hugh Ballantyne)*

Table 26

Standard Cl. 4 4-6-0s 75000-75079: Record of Boilers Fitted

Engine Number	Boiler Number and Fitting Date	Engine Number	Boiler Number and Fitting Date	Engine Number	Boiler Number and Fitting Date
75000	866 21.05.51 N	75023	1016 03.12.53 N	75053	1196 04.01.57 N
	1372 ? 01.56	75024	1017 18.12.53 N	75054	1197 17.01.57 N
75001	867 ? 08.51 N	75025	1018 29.04.54 N	75055	1198 23.01.57 N
75002	868 24.08.51 N		1015 ? 06.59	75056	1199 28.02.57 N
	875 ? ?.56	75026	1019 13.05.54 N	75057	1200 15.03.57 N
	1220 02.05.64		1036 08.01.59	75058	1201 08.04.57 N
75003	869 30.08.51 N		873 14.10.60	75059	1202 15.04.57 N
	873 ? 02.57	75027	1020 17.05.54 N	75060	1203 02.05.57 N
	1016 ? 12.59		1017 ? 05.59	75061	1204 15.05.57 N
75004	870 27.08.51 N		871 09.07.65 ★	75062	1205 28.05.57 N
	1222 12.12.56	75028	1021 27.05.54 N	75063	1206 13.06.57 N
	1014 16.06.59		1019 02.04.59	75064	1207 26.06.57 N
	869 10.10.62	75029	1022 28.05.54 N	75065	1208 26.08.55 N
75005	871 07.09.51 N		1018 11.02.60		1024 22.04.61
	1374 ? 09.56	75030	1023 15.06.53 N	75066	1209 01.09.55 N
	1372 09.02.62		1030 17.09.58		1214 01.04.61
75006	872 14.09.51 N	75031	1024 17.06.53 N	75067	1210 12.09.55 N
	871 ? 12.56		1013 08.04.59		1215 03.12.60
	1022 16.12.60	75032	1025 30.06.53 N	75068	1211 15.09.55 N
75007	873 ? 09.51 N		1032 14.10.58		1210 21.01.61
75008	874 ? 10.51 N	75033	1026 03.07.53 N	75069	1212 26.09.55 N
	1373 ? 11.55		1027 26.09.58		874 22.10.60
	868 ? 09.58	75034	1027 10.07.53 N	75070	1213 13.10.55 N
	1222 ? 12.60		1039 19.08.58		1211 25.02.61
	1017 ? 08.62	75035	1028 13.08.53 N	75071	1214 26.10.55 N
75009	875 16.10.51 N		1033 06.02.59		1213 18.03.61
75010	876 02.11.51 N	75036	1029 14.08.53 N	75072	1215 01.11.55 N
	1597 30.11.56		1042 14.03.58		1212 12.11.60
75011	877 12.11.51 N	75037	1030 14.08.53 N	75073	1216 03.12.55 N
	876 16.01.57		882 01.08.58		1371 19.08.61
	1021 07.06.61	75038	1031 25.08.53 N	75074	1217 18.10.55 N
75012	878 23.11.51 N		884 30.01.58		1218 29.07.61
	880 12.12.56	75039	1032 27.08.53 N	75075	1370 25.11.55 N
	881 10.03.65 ★		1040 02.09.58		1217 30.09.61
75013	879 20.11.51 N	75040	1033 02.09.53 N	75076	1371 09.12.55 N
	881 04.01.57		1026 31.10.58		1208 24.06.61
	870 04.04.64 ★	75041	1034 10.09.53 N	75077	1218 19.12.55 N
75014	880 06.12.51 N		1028 26.03.59		1209 10.06.61
75015	881 20.12.51	75042	1035 11.09.53 N	75078	1219 20.01.56 N
	1596 09.11.56		1037 04.10.57		1370 14.10.61
75016	882 03.01.52 N	75043	1036 17.09.53 N	75079	1220 20.01.56 N
	1031 05.06.58		1023 23.10.58		1219 25.11.61
75017	883 18.01.53 N	75044	1037 25.09.53 N		
	877 05.04.57		879 15.02.57		
75018	884 07.03.52 N	75045	1038 20.09.53 N		
	885 31.05.57		1034 12.05.59		
	1206 04.11.64 ★	75046	1039 05.10.53 N		
75019	885 21.03.52 N		1041 12.06.58		
	878 24.01.57	75047	1040 16.10.53 N		
	876 17.09.65 ★		1029 11.07.58		
75020	1013 13.11.53 N	75048	1041 23.10.53 N		
	1025 28.11.58		? 12.02.58		
	1036 29.05.62	75049	1042 23.10.53 N		
75021	1014 23.11.53 N		883 29.01.58		
75022	1015 01.11.53 N	75050	1193 09.11.56 N		
	869 ? 01.59	75051	1194 27.11.56 N		
	1374 25.06.62	75052	1195 20.12.56 N		

Notes N: Fitted from new.

★ : Boiler number noted during overhaul at Eastleigh; unclear if fitted as replacement at that date.

Table 27

Standard Cl. 4 4-6-0s 75000-75079: Initial Tender Allocation

Tender Type	Tender Side	Water Capacity (gallons)	Coal Capacity (tons)	Weight in Working Order (tons)	Allocated to Engine Numbers	Tender Serial Numbers	Tender Notes
BR1B	Flush	4725	7	51.25	75065-79	1029-1043	Fall plate and gangway doors fitted. High water capacity tender not fitted with water pick-up gear as engines were allocated to SR which had no water troughs.
BR2	Inset at top	3500	6	42.15	75000-19 75020-49	824-843 884-913	No fall plate fitted. Modified with draught excluders after service experience.
BR2A	Inset at top	3500	6	42.15	75050-64 75080-89★	1014-1028 1216-1225★	Identical to BR2 but with addition of a fall plate and gangway doors.

★ Orders cancelled September 1956.

3.4 Tenders

Different batches of the Standard Cl. 4 4-6-0s were furnished with different tender types; details are shown in Table 27. The first 50 locomotives, 75000-49, were provided with BR2 type tenders which, like the BR1 tenders supplied to the Cl. 5 4-6-0s, suffered from the draughtiness problem described in section 2.4; they were modified with draught excluders in the same way. The original BR2 tenders did not have foot platforms adjacent to the water filler cap to provide the fireman with a stable foothold when filling the tender but this feature was incorporated on later batches and fitted to the earlier examples as the engines passed through works for overhaul. The next 15 engines, 75050-64 carried the BR2A tender, identical to the BR2 type, except that it was fitted with a fall plate (and gangway doors) to reduce cab draughts more effectively. The 15 locomotives for the SR, 75065-79, carried the flush-sided BR1B tender which had a higher water capacity to allow for the lack of water troughs on that Region. These tenders were furnished with Timken roller bearing axleboxes which were identified by being painted yellow with a horizontal red stripe.

Engines tended to stay paired with the same tender for the whole of their working lives. Towards the end of steam operation on the SR however, some cannibalisation occurred with at least one member of the class, 75075, being noted coupled to the very high water capacity BR1F tender from a withdrawn SR based Standard Cl. 5 4-6-0. The BR2 tender in common with the BR1 type had the shovelling plate and brake cylinder drains which discharged over the the leading - axle. This arrangement was found to lead to corrosion fatigue on the axle and a programme of protection shield fitting was authorised in late 1956. Not all the BR2 tenders had been thus modified by the time the programme was discontinued

in October 1964. Tender nos. 1216-1225 allocated to the cancelled lot no. 413, 75080-89, were not built, neither were their serial numbers used for other tender types.

3.5 Construction Costs

A comparison of estimated, record card and official construction costs for the Standard Cl. 4 4-6-0s is given in Table 28. The final batch of engines, 75050-64 delivered in 1956/7 at £21,194 each shows an increase of over 40% in official cost compared with the 1951 batch. Labour inflation accounted for much of the increase but the later engines incurred extra expense by being fitted from new with refinements such as the Smith-Stone speedometer. Once again, official costs exceeded estimated costs by between 22% and 40%.

3.6 Liveries

All the Standard Cl. 4 4-6-0s were turned out in mixed traffic lined black livery when new, 75057-64 appearing with the smaller, second style BR emblem; full details of the lining style are given in section 2.6. At least three of the LMR allocation, 75009/38/48, overhauled at Derby in 1961/2, were observed with the running plate lining positioned higher up from the lower edge, as noted on Standard Cl. 5 4-6-0s 73125-54 fitted with Caprotti valve gear. On the WR, the class was one of those selected by Swindon to receive BR lined Brunswick green livery, 75029 being the first to emerge in May 1957; full details of the green livery style are given in section 2.6. All the original WR allocation, 75000-9 and 75020-9 eventually received the green livery with the exception of 75009/28 transferred to the LMR (the former to Gloucester Barnwood in August 1958 and the latter to Rhyl in June 1959) before they could revisit Swindon for overhaul.

Table 28

Standard Class 4 4-6-0s 75000-79: Manufacturing Cost Comparisons

Programme Year	Locomotive Number	Delivery Year	Estimated Cost (£)	Record Card Final Cost (£)	Official Final Cost (£)
1951	75000-09	1951	11,900	16,621	15,163
	75010-19	1951/2	11,900	16,202	14,745
1952	75020-29	1953/4	12,930	17,775	17,727
	75030-49	1953	12,930	17,246	17,198
1953	75050-64	1956/7	15,190	19,682	21,194
	75065-79	1955/6	15,190	18,523	18,452
1954	75080-89	Cancelled 09.56			

Table 29

Standard Cl. 4 4-6-0s 75000-75079: Locomotives Acquiring BR Green Livery

Engine Number	BR Green Livery Date	Applied at	Engine Number	BR Green Livery Date	Applied at
75000	9.57	Swindon	75020	11.58	Swindon
	9.60	Wolverhampton		2.62	Swindon
75001	9.57	Swindon		7.65	Cowlairs★
	10.59	Swindon	75021	2.59	Swindon
75002	11.57	Swindon		11.61	Swindon
	10.59	Swindon		2.64	Darlington
	5.64	Eastleigh	75022	2.59	Swindon
75003	5.59	Swindon		6.62	Swindon
75004	9.59	Swindon	75023	9.59	Swindon
	10.62	Swindon		3.61	Swindon
75005	4.62	Swindon		6.62	Swindon
	5.64	Eastleigh	75024	2.59	Swindon
75006	12.60	Swindon		6.62	Wolverhampton
	4.64	Darlington		7.65	Cowlairs★
75007	3.59	Swindon	75025	8.59	Swindon
	1.61	Doncaster	75026	6.62	Swindon
	7.62	Wolverhampton		9.65	Cowlairs★
75008	6.57	Swindon	75027	5.59	Swindon
	10.58	Swindon	75029	5.57	Swindon
	9.62	Swindon		4.58	Swindon
75016	7.64	Eastleigh		8.60	Swindon
				4.64	Eastleigh

★ 75020/4/6 were overhauled at Cowlairs in 1965 and were reported to have emerged in green livery but it is not clear whether green repaints were applied during the visits.

The green repaints had the WR 'blue spot' route restriction indicator applied below the cabside numerals. The 'blue spot' was also applied new to 75030-4 on delivery in June and July 1953 even though the engines were destined for the LMR. The Swindon paint dates described in section 2.6 were applied to some of the WR allocation; examples included 75006 (21/12-60W) and 75026 (21/6-62K). Dates and Works of application of the green livery are given in Table 29.

From January 1961 to the autumn of 1963, Doncaster works undertook the overhaul of some of the LMR and WR based Standard Cl. 4 4-6-0s as did Darlington from September 1963 to mid-1964. Both works re-applied the green livery to engines already carrying it. In later years, some engines were turned out in unlined green as an economy measure. There is no record of any of the class being re-painted with the large Doncaster or Darlington cabside numerals or having the

Fig. 103
75007 waits to restart the 11.40am Bournemouth West-Bristol Temple Meads out of Evercreech Junction on 14th September 1963. The fireman appears to be pulling coal forward in the rather empty-looking tender. The engine had received an unlined green livery during an intermediate overhaul at Wolverhampton Works in July 1962.
(Courtney Haydon)

Fig. 104
75013 heads a mixed freight at an unidentified location on 2nd May 1964; the engine was allocated to Bletchley at this time. It had recently returned from a Works visit to Eastleigh but does not appear to have had the benefit of a repaint. *(P.H. Wells)*

Fig. 105
On the 6th September 1962, double chimney 75020 approaches Towyn with the Pwllheli portion of the down 'Cambrian Coast Express', the 10.10am from Paddington. The train divided at Machynlleth, the other portion continuing through to Aberystwyth; 75020 is in lined green livery. *(P.H. Wells)*

assigned RA4 route availability code applied to the cabside by Doncaster. The SR locomotives, 75065-79 received the thicker style Swindon cabside numerals on delivery. The classification number '4' above the running numbers on the cabside was expanded by the SR to '4P/4F' or '4P 4F' on some of the class. Later the SR re-paints at Eastleigh reduced this to '4' again. All SR members of the class carried first the yellow circle and later the yellow triangle below the cabside numerals to denote the fitting of a water softening treatment system. Initially the French T.I.A. apparatus (yellow circle) was fitted but from 1957 onwards, this was replaced by the standard BR briquette system (yellow triangle). From May 1964, Eastleigh began handling overhauls for the class operating on the LMR and WR, reapplying their version of the green livery to those engines already carrying it. Black liveried 75016 allocated to the LMR was repainted lined green at Eastleigh in July 1964 possibly in error. It is believed there are no examples of green liveried locomotives reverting to mixed traffic black. Towards the end of steam working, engines from all three operating Regions, WR, LMR and SR carried non-standard front numberplates probably fitted as replacements for the originals 'collected' by souvenir hunters; towards the end of steam, some engines ran without front numberplates.

3.7 Allocation and Duties

3.7.1 Delivery Period, 1951-1957

The first batch of ten engines 75000-9 was delivered to the WR from Swindon Works over the period May to October 1951. The proposed initial allocation for 75001 was Bristol Bath Road with 75002/3 destined for Wolverhampton Stafford Road. This plan was not followed through and the engines were all delivered new as shown:

Swindon	(2)	75000/6
Shrewsbury	(7)	75001-3/5/7-9
Bristol Bath Road	(1)	75004

75000 arrived in May, the rest following between August and October. Together with other new designs, 75000 was on view at Marylebone station on 23rd May at a private exhibition. Over the next two months, the engine carried out running-in trials on the Swindon to Gloucester, Reading and Westbury routes. During its short spell at Bristol, 75004 was used on Cardiff locals and reached Paddington at least once on a Trowbridge semi-fast. By October, apart from 75006 which followed later, the engines were all operating from Shrewsbury. This was part of a complex regional locomotive exchange in which fifty large freight engines (ex-WD Cl. 8F 2-8-0s and LNER Cl. O4 2-8-0s) were sent from the ScR and NER to the WR, ER and LMR in exchange for freight and mixed traffic engines of a lighter design. Five Stanier Cl. 5 4-6-0s moved from Shrewsbury to Scotland.

The new Standard Cl. 4s began assisting LMS Fowler Cl. 4 2-6-4 tank engines on the Shrewsbury-Swansea Victoria services via the Central Wales line and were also noted on Shrewsbury-Crewe local passenger trains. They soon began putting in appearances at Manchester London Road (now Piccadilly), for example on the 8.55am ex-Cardiff returning on the 5.11pm London Road-Crewe parcels. On the North to West route from Manchester and Liverpool to South Wales

via Hereford, it quickly became apparent that due to poor steaming characteristics and a lower power rating compared with other classes used on these heavily loaded trains, the Standard Cl. 4s had difficulty keeping time. Later, workings to Stafford and Derby were introduced and the engines also began appearing on what was nominally a Stanier Cl. 5 4-6-0 diagram for fitted freights to and from Carlisle. The duty involved the daily 4.40am Shrewsbury-Carlisle and the 5.15pm (6.30pm Sundays) Carlisle to Bushbury. Return to Shrewsbury was light engine or on a suitable freight working as required.

The Standard Cl. 4s were not popular on this roster as they again got into trouble through poor steaming. The defect was eventually remedied by the adoption of modified firebars but by September 1953 the Shrewsbury engines had been replaced by higher powered Standard Cl. 5 4-6-0s, 73012-5/7/8/25/6/33-7, initially on loan from the LMR and the ScR but then transferred permanently. 75000-4 departed for Swindon whilst 75005-9, initially earmarked for St Philips Marsh, were eventually re-allocated Cardiff Canton.

Swindon's new engines regularly worked freight turns to Oxford and the Midlands. 75004 was one of the first of its class recorded on a passenger train in the West Country in March 1954 when on one occasion it was in charge of the first part of the 12.00 noon Penzance to Manchester London Road from Plymouth as far as Bristol, having worked down with the 10.50pm Marston Sidings to Plymouth Millbay fish. Later that year, in September, 75001/4 were transferred to Oxford and began to appear regularly on a new freight service which left Oxford at 6.55pm(SX) for the Longbridge car production facility near Birmingham, conveying car bodies from the Cowley plant of the British Motor Corporation (BMC) as it was then known; the return working was at 12.17am (MX). The Oxford engines were also noted on passenger turns on the Worcester and Hereford lines, whilst the Swindon group was by now used on pick-up freights on the M&SWJR line between Cheltenham and Andover as well as on freights to Bristol East depot.

In February 1957, 75001 was involved in a collision at the north end of Leamington Spa General station whilst hauling a Wednesbury-Banbury freight, when it ran into a train loaded with prefabricated track which was crossing over to the down line. The Rugby breakdown crane was sent and through traffic was diverted from Tyseley via Stratford-on-Avon and Honeybourne Junction to Oxford.

The Cardiff allocation, 75005-9 arrived during September 1953 and was observed working Cardiff-Bristol locals and Birmingham Snow Hill-Cardiff semi-fasts forward from Hereford. There were occasional visits to Salisbury on Cardiff-Portsmouth trains and freights to the Oxford area.

The LMR Central Division received the next batch of ten engines, 75010-9 over the period November 1951 to March 1952. They were allocated as shown, displacing a comparable number of Stanier Cl. 5 4-6-0s to Western and other Central Division depots:

Patricroft	(5)	75010-4
Southport	(5)	75015-9

For a short period, the Patricroft engines took over some of the former Stanier Cl. 5 duties on the Manchester Exchange-North Wales Coast line and trans-Pennine Liverpool Lime

Fig. 106
75021 passes Forden with the last westbound 'Cambrian Coast Express' on 4th March 1967. The laurel wreath has been demoted to the coupling hook to make way for the traditional reporting number display, added at Welshpool. Fireman Evan Hughes of Aberystwyth leans from the cab. *(Courtney Haydon)*

Fig. 107
75026 with double chimney leaves Towyn with an up train which includes through coaches to Paddington on 5th September 1962. The engine is in green livery applied at Swindon Works three months previously and is also fitted with WR type ATC apparatus. 75026 ended its days allocated to Tebay where it was used for banking duties on the 1 in 75 climb to Shap summit.
(P.H. Wells)

Fig. 108
On 1st July 1961, 75027 pilots Bulleid light Pacific 34039 *Boscastle* past Templecombe shed yard which features LMS Cl. 2P 4-4-0 40634 on the ash pit. The train is 1O97, the 10.20am Liverpool Lime St–Bournemouth West with through carriages from Manchester Piccadilly; it is restarting its southbound journey after reversing down the bank from Templecombe station, the platforms of which are situated on the Salisbury-Exeter main line. 75027 is restored to full working order on the Bluebell Railway in East Sussex.

(Courtney Haydon)

Street-Hull expresses as far as Leeds City; they were occasionally noted on Manchester Exchange pilot and Miles Platting banking duties. Again however, reports of poor steaming and bad time-keeping resulted in the return of the Stanier 5s. By October 1953, 75010-4 had moved on to Llandudno Junction and examples of the class remained in the North Wales area on local and semi-fast traffic until replaced by diesels a decade later. The Southport engines were used on the Preston line and on the Manchester services, which regularly loaded up to ten coaches. Some fast runs were noted on the race track between Wigan Wallgate and Southport; details of two such performances are given in Table 37. By the summer of 1953, the Southport engines were frequent visitors to Bradford Exchange on the through services via the Calder Valley main line through Todmorden. In September 1952, a BR freight exhibition was held at Battersea Wharf in London where Southport's 75019 was on show together with LMS 0-6-0 diesel shunter 12120 and Standard Cl. 7 Britannia Pacific 70025 plus various types of wagons.

The third batch of ten Standard Cl. 4s 75020-9 was initially intended for the LMR but then re-assigned to the WR. Before a start was made on this order, a further twenty engines, 75030-49 were delivered to the LMR from June to October 1953, allocated as follows:

Bletchley	(10)	75030-9
Bedford	(5)	75040-4
Accrington	(5)	75045-9

The Bletchley engines were delivered in the period June to August 1953, displacing a similar number of Stanier Cl. 5 4-6-0s to Willesden, Crewe and Carlisle Upperby. They undertook duties on Northampton trains and on the Cambridge-Oxford line as well as working parcels trains to Marylebone and semi-fasts to Euston. Some of these engines were among the first of the class to visit East Anglia the following year when 75035/9 were noted on excursions at Ipswich and Clacton-on-Sea. 75030 moved to Llandudno Junction in June 1954, briefly returning to Bletchley in the following February, before returning to North Wales with the majority of the Bletchley contingent in the same month; the engines were replaced at Bletchley with an equal number of Stanier 5s from other LMR Western Division depots. The latter took over the longer suburban workings out of Euston on which the remaining Standard Cl. 4s became increasingly rare performers.

75040-4 had arrived at Bedford by September 1953 and began work on the commuter services to St Pancras taking over from LMS Compound 4-4-0s, several of which departed for the scapyard over the following few weeks. The new Standard Cl. 4s were hardly at Bedford for a month before they were sent to join newly received 75045-9 at Accrington. This resulted in a reprieve for the remaining Compound 4-4-0s on fasts and semi-fasts to St Pancras, Kettering and Leicester although the majority of the Standard Cl. 4's work at Bedford was taken over by the new Brighton-built Standard Cl. 4 2-6-4 tank engines (80XXX). These eventually proved to have insufficient water capacity for their duties and by early 1955 75040-4 were back from Accrington, the tank engines moving north to a neighbouring part of East Lancashire, Bury. With rearranged rosters, Compound 4-4-0s were seen less frequently on the St Pancras services. It was possible to see a

regular double-heading of Standard Cl. 4s on the 10.40am St Pancras-Leicester semi-fast. The assisting engine was detached at Bedford to take over the 4.14pm local back to St Pancras. This train produced the only regular working for a Bedford Standard Cl. 4 to Leicester. Several new passenger trains were introduced on the St Pancras service during 1955 and the Standard Cl. 4s began to make a name for themselves for fast running. For example, on 15th April, the 5.05pm St Pancras arrival from Nottingham had delayed the following up semi-fast due to brake failure. 75040 left Luton with the latter train some fourteen minutes late and in spite of three intermediate stops, ran through to St Pancras in less than forty minutes, gaining seven minutes on the schedule with a maximum of 68mph at Harpenden and 75mph through Radlett. At the beginning of 1956, the Standard Cl. 4s were responsible for Bedford's five stopping train duties to St Pancras with the expresses now handled by three newly arrived Stanier Cl. 5 4-6-0s. Other work carried out by the Standard Cl. 4s at Bedford involved several visits to the South Coast on excursions during the summer months.

The original Accrington allocation, 75045-9 was delivered during September and October 1953 and together with 75040-4 newly arrived from Bedford displaced Stanier Cl. 5 4-6-0s on East Lancashire and Todmorden-Burnley line work. The engines were also employed on banking duties on the 1in 68/70 incline out of Burnley to Copy Pit sidings. On the last Saturday in January 1954 for example, 75043/4/8 were seen busily assisting FA Cup Tie excursions returning home to Newcastle upon Tyne.

Later, a strange malady began to affect the Accrington based engines, the phenomenon of 'groaning' brakeblocks, the noise from which was audible over a mile away. Several attempts by the shed staff to cure the fault were in vain, although some improvement was achieved. One of the turns booked for these engines involved shunting Ramsbottom yard in the small hours of the morning which caused the local residents to complain bitterly at the disturbance to their night's rest. A formal complaint was made through the police and as a result, a Hughes-Fowler Cl. 6P/5F Crab 2-6-0 was borrowed from Rose Grove depot to take on the duty.

By November 1955, the remaining Standard Cl. 4 4-6-0s at Accrington, 75045-9 (75040-4 having returned to Bedford earlier in the year) had moved to Liverpool Bank Hall in exchange for Stanier Cl. 5 4-6-0s. Although some work in the Accrington area, such as short distance freights and Copy Pit banking duties, was suited to the smaller-wheeled Standard Cl. 4s, other diagrams were more in the province of the Stanier Cl. 5s. One such roster on which the Standard Cl. 4s had been used is noted below:

4.06am Accrington-Colne parcels
7.30am Colne-Blackpool Central local
1.30pm Blackpool Central-Wakefield Kirkgate
7.15pm Wakefield-Preston slow
via Brighouse and Accrington
11.25pm Preston-Accrington local

At Bank Hall, the Standard Cl. 4 4-6-0s were noted on the Preston and Blackpool lines and appeared regularly on semi-fasts to Manchester Victoria and as far as Bradford Exchange on the through service from Liverpool Exchange to Leeds Central on the Calder Valley line via Todmorden.

Work on the next batch of ten Standard Cl. 4s, 75020-9 outstanding from the 1952 building programme was not started until October 1953. The engines were delivered to the WR over the six month period from November and were allocated as follows:

Oswestry	(3)	75020/3/4
Cardiff Canton	(2)	75021/2
Laira	(5)	75025-9

The Oswestry engines, together with newly acquired 75006, had arrived by December displacing GWR Manor Cl. 4-6-0s 7807/8/20/1 to Bristol, Chester and Shrewsbury. Initially, the Standard Cl. 4 4-6-0s worked regularly between Oswestry and Aberystwyth and had difficulty keeping time, appearing light on their feet compared with the Manor Cl. 4-6-0s. As the drivers gained experience the performance of the new engines improved markedly and the slipping problem was largely cured, the engines being successfully used turn and turn about with the remaining Manor Cl. 4-6-0s. By the middle of 1957, there were six Standard Cl. 4s at Oswestry, 75005/6/20/4/6/8. Around this time, the coastal section of the Cambrian line from Dovey Junction to Barmouth Junction and northwards was upgraded to take heavier engines and Standard Cl. 4s, Manor Cl. 4-6-0s and the GWR 43XX 2-6-0s were permitted along the route working heavier trains. The 5.40pm Machynlleth-Pwllheli was regularly a Standard Cl. 4 turn. Later, in the 1960s based at Machynlleth, Croes Newydd and Shrewsbury, the class became well entrenched on the Cambrian lines, remaining until the end of steam-working in the area.

The Laira engines appeared during April and May 1954 and at first were employed mainly on pilot duties on the South Devon banks, displacing Manor Cl. 4-6-0s 7809/14/5/24 to other Newton Abbot Division depots and 7804 to Carmarthen. In June, 75025 was observed heading the 9.18am Exmouth-Manchester London Road at Exeter Central. During July, one of the class was tested on the SR Exeter Central-Plymouth Friary route over Dartmoor via Okehampton. 75026 was regularly noted on the 2.33pm Plymouth Friary-Exeter Central and 6.44pm return (3.00pm ex-London Waterloo) instead of the usual GWR 43XX 2-6-0. In September, 75027/9 were on the move to Reading. Three months later they were transferred to Oxford where they appeared on the freights to the Midlands and passenger trains to Paddington. Of the remaining Laira engines, 75025 was maintained in the splendid condition usually associated with Laira's favourite Castle Class 4-6-0s. The Standard Cl. 4s now took their turn on a regular Newton Abbot district working, the 9.00pm Exeter-Crewe freight as far as Birmingham Tyseley. In June 1956, all three engines were displaced by GWR Hall Cl. 4-6-0s, 4900/76/7, 75025/6 moving to Swindon and 75028 to Oswestry. Meanwhile, on Whit Monday 1957, 75029 still nominally at Oxford was noted, painted in lined green livery and fitted with a double chimney, on an excursion from Swindon to Weston-super-Mare. 75029 was the first of the class to be so fitted following successful double draughting tests at Swindon. It was intended to equip the whole class with double chimneys but only twenty two were modified, fifteen on the SR and seven on the WR. On the latter Region, a total of nine members of the class were observed at various times with double chimneys, as

a result of re-use of smokeboxes and boilers from withdrawn locomotives.

75021/2 joined other members of the class at Cardiff and were employed on similar duties. 75022 was transferred to Swansea Victoria for a short period in 1957 and was used mainly on Central Wales line trains to Craven Arms and Shrewsbury. Its regular duty was the 10.25am to Shrewsbury and the 5.10pm return.

The next batch consisting of fifteen engines, 75050-64 was destined for the LMR. Construction was delayed until November 1956, precedence being given to 75065-79 for the SR. The latter batch of fifteen engines was begun in August 1955, a gap of over a year since 75020-9 had appeared. Delivery was over the six month period to January 1956 with allocation as shown:

| Dover | (5) | 75065-9 |
| Exmouth Junction | (10) | 75070-9 |

The Dover engines were in place by September 1955, running in on the usual Swindon-Oxford turns and reaching Dover via the Reading-Redhill route. Their arrival coincided with the storage of Dover allocated Maunsell Schools 4-4-0 30919 and King Arthur N15 4-6-0s 30775/97/8 at their home depot. The new Standard Cl. 4s were employed mainly on van and freight workings including continental ferry van trips to and from the London area goods depots at Bricklayers' Arms, Hither Green and Southwark. By early 1956, they were being used increasingly on passenger workings. Examples included 75069 replacing the Hither Green Cl. N15 4-6-0 on the 5.40pm London Cannon Street-Dover on 29th March and on 2nd April 75065 appearing on a Tonbridge-Redhill working. By June, 75065 was being used by Ramsgate depot on the heavy 6.06am Ramsgate-Cannon Street commuter express, officially a Bulleid light Pacific duty, whilst other Standard Cl. 4s took on the 8.59am to Charing Cross and the 9.20am to Victoria. During the summer season, the engines were frequently seen on Chatham line holiday services at weekends as well as the regular 'Kentish Belle' Pullman linking Victoria with Herne Bay, Margate, Broadstairs and Ramsgate.

The Southwark ferry van trains were only run on demand and often had no balancing return working. Hence the Standard Cl. 4 4-6-0s were frequently borrowed by the nearest depots, Stewarts Lane and Hither Green for summer Saturday services at times of pressure. One instance was recorded in June 1957 when 75067 was used by Stewarts Lane to cover a Schools 4-4-0 duty on a round trip to Hastings via Ashford, returning on the 10.10am to Charing Cross via the Bopeep Junction-Tonbridge route, officially barred to Standard Cl. 4s for clearance reasons. The engines regularly appeared on South Coast to North West holiday through trains via the Reading-Redhill line in the summer months.

The Exmouth Junction allocation was delivered between October 1955 and January 1956. Their appearance seemed to foretell early withdrawal of the LSWR Cl. T9 4-4-0s and gradual replacement of the Cl. N 2-6-0s in the area but this aim was not to be fulfilled. With their 50 ft wheelbase, the new engines were, not surprisingly, a fairly tight fit on the 50 ft turntables at places such as Barnstaple, Bude, Launceston and Wadebridge. Hence they could not take over the intricate cyclic diagrams of the T9s and Ns. As a result, the only

Fig. 109
The first of the class to acquire a double chimney (in May 1957), 75029 rolls into a rather weed-overgrown platform at Llangybi with a Carmarthen–Aberystwyth train on 18th July 1962. The engine is based at Tyseley and is being utilised by Aberystwyth for a 'filling-in' turn before being returned to Birmingham. Llangybi was one of several unstaffed 'request stop' stations on the line. The branch was closed to passengers between Aberystwyth and Strata Florida on 14th December 1964 as a result of severe flooding; closure of the remainder followed on 22nd February 1965. *(Rodney Lissenden)*

Fig. 110
75030 enters Oxford with a Bletchley train on 15th August 1959. Note the rectangular cross-section coupling rods fitted instead of the fluted type from 75020 onwards. *(R.C. Riley)*

Fig. 111
75030 waits to leave Cambridge with the 11.26am to Bletchley on 31st August 1959. The engine was fitted with manganese steel axlebox liners (on the coupled axleboxes only) and had visited Derby Works one year previously for its first general overhaul having accrued a mileage of around 173,000. *(Peter Groom)*

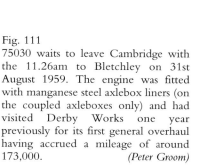

Fig. 112
75032 heads a mineral train at Southam Road and Harbury between Leamington Spa and Banbury in the spring of 1963. By this time, the engine had achieved a mileage of around 275,000.

(Top Link Prints)

Fig. 113
75032 leaves Skipton with the 9.55am Bradford Forster Square -Morecambe Promenade on 31st July 1965. Note the draught screens attached to the tender, the non-standard front number-plate and the depot name, Bank Hall, painted on the front buffer beam; the latter feature indicates the engine had recently been overhauled at Cowlairs Works which dealt with several LMR class members in 1965.

(Courtney Haydon)

Fig. 114
The 3.35pm Swindon-Grimsby and Hull goods, conveying empty fish wagons, passes under the modern concrete arch bridge at Wolvercote Junction in the charge of 75034 on 13th July 1953; 75034 is probably on a running-in turn from Swindon Works. The train is routed via Banbury, Woodford Halse and the GCR line. Note the provision of the Smith-Stone speedometer activated by the rear driving wheel; speedometers were fitted to the class new from 75020 onwards. Swindon has also applied the WR 'blue spot' route restriction indicator on the cabside even though the engine is destined for the LMR.

(E.D. Bruton)

booked turns for the Standard Cl. 4s were between Exeter and Plymouth via both the SR Okehampton and WR Newton Abbot routes. There was no doubt that they were masters of their work. A fine run behind 75074 on the 2.15pm Plymouth Friary-Waterloo on 3rd December 1955 showed a 2½ minute gain on the 34 minute schedule for the 25 miles from Okehampton to Exeter St Davids. Speeds of over 70mph were recorded at North Tawton and approaching Cowley Bridge.

At times of pressure, the Standard Cl. 4s deputised for Bulleid light Pacifics. An example was on Christmas Eve 1955 when 75074 was noted on the 11.30am Brighton-Plymouth service between Exeter Central and Plymouth taking eleven coaches in its stride. The engines worked the Meldon Quarry permanent way ballast freights on occasion and also featured on stopping trains to Salisbury but were obviously under-employed during their time at Exmouth Junction. When the last of the batch 75079 arrived in January 1956, it was almost immediately loaned to Yeovil. There it worked various Cl. U 2-6-0 duties such as the 4.25pm Cardiff-Portsmouth from Salisbury, returning on the 11.23pm Portsmouth-Eastleigh and the 1.55am Eastleigh-Yeovil.

By June 1956, all ten had been reallocated, 75070/1/2 to Bath Green Park, 75073/4 to Eastleigh and 75075-9 to Basingstoke. The Bath engines were fitted with tablet exchange apparatus for working on the single track portions of the S&DJR line replacing the trusty but ageing LMS Cl. 2P 4-4-0s on stopping trains to Bournemouth West. The Standard Cl. 4s were used on summer Saturday holiday services on both pilot and train engine rosters and it was not uncommon to see them in double harness on these trains.

The Eastleigh engines, 75073/4 were used interchangeably on the Standard Cl. 4 2-6-0 (76XXX) rosters and also worked far and wide on permanent way sleeper trains from the Redbridge Works at Southampton. On 15th November 1956, 75073 reached Eastbourne on one of these duties and later worked its train to the track relaying site at Heathfield.

The Basingstoke group, 75075-9 took over commuter services to and from Waterloo, displacing Urie King Arthur Cl. N15 and Remembrance Cl. N15X 4-6-0s from this service. On Saturdays the Standard Cl. 4s assisted with main line summer reliefs, becoming regular power for the 10.30am Lymington Pier-Waterloo, one of the trains run in connection with the Isle of Wight boat service.

The last batch of fifteen Standard Cl. 4s, 75050-64 was for the London Midland Region. Delivery was in the period November 1956 to June 1957 with allocation as shown:

Llandudno Junction	(1)	75050
Chester Midland	(3)	75051/3/4
Bletchley	(1)	75052
Bedford	(1)	75055
Nottingham	(4)	75056/62-4
Leicester Midland	(5)	75057-61

Only two new depots featured in this group, Leicester Midland and Nottingham. The Leicester engines took over the last remaining LMS Compound 4-4-0 duty on the London line, the 3.20pm St Pancras-Kettering, releasing 41095 and 41181 to Gloucester. The Standard Cl. 4s performed well on this route even with the heavy 5.30pm St Pancras-Leicester. Other duties involved stopping and branch line trains to Kettering, Peterborough, Derby, Burton-on-Trent via Moira and the Nottingham and Birmingham line locals. The 12.46pm Worcester-Birmingham New Street was regularly piloted by a Leicester engine which had arrived overnight and the Standard Cl. 4s were commonly observed on this duty.

The Nottingham engines were similarly employed on local and stopping trains on the Derby and Lincoln lines and excursion work, for example to the now defunct Belle Vue Zoo and theme park in Manchester. On 24th August 1957, 75064 was observed at Skipton on the 5.50am Nottingham Midland-Morecambe through train. Several elderly LMS Cl. 2P 4-4-0s were displaced by the new engines.

With the whole class of Standard Cl. 4s in service by June 1957, the LMR had the lion's share of forty five engines with the WR having twenty and the SR fifteen examples.

A further group, 75080-9 planned for construction at Swindon in 1958 for the ER, was earmarked for the former Midland and Great Northern Joint Railway which linked the East Midlands with Kings Lynn, Melton Constable, Cromer and Yarmouth. Apart from summer Saturday holiday traffic, the line was lightly used and the order was cancelled when it was obvious the route had no future; closure occurred in November 1959.

3.7.2 From 1957 to Withdrawal

Western Region

In July 1957, the twenty Standard Cl. 4 4-6-0s allocated to the WR 75000-9/20-9 were distributed as shown; duties remained much as before.

Swindon	(5)	75000/2/3/23/5
Oxford	(3)	75001/27/9
Cardiff Canton	(6)	75004/7-9/21/2
Oswestry	(6)	75005/6/20/4/6/8

Regular workings for the Cardiff engines were Cardiff-Bristol stopping trains and the 8.30am Cardiff-Newcastle as far as Gloucester Central. By the end of 1958, Canton's Standard Cl. 4s had been moved to Oxford, Gloucester Barnwood and Bristol Barrow Road, the last two former LMR depots by now under the control of the WR. Double chimneyed 75029 was loaned to Southport (LMR) for three months from October 1958 for test purposes.

In early 1959, 75027/9 and 75024 by then also at Oxford were reallocated to Swindon. This move was made as their regular loads of car bodies to Longbridge now originated from the Pressed Steel company's plant at Swindon instead of Morris Cowley. Their tender capacity was now even more taxed by the additional mileage resulting in occasional calls at Oxford for coal on the return journey. The Oxford engines were rostered to take over 7.15pm Ipswich-South Wales area freight from Oxford at this time, returning on the 12.10pm Llandilo-Cambridge freight. Along with GWR Hall Cl. 4-6-0s, the Standard Cl. 4s regularly appeared on the Oxford-Bournemouth leg of the 10.23am from York (which reached Oxford via the GCR route through Leicester Central) returning on the 9.20pm Bournemouth-Reading semi-fast; in late 1959, they could occasionally be observed working the regular freight from Cowley to Birkenhead.

In August 1958, responsibility for Chester West depot was

transferred from the WR to the LMR; 75005/6/20/6/8 from Oswestry went to Chester West in exchange for its remaining GWR Manor Cl. 4-6-0s. There were no further allocations of the class to Oswestry from this time on but they continued to receive attention at the former Cambrian Railways' Oswestry Works, 75024 being the last engine to be repaired there before the facility closed in January 1967.

In May 1961 the WR allocation was twenty two engines. The depots now included Bath Green Park and Templecombe, transferred from the SR when the WR took over responsibility for the Somerset and Dorset line (S&DJR) in early 1958; distribution in May 1961 was as shown:

Oxford	(5)	75000/1/7/8/21
Gloucester Barnwood	(3)	75002/9/23
Tyseley	(4)	75003/6/24/9
Bristol Barrow Road	(2)	75004/22
Worcester	(2)	75005/25
Machynlleth	(2)	75020/6
Templecombe	(1)	75027
Bath Green Park	(3)	75071-3

The responsibilty for Bristol Barrow Road and Gloucester Barnwood had been transferred from the LMR to the WR early in 1958 and by the following September both had received allocations of the class. Together with the Worcester engines they were used on the Bristol-Gloucester Eastgate-Birmingham New Street stopping passenger services replacing former LMS Compound 4-4-0s. Regular workings were the 11.30am Gloucester-Birmingham and the 5.45pm return to Bristol. The Worcester allocation was noted on the 9.24am Great Malvern to Birmingham New Street and the 1.56pm return to Worcester as well as on passenger and freight turns on the Hereford and Oxford lines.

The Tyseley group, 75003/6/24/9, was used on secondary pasenger turns on the Shrewsbury and Oxford lines and had regular workings to the London area on fitted freights. They also appeared on summer Saturday holiday specials to the Cambrian coast. One through working for a short period was the 8.05am from Birmingham Snow Hill to Barmouth returning the following week with the 1.30pm from Barmouth. Aberystwyth depot provided the balancing engine for the cross-working, usually a GWR Manor Cl. 4-6-0. During its stay in the Aberystwyth area, the Tyseley engine often worked a turn over the Carmarthen line. 75020/6 at Machynlleth had transferred from Tyseley in June 1959 to assist GWR Manor Cl. 4-6-0s on the Cambrian line summer holiday traffic. They were also noted on the North Wales Radio Land Cruise train which took holidaymakers from Pwllheli to Rhyl via Corwen returning through Llandudno and Caernarvon on a tour of the splendours of Snowdonia; the service ran several times each week during the summer season. 75000/1/7/8/21 at Oxford continued as before on freights to London and the Midlands and passenger services to Bournemouth.

Templecombe had received 75027 in February 1960 for service on the Somerset and Dorset (S&DJR) line where 75071/2/3 were already operating from Bath Green Park. Later, in September 1961, 75002/9/23 were also at Templecombe. The new allocation was used on locals and summer Saturday holiday trains enabling the remaining LMS Cl. 2P 4-4-0s to be retired.

By June 1964, the WR allocation had been halved to eleven engines spread over four depots which now included the former SR sheds at Yeovil Town and Exmouth Junction taken over by the WR in early 1963. Several of the class were still working on the Cambrian section but responsibility for this area had passed to the LMR in January 1963.

Yeovil Town	(3)	75000/1/3
Exmouth Junction	(3)	75005/22/5
Templecombe	(4)	75007/71-3
Oxford	(1)	75008

The turntable problems which had confined Exmouth Junction's earlier allocation of the class in 1955 to working between Exeter and Plymouth appear to have been overcome. The engines were now used on the North Cornwall line to Wadebridge and on Meldon Quarry workings as well as freights to Okehampton and Plymouth. They replaced Standard Cl. 4 2-6-4 tanks (80XXX) and Cl. 3 2-6-2 tanks (82XXX) on these routes in an effort to improve time keeping. The Yeovil engines were noted on semi-fasts to Exeter and Salisbury with through workings from the latter to Bournemouth via the doomed Fordingbridge line. The North Cornwall line services were given over to diesel multiple units in early 1965. Both Yeovil Town and Exmouth Junction depots closed to steam in June 1965 and 75000/3/5/8/22/5 transferred to Worcester.

At Worcester, although there was little suitable work, a rostered passenger duty was the 5.37pm to Hereford, a continuation of the 3.15pm from Paddington; return was with the 7.10pm Hereford-Worcester parcels. Other regular duties were the daily Evesham pick-up freight and banking assistance for freights from Honeybourne Junction on the five mile 1 in 100 gradient to Campden on the Oxford line. It was one of Worcester's engines, 75005, which was involved in an accident when hauling the 2.45am Swindon Highworth Junction to Birmingham Bordesley class 7 freight on 14th September 1965. The engine was in charge of forty four loaded wagons when it crashed through the stop blocks on the Fosse Road loop between Harbury and Leamington Spa.

Fig. 115   75039 approaches Stamford Town on a local from Peterborough on 10th August 1963. In the ten years since delivery, 75039 had run over 300,000 miles, the highest individual year being 1954 when the engine's annual total was nearly 42,000.   *(P.H. Wells)*

Engine and tender finished up on their sides down the embankment where they were sheeted over and left for over two months. With the assistance of the Crewe and Saltley cranes, 75005 was rerailed and removed to Banbury depot on 21st November. There it remained covered in soil and grass until by the following March it had been taken to Birds' Commercial Motors' scrapyard at Morriston for disposal.

In July 1964, Templecombe's 75071 went to the LMR to be replaced by Oxford's 75008 although the latter was soon again on the move to Exmouth Junction. 75072/3, albeit latterly in poor condition were at Templecombe until withdrawal in December 1965 a few months before closure of the S&DJR line in March 1966. The remaining allocation at Worcester, 75000/3/8/22/5 was also withdrawn at the end of 1965; no further allocations of the class were made to the WR from this date.

Southern Region

In June 1957, the SR's fifteen engines were allocated as shown:

Dover	(5)	75065-9
Eastleigh	(2)	75070/4
Bath Green Park	(3)	75071-3
Basingstoke	(5)	75075-9

The Eastern Section engines at Dover 75065-9 continued on both passenger and freight work as before until June 1959 when they were displaced to Bournemouth on completion of the first phase of the Kent Coast electrification scheme. The Western Section already had 75076-9 operating from Basingstoke on semi-fasts on the Waterloo-Salisbury main line. The Standard Cl. 4s at Bournemouth took over from King Arthur Cl. N15 4-6-0s amongst others on local services to Southampton, Weymouth and Salisbury. They were also used on summer Saturday cross-country reliefs. Autumn 1959 found them under-employed and 75069 moved back to Stewarts Lane for Central Section work.

Before this, in early 1959, 75070/4/5 were moved to the Central Section, based at Stewarts Lane and Three Bridges. Here the trio performed some of the best work of the class's career on the tightly timed commuter expresses on the Oxted line. In a roundabout way their advent on these services was the result of the introduction of Bulleid light Pacifics on the 6.10pm Victoria-Uckfield, a heavily loading commuter express with a long standing reputation for poor time keeping. The Pacifics solved the problem of late running on the 6.10pm but on-time approaches to Oxted were now regularly met with adverse signals from the preceding train, the equally popular 5.49pm Victoria-Groombridge via East Grinstead whose Cl. 4 2-6-4 tank engine frequently took a long water-stop at Oxted. Accordingly, 75074 was borrowed from Basingstoke on the Western Section and tried out on the 5.49pm commencing 4th December 1958. Water-stop delays were now eliminated and 75074 was permanently allocated to Stewarts Lane in January 1959; 75070/5 were transferred from Eastleigh and Basingstoke to Three Bridges in the same month. The 5.49pm Victoria-Groombridge was part of the following diagram which 75074 worked almost without a break until mid-April:

6.29am	Victoria-Tunbridge Wells West via East Grinstead.
1.47pm	Tunbridge Wells-Victoria via East Grinstead, turning on the Ashurst Junction triangle
5.49pm	Victoria-Groombridge via East Grinstead Light Engine to Tunbridge Wells again turning on the Ashurst triangle
9.20pm	Tunbridge Wells-Victoria via Edenbridge Town.

A Sunday duty for 75074 at this time involved two return trips to Brighton leaving Victoria at 9.38am and 4.38pm. The regular turn for 75075 at Three Bridges was as shown:

7.07am	Three Bridges-Forest Row
8.24am	Forest Row-Victoria
3.50pm	Victoria-Brighton via Uckfield
7.14pm	Brighton-Horsham
9.54pm	Vans, Horsham-Three Bridges

The engines were also noted on the following roster:

5.20am	Goods, Three Bridges-East Grinstead
7.41am	East Grinstead-London Bridge
5.38pm	London Bridge-East Grinstead
7.26pm	East Grinstead-Victoria
9.31pm	Vans, Victoria-Three Bridges

A Standard Cl. 4 plus train proved to be rather a tight fit at London Bridge on the platform designated for the 5.38pm. As no other platform was available, the working ceased to be diagrammed for a 4-6-0 and 75070 was transferred to Brighton. Here it was noted on the 7.19am Brighton-London Bridge and 4.40pm return or the 8.20am or 9.55am Brighton-Victoria returning at 3.50pm. From the summer of 1959 the Central Section Standard Cl. 4s, 75070/4/5 were regularly used between Kensington Olympia and the coast on the Glasgow-Eastbourne car sleeper service and summer Saturday holiday specials from Manchester, Sheffield and the West Midlands to Brighton and Eastbourne.

In May 1961, the SR allocation was down to twelve engines, 75065-70/4-9, as Bath Green Park had retained 75071-3 when the S&DJR line came under the control of the WR in early 1958; the SR distribution was as shown:

Bournemouth	(3)	75065-7
Eastleigh	(1)	75068
Stewarts Lane	(2)	75069/74
Three Bridges	(2)	75070/5
Basingstoke	(4)	75076-9

Eastleigh's 75068 was noted on the South Wales trains between Portsmouth and Salisbury sharing the duties with Standard Cl. 4 and Cl. U 2-6-0s. Both Bournemouth and Basingstoke engines were regularly employed on summer Saturday reliefs sometimes ranging far afield as for example on 11th August 1962 when 75078 reached the West Midlands with the 9.32am Portsmouth Harbour-Wolverhampton.

Following the electrification and dieselisation of the London-Ashford-Kent Coast main line in the spring of 1961,

Fig. 116
75040 leaves Stamford Town with the 5.32pm Peterborough East-Leicester London Road local on 5th June 1963. The engine carries the electric warning flashes on the firebox and above the access steps from the buffer beam to the running plate. *(P.H. Wells)*

Fig. 117
75051, based at Wigan Springs Branch, heads south past Shap summit on a local from Carlisle to Preston on 28th June 1964. Three years later, several of the class were at Tebay for Shap banking duties.
(Rodney Lissenden)

Fig. 118
75052 approaches Euston with an up local composed of non-corridor stock on 19th March 1958. By the end of the year, on entry to Rugby Works for a casual repair at the end of its second year in service, the engine had run over 69,000 miles. *(Peter Groom)*

Fig. 119
75053, piloted by Ivatt Cl. 2 2-6-0 46521 nears the summit of Talerddig bank on the 6.05pm Aberystwyth- Shrewsbury on 7th May 1966. This train conveyed through mail coaches to York. 75053 was withdrawn four months later with an estimated total mileage of over 250,000, whilst the Ivatt Mogul is preserved on the Severn Valley Railway at Bridgnorth.

(M. Mensing)

Fig. 120
75055 approaches Elstree with the 1.02pm St Pancras–Bedford slow on 17th August 1957. Note the whitened lower hinge on the smokebox door. The class continued operating on these workings until displaced by diesel multiple units in early 1960.

(Frank Hornby)

Fig. 121
75055 is seen at the head of an RCTS rail tour at Bedford on 10th May 1958. Beginning at Liverpool Street, the tour had reached Bedford via Cambridge. 75055 took over for the last stage to St Pancras with a stop at Harpenden for enthusiasts to join a special train headed by MR Cl. 3F 0-6-0 43245 for a run up the Hemel Hempstead branch.   (J. Faithfull)

Fig. 122
75057 nears Stamford Town on a local for Leicester London Road on 6th June 1963. Six weeks earlier, the engine was fitted with the BR type AWS apparatus at a cost of £383.

(P.H. Wells)

Fig. 123
75059 hurries away from Skipton with the 12.22pm for Morecambe Promenade on 31st July 1965; twelve of the class were allocated to Skipton at this time. Apart from passenger and parcels work, the class had freight duties which included the ballast train workings on the Grassington branch.

(Courtney Haydon)

Fig. 124
75062 heads a down semi-fast passenger train near Melton Mowbray in 1958. The engine completed almost 37,000 miles on this and similar duties during 1958 and had achieved 117,000 miles in service by the time it was called to Derby Works for its first intermediate overhaul in August 1960.

(Peter Groom)

Stewarts Lane retained a small group of steam engines now including 75069/74 for Central Section work and the summer Saturday inter-regionals. By the summer of 1963 with the rundown of steam, the Standard Cl. 4s were the largest engines available at Stewarts Lane and they virtually monopolised the Glasgow sleeper as well as appearing on inter-regional reliefs and excursions. At that time, Race Day Specials were still prestige workings and on 7th June 75069/74 were both noted at Lingfield, each with nine corridors including Pullman cars. Otherwise dieselisation, mainly with Type 3 Cl. 33s, was gradually displacing steam from regular Oxted line work and on 28th June 75068 made the last steam run on the 3.54pm Victoria-Brighton. In September 1963, Stewarts Lane finally closed to steam. By then its Standard Cl. 4s 75067/8/74/5 had moved to Norwood Junction from where they worked the autumn programme of Saga holiday specials to Eastbourne as well as the Glasgow sleeper during the final weeks of the season. Their other duties at Norwood included the Caterham freight and passenger trips between Clapham Junction and Kensington. The Standard Cl. 4s were also prominent on the Christmas 1963 mails programme for the two weeks from the 9th December. Norwood's pretensions as a main line passenger depot were short-lived as the depot closed in January 1964. Its Standard Cl. 4s were moved to Eastleigh and thereafter the class was seldom seen on the Central Section.

In June 1964, the SR's allocation was concentrated at two depots, Eastleigh and Nine Elms as shown:

Eastleigh	(7)	75065-8/74/5/9
Nine Elms	(5)	75069/70/6-8

The Eastleigh stud continued on Portsmouth-South Wales trains and the daily Brighton-Plymouth service whilst the London engines were diagrammed for fairly low grade work on local freight and van trains, the longest regular run being to Reading. Other duties involved shunting Surbiton and Wimbledon yards and occasionally working a Reading-Redhill train or covering a Standard Cl. 5 4-6-0 turn on a semi-fast to Basingstoke or Salisbury.

In early 1965 the Standard Cl. 4s were increasingly in evidence as substitutes for absent Bulleid Pacifics on Waterloo-Bournemouth expresses. In March 1966, 75070 assisted with the RCTS 'Solent Limited' rail tour originating at Waterloo. It worked the nine coach special forward from Salisbury to Southampton Docks then from Southampton Terminus to Fareham and finally double-headed the return with Cl. U 2-6-0 31639 from Fareham to Waterloo via Havant and Putney.

Towards the end of 1966, some of the Standard Cl. 4s were being allowed to lapse into a run-down condition. This caused problems when they were called on to substitute for higher power on Waterloo-Bournemouth expresses. On 30th October 1966 for example, Nine Elms could produce nothing larger than a rather woebegone 75074 for the 7-30pm Waterloo-Weymouth. The train came to a halt a half mile short of Woking station, finally managing to gain the platforms at 8.25pm. Here the refreshment room did a brisk trade whilst 75074 paused to raise steam. A further attempt in the Weymouth direction was cut short at Farnborough to attach assistance in the form of a Type 3 Cl. 33 diesel. The cavalcade then proceeded to Eastleigh where both engines

were replaced by Standard Cl. 5 4-6-0 73002. On 19th November 75074 was again noted at Waterloo, this time in much better shape at the head of the 3.25pm from Bournemouth Central.

By January 1967 the SR's five remaining Standard Cl. 4s, 75068/74-7 were all at Eastleigh. From here, they were still at work on semi-fasts, local passenger, freight and parcels trains to Waterloo, Salisbury and Weymouth;one of the class was normally kept at Basingstoke as standby engine. 75075 worked a Waterloo-Bournemouth relief on 10th June 1967, whilst on 1st July, 75074 had a lively run from Portsmouth Harbour to Willesden with a return 'Wakes Week' special for Bolton Trinity Street via Haslemere, East Putney and the West London line. By the end of July, following commencement of the Bournemouth line electric service earlier in the month, 75074/5/7 were at Salisbury and 75068/76 at Weymouth together with other engines awaiting movement to the breaker's yard.

London Midland Region

In early July 1957, the LMR allocation of forty five engines was distributed as shown:

Llandudno Junction	(7)	75010-4/31/50
Southport	(5)	75015-9
Bletchley	(5)	75030/6-8/52
Chester Midland	(7)	75032/4/5/9/51/3/4
Rhyl	(1)	75033
Bedford	(6)	75040-4/55
Bank Hall	(5)	75045-9
Nottingham	(4)	75056/62-4
Leicester Midland	(5)	75057-61

With the number at Bletchley now five, the Standard Cl. 4s were appearing regularly at Euston on locals and semi-fasts. They continued to share the Oxford-Cambridge line workings with Standard Cl. 4 2-6-4 tank engines (80XXX) and Stanier Cl. 5 4-6-0s until the service was taken over by diesel multiple units in 1962. On the Banbury line, the 5.45am freight to Banbury and 11.20am return were a regular duty for the class in 1959. They continued to act as standby for non-availability of diesels, although Bletchley's 75038 was unable to take full advantage of its hour of glory on 6th April 1962 whilst deputising for a failed Type 4 Cl. 40 diesel on the down 'Caledonian', 3.35pm Euston-Glasgow Central. The unfortunate engine took over at Bletchley but was forced to halt at Castlethorpe to raise steam and was relieved at Rugby by Stanier Cl. 5 4-6-0 45050; another Cl. 40 took over at Crewe.

The North Wales contingent, now at Chester, Rhyl and Llandudno Junction continued work on semi-fasts and freights; several of the class including 75010/2/31/2/4-6 worked on similar services based at Bangor at various times. Chester engines were also noted on local passenger turns to Liverpool Lime Street and in 1959 operated on the Lime Street-Wigan North Western line prior to its dieselisation. The Rhyl engine, 75033 (and later 75034), was regularly employed in the summer months on the North Wales Land Cruise train, the LMR's counterpart to the WR's Radio Land Cruise train. With a mid-morning departure from Llandudno usually behind an Ivatt Cl. 2 2-6-2 tank engine, this popular train picked up passengers along the coast to Rhyl where it reversed. The Standard Cl. 4 4-6-0 then took over and spent a leisurely day meandering down the Clywd Valley line via Denbigh and Corwen to Barmouth, returning to Llandudno via Portmadoc, Caernavon and Bangor; passengers for Rhyl caught a connection to arrive back in time for tea. A former SR 'Devon Belle' Pullman observation car and several LMS 'Coronation Scot' coaches were included in the formation for a time. At the height of their popularity in the late 1950s and early 1960s, before the increase in family car ownership caused business to fall off, there were five Cruise trains operating on the circuit, three originating on the LMR and two from the WR; Standard Cl. 4 4-6-0s were regular performers on these services. In September 1958, Chester West depot was transferred from the WR to the LMR and its GWR Manor Cl. 4-6-0s, 7800/1/7/22/7 were exchanged for 75005/6/20/6/8 from Oswestry bringing to a total of twenty the number of class members regularly to be seen on the North Wales Coast lines. Two of the Chester West engines 75028/33 had a brief spell at Workington in the spring of 1960 before transferring back to the North Wales area at Mold Junction.

During summer 1958, shortage of power at Leicester Central led to the loan of Leicester Midland Standard Cl. 4s 75057/61 for use on semi-fasts and Saturday through trains from Newcastle and the then West Riding of Yorkshire to the South Coast as far as Banbury. Other work included excursions to such diverse destinations as Kings Lynn and Bognor Regis. By early 1960 the Bedford contingent 75040-4/55 had been displaced to Leicester by dieselisation of the St Pancras services. From October of that year, the Leicester allocation could be observed regularly working from Cambridge into the Kings Cross area during stopovers at March depot after powering freights and holiday services from the East Midlands into East Anglia. Later, the class was used to work through to Norwich, Ipswich and Clacton-on-Sea on similar turns. In the autumn of 1961 the Standard Cl. 4s were still operating on passenger trains to Peterborough and Kettering.

The Liverpool area saw the Standard Cl. 4-6-0s continuing to be deployed at Bank Hall and later from Walton on the Hill, Aintree and Edge Hill. The Bank Hall contingent worked as before on the Preston-Wigan line and on through semi-fasts to Rochdale and Bradford. The Southport engines, 75015-9, continued to be used mainly on the Manchester and Rochdale line semi-fasts. For three months at the end of 1958, the double-chimneyed 75029 was at Southport for test purposes. The engine was well received by some of the the footplatemen who regarded its performance as similar to that of a Stanier Cl. 5 4-6-0; other crews were less than impressed.

In May 1961, the LMR allocation was forty six engines, allocated as shown:

Llandudno Junction	(3)	75010-2
Mold Junction	(7)	75013/4/2
		75031/3/53/4
Southport	(5)	75015-9
Willesden	(2)	75030/52
Chester Midland	(6)	75032/4/5/9/50/1
Bletchley	(3)	75036-8
Leicester Midland	(10)	75040-4/57-61
Bank Hall	(5)	75045-9
Nottingham	(5)	75055/6/62-4

The seven engines at Mold Junction were employed on local passenger and freight duties to Crewe and along the coast to Bangor and Holyhead. Nottingham continued to use its allocation on local passenger turns. Together with Ivatt Cl. 2 2-6-0s the engines had by now displaced the LMS Compound 4-4-0s from the Nottingham to Chesterfield and Sheffield stopping trains via the Erewash Valley line. Excursions further afield still featured Standard Cl. 4 4-6-0 haulage such as in May 1961 when 75056 headed a train from Basford North to Windsor outward via High Wycombe and Maidenhead, returning via Reading and Oxford.

Early in 1960, Willesden had received 75030/52 from North Wales for a three year spell, joined later by 75031. The engines were employed alongside those at Bletchley on semi-fasts and locals from Euston. They were also used on the commuter trains serving the former North London Railway terminus at Broad Street, the 6.05pm departure for Tring being a regular working in the summer of 1962. Earlier, in March 1962, 75052 was involved in a 'failure to stop' incident when working the 5.48pm Euston-Watford local. Passengers for Harrow and Wealdstone, Hatch End and Bushey were alarmed to find their train non-stop to Watford Junction. Not surprisingly, arrival there was several minutes early, after which a large number of somewhat bewildered travellers caught the next available local electric service back towards the capital. A blackboard apology appeared the following morning at the stations concerned.

Freight duties for the Standard Cl. 4 4-6-0s at Willesden included working the lightly used Hammersmith branch of the former North and South West Junction Railway (NSWJR). Wagons for the branch were carried by the daily goods service from Willesden to Kew Bridge North (Midland) depot. About three times per week, a pick-up freight service was operated on the branch, the cargo consisting mostly of coal.

At the end January 1963, following the transfer of control of the Shrewsbury district from the WR, the LMR now had fifty eight of the class, allocated as shown.

Machynlleth	(12)	75002-4/6/9
		75020/1/3/4/6/7/9
Nuneaton	(10)	75010-2/30/2/3/5/6
		75050/2
Bletchley	(7)	75013/4/28/38/9/51/4
Southport	(5)	75015-9
Aston	(4)	75031/4/7/53
Derby	(15)	75040-4/55-64
Bank Hall	(5)	75045-9

Operations in the Shrewsbury district included the former Cambrian Railways' lines and the depots at Croes Newydd, Oswestry and Machynlleth. The class was a common sight on passenger workings on the Cambrian section until the end of steam working in March 1967. Three of the engines at Machynlleth were out-stationed at Pwllheli for fortnightly periods. From here they worked to and from Dovey Junction on the Pwllheli portion of the 'Cambrian Coast Express', serving Paddington, and also featured on the daily Machynlleth freight.

The ten engines at Nuneaton had arrived by January 1963 displacing Ivatt Cl. 4 2-6-0s to Bescot and Crewe South and LMS Jubilee Cl. 4-6-0s into store at Rugby. The new arrivals were used on freights and parcels work on the West Coast main line as well as on local passenger services and mineral trains to Coventry and the Leamington Spa area. When Nuneaton depot was closed in June 1966, the remaining Standard Cl. 4 allocation there, 75018/35/50, transferred to Stoke.

Bletchley received an influx of the class from North Wales for the Euston line duties in the period March to June 1962. By the time the depot closed in July 1965, the three remaining engines, 75013/28/55 had moved to Machynlleth. At the end of 1962 Aston was employing 75031/4/7/53 on local freight and passenger workings in the Birmingham area but by the following September they had all moved to Stoke. From September 1962 the Midland Division engines were concentrated at Derby when 75040-4/55-64 were transferred from Nottingham and Leicester. In reality there was little work for them following dieselisation of most of the local passenger services. By early 1964, the Derby engines had been dispersed to Stoke, Springs Branch, Walton on the Hill, Bletchley and Nuneaton. Stoke depot became a refuge for the class in the closing years of steam on the LMR and by October 1963 some eleven engines 75014/8/30/1/4/6/7/40/53/6/62 were allocated with more to follow later. They were used mainly on local freights although a number were already stored out of use.

By late 1963, Southport's Standard Cl. 4 4-6-0s had all been displaced by dieselisation, transferring to Aintree, Nuneaton and Springs Branch. The latter depot was host to twelve engines 75011/5/7/9/39/41/2/4/51/7-9 by April 1964. The class was used on trip and local freights and started to appear on West Coast Main Line locals as far as Carlisle as well as Bolton and Rochdale line passenger services following the closure of the former L&YR depot at Wigan Central in the same month. Bank Hall continued to use the class on the semi-fasts to East Lancashire although one diagram in 1964 saw them regularly assisting as pilot on the heavy 8.26am Newcastle Scotswood-Manchester Red Bank newspaper empties from York.

In April 1965, the LMR still had fifty eight of the class, distributed as shown:

Machynlleth	(2)	75002/4
Stoke on Trent	(13)	75006/18/20/3
		75030/1/4/6/7
		75040/54/6/62
Croes Newydd	(5)	75009/21/4/9/71
Chester Midland	(2)	75010/2
Skipton	(12)	75011/5/7/9/39
		75041/2/4
		75051/7-9
Bletchley	(3)	75013/28/55
Shrewsbury	(4)	75014/38/53/63
Nuneaton	(4)	75016/35/45/52
Bank Hall	(9)	75026/7/32/3/46-50
Aintree	(4)	75043/60/1/4

Skipton had received all of Springs Branch's Standard Cl. 4s during the previous month. Here they took over the daily Grassington branch freight and were used on the Leeds City-Morecambe Promenade passenger services which were regularly steam hauled until April 1966. In early 1967, Skipton's 75042 was loaned to Tebay to be tried out on banking duties on the six mile climb, mostly at 1 in 75, up Shap Fell on the West Coast main line to Carlisle; this resulted

in several of the class being transferred there in April and May 1967 replacing LMS Fairburn Cl. 4 2-6-4 tank engines and Ivatt Cl. 4 2-6-0s from these duties.

After dieselisation of the Liverpool-Preston line local services in October 1965, the only surviving working for Bank Hall's Standard Cl. 4 4-6-0s on this route was the 4.40pm Liverpool Exchange-Glasgow Central as far as Preston, returning at 9.45pm with the 5.30pm Glasgow-Liverpool. From Aintree the class worked local goods and trip freights to and from the Aintree sorting sidings and the Huskisson and Fazakerley yards. The engines were also observed on passenger turns at Manchester Central and Northwich. 75060 was at Edge Hill for almost a year from June 1965, mostly working local freights. By March 1966, the last remaining Standard Cl. 4s at Chester Midland 75010/2 had joined other class members for work on the Cambrian section based at Croes Newydd and Shrewsbury.

A regular duty for the Shrewsbury engines, 75014/38/53/63, in the summer of 1965 was a daily 325 mile double return trip to Aberystwyth. This consisted of the 4.10am mail from Shrewsbury (the previous night's 9.50pm from York), the 9.50am up 'Cambrian Coast Express' the down service of the same express (2.30pm from Shrewsbury, 11.10am from Paddington) and finally the 6.10pm York mail back to Shrewsbury. Both Shrewsbury and Croes Newydd engines worked local freights to Shotwick, Brymbo and Dee Marsh and also passenger services to Chester and Birkenhead Woodside. It was whilst working the 12.10pm ex-Paddington forward from Chester on 22nd September 1965 that 75024, a Holyhead engine probably in the area in connection with a visit to Oswestry Works, became involved in a rather unusual failure. At Hooton, the left-hand cylinder suddenly shot forth a jet of steam some 15 feet in length at right angles to the engine parallel to the ground. 75024 proceeded cautiously on one cylinder to Rock Ferry still with the steam jet extending across two adjoining tracks. At Rock Ferry, the train was terminated and passengers transferred to a following diesel multiple unit to complete their journey to Birkenhead. In February 1967, Standard Cl. 4 4-6-0s were still rostered for Croes Newydd's local trip freight workings to Llangollen, Weston Rhyn and Gobowen as well as performing the South Fork and Wrexham Exchange pilot duties. The depot closed to steam in June 1967, after which the Standard Cl. 4s were stored prior to withdrawal.

In November 1966, the LMR allocation had been reduced by withdrawals to forty three engines. Concentration of steam power was now in evidence as the engines were distributed over no more than six depots as shown:

Machynlleth	(7)	75002/9/13/24/47/52/5
Shrewsbury	(7)	75004/6/12/4/6/20/9
Croes Newydd	(7)	75010/21/33/46/8/60/71
Skipton	(10)	75015/7/9/26/7
		75039/41/2/58/9
Stoke on Trent	(9)	75018/30/2/4/5/7/40
		75050/62
Aintree	(3)	75043/61/4

More of the class had been drafted into the Shrewsbury district during the previous summer to improve timekeeping on the Cambrian section by allowing for double-heading of most passenger trains. This was the last summer for steam on

Fig. 125
On 5th January 1964, double chimney 75065 makes a spirited start out of Victoria with the 9.50am Ramblers' Excursion for Shalford (near Guildford), the first steam departure from the terminus for several months and also one of the last. The ten coach empty stock was brought in by Cl. U 2-6-0 31616, thus providing the sight of two steam locomotives in the station together, a very rare spectacle during the last years of SR steam.   (Courtney Haydon)

Fig. 126
An up parcels train leaves Ashford on 28th April 1959 headed by 75066, still with single chimney. The engine had undergone an intermediate overhaul at Eastleigh Works six months earlier and would return for its first general overhaul and installation of double chimney in February 1961, having run over 165,000 miles.   (Dennis Ovenden)

Fig. 127
On 31st May 1986, two Severn Valley Railway engines, double chimney 75069 and Stanier Jubilee 4-6-0 5690 Leander power a special train from Hereford to Swindon on their way to the Great Western Society depot at Didcot. The train is seen here approaching Severn Tunnel Junction heading for Gloucester. 75069 remains at work on the Severn Valley Railway. 5690 is now at the East Lancashire Railway at Bury.

(Hugh Ballantyne)

Fig. 128
75077 passes Mount Pleasant, Northam, Southampton with a Bournemouth bound express on 17th May 1958; the engine had achieved over 200,000 miles by the time of its first general overhaul at Eastleigh in May 1961. *(K.W. Wightman)*

Fig. 129
75074, only six months old and hence still with single chimney, heads the 2.35pm Portsmouth-Cardiff through train out of Southampton Central on 5th May 1956. The fifteen members of the class allocated to the SR, 75065-79, all carried the higher water capacity BR1B tenders (4725 gal.) which, in the absence of troughs on the SR, were not fitted with water pick-up gear. 75074 acquired a double chimney at Eastleigh in July 1961 during its first general overhaul. *(E.V. Fry)*

the route and the traditional chorus of whistles sounded at Shrewsbury depot to usher in the New Year was particularly vociferous in the first few minutes of the 1st January 1967, the Standard Cl. 4 4-6-0s playing their part to the full. In February 1967, 75033/48 were still regularly making the daily double return trip to Aberystwyth, both appearing to be in good external condition. Shrewsbury depot closed to steam on the weekend of 4th/5th March. This event coincided with the withdrawal of through services from Paddington to Chester, Birkenhead and the Cambrian line resorts. The last up 'Cambrian Coast Express' was hauled by 75033 and the final down working in charge of 75021. The latter engine returned on the York mail, its whistle sounding almost continuously for the whole trip to acknowledge the many small groups of people assembled by the lineside. Type 2 Cl. 24/25 and Type 3 Cl. 37 diesels took over most of the Cambrian line workings.

The duties for the Skipton, Stoke and Aintree engines remained much as before but by the end of May 1967, nine of the class 75019/24/6/7/30/2/5/7/9 had been moved to Tebay for banking duties to Shap summit. The engines were rostered for four diagrams on this work, although several were stored out of use at both Tebay and Carlisle Upperby. It was reported that the class was unpopular in adverse weather conditions due to draughty cabs when running in reverse. During the latter half of 1967 some 15 class members, 75009/10/5/20/1/33/4/40-3/8/58/9/62 were at Carnforth which also supplied engines for Shap banking turns. Other regular duties included the Grassington branch freight and yard shunting in the Ulverston area. It was one of these engines, 75042 which was involved in an accident one mile south of Lambrigg Crossing signalbox on 19th October 1967. 75042 was returning light from Shap summit to Oxenholme when it ran into the rear of a stationary permanent way inspection saloon coupled to Stanier Cl. 5 4-6-0 45374. Both tenders derailed with the coach chassis coming to rest at right angles across the main line with the body reared into the air. Traffic was diverted via the Midland Division Settle and Carlisle line until the obstruction was cleared early the following morning. The remaining locomotives moved to Carnforth when Tebay closed in January 1968. The class was displaced from Shap Fell duties by the short-lived Type 1 Clayton Cl. 17 diesels in the spring of 1968.

By January 1968, the class survivors 75009/19-21/7/32/4/41/8/62 were grouped at Carnforth where they were still used for a time to deputise for the frequent Cl. 17 diesel failures on the Shap banking duties. Carnforth was one of the last two depots on BR to operate steam locomotives, the other being Lostock Hall which retained Stanier Cl. 5 4-6-0 45110 mainly for steam specials. In August 1968, the last five Standard Cl. 4 4-6-0s, 75009/19/20/7/48 were withdrawn along with the remainder of the steam allocation at Carnforth and Lostock Hall thus marking the official end of steam on British Rail. *(continued on p.140)*

SECTION OF COLOUR ILLUSTRATIONS

Fig. 130   73026 passing Lapworth station with an up train of empty coaching stock in 1965. This locomotive was transferred from Leamington Spa to Tyseley sheds in June 1965, both these depots are indicated, Leamington Spa in former LNER style on the buffer beam and 2A plate on the smokebox door!   *(M. Mensing)*

Fig. 131   73054 ex works at Swindon in lined out Brunswick green livery. The red disc on the cabside denotes GWR/WR route availability.   *(R. C. Riley)*

Fig. 132   73110 passes through Farnborough with a London Waterloo to Bournemouth express 9th June 1962.   *(Rodney Lissenden)*

Fig. 133   73144 nearing Shap station with an up mixed goods train in August 1965   *(M. J. Burnett)*

Fig. 134   75019 leaving Swindon Quarry, Rylstone on the Grassington Branch with a load of stone ballast, 1st June 1968.

(G. W. Morrison)

Fig. 135   75022 just outshopped from Swindon Works after overhaul. Note the cab back plate and the GWR/WR blue route indicator disc on cabside, 18th June 1962.

(Rodney Lissenden)

Fig. 136   75024 with the 5.5pm Birmingham (Snow Hill) to Portsmouth and Southsea leaving Oxford, 15th August 1959.   *(R.C. Riley)*

Fig. 137   75069 climbing westwards up the 1 in 100 gradient to Hookagate after leaving Shrewsbury with a special for Aberystwyth, 22nd September 1991.
(Hugh Ballantyne)

Fig. 138   75070 at Southampton Ocean Terminal with the RCTS 'Solent' rail tour, 20th March 1966.   (M. J. Burnett)

Fig. 139   75071 with the 3.20pm Bath to Templecombe stopping train approaching Templecombe, 3rd July 1961.   (R. C. Riley)

Fig. 140   76015 passes over Tuckingham Viaduct with the local 4.35pm from Bath to Templecombe, 10th April 1965.   *(Hugh Ballantyne)*

Fig. 141   76017 about to reverse in Ropley Yard, Mid–Hants Railway. It was rescued from Woodham Bros. at Barry in January 1974.

(Hugh Ballantyne)

Fig. 142   77001 passes Wortley Junction at Leeds with a pick up goods train which includes four wagons of coal bound for the local gas works.
(G. W. Morrison)

Fig. 143   77003 and 76049 seen at Tebay taking water whilst working the 'Stainmore Limited' RCTS special from Darlington, Saturday 20th January 1962. This train was the last to traverse the Kirkby Stephen to Tebay former North Eastern Railway line.
(G. W. Morrison)

Fig. 144   78031 stands in Crewe South shed yard, 21st April 1963.   *(Rodney Lissenden)*

Fig. 145   78039 in Willesden shed yard in company with LMS 45716, 42431 and 42289, 10th June 1964.   *(Hugh Ballantyne)*

3.7.3 Allocation Summary

75000   5.51 Swindon; 9.51 Shrewsbury; 9.53 Swindon; 8.59 Tyseley; 2.61 Oxford; 7.62 Bristol Barrow Road; 9.62 Leamington Spa; 9.63 Yeovil Town; 6.65 Worcester; 12.65 Withdrawn.

75001   8.51 Shrewsbury; 9.53 Swindon; 9.54 Oxford; 3.63 Bristol Barrow Road; 9.63 Yeovil Town; 12.64 Withdrawn.

75002   8.51 Shrewsbury; 9.53 Swindon; 9.56 Oswestry; 1.57 Swindon; 1.60 Gloucester Barnwood; 9.61 Templecombe; 6.62 Bristol Barrow Road; 9.62 Machynlleth; 12.66 Croes Newydd; 6.67 Stoke on Trent; 8.67 Withdrawn.

75003   8.51 Shrewsbury; 9.53 Swindon; 2.58 Worcester; 7.60 Tyseley; 9.62 Machynlleth; 10.63 Yeovil Town; 6.65 Worcester; 10.65 Withdrawn.

75004   8.51 Bristol Bath Road; 10.51 Shrewsbury; 9.53 Swindon; 9.54 Oxford; 7.55 Cardiff Canton; 9.58 Bristol Barrow Road; 11.61 Templecombe; 5.62 Bath Green Park; 10.62 Machynlleth; 1.66 Shrewsbury; 3.67 Withdrawn.

75005   9.51 Shrewsbury; 9.53 Cardiff Canton; 2.54 Oswestry, 8.58 Chester West; 4.59 Tyseley; 7.60 Worcester; 1.64 Gloucester Horton Road; 3.64 Exmouth Junction; 4.65 Yeovil Town; 6.65 Worcester; 11.65 Withdrawn.

75006   9.51 Swindon; 4.52 Shrewsbury; 9.53 Cardiff Canton; 12.53 Oswestry; 8.58 Chester West; 4.59 Tyseley; 9.62 Machynlleth; 3.63 Croes Newydd; 11.64 Stoke on Trent; 7.65 Tyseley; 11.65 Shrewsbury; 3.67 Croes Newydd; 6.67 Stoke on Trent; 8.67 Withdrawn.

75007   9.51 Shrewsbury; 9.53 Cardiff Canton; 9.58 Oxford; 3.63 Templecombe; 9.64 Yeovil Town; 4.65 Withdrawn.

75008   10.51 Shrewsbury; 10.53 Cardiff Canton; 10.58 Oxford; 7.64 Templecombe; 9.64 Exmouth Junction; 6.65 Worcester; 12.65 Withdrawn.

75009   10.51 Shrewsbury; 9.53 Cardiff Canton; 5.58 Worcester; 8.58 Gloucester Barnwood; 9.61 Templecombe; 11.62 Machynlleth; 3.63 Croes Newydd; 2.66 Llandudno Junction; 6.66 Machynlleth; 12.66 Shrewsbury; 3.67 Croes Newydd; 5.67 Lostock Hall; 6.67 Carnforth; 8.68 Withdrawn.

75010   11.51 Patricroft; 10.53 Llandudno Junction; 5.57 Bangor; 7.57 Llandudno Junction; 10.62 Nuneaton; 3.63 Chester Midland; 3.66 Croes Newydd; 5.67 Lostock Hall; 6.67 Carnforth; 10.67 Withdrawn.

75011   11.51 Patricroft; 10.53 Llandudno Junction; 10.62 Nuneaton; 5.63 Derby; 11.63 Springs Branch; 3.65 Skipton; 11.66 Withdrawn.

75012   11.51 Patricroft; 10.53 Llandudno Junction; 5.57 Bangor; 7.57 Llandudno Junction; 10.62 Nuneaton; 3.63 Chester Midland; 1.66 Machynlleth; 3.66 Croes Newydd; 3.66 Shrewsbury; 7.66 Croes Newydd; 7.66 Shrewsbury; 1.67 Withdrawn.

75013   11.51 Patricroft; 10.53 Llandudno Junction; 9.59 Chester Midland; 4.60 Mold Junction; 4.62 Bletchley; 6.65 Machynlleth; 12.66 Shrewsbury; 3.67 Croes Newydd; 5.67 Stoke on Trent; 8.67 Withdrawn.

75014   12.51 Patricroft; 10.53 Llandudno Junction; 9.57 Chester Midland; 6.59 Llandudno Junction; 9.59 Chester Midland; 4.60 Mold Junction; 4.62 Bletchley; 5.63 Stoke on Trent; 6.64 Tyseley; 9.64 Shrewsbury; 12.66 Withdrawn. Preserved on the North York Moors Railway at Grosmont.

75015   12.51 Southport; 12.63 Aintree; 4.64 Springs Branch; 3.65 Skipton; 2.67 Carnforth; 12.67 Withdrawn.

75016   1.52 Southport; 5.63 Nuneaton; 6.65 Shrewsbury; 3.67 Croes Newydd; 6.67 Colwick as a stationary boiler; 7.67 Withdrawn.

75017   1.52 Southport; 12.63 Springs Branch; 3.65 Skipton; 1.67 Withdrawn.

75018   3.52 Southport; 5.63 Nuneaton; 6.63 Bangor; 9.63 Stoke on Trent; 4.66 Nuneaton; 6.66 Stoke on Trent; 6.67 Withdrawn.

75019   3.52 Southport; 12.63 Springs Branch; 3.65 Skipton; 1.67 Carnforth; 4.67 Tebay; 1.68 Carnforth; 8.68 Withdrawn.

75020   11.53 Oswestry; 8.58 Chester West; 4.59 Tyseley; 6.59 Machynlleth; 3.63 Croes Newydd; 1.65 Stoke on Trent; 1.66 Shrewsbury; 3.67 Aintree; 6.67 Carnforth; 8.68 Withdrawn.

75021   11.53 Cardiff Canton; 9.58 Bristol Barrow Road; 10.60 Oxford; 5.62 Machynlleth; 3.63 Croes Newydd; 3.66 Shrewsbury; 7.66 Croes Newydd: 4.67 Carnforth; 2.68 Withdrawn.

75022   12.53 Cardiff Canton; 6.57 Swansea Victoria; 7.57 Cardiff Canton; 9.58 Bristol Barrow Road; 9.61 Oxford; 4.64 Exmouth Junction; 1.65 Bristol Barrow Road; 2.65 Exmouth Junction; 6.65 Worcester; 12.65 Withdrawn.

75023   12.53 Oswestry; 9.56 Swindon; 11.57 Worcester; 8.58 Gloucester Barnwood; 9.61 Templecombe; 9.62 Machynlleth; 3.63 Croes Newydd; 1.65 Stoke on Trent; 1.66 Withdrawn;

75024   12.53 Oswestry; 2.58 Shrewsbury; 12.58 Oxford; 3.59 Swindon; 8.59 Tyseley; 11.62 Machynlleth; 3.63 Croes Newydd; 6.65 Holyhead; 7.66 Machynlleth; 12.66 Stoke on Trent; 5.67 Tebay; 11.67 Withdrawn.

75025   4.54 Laira; 6.56 Swindon; 11.57 Worcester; 8.60 Machynlleth; 11.60 Worcester; 1.64 Gloucester Horton Road; 3.64 Exmouth Junction; 6.65 Worcester; 12.65 Withdrawn.

75026   5.54 Laira; 6.56 Swindon; 1.57 Oswestry; 8.58 Chester West; 4.59 Tyseley; 6.59 Machynlleth; 3.63 Croes Newydd; 2.65 Bank Hall; 10.66 Aintree; 11.66 Skipton; 3.67 Carnforth; 4.67 Tebay; 12.67 Withdrawn.

75027   5.54 Laira; 9.54 Reading; 12.54 Oxford; 2.59 Swindon; 2.60 Templecombe; 11.62 Machynlleth; 3.63 Croes Newydd; 2.65 Bank Hall; 10.66 Aintree; 11.66 Skipton; 1.67 Carnforth; 4.67 Tebay; 1.68 Carnforth; 8.68 Withdrawn; Preserved on the Bluebell Railway at Horsted Keynes.

75028   5.54 Laira; 6.56 Oswestry; 8.58 Chester West; 6.59 Rhyl; 9.59 Chester West; 4.60 Workington; 6.60 Mold Junction; 6.61 Rhyl; 9.61 Mold Junction; 4.62 Bletchley; 6.65 Machynlleth; 12.65 Withdrawn.

75029   5.54 Laira; 9.54 Reading; 11.54 Gloucester Horton Road; 12.54 Oxford; 10.58 Southport; 1.59 Oxford; 2.59 Swindon; 11.60 Oxford; 1.61 Tyseley; 11.62 Machynlleth; 3.63 Croes Newydd; 6.65 Llandudno Junction; 9.66 Shrewsbury; 3.67 Croes Newydd; 6.67 Stoke on Trent; 8.67 Withdrawn.
Preserved on the East Somerset Railway at Cranmore.

75030   6.53 Bletchley; 6.54 Llandudno Junction; 2.55 Bletchley; 2.55 Llandudno Junction 12.56 Bletchley; 11.59 Chester Northgate; 1.60 Willesden; 1.63 Nuneaton; 9.63 Stoke on Trent; 5.67 Tebay; 12.67 Withdrawn.

75031   6.53 Bletchley; 2.55 Llandudno Junction; 12.55 Chester Midland; 5.57 Bangor; 7.57 Llandudno Junction; 9.57 Chester Midland; 6.59 Llandudno Junction; 9.59 Chester Midland; 4.60 Mold Junction; 6.61 Rhyl; 9.61 Willesden; 12.62 Aston; 9.63 Stoke on Trent; 2.66 Withdrawn.

75032   6.53 Bletchley; 2.55 Llandudno Junction; 12.55 Chester Midland; 6.56 Llandudno Junction; 10.56 Chester Midland; 7.57 Bangor; 11.57 Llandudno Junction; 9.59 Chester Midland; 6.62 Llandudno Junction; 10.62 Nuneaton; 5.63 Southport; 7.63 Bank Hall; 2.66 Stoke on Trent; 5.67 Tebay; 1.68 Carnforth; 2.68 Withdrawn.

75033   7.53 Bletchley; 2.55 Chester Midland; 6.56 Llandudno Junction; 10.56 Chester Midland; 7.57 Rhyl; 8.57 Chester Midland; 6.59 Rhyl; 9.59 Chester West; 4.60 Workington; 6.60 Mold Junction; 4.62 Rhyl; 9.62 Llandudno Junction; 10.62 Nuneaton; 5.63 Southport; 7.63 Bank Hall; 4.66 Heaton Mersey; 4.66 Chester Midland; 5.66 Croes Newydd; 1.67 Shrewsbury; 3.67 Croes Newydd; 4.67 Carnforth; 12.67 Withdrawn.

75034   7.53 Bletchley; 2.55 Chester Midland; 5.56 Accrington; 8.56 Chester Midland; 8.57 Rhyl; 9.57 Bangor; 11.57 Llandudno Junction; 9.58 Chester Midland; 6.61 Rhyl; 9.61 Mold Junction; 4.62 Rhyl; 9.62 Llandudno Junction; 10.62 Nuneaton; 12.62 Aston; 9.63 Stoke on Trent; 6.67 Carnforth; 2.68 Withdrawn.

75035   8.53 Bletchley; 2.55 Chester Midland; 8.57 Bangor; 11.57 Llandudno Junction; 9.58 Chester Midland; 6.62 Rhyl; 9.62 Llandudno Junction; 10.62 Nuneaton; 6.63 Bangor; 12.64 Nuneaton; 6.66 Stoke on Trent; 5.67 Tebay; 7.67 Withdrawn;

75036   8.53 Bletchley; 6.61 Llandudno Junction; 10.62 Nuneaton; 6.63 Bangor; 7.63 Nuneaton; 9.63 Stoke on Trent; 6.66 Withdrawn;

75037   8.53 Bletchley; 12.62 Aston; 9.63 Stoke on Trent; 5.67 Tebay; 12.67 Withdrawn.

75038   8.53 Bletchley; 10.64 Shrewsbury; 12.65 Withdrawn.

75039   8.53 Bletchley; 2.55 Chester Midland; 3.62 Bletchley; 5.63 Derby; 11.63 Springs Branch; 3.65 Skipton; 1.67 Carnforth; 4.67 Tebay; 9.67 Withdrawn.

75040   8.53 Bedford; 10.53 Accrington; 1.55 Bedford; 1.60 Derby; 2.60 Leicester Midland; 9.62 Derby; 10.63 Stoke on Trent; 6.67 Carnforth; 10.67 Withdrawn.

75041   9.53 Bedford; 10.53 Accrington; 1.55 Bedford; 1.60 Leicester Midland; 9.62 Derby; 11.63 Springs Branch; 3.65 Skipton; 4.67 Carnforth; 1.68 Withdrawn.

75042   9.53 Bedford; 10.53 Accrington; 1.55 Bedford; 4.59 Leicester Midland; 9.62 Derby; 11.63 Springs Branch; 3.65 Skipton; 4.67 Carnforth; 11.67 Withdrawn.

75043   9.53 Bedford; 10.53 Accrington; 1.55 Bedford; 1.60 Leicester Midland; 9.62 Derby; 11.63 Walton on the Hill; 12.63 Aintree; 6.67 Carnforth; 12.67 Withdrawn;

75044   9.53 Bedford; 10.53 Accrington; 1.55 Bedford; 1.60 Nottingham; 2.60 Leicester Midland; 9.62 Derby; 11.63 Springs Branch; 3.65 Skipton; 3.66 Withdrawn.

75045   9.53 Accrington; 10.55 Bank Hall; 5.63 Nuneaton; 4.66 Withdrawn.

75046   10.53 Accrington; 11.55 Bank Hall; 4.66 Heaton Mersey; 4.66 Chester Midland; 5.66 Croes Newydd; 5.67 Stoke on Trent; 8.67 Withdrawn.

75047   10.53 Accrington; 11.55 Bank Hall; 2.66 Stoke on Trent; 3.66 Croes Newydd; 7.66 Machynlleth; 12.66 Croes Newydd; 1.67 Shrewsbury; 3.67 Croes Newydd; 6.67 Stoke on Trent; 8.67 Withdrawn.

75048   10.53 Accrington; 11.55 Bank Hall; 4.66 Chester Midland; 5.66 Croes Newydd; 5.67 Lostock Hall; 6.67 Carnforth; 8.68 Withdrawn.

75049   10.53 Accrington; 11.55 Bank Hall; 5.56 Chester Midland; 8.56 Bank Hall; 10.66 Withdrawn.

75050   11.56 Llandudno Junction; 9.57 Chester Midland; 6.62 Bangor; 9.62 Llandudno Junction; 10.62 Nuneaton; 5.63 Bank Hall; 2.66 Stoke on Trent; 3.66 Nuneaton; 6.66 Stoke on Trent; 11.66 Withdrawn.

75051   11.56 Chester Midland; 6.58 Rhyl; 9.58 Chester Midland; 6.62 Bletchley; 5.63 Derby; 11.63 Springs Branch; 3.65 Skipton; 10.66 Withdrawn.

75052   12.56 Bletchley; 12.59 Chester Northgate; 1.60 Willesden; 1.63 Nuneaton; 6.65 Holyhead; 7.66 Machynlleth; 12.66 Croes Newydd; 6.67 Stoke on Trent; 8.67 Withdrawn.

75053   1.57 Chester Midland; 6.58 Rhyl; 9.58 Chester Midland; 6.60 Rhyl; 9.60 Mold Junction; 4.62 Bletchley; 12.62 Aston; 9.63 Stoke on Trent; 9.64 Shrewsbury; 9.66 Withdrawn;

75054   1.57 Chester Midland; 6.58 Rhyl; 9.58 Chester Midland; 6.60 Rhyl; 9.60 Mold Junction; 4.62 Bletchley; 1.65 Stoke on Trent; 8.66 Withdrawn.

75055   1.57 Bedford; 1.60 Nottingham; 2.60 Leicester Midland; 1.61 Nottingham; 2.62 Leicester Midland; 9.62 Derby; 5.63 Bletchley; 9.64 Shrewsbury; 10.64 Bletchley; 6.65 Machynlleth; 12.66 Shrewsbury; 3.67 Croes Newydd; 5.67 Stoke on Trent; 5.67 Withdrawn.

75056   3.57 Nottingham; 9.62 Derby; 5.63 Bletchley; 9.63 Stoke on Trent; 6.66 Withdrawn.

75057   3.57 Leicester Midland; 9.62 Derby; 11.63 Springs Branch; 3.65 Skipton; 2.66 Withdrawn.

75058   4.57 Leicester Midland; 9.62 Derby; 1.64 Springs Branch; 3.65 Skipton; 4.67 Carnforth; 12.67 Withdrawn.

75059   4.57 Leicester Midland; 9.62 Derby; 11.63 Springs Branch; 3.65 Skipton; 4.67 Carnforth; 7.67 Withdrawn.

75060   5.57 Leicester Midland; 9.62 Derby; 11.63 Walton on the Hill; 12.63 Aintree; 6.65 Edge Hill; 4.66 Heaton Mersey; 4.66 Chester Midland; 5.66 Croes Newydd; 4.67 Withdrawn.

75061   5.57 Leicester Midland; 9.62 Derby; 11.63 Walton on the Hill; 12.63 Aintree; 2.67 Withdrawn.

75062   5.57 Nottingham; 9.62 Derby; 10.63 Stoke on Trent; 5.67 Lostock Hall; 6.67 Carnforth; 2.68 Withdrawn.

75063   6.57 Nottingham; 9.62 Derby; 5.63 Nuneaton; 9.64 Shrewsbury; 5.66 Withdrawn.

75064   6.57 Nottingham; 9.62 Derby; 11.63 Walton on the Hill; 12.63 Aintree; 5.67 Withdrawn.

75065   8.55 Dover; 6.59 Bournemouth; 8.61 Eastleigh; 11.62 Basingstoke; 3.63 Eastleigh; 9.66 Withdrawn;

75066   9.55 Dover; 6.59 Bournemouth; 7.61 Eastleigh; 11.62 Basingstoke; 3.63 Eastleigh; 1.66 Withdrawn.

75067   9.55 Dover; 6.59 Bournemouth; 8.61 Eastleigh; 11.62 Brighton; 4.63 Stewarts Lane; 9.63 Norwood Junction; 12.63 Eastleigh; 10.64 Withdrawn.

75068   9.55 Dover; 6.59 Bournemouth; 5.61 Eastleigh; 11.62 Brighton; 4.63 Stewarts Lane; 9.63 Norwood Junction; 12.63 Eastleigh; 7.67 Withdrawn.

75069   9.55 Dover; 6.59 Bournemouth; 11.59 Stewarts Lane; 8.63 Nine Elms; 5.65 Eastleigh; 9.66 Withdrawn; Preserved on Severn Valley Railway at Bridgnorth

75070   10.55 Exmouth Junction; 6.56 Bath Green Park; 3.57 Eastleigh; 1.59 Three Bridges; 2.59 Brighton; 1.60 Three Bridges; 10.62 Stewarts Lane; 8.63 Nine Elms; 5.65 Eastleigh; 9.66 Withdrawn.

75071   10.55 Exmouth Junction; 6.56 Bath Green Park; 11.62 Templecombe; 7.64 Croes Newydd; 6.67 Stoke on Trent; 8.67 Withdrawn.

75072   11.55 Exmouth Junction; 6.56 Bath Green Park; 10.62 Templecombe; 12.65 Withdrawn.

75073   11.55 Exmouth Junction; 6.56 Eastleigh; 3.57 Bath Green Park; 11.62 Templecombe; 12.65 Withdrawn.

75074   11.55 Exmouth Junction; 6.56 Eastleigh; 8.57 Basingstoke; 1.59 Stewarts Lane; 7.63 Norwood Junction; 12.63 Eastleigh; 8.64 Nine Elms; 5.65 Eastleigh; 7.67 Withdrawn.

75075   11.55 Exmouth Junction; 6.56 Basingstoke; 1.59 Three Bridges; 10.62 Stewarts Lane; 7.63 Norwood Junction; 12.63 Eastleigh; 7.67 Withdrawn.

75076   12.55 Exmouth Junction; 6.56 Basingstoke; 3.63 Nine Elms; 5.65 Eastleigh; 7.67 Withdrawn.

75077   12.55 Exmouth Junction; 6.56 Basingstoke; 3.63 Nine Elms; 5.65 Eastleigh; 7.67 Withdrawn.

75078   1.56 Exmouth Junction; 6.56 Basingstoke; 3.63 Nine Elms; 5.65 Eastleigh; 7.66 Withdrawn. Preserved on the Keighley & Worth Valley Railway at Haworth.

75079   1.56 Exmouth Junction; 6.56 Basingstoke; 3.63 Eastleigh; 11.66 Withdrawn. Stored on the Plym Valley Railway at Marsh Mills Plymouth with a view to preservation.

3.8 Maintenance

For the Standard Cl. 4 4-6-0s, the official recommended period between works visits was 28 months to intermediate and 56 months to general overhauls; the schedule for repairs was the same as that described for the Cl. 5 4-6-0s in section 2.8. Figures for average mileage to intermediate and general overhaul are given in Table 30. Also included is a comparison of representative repair costs between the Standard Cl. 4 4-6-0s and the GWR Manor and Grange Cl. 4-6-0s; the latter two classes although showing similar repair costs per mile achieved significantly less mileage before requiring general overhaul.

For the LMR allocation of Standard Cl. 4 4-6-0s over the 1954-7 period, intermediate overhaul on average was carried out at 30.9 months at a cost of around £1,600 whilst for general overhaul, equivalent figures were 60.8 months and £3,150. For the SR allocation, average time to intermediate

and general overhauls was 31.3 and 69.4 months respectively for the four years 1958-61. Average mileage for the whole of the LMR allocation over the seven years from 1957-63 is given in Table 31. The figures are shown for groups of five engines, reflecting each group's shed allocation over this period. The 30,000 average annual mileage per locomotive masks significant differences between groups. For Group 2, 75015-9 based at Southport and Group 6, 75045-9 at Bank Hall, their duties included intensive use on semi-fasts to Manchester and also to Bradford Exchange via the Calder Valley main line. This work provided opportunity to achieve higher daily mileages on a regular basis. In contrast, engines based in North Wales were used on shorter distance work which generated lower annual mileage rates. With the advent of diesel power in the early 1960s, all groups were displaced from their traditional work as seen by the drop in annual

Table 30

Standard Cl. 4 4-6-0s 75000-75079

Comparison with Selected Classes

Representative Repair Costs and Average Mileage to Overhaul

Class	Data For Year	Cost per Mile (New Pence)			Average Mileage ('000s) to:	
		Engine & Boiler	Tender	Total	Intermediate Overhaul	General Overhaul
BR Standard 4 4-6-0	1956-7	3.40	0.51	3.91	93.4	166.7
BR Standard 4 4-6-0★	1954-7	-	-	-	80.6	188.8
BR Standard 4 4-6-0★★	1957	-	-	-	91.2	175.0
GWR Manor 4-6-0	1957	3.45	0.50	3.95	-	136.3
GWR Grange 4-6-0	1957	3.20	0.52	3.72	-	158.9
LMS Compound 4-4-0	1956	-	-	-	53.8	116.9

★ Data for LMR allocation
★★ Data for WR allocation

Table 31

Standard Cl. 4 4-6-0s LMR Allocation: Annual Mileage Statistics 1957-1963

Year	Average Annual Mileage ('000s) per locomotive. LMR Allocation: Forty five locomotives, 75010-9, 75030-64.									
	(1) 75010-4	(2) 75015-9	(3) 75030-4	(4) 75035-9	(5) 75040-4	(6) 75045-9	(7) 75050-4	(8) 75055-9	(9) 75060-4	Total Allocation
1957	30.0	36.2	31.7	32.0	36.3	44.8	35.5	32.3	23.0	33.5
1958	30.3	36.7	24.8	28.5	34.6	44.7	32.7	39.9	40.4	34.7
1959	29.1	38.7	33.6	32.6	35.2	45.0	29.7	37.2	38.3	35.5
1960	28.8	34.9	27.9	30.8	31.9	39.7	29.1	32.5	29.1	31.6
1961	24.6	34.9	22.2	25.0	30.2	43.9	21.2	28.9	28.8	28.9
1962	21.5	31.8	18.6	23.8	24.3	38.5	21.9	24.5	21.9	25.2
1963	18.8	24.5	19.4	18.2	16.5	34.3	15.5	19.1	17.8	20.5
Average per loco per year	26.2	34.0	25.5	27.3	29.9	41.6	26.5	30.6	28.5	30.0

Allocations
(1) 75010-4 mainly in North Wales.
(2) 75015-9 at Southport.
(3) 75030-4 mainly at Bletchley and in North Wales.
(4) 75035-9 mainly at Bletchley and in North Wales.
(5) 75040-4 at Bedford, Leicester Midland and Derby.
(6) 75045-9 at Bank Hall.
(7) 75050-4 mainly at Bletchley, Willesden and in North Wales.
(8) 75055-9 at Bedford, Leicester Midland, Nottingham and Derby.
(9) 75060-4 at Leicester Midland, Nottingham and Derby.

Fig. 146
Homeward bound commuters leave Woldingham on the 5.37pm London Bridge-East Grinstead on 24th May 1962 with double chimney 75075 in charge. Note the triangle below the cabside numerals indicating the engine has been fitted with water softening apparatus.   (Courtney Haydon)

Fig. 147
Double chimney 75078 speeds a Bournemouth line semi-fast through Raynes Park on 24th March 1962. The engine is now preserved on the Keighley and Worth Valley Railway at Haworth.   (Rodney Lissenden)

Fig. 148
Double chimney 75078 is bound for Reading with a train from Redhill at Ash Junction on 3rd October 1964. The engine had accrued around 300,000 miles by this date.   (Rodney Lissenden)

Fig. 149
75079, still with single chimney, hurries the 12.39pm Waterloo-Basingstoke semi-fast towards Wimbledon past Durnsford Road power station and carriage sidings on 2nd March 1957; Bo-Bo electric locomotive DS 74 is at rest on the approach line to the power station. 75079 is at present stored awaiting restoration on the Plym Valley Railway at Marsh Mills near Plymouth.
(R.C. Riley)

Fig. 150
75000 reposes in fully lined green at Swindon depot on 22nd February 1959. The 'blue spot' route restriction indicator applied below the cabside numerals is prominent.
(G. Wheeler)

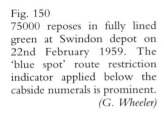

Fig. 151
75001 is seen under construction in Swindon 'A' Shop in July 1951. The engine carries the Bristol Bath Road shed code 82A, its proposed initial allocation but the move was cancelled before delivery in favour of Shrewsbury.
(G. Wheeler)

Table 32

Standard Cl. 4 4-6-0s
Original LMR Allocation: 75010-9, 75030-64
Cumulative Mileage at end 1963

Engine Number	Mileage at 12.63	Engine Number	Mileage at 12.63
75010	334,305	75046	392,464
75011	331,606	75047	395,398
75012	331,047	75048	398,848
75013	333,790	75049	411,070
75014	332,859	75050	192,040
75015	414,255	75051	202,661
75016	403,922	75052	164,631
75017	401,163	75053	181,507
75018	403,552	75054	186,935
75019	423,228	75055	205,635
75030	285,918	75056	205,631
75031	307,544	75057	226,257
75032	305,887	75058	220,646
75033	308,003	75059	213,369
75034	294,581	75060	221,374
75035	294,513	75061	190,940
75036	323,951	75062	189,708
75037	312,510	75063	189,973
75038	335,504	75064	184,372
75039	321,992		
75040	325,151		
75041	308,513	Note: These figures do	
75042	319,885	not represent the final	
75043	319,262	mileages for these	
75044	324,001	engines.	
75045	416,330		

mileage to just over 20,000 per locomotive. Cumulative mileage achieved by the end of 1963 for each of the LMR class members is given in Table 32. For the WR and SR allocation, cumulative mileage at various dates where known is given in Table 33.

Annual mileages in excess of 45,000 for several of the class are recorded as follows:

Engine	Miles	Year	Engine	Miles	Year
75045	49,083	1956	75048	49,029	1957
	47,911	1958		45,638	1959
	47,000	1960	75049	47,824	1956
75046	45,350	1957		48,344	1959
75047	46,941	1957		46,460	1961
	45,512	1959	75057	46,294	1958
			75060	49,769	1958

At the other end of the scale, a few engines recorded annual mileages of less than 15,000.

Engine	Miles	Year	Engine	Miles	Year
75030	12,126	1961	75050	11,323	1963
75037	14,979	1963	75052	14,415	1963
75042	10,257	1963	75053	11,224	1963

Works responsibility for all major overhauls of the Standard Cl. 4 4-6-0s is given in Table 34. Also included is a list of Works in which the class was noted from time to time undergoing light and non-classified repairs. A 1959 proposal to maintain the SR allocation, 75065-79, at Swindon was not pursued. The engines repaired at Darlington were 'run in' on freight turns to Tyneside and York as well as on local parcels workings to Bishop Auckland, Middlesbrough and Saltburn. These workings represented some of the very few occasions when the class was noted on revenue service in the North East. In addition, it was reported that Cowlairs Works gave several LMR-based engines general overhauls between May 1965 and January 1966. Typical of Cowlairs practice most, if

Table 33
Standard Class 4 4-6-0s 75000-75079
Original WR and SR Allocation
Cumulative Mileage at Various Dates

WR Allocation 75000-9/20-9			SR Allocation 75065-79		
Engine Number	Cumulative Mileage	Date	Engine Number	Cumulative Mileage	Date
75000-4	No information		75065	244,436	10.63
75005	380,205	12.63	75066	247,857	1.64
75006	275,652	12.63	75067	195,790	8.62
75007-9	No information		75068	156,483	12.60
75020	233,702	12.63	75069	240,501	7.63
75021-4	No information		75070	237,215	7.63
75025	245,333	12.63	75071	171,757	2.61
75026-7	No information		75072	155,014	10.60
75028	115,305	02.60	75073	260,214	10.63
75029	No information		75074	256,933	1.64
			75075	196,624	8.61
			75076	205,132	5.61
			75077	279,071	1.64
			75078	257,166	1.63
			75079	241,192	2.63

Note 1: 75009/28 transferred to LMR in August 1958 and June 1959 respectively.
75071/2/3 transferred to WR in February 1958.
Note 2: The figures do not represent the final mileages for these engines.

Table 34

Standard Cl. 4 4-6-0s 75000-75079

Works Repairs

Region	All Repairs including Intermediate and General Overhauls	Light Casual and Non-classified Repairs Only
WR	Swindon (to end 1962) Derby (September 1958 - April 1959) (July 1962- November 1963) Oswestry Wolverhampton Caerphilly Doncaster (January 1961-September 1963) Darlington (September 1963-mid 1964) Eastleigh (from March 1964)	Newton Abbot Bristol Barrow Road depot
LMR★	Derby (to November 1963) Darlington (September 1963 to mid-1964) Eastleigh (from March 1964)	Crewe, Horwich, Bow, Rugby
SR	Eastleigh	Ashford (Eastern Section engines, 75065-9 to April 1959) Stewarts Lane electric depot
★	Cowlairs was reported to have given general overhauls to several LMR based members of the class in 1965; see section 3.8.	

not all, of these engines emerged with their shed allocations painted in full on the bufferbeam. Among those noted were:

75010	01.66	75026	09.65
75012	05.65	75032	07.65
75020	07.65	75048	09.65
75024	07.65	75071	09.65

The engines were noted on 'running-in' turns from Corkerhill, Eastfield, Motherwell, Polmadie and St Rollox depots; these visits were virtually the only occasions when the class was observed in Scotland.

3.9 Modifications in Service

The main modifications carried out on the Standard Cl. 5 4-6-0s were also applied to the Cl. 4 4-6-0s. These included changes to the rocking grate bars, the system of cylinder lubrication, the Downs pattern sanding gear and the cab-tender arrangements; full details are given in section 2.9. Further modifications to improve steaming characteristics together with other detail changes are discussed below in section 3.9.1.

An insight into some of the problems associated with the construction and early testing of the class in 1951/2 has been made available by Mr. Alan Clothier, employed in the Swindon Works drawing office at the time.

Standard Class 4 4-6-0s: Early experience at Swindon Works by Mr. Alan Clothier.

Frames for 75000 were set up and erecting commenced in the AE Shop at Swindon Works during the week ending 7th April 1951. With myself present as the Drawing Office representative from the Boiler Section, the boiler was first tried, minus cleating, on 16th April. It would not fit between the frames owing to poor lapping of the corner joints making the firebox wide with respect to drawing. This produced repercussions later as, combined with over-thick seatings, it had the result of making the mud plugs project outside the frames sufficient for them to foul the driving wheel balance weights. The boiler was finally fitted successfully on 9th May and on the following day, 75000 went on its Works trial to Dauntsey with Mr. K.J. Cook (Regional Mechanical and Electrical Engineer) and Mr. C.T. Roberts (Works Manager) aboard. 75000 was then held in works for about a fortnight for adjustments and for preparation for its trip to Marylebone on 23rd May where it was inspected by Mr. R.A. Riddles and again by Mr. E.S. Cox at Swindon Works on 28th May; inside, the cab was painted light cream!

On 31st May, 75000 travelled to Eastbourne for display before the Railway Congress there on 2nd June and was exhibited along with Standard Cl. 5 4-6-0 73001, Britannia Pacific 70009 (straight from trial running with Waterloo-Bournemouth expresses), English Electric/Bulleid 0-6-0 diesel electric shunter 15227, Ivatt/Fell 4-8-4 diesel mechanical 10100, and Bulleid/Raworth Co-Co electric CC 20003. Several days later, 75000 returned to Swindon Works and attempts were made to rectify the trouble experienced with the steam sanding gear, together with other other minor modifications.

During the week ending 14th July 1951, 75000 was placed in traffic working from Swindon shed, its allocated depot. The engine commenced by working local passenger services to Reading and on 11th July was on 10.25am Swindon-Reading, 2.40pm Reading-Swindon, 5.00pm Swindon-Bristol and 8.25pm Bristol-Swindon. That evening, I travelled from Christian Malford Halt back to Swindon behind 75000 and was favourably impressed, as were the crew, with whom I had a long conversation on arrival at Swindon. 75000 worked this and other local passenger turns including the 2.42pm Swindon-Paddington on 16th July (see photograph in Railway Magazine, Vol. 605, No.97 September 1951, page 603) until on 12th August, one of the tender roller bearings developed a fault whilst the engine was at Moreton Cutting. 75000 was immediately returned to Swindon Works for inspection and enquiry.

The first Lot of ten engines was completed in October when, apart from 75006 now allocated to Swindon, the remaining nine engines were at Shrewsbury. Originally, it had been planned to follow this Lot at Swindon with the initial Lot of Standard Cl. 3 2-6-2 tank engines (82XXX) but owing to late delivery of materials, etc., to the shops, the next batch of Standard Cl. 4 4-6-0s, Lot 391, 75010-19, was commenced. 75006 was used principally on the 9.28am Swindon-Gloucester, 2.40pm Gloucester-Swindon, 6.10pm Swindon-Westbury passenger and milk empties, returning from Trowbridge with the 10.00pm express as far as Swindon. On 5th November 1951 75006, by now in filthy condition, was returned to Swindon Works and prepared for tests, initially on the Swindon Test Plant. By 31st December, 75006 had been fitted up with the customary front-end shelter for road testing with the dynamometer car and 18 'eights' (bogies) between Moreton Cutting and Stoke Gifford which commenced on 15th January 1952. Two days later, with the same load and a constant steaming rate of some 19,000lb per hour, the tubeplates began to leak excessively and the return trip was terminated at Swindon. Firing had been at the rate of one hundredweight of coal every 1.8 minutes. Mr. E.S. Cox accompanied a further test run with the same load and steaming rate on 24th January when the train passed Swindon three minutes early at a speed of 57mph and the boiler blowing off hard!'

Further reference to these tests is given in the following section.

3.9.1 Steaming Characteristics

Performance and efficiency tests on the Standard Cl. 4 4-6-0 design were commissioned in January 1952. The locomotive selected for testing was 75006 which was built in September 1951 and had run 4,600 miles in traffic; a further 2,910 miles was completed during the test period. Static experiments at the Swindon testing plant established the boiler and cylinder performances and efficiencies and these were supplemented by road tests. Continuous rates of water evaporation of 19,600 lbs per hour were maintained with both types of coal used, a Welsh sourced grade 2A soft fuel from Bedwas colliery and grade 2B Blidworth Cobbles, a hard coal from the East Midlands. Calorific values at 14,220 and 13,890 British Thermal Units per dry lb. respectively were similar as was the chemical analysis. At the above steaming rate, 75006 had still not reached its 'grate limit', defined as the point where no increase in steam production with respect to firing rate can be obtained even if the air necessary for combustion can be supplied. Extrapolation of the boiler efficiency characteristics indicated that steaming rates of up to 22,490 lb per hour were theoretically possible. Accordingly, further work was authorised at Swindon to improve the efficiency of the 'front-end' draughting arrangement by developing a double blastpipe and chimney. The first engine to receive the modification was 75029 in May 1957. Subsequent testing confirmed a water evaporation rate of 22,400 lb per hour prompting the announcement that all 80 of the class would receive double blastpipe and chimney in due course. In the event, only nine engines on the WR were noted with double chimneys, one or two probably with boilers and smokeboxes taken from withdrawn engines. The whole of the SR allocation was converted between October 1960 and November 1961. The original experimental chimney for 75029 was designed and fabricated from sheet steel at Swindon; it was built to the limit of the L1 loading gauge and appeared disproportionately large and ungainly. The shorter, more elegant production chimneys were designed at Brighton for both the WR and SR engines. They were made of cast iron and all were produced at Swindon. The WR engines were converted at Swindon and the SR allocation at Eastleigh as they passed through for overhauls. 75029 eventually received a production chimney in February 1960. Dates of conversion are given in Table 35. Many SR enginemen considered the new draughting arrangements transformed the engines almost to the level of the Standard Cl. 5 4-6-0s in

Table 35

**Standard Cl. 4 4-6-0s 75000–75079
Provision of
Double Blastpipe and Chimney**

Region	Engine Number	Date of Fitting
WR	75003	? .12.59
	75004	10.10.62
	75005	09.02.62
	75006	16.12.60
	75008	12.02.61
	75020	28.11.58
	75022	? .01.59
	75026	25.06.62
	75029	20.05.57 E
		11.02.60 P
SR	75065	22.04.61
	75066	01.04.61
	75067	03.12.60
	75068	21.01.61
	75069	22.10.60
	75070	25.02.61
	75071	18.03.61
	75072	12.11.60
	75073	19.08.61
	75074	29.07.61
	75075	30.09.61
	75076	24.06.61
	75077	10.06.61
	75078	14.10.61
	75079	25.11.61

Notes E: Experimental chimney
P: Production series chimney

performance. Other crews, for example on the S&DJR and later on the Cambrian lines, could detect little if any advantage over their single chimney stablemates. None of the LMR-based engines received double chimneys but it was reported that the blastpipe cap orifice diameter was reduced by $1/8$" for 75010-9 and 75030-49, the conversion being completed by the 3rd of March 1958. It is believed the final LMR batch, 75050-64, was fitted with the modification from new.

3.9.2 Detail Modifications

The WR and SR allocations of Standard Cl. 4 4-6-0s acquired lamp brackets of their respective Region's pattern as detailed in section 2.9.2. The WR contingent also acquired the GWR pattern ATC apparatus which was usually removed before any subsequent transfer to another Region. There were other detail modifications made to various members of the class and these are listed in Table 36. The information is incomplete as changes were not always faithfully recorded, particularly from the early 1960s onward. The modification reference numbers are given below together with a brief description of the work and costs involved. Reference numbers 3980 and 4175 appear to relate to the same

Fig. 152   75002 rests on Swindon depot after delivery from the Works on 26th August 1951. Although carrying a Wolverhampton Stafford Road shed plate, 75002 began working life at Shrewsbury, the proposed Stafford Road allocation being cancelled before delivery.   *(L. Elsey)*

Fig. 153   75002 in lined green livery stands at Willesden depot LMR on 30th May 1964. The engine was working back to its home depot, Machynlleth, after receiving a general overhaul at Eastleigh Works. Note the Eastleigh version of the running plate lining on green painted engines, where both top and bottom edges are lined, the lining being joined   at the footplate and buffer beam to form a panel. Also the electric warning flash is in the eccentric frame angle position sometimes adopted at Eastleigh.   *(Rodney Lissenden)*

Fig. 154
75003 and its BR2 type tender await union outside 'A' Shop at Swindon Works on 24th August 1951. The BR2 tender, in common with the BR1 and BR1A types, had no fall plate which led to increased draughtiness in the cab. This was partly remedied by the fitting of draught screens; subsequent tender designs reinstated the fall plate which largely solved the problem.

(G. Wheeler)

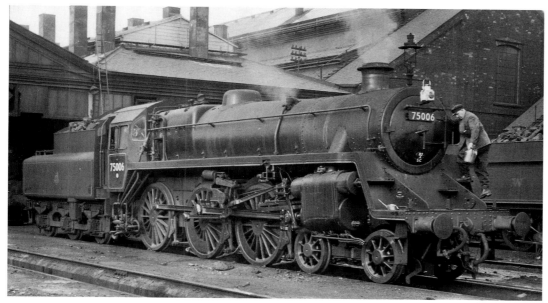

Fig. 155
75006 is pictured at Swindon shed in the early 1950s. Judging by the shed plate Bristol Bath Road depot still appears determined to get in on the act despite the fact that 75006 was never officially allocated there. The only member of the class to be at Bath Road was 75004 for two months from August 1951. (E.V. Fry)

Fig. 156
Type BR2 tender No. 832 awaits connection to 75008 at Swindon Works on 30th September 1951.
(W. Potter)

Table 36
Standard Cl. 4 4-6-0s 75000–75079: Detail Modifications

Mod.★	Locomotive Modified and Date of Modification				
3329	75040:16.06.57	75041:16.06.57	75042:05.10.57	75044:16.06.57	75045:23.05.57
3400	75010:02.12.56	75012:19.06.54	75013:28.11.59	75014:11.09.54	75016:01.10.55
	75017:26.03.55	75019:26.03.55			
3622	75011:30.01.54	75012:30.01.54	75013:30.01.54	75014:11.09.54	75015:06.11.54
	75016:01.01.55	75017:26.03.55	75018:29.01.55	75019:26.03.55	
3698	75010:02.12.56	75012:31.12.56	75019:27.01.57		
3980	75012:23.02.57	75014:no date	75015:19.06.54	75016:19.06.54	75017:19.06.54
	75018:19.06.54	75019:19.06.54			
4175	75010:19.06.54	75011:09.10.54	75013:14.08.54		
4341	75010:16.06.62	75012:07.09.63	75013:29.12.62	75017:20.04.57	75019:24.02.62
4542	75044:26.01.63				
4983	75009:no date	75013:29.12.62	75014:02.12.62	75016:19.05.62	75018:02.12.62
	75020:no date	75023:no date	75025:no date	75027:no date	75028:02.12.62
	75030:26.12.59	75035:24.03.62	75036:26.12.59	75037:26.12.59	75038:27.02.60
	75044:26.01.63	75045:26.01.63	75047:06.10.62	75052:23.04.60	75054:06.10.62
	75055:26.01.63	75057:14.07.63	75060:23.02.63	75063:08.09.62	
	75065-78:no date	75079: 11.58			
5900	75010:02.12.56	75011:27.01.57	75012:31.12.56	75015:03.11.57	75018:31.05.57
	75030:04.10.58	75031:18.04.59	75032:01.11.58	75033:04.10.58	75035:23.02.59
	75036:22.03.58	75037:09.08.58	75038:22.02.58	75039:06.09.58	75040:01.11.58
	75041:18.04.59	75042:03.11.57	75043:01.11.58	75044:23.05.57	75045:23.05.57
	75047:12.07.58	75048:22.02.58	75049:22.02.58		
	75066: 04.61	75069: 10.60	75071: 03.57	75072: 04.57	75074: 08.58
	75075: 05.57	75076: 03.57	75077: 07.58	75078: 10.61	
6132	75011:16.07.60	75038:22.02.58	75048:22.02.58	75049:22.02.58	
7192	75010:27.12.58	75011:17.05.58	75012:12.09.57	75013:04.10.58	75015:17.05.58
	75016:14.06.58	75017:04.10.58	75018:16.05.59	75019:09.08.58	
9089	75065: ? 03.58	75066: 10.58	75067:no date	75068: ? 03.58	75069: 04.58
	75070:no date	75071:no date	75072:no date	75073: 10.58	75074: 08.58
	75075: 07.58	75076: 10.58	75077: 08.58	75078: 08.58	75079: 11.58
SR01	75067: 12.60	75069: 10.60	75072: 11.60		
SR03	The whole SR allocation, 75065-79, was modified; dates recorded for the following:				
	75065: 04.61	75066: 04.61	75067: 08.58	75068: 01.61	75069: 10.60
	75072: 11.60	75073: 08.61	75076: 06.61	75078: 10.61	
SR05	75065: 03.58	75067: 03.58	75068:no date	75071:no date	75072:no date
	75075: 07.58	75077: 08.58	75079: 11.58		
SR07	75067:no date	75071:no date	75073: 10.58	75074: 08.58	75075: 08.58
	75077: 08.58	75079:no date			
SR09	75065: 03.58	75066: 04.61	75067: 03.58	75068: 03.58	75069: 04.58
	75070:no date	75071: 03.57	75072: 04.57	75073: 11.56	75074: 07.61
	75075: 07.58	75076: 06.61	75077: 08.58	75078: 10.61	75079: 11.58
SR11	75065: 04.61	75066: 04.61	75068: 01.61	75070: 02.61	75073: 08.61
	75075: 09.61	75076: 06.61	75077: 06.61	75078: 10.61	75079: 11.61
SR12	The whole SR allocation, 75065-79 was modified; dates recorded for the following:				
	75065: 04.61	75067: 04.61	75068: 01.61	75069: 10.60	75072: 11.60
	75073: 08.61	75076: 06.61	75077: 08.58	75078: 10.61	75079: 11.58
SR13	75067:no date	75068: 03.58	75069: 04.58	75071: 05.58	75072: 08.58
	75073: 10.58	75075:no date	75077: 07.58	75078: 08.58	75079: 11.58
SR20	75070:no date				
SR28	75065: 04.61	75073: 08.61			

★ See text for key to work carried out under individual modification numbers

modification, ie. the provision and fitting of cab draught shields and a padded back to the fireman's seat; engines modified are recorded under the specified reference number. It is not clear why two different reference numbers should be used for the same modification at the same cost.

Ref. No.	Work Involved
3329	Modified pistons for continuous blowdown valves. Cost £1.00.
3400	Fitting manganese liners to intermediate rubbing plates and buffer faces. Cost £25.15s.0d (£25.75).
3622	Alteration to spring balancing arrangement and fitting stops to prevent reversing gear jamming. Cost £14.7s.0d (£14.35).
3698	Provision and fitting of new tank holding down bracket and packing. Cost £5.12s.0d (£5.60).
3980 and 4175	Fitting of: (1) padded backs to fireman's seat. Cost £3.9s.0d (£3.45) and (2) cab draught shield. Cost £49.2s.0d (£49.10); from 75015 onwards, cost was £64.19s.6d (£64.98)
4341	Removal of Downs sanding gear. Cost £47.7s.2d (£47.36).
4542	Additional cross-bracings to frame. Cost £27.14s.1d (£27.70).
4983	Fitting of BR type ATC equipment. Cost £383.0s.0d.
5900	Fitting of safety links between engine and tender. Cost £13.1s.0d (£13.05).
6132	Fitting of protective shield over tender leading axle. Cost £11.17s.5d (£11.87).
7192	Provision and fitting of atomiser control. Cost £160.00.
9089	Modification to briquette tube feeder, part of the BR water softening system. No cost quoted.

A list of LMR experimental fittings to Standard Cl. 4 4-6-0s, dated March 1959, is as follows.

Mod. No.	Modification Detail
MDL/1322	Provision of draught shield supports. Engine: 75015
MDL/1323	Piston valve liners; shape of ports Engine: 75034
MDL/1330	Specification not identified. Engine: 75037
MDL/1332	Specification not identified. Engine: 75046
MDL/1335	Fitted with special brake hangers to support brake blocks. Engine: 75035
MDL/1346	Tender has axles treated with zinc rich primer and black enamel to reduce corrosion. Engine: 75037
MDL/1385	To obtain improved steaming; engines also fitted with ash arrester screens of wedge section; modification later removed (recorded as 'deleted'). Engines: 75040-4 (all deleted)

On the WR, two modifications were recorded for the class, as shown.

W/SW/L/131 Details have not been confirmed but it is probable that this was the same modification as MDL/1385, the attempt to improve steaming with arrester screens of wedge section.
 Engine: 75025 (25.04.59)
W/SW/L/135 Specification not indicated.
 Engine: 75025

All the Standard Cl. 4 4-6-0s originally allocated to the SR, 75065-79, had their cabs modified at Eastleigh to incorporate glazed rear draught screens similar to those fitted to Bulleid Pacifics. It was also reported that Eastleigh applied 'lifting brackets' to the cab roofs of all Standard locomotives visiting the Works from around 1960 onwards to facilitate ease of handling by overhead cranes during overhauls. The SR allocation was fitted with the French T.I.A. water softening apparatus, later replaced by the standard BR briquette system, which proved successful in reducing boiler corrosion.

In addition to these modifications the SR made a number of other detail alterations to the majority of their allocation. These were associated with a specific 'Test Number' but it has been possible to link only a few of the numbers to particular modifications; these are given where known. For the purposes of reference to Table 36, arbitrary numbers for each alteration are assigned as shown; no cost information is available.

Ref. No.	Work Involved
SR01	Fitting of injector overflow pipes and brackets.
SR03	Modification to allow atomiser steam for lubrication to be controlled by cylinder cock gear.
SR05	Piston head modification: SR Test Number 2272.
SR07	Smokebox door safety chains fitted.
SR09	Piston rod modified packing. SR Test Number 2263. Same as Ref. Mod. 8895.
SR11	Tender coal hole door plates modification.
SR12	Provision of 'Melesco' type superheater.
SR13	Isolating cocks and pipe gear.
SR20	Modification of BR Standard firebars to permit improved steaming by reducing clinker build-up. SR Test No. 2298.
SR28	Modification of intermediate drawgear.

The test numbers were shown on the engine record cards but several of these were subsequently crossed out. This could mean that the tests were either not carried out, were terminated or were regarded as successful and hence became adopted as a permanent feature of the locomotive. Engines on the SR subjected to the tests usually carried details of the test number on a small brass plate attached to the cabside under the numerals. A copy of The Railway Executive's protocol for dealing with experimental modifications to locomotives, entitled 'Proposals for Standard Procedure for Dealing with Experiments' is reproduced as Appendix 5.

3.10 Names and Nicknames

None of the Standard Cl. 4 4-6-0s received names during their service with British Railways. In preservation, 75029 carries the name *The Green Knight*, whilst 75014 was named *Braveheart* at Fort William station on 19th June 2000 (the first day of that season's 'Jacobite' workings to Mallaig) in connection with a new film release. There does not appear to have been a network wide nickname, neither were local nicknames common. Occasionally heard were terms such as

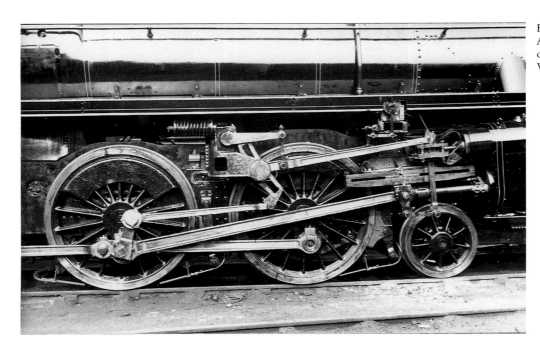

Fig. 157
A close up view of the valve gear of 75008 is seen at Swindon Works on 30th September 1951.
(W. Potter)

Fig. 158
75008 in lined green livery at Swindon shed on 20th June 1957. The engine acquired a double chimney in February 1961, one of nine class members operating on the WR to do so.
(G. Wheeler)

Fig. 159
75016 allocated to Nuneaton depot LMR entered Eastleigh Works for an intermediate overhaul on 4th June 1964 in mixed traffic black livery and emerged on 31st July in Eastleigh's version of lined green, fully applied apart from the cylinder casings; 75016 had accrued a mileage of more than 400,000 by this time.
(G. Wheeler)

Fig. 160   75029 is captured on shed at Swindon on 26th May 1957 after acquiring the 'one-off' Swindon designed double chimney. The engine has also received a lined green livery during the same Works visit , the first of the class to do so. Note the draught screens fitted to the BR2 type tender.   (G. Wheeler)

Fig. 161   Complete with 'Cambrian Coast Express' headboard, 75029 stands in Swindon style green livery at Longmoor on 5th July 1969 in the early days of preservation. The engine has acquired the name *The Green Knight* and is now preserved on the East Somerset Railway at Cranmore. Note 75029 now has the Brighton designed lower profile double chimney, fitted in February 1960 as replacement for the original Swindon type.

(Rodney Lissenden)

Fig. 162   75030 is pictured at Eastleigh shed on 11th September 1965 after an intermediate overhaul at the Works. Full mixed traffic lined black livery is apparently still being applied in the paint shop at this late date.   *(Courtney Haydon)*

'Basingstoke Arthurs' derived from the exploits of 75075-9 when they were allocated there for work on the Waterloo main line from 1956-63 (75075 until January 1959 only). Further north, reference was made to 'Lancashire (or Merseyside) Runners' as applied to 75015-9 at Southport and 75045-9 at Bank Hall for their work on the semi-fasts to Manchester and Yorkshire. On the S&DJR, the class was known as the 'Baby 4-6-0s', a reference to their lower power classification compared with their Standard and Stanier Cl. 5 4-6-0 stablemates at Bath Green Park.

3.11 Performance

Opinions varied as to the effectiveness of the Standard Cl. 4 4-6-0s in their daily work. The first engines on the WR, 75000-9, were at Shrewsbury for a period from the autumn of 1951. Here they were used on nominally Cl. 5 4-6-0 duties and were not a success due to poor steaming characteristics, later greatly improved by adoption of the modified firebars described in section 2.9. The class was also used on the Central Wales line from Shrewsbury to Swansea Victoria. On passenger turns with frequent stops on this hilly route the class was much more at home, regularly rostered for the return trip of 236 miles in around 9 hours. From 1953-8, several of the class were at Oswestry for Cambrian line work to Aberystwyth. Here, despite the more comfortable cabs compared with the GWR Manor Cl. 4-6-0s, enginemen were unhappy with their performance. The class was regarded as 'light on its feet' and, according to some observers, seldom set out on the level start from Aberystwyth without vigorous slipping. The cabs were noisy and the stiff reversing gear was seen as 'clumsy' and a great nuisance to operate, for example, on pick-up goods work. From 1963, however, when the Cambrian lines became part of the LMR, several members of the class were reallocated to the route and came to be regarded as free-running able performers, successfully tackling the formidable Talerddig summit single-handed with nine coach loads on a regular basis.

In contrast on the S&DJR, the class became popular with crews who regarded them as free runners from the start. One unfortunate characteristic was reported however. When coasting downhill at 60-70mph, there was a tendency for a 'shuttle' motion to develop between engine and tender, spilling coal all over the footplate. The class could run to a Cl. 5 4-6-0 schedule with the route's prestige working, the Pines Express linking Manchester and Liverpool with Bournemouth but had to be worked hard to achieve point to point timings. Both the single and double chimney types were in use on the line with no significant advantage being reported for the double chimney examples.

On the SR, the Basingstoke engines were considered indifferent steamers until modified with double blastpipe and chimney. From then on they were used turn and turn about with the Standard Cl. 5 4-6-0s. The class was considered ideal for the LSWR main line semi-fasts from Waterloo to Salisbury and Bournemouth.

On the LMR in Lancashire the Standard Cl. 4 4-6-0s soon gained the reputation as 'erratic' steamers, no match for the Stanier Cl. 5 4-6-0s and Cl. 4 2-6-4 tank engines they replaced on the Southport-Manchester semi-fasts. The loan of the WR's double chimney 75029 to Southport for three months in October 1958 was not a complete success, although some crews put it on a par with a Stanier Cl. 5 4-6-0. Later however some lively turns of speed were obtained with the class on the Wigan-Southport race track as displayed in Table 37. The engines were better received both on the St. Pancras-Bedford semi-fasts, where they took over from ageing LMS Cl.4 Compound 4-4-0s and on the Euston-Bletchley services, where no fewer than six of the Bletchley allocation, 75031/2/3/6/8/9, each ran an annual mileage in excess of 40,000 in 1954. The contingent based in the Midlands at

Fig. 163   75035 is at rest on Cheltenham shed on 30th August 1953 after working an M&SWJR line train during a running-in turn from Swindon. 75035 was an LMR–based engine for the whole of its 14 years of life.   *(Frank Hornby)*

Fig. 164   75042 pauses at Derby Midland station on 29th September 1963 after overhaul at the adjacent Works. By the end of the year, 75042 had completed almost 320,000 miles in traffic.

(Courtney Haydon)

Fig. 165   75057, only three months old, stands at Leicester Midland depot on 2nd June 1957. The following year, 75057 ran some 46,294
miles, one of the highest annual mileages recorded for any of the class.
(Alan Bowman, John S. Phillips Collection)

Leicester, Derby and Nottingham displaced the likes of LMS
Cl. 2P 4-4-0s on local passenger services and were regarded as
a significant improvement in cab comfort and ease of
preparation and disposal.

3.11.1 Performance in Day to Day Service
Several performance logs of the Standard Cl. 4 4-6-0s are
given in the accompanying tables. The services involved are:

    LMR   Wigan Wallgate-Southport St. Lukes
             Nottingham- St. Pancras
    SR   Victoria-Chatham

Table 37 compares the work of the class with that of an
LMS Cl. 4 2-6-4 tank engine and a Stanier Cl. 5 4-6-0 on the
evening commuter services from Manchester Victoria to
Southport. There were two fast trains to the coast around tea-
time, the 5.00pm non-stop and the 5.22pm stopping at Wigan
Wallgate only; the Standard Cl. 4 4-6-0s and the Cl. 4 2-6-4
tank engine were timed on the 5.22pm whilst the Stanier Cl.
5 4-6-0 was in charge of the non-stop. The line has a
generally falling gradient from Wigan with a 1¼ mile
downhill stretch at 1 in 282/120/215 through Parbold where
high speeds were often achieved. The schedule for the 16.4
miles from Wallgate to St. Lukes was a sharp 20 minutes; the
timings were made by Messrs. J. C. Natzio and G. H.
Hammersley. Despite 75018 encountering a series of signal
checks from Bescar Lane onward, all four engines maintained
schedule, although 75017/8 ceded maximum speed honours
to the other two locomotives. Elsewhere on the LMR

however, between Nottingham and St. Pancras, a Standard
Cl. 4 4-6-0 was shown to be capable of speeds up to 85mph,
albeit with some help. The log timed by Mr. H.J.J. Griffith
concerned 75063 acting as pilot to Stanier Jubilee Cl. 4-6-0
45627 on the 11.40am from Nottingham (8.55am ex-
Bradford Forster Square); details are given in Table 38. The
service was one of the 'XL Limit' timings introduced on the
Midland main line in June 1957; the 11 coach load of 390
tons gross was in excess of the prescribed limit of nine
coaches/300 tons tare for a Jubilee Cl. 4-6-0, hence the
presence of the pilot. The two engines made a vigorous attack
on the 1 in 200 out of Nottingham and by Widmerpool had
attained a speed of 56mph. The sustained 64mph up the 1 in
280 grade past Whissendine was also good as was the
minimum of 58mph up the six miles at 1 in 200 from
Harringworth to Corby. Kettering would have been passed in
'even time' (ie mile a minute) but for the Glendon South
Junction signal check. Time was gained with the minimum
57mph to Sharnbrook summit but a permanent way slowing
brought the train back to schedule through Bedford. From
here the climb to Luton was noteworthy with a minimum of
65½ mph up the 1 in 200 to Ampthill, 71½ mph in the dip
at Flitwick and a second minimum of 60½ mph on the 1 in
200 up to Milepost 34 just north of Leagrave. The time to the
Luton stop was 92 min. 57 sec., or 89 min. net. The
remaining 30.2 miles to St. Pancras were run in 29 min. 11
sec. or 28½ min. net with the top speed of 85mph being
reached at Mill Hill.

158

Table 37

Standard Cl. 4 4-6-0s 75000–75079

LMR   Wigan Wallgate–Southport St Lukes

Engine Number		75017 (Southport)		75018 (Southport)		42063 (Southport)		45228 (Southport)	
Class		BR 4 4-6-0		BR 4 4-6-0		LMS 4 2-6-4 Tank		LMS Stanier 5 4-6-0	
Load, coaches		8		9 (non-corridor)		7		9	
Load, tons tare		262		263		208		296	
Load, tons gross		285		300		230		320	
	Sch. Min.	Actual min.sec	Speeds mph	Actual min.sec	Speeds mph	Actual min.sec	Speeds mph	Actual min.sec	Speeds mph
Distance Miles									
0.00 WIGAN Wallgate	0	0.00	–	0.00	–	0.00	–	**00.0	**20
1.10 Douglas Bank		1.49	40	1.46	–	1.38	–	1.30	41
2.70 Gathurst		4.25	50/58	4.21	54½/57	4.01	60/63	3.56	55/64
4.50 Appley Bridge		6.25	*52	6.17	*55	5.54	*55	5.44	*60
6.75 Parbold		8.47	64/70	8.30	68	8.06	73	7.53	72
8.20 Hoscar		10.03	68	9.44	75	9.18	76½	9.03	79
9.60 Burscough Bridge		11.32	65	11.05	69	10.37	70	10.18	76
10.95 New Lane		12.35	70	12.05	75	11.32	78	11.12	80
				sigs.					
13.05 Bescar Lane		14.20	74	13.52	66	13.08	81	12.48	82
14.65 Pool Hey Junction		15.51	72	15.19	60	14.24	72	14.00	81
				sigs.	*15				
15.70 Blowick		16.52	*65	16.50	–	15.17	*65	14.50	*73
				sigs.					
16.40 SOUTHPORT St Lukes	20	17.58	–	19.33	–	16.22	–	15.55	–
16.40 Net times (min.)		18.00		17.15		16.15		***16.30	

*Speed restriction   **Passing time and speed   ***Equivalent start to stop time.

First published in Modern Railways, Vol 15, No. 162, March 1962

Table 38

Standard Cl. 4 4-6-0s 75000-75079

LMR Nottingham-St Pancras
Engine: Stanier Jubilee Cl. 4-6-0 45627 piloted by Standard Cl. 4 4-6-0 75063
Load: 11 coaches, 367 tons tare, 390 tons gross
Driver 45627: Driver Brooks (Kentish Town), 75063: Driver Cowdell (Nottingham)

Distance Miles		Schedule min.	Actual min.sec.	Speeds mph
0.0	NOTTINGHAM Midland	0	0.00	–
2.8	Edwalton		4.58	50
5.4	Plumtree		7.49	55½
8.3	Widmerpool		10.57	56
12.1	Old Dalby		14.50	65
14.3	Grimston		16.53	★77½
17.6	Melton Junction	21	19.41	★40
18.2	MELTON MOWBRAY	22	20.36	–
22.0	Saxby		24.56	59
24.3	Whissendine		27.13	64
26.6	Ashwell		29.23	64
29.7	Oakham		32.12	70
33.4	Manton	37	35.10	77½/66
38.6	Harringworth		39.32	75
40.5	Gretton		41.17	63½
44.0	Corby		44.48	58
46.5	Geddington		47.09	72
			sigs.	★34
48.9	Glendon South Junction		49.35	–
51.5	KETTERING	54	52.47	56
52.8	Kettering Junction	56	54.18	★33
55.3	Finedon		57.21	64
58.5	WELLINGBOROUGH	61	60.09	69/72½
60.8	Irchester		62.12	69
63.8	Milepost 59¾	67	65.02	57
66.9	Sharnbrook		67.39	77½
			p.w.s	★26
70.5	Oakley	72	72.22	–
73.6	Bedford North Junction	75	75.06	77½
78.5	Milepost 45		79.00	73
81.7	Ampthill		81.48	65½
83.3	Flitwick		83.11	71½
86.2	Harlington		85.46	65
90.7	Leagrave		90.06	60½/65
93.3	LUTON	95	92.57	–
2.9	Chiltern Green		4.25	67
5.6	Harpenden		6.48	69/73½
8.9	Sandridge		9.36	72
			p.w.s.	★45
10.3	ST ALBANS	10	10.52	–
15.0	Radlett		15.07	80½
17.8	Elstree		17.18	73
20.9	Mill Hill		19.38	85
23.3	Hendon	21	21.24	82
			eased	
26.3	West Hampstead		24.02	62
28.7	Kentish Town	27	26.40	–
30.2	ST PANCRAS	30	29.11	–

★ Speed restriction   ★★Maximum before Melton Junction
First published in Railway Magazine, Vol. 104, No. 682, February 1958

Table 39

Standard Cl. 4 4-6-0s 75000-75079

SR Kent Coast Line Victoria-Chatham

			75069 (Dover) BR 4 4-6-0 10 — 337		73081 (Stewarts Lane) BR 5 4-6-0 9 — 301		30796 (Hither Green) SR King Arthur N15 4-6-0 8 — 266	
Distance Miles		Sch. Min.	Actual min.sec	Speeds mph	Actual min.sec	Speeds mph	Actual min.sec	Speeds
0.0	VICTORIA	0	0.00	–	0.00	–	0.00	–
3.2	Brixton				sigs.			
4.0	HERNE HILL	8	9.00	30	13.30	32	8.40	–
					sigs.			
5.7	Sydenham Hill		12.50	22	17.50	24	11.40	–
8.7	Beckenham Junction	16½	18.10	40	21.35	50	16.35	–
				★15		★15		★15
9.9	Shortlands		23.30	28		★15	19.45	–
10.9	BROMLEY SOUTH arr:	20	25.20	–	27.30	–	21.40	–
	dep:	22	28.30	–	28.50	–	22.30	–
12.6	Bickley Junction	27	33.00	18	32.10	26	27.20	–
				★30		★20		★30
14.8	St. Mary Cray	33	38.20	–	37.50	48	32.35	–
				★15		★15		★15
17.7	Swanley Junction		44.20	32	43.20	40	38.40	–
20.5	Farningham Road		48.05	64	46.55	70	42.3	62
23.4	Fawkham		51.10	53	49.45	60	45.45	56
25.9	Meopham		54.05	50	52.25	54	48.35	53
26.9	Sole Street	43	55.20	50/72	53.35	52/78	49.50	56/64
30.9	Cuxton Road	48	59.05	69	57.05	76	53.20	60
33.2	Rochester Bridge Jct.	51½	62.20	36	60.15	34	56.15	34
					sigs.			
34.3	CHATHAM	54	64.35	–	63.45	–	59.00	–

★ Speed restriction

First published in Trains Illustrated Vol. 12, No. 127, April 1959

Fig. 166
75068 with Brighton double chimney reposes at Eastleigh shed on 9th May 1964 after a heavy intermediate overhaul at the Works. 75068 was one of the SR-based engines which survived until the end of steam on that region in July 1967. *(P.H. Wells)*

Fig. 167
75069 is pictured new at Swindon shed in September 1955. The engine carries the high water capacity (4725 gal.) BR1B type tender as paired to all fifteen SR allocated class members, 75065-79. The SR group had all acquired double chimneys by the end of 1961, 75069 being the first to be so fitted in October 1960. *(G. Wheeler)*

Fig. 168
Double chimney 75071 by now based on the LMR stands at St Rollox shed in October 1965 in connection with a visit to Cowlairs Works. Several LMR class members received attention at Cowlairs during 1965.

(J.B. Arnold)

Table 40

Standard Cl. 4 4-6-0s 75000-75079: Dates when Stored Serviceable

Loco Number	Date of Storage	Loco Number	Date of Storage
75009	10.10.66 – 04.05.67	75030	19.04.67 – 03.05.67
	26.06.67	75032	08.11.65 – 30.01.66
75010	22.04.67 – 04.05.67	75033	08.11.65 – 07.02.66
	07.06.67		27.03.66 – 30.03.66
75013	01.10.66 – 02.05.67	75034	25.09.67 – 10.02.68
75015	09.01.67 – 30.01.67	75035	19.04.67 – 03.05.67
75019	17.10.65 – 04.11.65	75039	09.01.67 – 20.03.67
	14.02.66 – 18.04.66		27.03.67 – 17.04.67
	30.01.67 – 20.03.67	75047	22.04.67 – 01.06.67
	27.03.67 – 24.02.68		07.06.67
75020	19.09.66 – 02.03.67	75048	03.01.66 – 30.03.66
	24.06.67		22.04.67 – 07.05.67
75021	25.09.67 – 10.02.68	75052	22.04.67
75026	08.11.65 – 31.10.66	75055	01.10.66 – 06.05.67
75027	08.11.65 – 31.10.66	75058	25.09.67
	09.01.67 – 20.03.67	75062	25.09.67 – 10.02.68
	27.03.67 – 27.02.68		

On the SR Kent Coast line from Victoria to Chatham, the work of 75069, still with single chimney, is compared with a Standard Cl. 5 4-6-0 and a Maunsell N15 King Arthur 4-6-0. All three runs were timed by Dr. P. Ransome-Wallis in 1958 whilst the engineering work was in progress for the first stage of the Kent Coast electrification and were hence subject to several severe speed restrictions: details are given in Table 39. 75069 was timed on the 3.35pm Victoria-Ramsgate, substituting at the last moment for a failed Standard Cl. 5 4-6-0. With the assistance of a banker, full regulator was used on 75069 for the 1 in 62 climb out of Victoria with cut-off brought back to 40% by Grosvenor Bridge. The engine's fire was very thick, consisting of very small coal and slack. Despite hard work with the pricker, shovel and rocking grate, boiler pressure fell to 140 p.s.i. at Brixton and was down to 120 p.s.i. by the time the stop was made at Bromley South. On the restart, pressure was still only 150 p.s.i. but by Bickley was back up to 190 p.s.i. and with full regulator and 40% cut-off, 48mph was achieved before slowing for the restrictions after St. Mary Cray. Despite all the difficulties, a speed of 72mph down Sole Street bank got the 3.35pm into Chatham only 10½ minutes late. The second run on the same train with Standard Cl. 5 4-6-0 73081 told a similar story, the speed restrictions again resulting in 10 minute late arrival at Chatham despite a 78mph maximum after Sole Street For N15 4-6-0 30796 on the 2.35pm from Victoria running to the same schedule as far as Chatham, arrival at Bromley South was less than two minutes late. Again speed restrictions and a maximum of only 64mph past Sole Street resulted in Chatham being reached five minutes late.

3.12 Storage, Withdrawal and Disposal

Towards the end of steam operation by British Railways, many locomotives were stored prior to withdrawal. A list of Standard Cl. 4 4-6-0s known to have been mothballed for a period are given in Table 40 together with approximate storage dates. Table 41 gives dates of withdrawal and place of disposal; reported cutting-up dates appear to be unreliable and have been omitted. The first to be withdrawn was 75067 in October 1964, whilst 75009/19/20/7/48 lasted until the end of BR steam in August 1968.

3.13 Preservation

Six Standard Cl. 4 4-6-0s have been preserved, two purchased directly from BR and four rescued from Woodham's scrapyard at Barry in South Wales.

75014

The engine was retrieved from Barry in 1981 and resteamed in 1994. It is now owned by the 75014 Locomotive Operators' Group with its home base on the North York Moors Railway at Grosmont. 75014 has been used on mainline rail tours and often spends the summer in the Scottish Highlands, working on the 'Jacobite' steam specials between Fort William and Mallaig; it carries the name *Braveheart*.

75027

Purchased direct from BR, 75027 is now at work on the Bluebell Railway line at Horsted Keynes and Sheffield Park in East Sussex.

75029

The artist David Shepherd purchased the double chimneyed 75029 direct from BR. The engine arrived at the East Somerset Railway after storage on the Longmoor Military Railway. 75029 was taken out of service in July 1976 and after an extensive overhaul at the railway's Cranmore workshops, was re-steamed in January 1986. The engine carries the name *The Green Knight* and is appropriately painted in BR green livery. 75029 was transferred to the North York Moors Railway in 1998 for completion of a general overhaul.

Table 41

Standard Cl. 4 4-6-0s 75000-75079

Construction, Withdrawal, and Disposal Information

Engine	Built	With-drawn	Disposal	
75000	5.51	12.65	4.66	T. W. Ward, Killamarsh
75001	8.51	12.64	4.65	J. Cashmore, Newport
75002	8.51	8.67	2.68	Birds Commercial Motors, Long Marston
75003	8.51	10.65	2.66	R. & S. Hayes, Bridgend
75004	8.51	3.67	8.67	J. Cashmore, Newport
75005	9.51	11.65	2.66	Birds Commercial Motors, Morriston
75006	9.51	8.67	2.68	Birds Commercial Motors, Long Marston
75007	9.51	4.65	8.65	Birds Commercial Motors, Bynea
75008	10.51	12.65	4.66	T. W. Ward, Killamarsh
75009	10.51	8.68	11.68	G. H. Campbell, Airdrie
75010	11.51	10.67	2.68	Motherwell Machinery and Scrap Co, Wishaw
75011	11.51	11.66	2.67	T. W. Ward, Beighton, Sheffield
75012	11.51	1.67	6.67	T. W. Ward, Beighton, Sheffield
75013	11.51	8.67	2.68	Birds Commercial Motors, Long Marston
75014	12.51	12.66		Preserved on the North York Moors Railway, Grosmont
75015	12.51	12.67	6.68	Arnott Young, Carmyle
75016	1.52	7.67	6.68	T. W. Ward, Killamarsh
75017	1.52	1.67	5.67	T. W. Ward, Beighton, Sheffield
75018	3.52	6.67	11.67	J. Buttigieg, Newport
75019	3.52	8.68	11.68	G. H. Campbell, Airdrie
75020	11.53	8.68	11.68	G. H. Campbell, Airdrie
75021	11.53	2.68	6.68	T. W. Ward, Inverkeithing
75022	12.53	12.65	4.66	T. W. Ward, Killamarsh
75023	12.53	1.66	4.66	T. W. Ward, Killamarsh
75024	12.53	11.67	4.68	Birds Commercial Motors, Long Marston
75025	4.54	12.65	4.66	T. W. Ward, Killamarsh
75026	5.54	12.67	7.68	Arnott Young, Carmyle
75027	5.54	8.68		Preserved on the Bluebell Railway, Horsted Keynes
75028	5.54	12.65	4.66	T. W. Ward, Beighton, Sheffield
75029	5.54	8.67		Preserved on the East Somerset Railway, Cranmore
75030	6.53	12.67	7.68	Arnott Young, Carmyle
75031	6.53	2.66	5.66	T. W. Ward, Beighton, Sheffield
75032	6.53	2.68	5.68	T. W. Ward, Beighton, Sheffield
75033	7.53	12.67	6.68	T. W. Ward, Killamarsh
75034	7.53	2.68	7.68	T. W. Ward, Inverkeithing
75035	8.53	7.67	1.68	G. H. Campbell, Airdrie
75036	8.53	6.66	8.66	Birds Commercial Motors, Long Marston
75037	8.53	12.67	7.68	Arnott Young, Carmyle
75038	8.53	12.65	4.66	T. W. Ward, Beighton, Sheffield
75039	8.53	9.67	2.68	Motherwell Machinery and Scrap Co., Wishaw
75040	8.53	10.67	3.68	G. Cohen, Kettering
75041	9.53	1.68	8.68	G. Cohen, Kettering
75042	9.53	11.67	3.68	G. Cohen, Kettering
75043	9.53	12.67	4.68	Arnott Young, Carmyle
75044	9.53	3.66	6.66	T. W. Ward, Beighton, Sheffield
75045	9.53	4.66	8.66	Birds Commercial Motors, Long Marston
75046	10.53	8.67	2.68	Birds Commercial Motors, Long Marston
75047	10.53	8.67	2.68	Birds Commercial Motors, Long Marston
75048	10.53	8.68	11.68	G. H. Campbell, Airdrie
75049	10.53	10.66	3.67	A. Draper, Kingston upon Hull
75050	11.56	11.66	6.67	Garnham, Harris and Elton, Chesterfield

Engine	Built	Withdrawn	Disposal	
75051	11.56	10.66	2.67	T. W. Ward, Beighton, Sheffield
75052	12.56	8.67	2.68	Birds Commercial Motors, Long Marston
75053	1.57	9.66	2.67	A. Draper, Kingston upon Hull
75054	1.57	8.66	1.67	J. Cashmore, Great Bridge
75055	1.57	5.67	2.68	Garnham, Harris and Elton, Chesterfield
75056	3.57	6.66	8.66	Birds Commercial Motors, Long Marston
75057	3.57	2.66	6.66	T. W. Ward, Beighton, Sheffield
75058	4.57	12.67	4.68	Arnott Young, Carmyle
75059	4.57	7.67	12.67	G. H. Campbell, Airdrie
75060	5.57	4.67	10.67	Hughes Bolckow, North Blyth
75061	5.57	2.67	6.67	T. W. Ward, Killamarsh
75062	5.57	2.68	6.68	T. W. Ward, Inverkeithing
75063	6.57	5.66	8.66	Birds Commercial Motors, Long Marston
75064	6.57	5.67	9.67	J. Cashmore, Newport
75065	8.55	9.66	3.67	J. Buttigieg, Newport
75066	9.55	1.66	4.66	J. Cashmore, Newport
75067	9.55	10.64	11.65	G. Cohen, Morriston
75068	9.55	7.67	2.68	Birds Commercial Motors, Risca
75069	9.55	9.66		Preserved on the Severn Valley Railway, Bridgnorth
75070	10.55	9.66	3.67	J. Cashmore, Newport
75071	10.55	8.67	2.68	Birds Commercial Motors, Long Marston
75072	11.55	12.65	4.66	T. W. Ward, Ringwood, Hants
75073	11.55	12.65	4.66	T. W. Ward, Ringwood, Hants
75074	11.55	7.67	2.68	R. A. King, Norwich
75075	11.55	7.67	2.68	R. A. King, Norwich
75076	12.55	7.67	12.67	Birds Commercial Motors, Risca
75077	12.55	7.67	2.68	R. A. King, Norwich
75078	1.56	7.66		Preserved on the Keighley & Worth Valley Railway, Haworth.
75079	1.56	11.66		Stored at Plym Valley Railway with a view to preservation.

Fig. 169   Still with single chimney, 75077 stands at Nine Elms shed on 19th April 1959. The engine will enter Eastleigh Works in May 1961 for the fitting of a double chimney during its first general overhaul, having completed over 200,000 miles.

(L.Hanson)

75069

Rescued from Barry in March 1973, the double chimney 75069 is owned by the 75069 Fund and has its home base on the Severn Valley Railway at Bridgnorth in Shropshire. 75069 is also used on mainline rail tours.

75078

Moved from Woodham's yard in June 1972, the double chimney 75078 was restored in BR mixed traffic lined black livery and is now working on the Keighley and Worth Valley Railway. It was purchased by the Standard 4 Preservation Group which also owns preserved Standard Cl. 2 2-6-0 78022 operating on the same line.

75079

The engine was purchased from Barry in March 1982 using a contribution from the City of Plymouth Lottery Fund. Double chimney 75079 is stored awaiting restoration at Marsh Mills on the Plym Valley Railway, now known as the Woodland Line, a short stretch of track from Marsh Mills to Plym Bridge on the former GWR branch from Plymouth to Launceston and Princetown.

Fig. 170
A close-up of BR1B type tender No. 1041 fitted to 75077, as viewed at Nine Elms shed on 13th January 1957. Note the 4P/4F class power mark above the cabside numerals.

(A.R. Goult)

Fig. 171
A view in Swindon Works 'A' Shop on 18th May 1957 of components for 75029; prominent are the blastpipes and nozzles for the experimental double chimney. *(G. Wheeler)*

Fig. 172   75077 is pictured at Banbury shed on 16th October 1965. The engine had acquired a double chimney in June 1961 and was withdrawn from service in July 1967, the last month of steam operation on the SR.

(Rodney Lissenden)

4. Class 4 2-6-0 76000-76114

4.1 Purpose

The design for the Standard Cl. 4 2-6-0 closely followed that of the LMS Ivatt Cl. 4 2-6-0 introduced in 1947. The latter was developed as a replacement for the LMS Cl. 4 0-6-0 freight engine but was intended also for passenger duties on secondary routes where weight restrictions precluded the use of a Cl. 5 locomotive. Comparison of leading dimensions of selected mixed traffic 2-6-0s is given in Table 42.

4.1.1 Design Development

The external appearance of the LMS version with its double chimney and high running plate was regarded by traditionalists as one of the least attractive ever seen in Britain. So much so that the engines were dubbed 'Doodlebugs', probably referring to the missiles of the same name targeted on southern England during the later stages of World War II, ie. 'something of alien origin which it would be better not to experience!'. A later generation of railway enthusiasts coined the other less than flattering nickname of 'Flying Pig'. The Standard version, tidied up and provided with the trademark running plate valance and other cosmetic refinements, had an altogether more finished appearance and hence managed to avoid both the 'Doodlebug' and 'Flying Pig' sobriquets. Apart from these changes and certain alterations to external boiler mountings to accept the BR design fittings the Standard Cl. 4 2-6-0 was virtually identical to later examples of the LMS Ivatt, the original design of which had been modified following steaming trials described below.

The development of the Standard Cl. 4 2-6-0s benefitted greatly from the work done on the LMS design over the three years before their appearance of the Standard version at the end of 1952. It had quickly became apparent that the first fifty Ivatt engines (BR 43000-49) did not have good steaming characteristics. This was largely attributed to the inefficient draughting arrangements associated with the double chimney with which they were originally equipped. In dynamometer car trials between Crewe and Holyhead during April and May 1949, 43027, new from Horwich in February, was fitted successively with two versions of single chimney; reportedly one was a Stanier Cl. 5 4-6-0 type and the other similar to that fitted to the Fairburn Cl. 4 2-6-4 tank engine. Considerable improvement in steaming was noted and, based on these results, a new-style single chimney was designed and fitted to the rest of the class from 43050 onwards. Even so, it was considered that further improvements in steaming could still be possible. Accordingly in the spring of 1952, a few months before delivery of the new Standard Cl. 4 2-6-0s was due to commence, tests were conducted on two of the Ivatt locomotives, 43027/94. The latter, one of the single chimney batches, was taken into Swindon testing plant where further alterations were made to the draughting arrangements and the inside diameter of the chimney was reduced by the introduction of a metal sleeve. Test results with these modifications indicated that a maximum sustained evaporation of 17,000lb steam per hour could be reached, almost double that of the 9,000lb per hour achieved with the

Fig. 173   76005 heads a rake of pre-grouping LSWR stock on the 12.30pm Southampton Central-Portsmouth in March 1953. 76005 spent the whole of its working life on the SR, surviving until the end of steam on the Region in July 1967.   *(G. Wheeler)*

Table 42

Standard Cl. 4 2-6-0s 76000-76114

Comparison of Leading Dimensions of Selected Mixed Traffic 2-6-0s

Class	Date of Introduction	Cylinders Diameter x Stroke	Coupled Wheel Diameter	Boiler Pressure p.s.i.	Total Heating Surfaces sq. ft.	Superheater sq. ft.	Grate Area sq. ft.	Tractive Effort at 85% boiler pressure lb.	Engine Weight in Working Order
BR Standard 4 (1)	1952	17½" x 26"	5' 3"	225	1453	247	23.0	24,170	59 tons 2 wt
GWR 43XX	1911 (2)	18½" x 30"	5' 8"	200	1691	213	20.6	25,670	62 tons 0 wt
LNER Proposed design (3)	1947	17" x 26"	5' 2"	200	1155	160	19.4	20,603	50 tons 5 wt
SR U	1928	19" x 28"	6' 0"	200	1729	203	25.0	23,865	(4)
SR U1 (Three cylinders)	1928	16" x 28"	6' 0"	200	1729	203	25.0	25,385	65 tons 6 cwt

(1) Dimensions identical to LMS Ivatt Cl. 4 2-6-0 introduced 1947.
(2) Dimensions applicable to engines built from 1913 onwards.
(3) Scaled down version of LNER K1 Cl. 2-6-0; abandoned by BR in favour of further batches of LMS Ivatt Cl. 4 2-6-0s.
(4) Class consisted of 50 engines; twenty were rebuilds of Maunsell's 'River' Cl. 2-6-4 tank engines introduced in 1917 and weighed 63 tons 0 cwt. The thirty engines built new to Class U design weighed 62 tons 6 cwt.

double chimney version. Road trials confirming these results were carried out between Wantage Road and Filton Junction, Bristol. The other engine, 43027 originally built with double chimney, had taken part in the earlier trials at Crewe. It was fitted with the modified draught arrangement and a single stovepipe chimney for trials on the Midland main line. Based at Derby, the engine was noted on fast fitted freights to Leeds and semi-fasts to Leicester and St Pancras. After the trials the stovepipe chimney was replaced with a conventional one to the same specification. The remaining double chimney locomotives in the 43000-49 group acquired the modified single chimneys, blastpipes and draughting arrangements during works visits over the 1953-6 period. The trials generated much useful data which were invaluable when finalising the design for the new Standard Cl. 4 2-6-0s.

Before Horwich and Doncaster could begin on the first batches of the Standard Cl. 4 2-6-0s, they were completing, along with Darlington, the last of some 92 examples of the modified Ivatt Cl. 4 2-6-0s for the ER, NER and ScR. These engines were to be used mainly to displace several ageing 0-6-0 types on freight work in Scotland and the North East and for both freight and passenger duties on the M&GN lines in East Anglia. The Ivatt design had been chosen over a 1947 LNER proposal to build a lightweight 5' 2" 2-6-0, (see Table 42 for details); this was a scaled down version of the K1 2-6-0 but with a tender cab for employment on lines such as the exposed Stainmore route from Barnard Castle to Kirkby Stephen. With the Ivatt design already in production, the LNER proposal had been abandoned.

Following completion of the Ivatt Cl. 4 2-6-0 batches, both Horwich and Doncaster began delivery of the Standard version in December 1952. Ten tons lighter than the Standard Cl. 4 4-6-0s, the class had wider route availability. Examples were allocated initially to all regions except the WR, although towards the end of steam, several of the class operated from former WR depots on the Cambrian lines. Primarily thought of as freight locomotives, the class was used extensively by the SR and the ER on secondary passenger duties. The SR engines were employed on locals and semi-fasts in the Salisbury-Bournemouth-Portsmouth triangle and on the main line to Waterloo whilst the ER used them for similar duties on both the former GC lines from Marylebone and GE section routes from Liverpool Street.

A summary of the annual building programme for the class is given in Table 43. Appendix 1 details year end class totals from 1952-1967.

Table 43

Standard Cl. 4 2-6-0s 76000-76114: Annual Building Programme

Programme Year	Works	Lot Numbers	Engine Numbers	Total	Delivery Date	Initial Allocated Region
1952	Horwich	108	76000-04	5	12.52	Scottish
			76005-19	15	12.52-07.53	Southern
	Doncaster	395	76020-24	5	12.52-01.53	North Eastern
1953	Doncaster	396	76025-29	5	10.53-11.53	Southern
			76030-34	5	11.53-12.53	Eastern
	Doncaster	397	76035-44	10	05.54-08.54	Eastern
1954	Doncaster	399	76050-52	3	08.56-09.56	North Eastern
			76063-69	7	07.56-08.56	Southern
	Doncaster	400	76053-62	10	04.55-07.55	Southern
	Doncaster	401	76045-49	5	03.55-04.55	North Eastern
	Doncaster	405	76070-74	5	09.56-11.56	Scottish
1956	Horwich	109	76075-89	15	12.56-06.57	London Midland
			76090-99	10	06.57-11.57	Scottish
	Doncaster	408	76100-09	10	05.57-08.57	Scottish
	Doncaster	409	76110-14	5	08.57-10.57	Scottish

Fig. 174
76005 brings empty stock into Bournemouth Central to form a football special to Southampton Central on 19th November 1966; on shed in the background are Standard Cl. 5 4-6-0 73002 and a Standard Cl. 4 2-6-4 tank engine.

(Courtney Haydon)

Fig. 175
Last day for the station at West Moors for Ferndown; 76005 pauses with the 10.04am Bournemouth West–Salisbury on 2nd May 1964; the station was obviously kept in immaculate condition to the very end. It is estimated that 76005 had accrued almost 400,000 miles by this date.

(Courtney Haydon)

Fig. 176
76011 heads up the South Western main line near Winchfield with the 4.08pm Southampton Western Docks–Feltham freight on 26th June 1965. Note the triangle below the cabside numerals indicating the engine is fitted with water softening apparatus.

(Courtney Haydon)

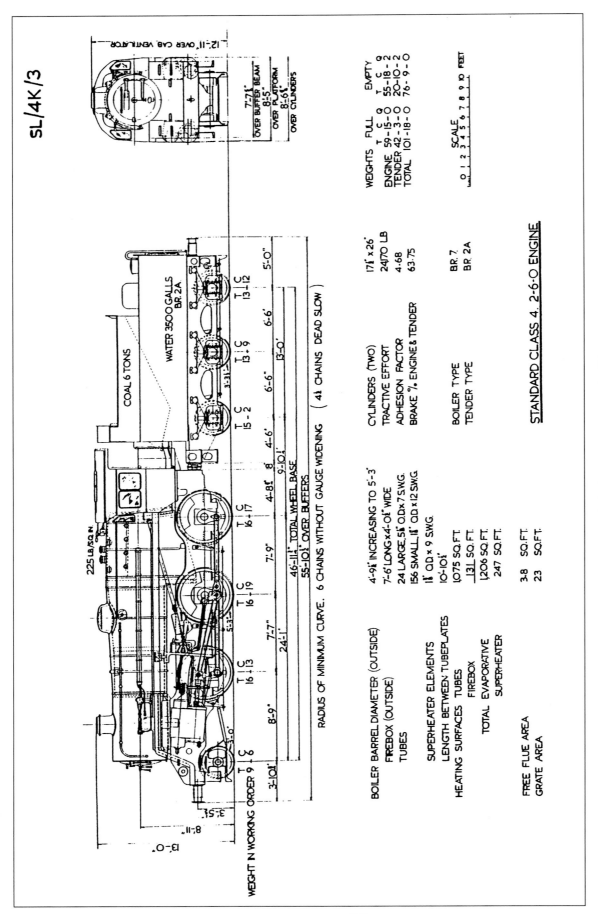

SL/4K/3

12'-11" OVER CAB VENTILATOR

7'-7½"
OVER BUFFER BEAM
8'-5"
OVER PLATFORM
8'-6½"
OVER CYLINDERS

WEIGHTS	FULL			EMPTY		
	T	C	Q	T	C	Q
ENGINE	59-15-0			55-18-2		
TENDER	42-3-0			20-10-2		
TOTAL	101-18-0			76-9-0		

SCALE
0 1 2 3 4 5 6 7 8 9 10 FEET

COAL 6 TONS

WATER 3500 GALLS
BR. 2A

225 LB/SQ IN

WEIGHT IN WORKING ORDER 9-6

T C
3-10½

T C
16-13

T C
16-19

T C
16-17

T C
15-2

T C
13-9

T C
13-12

8-9"   7-7"   7-9"   4-8½"   8   4-6'   6-6"   13-0'   6-6"   5-0"
24-1'   3-11½"
9-10½"
46-11¾" TOTAL WHEEL BASE
55-10½" OVER BUFFERS

3-5½"
8-11"
13'-0"

RADIUS OF MINIMUM CURVE. 6 CHAINS WITHOUT GAUGE WIDENING   (4½ CHAINS DEAD SLOW)

BOILER BARREL DIAMETER (OUTSIDE)	4'-9¼" INCREASING TO 5'-3"	
FIREBOX (OUTSIDE)	7'-6" LONG × 4'-0¼" WIDE	
TUBES	24 LARGE, 5⅛" O.D × 7 SWG.	
	156 SMALL, 1⅝" O.D × 12 SWG.	
SUPERHEATER ELEMENTS	1⅛" O.D × 9 SWG.	
LENGTH BETWEEN TUBEPLATES	10'-10⅜"	
HEATING SURFACES TUBES	1075 SQ.FT.	
FIREBOX	131 SQ.FT.	
TOTAL EVAPORATIVE	1206 SQ.FT.	
SUPERHEATER	247 SQ.FT.	
FREE FLUE AREA	3.8 SQ.FT.	
GRATE AREA	23 SQ.FT.	

CYLINDERS (TWO)	17½" × 26"
TRACTIVE EFFORT	24,170 LB
ADHESION FACTOR	4.68
BRAKE % ENGINE & TENDER	63.75
BOILER TYPE	BR. 7
TENDER TYPE	BR. 2A

STANDARD CLASS 4. 2-6-0 ENGINE

Diagram 5: Standard Cl. 4 2-6-0s : Locomotive Diagram

172

4.2 Dimensions and Data

Doncaster was the main design office for the Standard Cl. 4 2-6-0s with certain components designed at Swindon, Derby and Brighton. Principal dimensions and axle loads are given in Diagram 5.

Details of the BR 7 boiler fitted to the class are given in section 4.3; firebox dimensions appear in Appendices 2 and 2A. A copper inner firebox with a $^5/_8$" thick wrapper plate and a 1" thick tube plate was fitted. All firebox water stays were of Monel metal and fitted with steel nuts inside the firebox; longitudinal and transverse stays were of steel whilst both firebox and boiler were lagged with fibreglass mattresses. The main frames were $1^1/_8$" thick with plates spaced 4' $1^1/_2$" apart, well braced horizontally and vertically by fabricated plate stays. Pin jointed cross stays were attached to each of the axlebox guides. Both guides and axleboxes were fitted with manganese steel liners, those on the guides being bolted in position and the others welded to the axleboxes. The class had plain bearings on all wheels, pressed-in white metalled brasses in cast steel axleboxes for the axles and for pony truck boxes, white metalled bronze castings. The rocking grate, ashpan, self cleaning smokebox, frame design, piston, crosshead, slidebars, method of lubrication, sanding arrangements, reversing gear, bogie and cab design were similar to those described for the Standard Cl. 5 4-6-0s, see section 2.2. Valve gear was of the conventional Walschaerts type, also detailed in section 2.2; cylinder and valve dimensions appear in Appendices 3 and 3A.

Apart from the provision of different tenders, discussed in section 4.4, there were no significant variations between the production batches of the class. Minor changes included the provision of the Smith-Stone speedometer beginning with 76025 and the substitution of fluted-type coupling rods by the rectangular type from 76035 onwards. 76030-4, allocated to

Table 44

**Standard Cl. 4 2-6-0s 76000-114:
Initial Boiler Allocation**

Locomotive Number	Boiler Number Nominal Allocation	Date of Boiler Construction	Boiler Built at
76000-09	1043-1052	05.52-11.52	Darlington
76010-19	1053-1062	?? -11.52	Doncaster
76020-24	1063-1067	11.52	Doncaster
76025-44	1223-1242	08.53-06.54	Doncaster
76045-74★	1517-1546	03.55-06.57	Doncaster
76075-99	1797-1821	08.56-09.57	Swindon
76100-14★	1822-1831	06.56-10.56	Darlington
	1832-1836	08.57-11.57	Doncaster
Spare Boilers	1600	12.54	Doncaster
	1604-1605	08.56	Doncaster
	1874	04.57	Doncaster
	1899-1900	10.59-01.60	Crewe
	1943	08.59	Doncaster

★ Boilers not installed in numerical sequence. Several boilers nominally allocated to 76045-74 were fitted to engines numbered in the 76100-14 range and vice versa.

the ER, had recesses in both sides of the cab to accommodate tablet exchange apparatus for single line working, probably with the M&GN routes in mind. The tablet equipment was never installed as the group spent most of its time when on the ER working in the London area based on Stratford depot.

4.3 Boilers

The BR7 boiler fitted to the Standard Cl. 4 2-6-0s was very similar to that fitted to the LMS Ivatt Cl. 4 2-6-0s with the same flange plates and working pressure of 225 p.s.i. The shell plates were of standard quality steel and the barrel consisted of two rings, the second of which was tapered; dimensional details are given in Appendices 2 and 2A. A slide valve regulator was fitted in the dome and operated by an external pull rod on the left hand side of the barrel. It was connected to a transverse shaft which operated through a stuffing box on the second barrel plate. Boiler mountings, manifold, safety valves and clack valves were as carried by the other Standard BR locomotives with their controls operated similarly. Boilers for the class were constructed at Darlington, Doncaster, Swindon and Crewe; details are given in Table 44. The record of which boilers were carried by individual members of the class after general overhaul is incomplete and appears to be unreliable.

4.4 Tenders

The Standard Cl. 4 2-6-0s were equipped with the same three types of tender carried by the Standard Cl. 4 4-6-0s; details are given in Table 45. In general, the tenders were constructed alongside the engines at the same Works, but it is known that the tenders for Horwich-built 76000-19 were produced at Derby. Type 2 tenders for several members of the class were modified to reduce the problem of draughtiness discussed in section 2.4. The last batch allocated to the SR, 76053-69, had the BR1B higher water capacity tender to compensate for the absence of water troughs on that Region. These tenders were furnished with Timken roller bearing axleboxes which were identified by being painted yellow with a horizontal red stripe. There is evidence to indicate that the paint finish on tenders for the SR batch 76053-69 was of poor durability, at least one, 76057's, being given a full repaint before general overhaul. Again, engines tended to stay paired with the same tender for the whole of their working lives. It is not clear whether any of the Type 2 tenders allotted to the class were modified with the protection shield over the leading axle to prevent corrosion from the shovelling plate and brake cylinder drain discharge.

4.5 Construction Costs

Representative departmental first costs for the Standard Cl. 4 2-6-0s for 1952 and 1957 were £16,892 and £20,577 respectively, indicating a wage and raw material inflation of almost 22% over the period. Record card costs for the final batches from Horwich and Doncaster were £22,082 and £20,648 respectively; further details are shown in Table 46. Final costs are not available but using comparable figures from other Standard classes under construction over the same period, it is possible that they could have exceeded the estimate by up to 20%.

Table 45

Standard Cl. 4 2-6-0s 76000-76114: Initial Tender Allocation

Tender Type	Tender Side	Water Capacity (gallons)	Coal Capacity (tons)	Weight in Working Order (tons)	Allocated to Engine Numbers	Tender Serial Number	Tender Notes
BR1B	Flush	4725	7	51.25	76053-69	1234-1250	Fall plate and gangway doors fitted. High water capacity tender not fitted with water pick-up gear as engines were allocated to SR which had no water troughs
BR2	Inset at top	3500	6	42.15	76000-24 76025-44	914-938 1044-1063	No fall plate fitted. Modified with draught excluders after service experience.
BR2A	Inset at top	3500	6	42.15	76045-52 76070-74 76075-76114	1226-1233 1251-1255 1460-1499	Identical to BR2 but with addition of a fall plate and gangway doors.

Table 46

Standard Cl. 4 2-6-0s 76000-76114: Manufacturing Cost Comparisons

Programme Year	Locomotive Number	Delivery Year	Estimated Cost (£)	Record Card Final Cost (£)	Official Final Cost (£)
1952	76000-19	1952/3	16,892	–	–
	76020-24	1952/3	16,892	16,341	–
1953	76025-34	1953	–	16,110	–
	76035-44	1954	–	16,111	–
1954	76045-74	1955/6	–	17,037	–
1956	76075-89	1956/7	–	22,083	–
	76090-99	1957	20,577	22,082	–
	76100-14	1957	20,577	20,648	–

Key: – Information not traced.

Fig. 177
76011 heads a train on the S&DJR on 2nd May 1958; the Smith-Stone speedometer activated by the rear driving wheel was fitted a short time after delivery to the SR. A few weeks later, 76011 would enter Eastleigh Works for its first general overhaul, having completed over 185,000 miles.

(P.H. Wells)

Fig. 178
76013 passes Allbrook Signal Box with a Birmingham Snow Hill-Bournemouth train on 30th June 1956. 76013 had probably taken over the train from the WR at Oxford.

(L. Elsey Collection)

4.6 Liveries

The Standard Cl. 4 2-6-0s carried the designated standard BR mixed traffic lined black livery as outlined in section 2.6. None of the class appeared in the BR green livery applied to some other mixed traffic Standard classes whilst in BR service, probably as a consequence of there being no allocation to the WR. Both Horwich and Doncaster used 8" size numerals for the cabsides. For Doncaster, this represented a departure from the practice of using 10" size numerals for all the other BR Standard classes built there. Engines repaired at Darlington, Cowlairs and St. Rollox received 10" numerals which were usually replaced by the 8" type in the event of repainting at other works. Later, Darlington adopted 8" numerals for engines passing through for overhaul. In accordance with its usual practice, Doncaster applied the ER/NER 'RA4' route availability designation to the cabside with the power classification mark 'CLASS 4' painted on the fireman's side of the front buffer beam. This scheme was applied to all Doncaster-built class members including the two batches for the SR, 76025-9 and 76053-69; on the latter batch, as with the NER group 76045-52, the 'RA4' code was centrally placed under the numerals rather than being offset towards

the cab. Doncaster also adopted this scheme for engines sent for overhaul from the ER, NER and ScR; 76000-4 from the latter Region were nominally maintained by Doncaster until early 1956. The five engines with the cabside recesses, 76030-4 referred to in section 4.2, had their numerals applied high on the cabside to avoid the recessed panel; the 'RA4' route availability designation was placed centrally at the base on the cabside. Later, in visits to Stratford Works, the 'RA4' was replaced by the power classification mark '4' directly under the high placed numerals. With the exception of 76030-4 transferred to the SR in November 1962, all of the SR allocation carried either the yellow spot or later the yellow triangle underneath the cabside number denoting that they had been fitted with water softening treatment apparatus. The French T.I.A softening system (yellow spot) was later replaced by the standard BR briquette system (yellow triangle).

There was a variation in the tender livery applied by the LMR and ScR from the late 1950s. The lining at the front and rear edges of the tender was shortened significantly to allow for the second style BR logo introduced in 1957 to be centralised within the panel area whilst avoiding as many rivet heads as possible.

4.7 Allocation and Duties

4.7.1 Delivery Period 1952-1957

The first two batches, consisting of twenty five engines, 76000-24 were delivered in late 1952 and early 1953, 76000-19 from Horwich and 76020-4 from Doncaster. Initial allocations were to the ScR, SR and NER as follows:

ScR	Motherwell	(5)	76000-4
SR	Eastleigh	(15)	76005-19
NER	Darlington	(1)	76020
	York	(1)	76021
	Hull Dairycoates	(1)	76022
	Sunderland	(1)	76023
	Gateshead	(1)	76024

The new 2-6-0s were reportedly well received at Motherwell, although No 76000 had an inauspicious start on its first appearance in Scotland on 4th December 1952. It was working the 3.12pm Carlisle Kingmoor-Kilbirnie freight when, at Auchinleck between Dumfries and Kilmarnock on the former Glagow and South Western main line, it came into collision with a preceding freight, the 1.30pm Kingmoor-Ayr Falkland Junction. Both lines were blocked and the engine and a number of wagons sustained considerable damage. 76000 was sent to St Rollox works in Glasgow for attention to the twisted front end framing, emerging restored on 20th December. 76002 was also out of action before Christmas when the motion on one side was damaged during a collision at Newton between Hamilton and Glasgow. The engine was sent to Doncaster for repair and did not return to Scotland until the end of March.

Motherwell employed the new 2-6-0s on freight and local passenger turns to Glasgow and Ayr, including local football excursions to such places as Bonnybridge and Kilmarnock. They were noted on longer distance freights including the Law Junction to Forfar workings and made appearances on goods trains to Perth and Aberdeen. The arrival of the new engines enabled Motherwell's remaining former Caledonian Railway Cl. 4P 4-6-0s to be transferred to Hamilton.

In June 1953 the engines were noted on the Clyde Coast service from Glasgow Central to Greenock, Gourock and Wemyss Bay, an embarkation point for Caledonian sailings to the Isles of Bute and Cumbrae. The same month saw them on freight duties in the Ardrossan area, a regular turn being the night freight from Mossend which was shared between Motherwell and Ardrossan depots; the return working was a Glengarnock-Dalzell Junction freight. In April 1955, 76001 was transferred to Blair Atholl on the former Highland Railway main line from Perth to Inverness. From here it was tried out on banking duties on the seventeen mile 1 in 70 ruling gradient to Druimuachdar summit, 1484 feet above sea level. 76001 was not deemed a success and returned to Motherwell the following month.

The Eastleigh allocation, 76005-19, was put to work on passenger trains on the cross-country Portsmouth-Cardiff service as far as Salisbury, displacing the LSWR Drummond Cl. D15 4-4-0s. One roster included the 6.15am Southampton-Portsmouth, a return trip from there to Salisbury followed by a round trip to Fareham, ending the day

with the 6.45pm Portsmouth-Southampton. The new 2-6-0s became regular performers on the Southampton-Bournemouth line where one roster included a return to Eastleigh on services via Salisbury and Andover Junction. They also worked the Portsmouth-Reading trains throughout, displacing GWR Hall Cl.4-6-0s from the Eastleigh-Reading leg.

Following the closure of Winchester depot in 1953, the summer schedules on the Didcot, Newbury and Southampton route were considerably revised. As a result the new Standard Cl. 4 Moguls began working passenger services on this line, having already operated freight services for some time. A regular turn was as shown:

7.20am	Winchester Chesil-Reading General
3.45pm	Reading General-Didcot
5.52pm	Didcot-Southampton Terminus

In July, further routes to succumb to the Standard Cl. 4 Mogul invasion were the Southampton-Oxford and Bournemouth-Brighton passenger trains and the Bournemouth-Banbury freights. The Eastleigh engines also took over the heavy Bournemouth-South Wales passenger workings as far as Salisbury via the single track Wimborne

Fig. 179
76014 leaves Fratton with a Portsmouth-Cardiff train on 1st October 1961. It is estimated the engine had accrued almost 300,000 miles by this date operating mainly on the SR's Western Section. (P.H. Wells)

Fig. 180
76016 leaves Salisbury with the mid-morning Bristol Temple Meads-Portsmouth semi-fast in the mid-1950s. A Waterloo train headed by S15 4-6-0 30826 and the 12.42pm diesel electric for Southampton wait in adjacent platforms. 76016 spent all its time on the SR's Western Section, allocated to either Eastleigh or Guildford until withdrawal in October 1966. *(Peter Groom)*

Fig. 181
76016 heads a holiday extra at an unidentified location on 2nd August 1958. The engine had undergone a heavy intermediate overhaul at Eastleigh at the beginning of the year having run a total mileage of 161,825 from new. *(L. Elsey)*

Fig. 182
Preserved 76017 is seen on the Mid-Hants Railway near Ropley on 2nd June 1985 with an Alresford-Alton train shortly after the extension of the line to Alton; the engine has since been named *Hermes*.
(Hugh Ballantyne)

branch through Fordingbridge.

The NER allocation of five engines, 76020-4, was spread over the same number of motive power depots. The Darlington engine, 76020, began work on the Saltburn passenger trains whereas Sunderland used 76023 on local goods workings during the week and local passenger trains on Saturdays. 76022 at Dairycoates worked to Hornsea, Scarborough and Leeds whilst the Newcastle-Middlesbrough hourly services saw the first use of 76024, the Gateshead engine. Within a few weeks the latter was transferred, first to Blaydon, then to Percy Main, a freight depot where it was used alongside LNER Cl. J27 0-6-0s on local mineral turns. From here 76024 transferred to Alnmouth, a sub-depot of Tweedmouth for use on trains to Newcastle, which were nominally Cl. D20 4-4-0 workings. In April 1954, it was again on the move to Alston, a sub-shed of Blaydon and by the summer was in charge of the majority of the passenger and freight services on the branch from Haltwhistle.

York's 76021 began working on the Leeds and Scarborough lines but was soon moved to Neville Hill. From here it was used on services to Northallerton, West Hartlepool, Selby and Scarborough. One roster involved the 7.24am Leeds City-West Hartlepool which later included piloting the 9.20am Newcastle-London Holloway empty coaching stock train between Stockton and Thirsk. The engine then took the Leeds section of this train forward from Thirsk. After a short spell at Selby where it was noted on Leeds line passenger trains, 76021 was reallocated to Malton where it found employment on local freights. During Saturdays in the summer months its main duty was as a standby engine for the heavy holiday traffic on the Scarborough line.

The third batch of Standard Cl. 4 2-6-0s 76025-34, was delivered from Doncaster to the SR and ER during the last three months of 1953; allocation was as shown:

SR	Eastleigh	(5)	76025-9
ER	Stratford	(5)	76030-4

The class total at Eastleigh was now twenty which enabled 76005/6 from the earlier allocation to be loaned to Brighton for trial on Oxted line trains to London. The engines were a substitute for LMS Cl. 4 2-6-4 tank engines and SR Cl. U1 Moguls. Regular duties were the 8-20am, 11-02 am and 5-18pm from Brighton to Victoria and the 12-03pm, 3-52pm and 9-30pm (vans) return. The engines were also tried out on the heavily-loading 5-40pm from London Bridge and 6-10pm from Victoria. The newcomers were not popular as they were reportedly indifferent steamers and could not keep time. After only a few months 76005/6 moved to Dorchester from where they worked local passenger and goods traffic on the Bournemouth line becoming Eastleigh-based engines again early in 1955 when Dorchester depot lost its independent status.

The Eastleigh Standard Cl. 4 Moguls were always in demand for extra workings such as the two twelve coach specials run in June 1954 from Southampton to Winchester Chesil in connection with the King Edward's School thanksgiving service at the Cathedral. They also appeared at Waterloo on Channel Islands boat train reliefs, and were still regular performers on the Bournemouth-Brighton through service. In September 1954, 76017 was involved in a mishap

at the southern end of the single line crossing loop at Whitchurch Town when working the 9.50am Didcot-Eastleigh goods. Due to brake failure it was unable to halt in the loop to cross the 10.22am Eastleigh-Newbury passenger train. After diverting the runaway into the shunting spur, the signalman was able to run down the track to stop the passenger train clear of the wreckage.

In November 1954, the Standard Cl. 4 2-6-0s were rostered for use on the former M&SWJR line from Andover Junction to Cheltenham in place of SR Cl. U Moguls. The engines became regulars on the 10.10am Southampton Terminus-Cheltenham Spa Lansdown which took nearly three and a half hours for the ninety six mile journey calling at most stations. Return was on the 3.20pm Cheltenham-Eastleigh goods. In March 1955, altered engine workings brought the Eastleigh engines on regular trips to the former Somerset and Dorset line (S&DJR). Tablet exchange apparatus for these single line duties was duly fitted to 76007/11-13. Typical turns involved the 6.55am and 7.05pm Bath Green Park-Bournemouth West and 12.55pm return. Again, through passengers were not expected to be in a hurry as these stopping trains took anything up to four hours or more for the seventy one mile trip. The class now had fewer duties on the Didcot line services which were given back to the venerable LSWR Cl. T9 4-4-0s.

In June 1955, Salisbury received its first allocation of the class when 76027-9 were transferred from Eastleigh, to be replaced almost immediately by 76005/6/8. They were used on semi-fasts and stopping trains to Exeter and on the Portsmouth and Bournemouth line passenger services. The Bulford branch freights were also regular duties as the improved cab protection allowed more comfortable tender-first working for the crews.

In the summer of 1956, the Standard Cl. 4 2-6-0s were regularly seen in London on a Southampton-Kensington Olympia parcels working, the Saturdays only 10.30am Lymington Pier-Waterloo Isle of Wight boat service and the occasional Bournemouth semi-fast. From November 1957, the Hampshire diesel multiple units were scheduled to take over the local services on the Portsmouth, Southampton, Salisbury, Andover and Alton routes in two stages. Late delivery of some of the units meant that the services could not be entirely dieselised by that date. To cover this, a steam interval service was introduced between Portsmouth and Andover Junction using several classes of steam engine including Standard Cl. 4 2-6-0s.

The ER allocation 76030-4 at Stratford arrived in the last two months of 1953. They had a large section cut out of both sides of the cab for the fitting of tablet exchange apparatus for either forward facing or tender first single line working although there is no evidence that the apparatus was ever fitted. The engines were used on cross-London freights from Temple Mills to Acton via the North London line, to Hither Green via the West London line and on Southend line passenger duties. The class made occasional appearances on the Liverpool Street to Bishop's Stortford, Cambridge and Hertford services and were regulars on Clacton line duties. Occasionally they were pressed into service on busy summer weekends on trains to Yarmouth South Town and Lowestoft Central although this was usually seen as a last resort as the higher powered B1, B12 and B17 Cl. 4-6-0s were much better timekeepers. The class also had a spell on the

Wickford-Southminster branch and was noted on Tilbury line freights from time to time.

The fourth batch consisting of ten engines, 76035-44 for the ER was delivered to Neasden depot from Doncaster over the period May to August 1954 displacing B1 Cl. 4-6-0s and Ivatt Cl. 4 2-6-0s. The engines were employed on the suburban and parcels services from Marylebone to Aylesbury and the Aylesbury-Princes Risborough locals as well as Neasden-Woodford Halse and Aylesbury-Quainton Road freights. They were also noted on the 9.05pm Marylebone-Crewe parcels and the 7.30pm milk empties to Shrewsbury as far as Banbury returning with the up milk train arriving Marylebone around 1.00am. In March 1955, 76035 moved to Hitchin from where it worked on the Kings Cross to Hitchin and Cambridge trains and the Broad Street-Baldock commuter service. It occasionally appeared on the morning pick-up freight to Hertford. By June 76035 was back on the Marylebone line at Woodford Halse depot and was noted on semi-fasts between Leicester Central and the capital.

In the early summer of 1955, some Neasden Standard Cl. 4 2-6-0s were fitted with trip cocks to conform to the automatic train control requirements when operating on the London Transport Executive's Metropolitan lines. The class could be seen working freights from Harrow on the LTE Uxbridge line and coal trains to both the Metropolitan yard at Willesden Green and the Metropolitan power station sidings at Neasden. The class continued operating on the Metropolitan lines until replaced by Type 2 Cl. 24 diesels in the early 1960s. Neasden's Standard Cl. 4 2-6-0s were also observed on the Epping-Ongar branch passenger service, normally the preserve of LNER Cl. F5 2-4-2 tank engines, motor fitted for push and pull work.

The next batch of fifteen Doncaster built engines 76045-9/53-62 was delivered over the period March to July 1955; 76045-9 went to Gateshead depot on the NER and 76053-62 to Redhill on the SR. Manufacture of the missing 76050-2, also for the NER was deferred for a year in favour of the SR requirements.

The Gateshead allocation arrived in March and April and was found work on Park Lane goods depot's freight rosters to Ferryhill, Stockton, Newport, Middlesbrough and Darlington. The engines also appeared on the Middlesbrough and Carlisle line passenger services from Newcastle, although timekeeping on the latter service suffered as a result. At the start of the winter timetable in September some of the Gateshead engines were sharing workings on the Middlesbrough to Whitby and Scarborough line with LMS Cl. 4 2-6-4 tank engines and Standard Cl. 3 2-6-0s (77XXX). By October 76045-9 were all at Blaydon. In addition to local passenger and freight duties in the Newcastle area, they took over some of the services on the Border Counties line, the former North British Railway branch between Hexham and Riccarton Junction through the Kielder forest. From Hawick they had a regular working on the Sunday 9.00am to Edinburgh Waverley and the 8.25pm return.

The delayed batch, 76050-2, was finally delivered from Doncaster in August and September 1956; initially allocation was to Darlington (76050) and York (76051/2). The York engines were employed for a short time on freight turns to Mexborough and as far afield as Peterborough but were deemed insufficiently powerful for these duties. 76051/2 were also noted on freight workings to Darlington Croft Yard

and Gateshead Park Lane. They appeared on Scarborough line passenger duties, local freight trips, for example the Thirsk Junction pick-up goods and the Foss Islands freights as well as on the Leeman Road pilot duty and the occasional officers' special.

In May 1956, LMS Ivatt Cl. 4 2-6-0s operating on the Darlington-Kirkby Stephen line over the 1370 feet Stainmore summit began to be displaced, mainly to Tyneside, by Standard Cl. 4 2-6-0s. By October, the whole NER allocation was either at Kirkby Stephen (76020/2/3/47/8/51/2) or West Auckland (76021/4/45/6/9/50) for work on this route. Despite the inhospitable nature of the terrain, the South Durham and Lancashire Union Railway Company had opened the Stainmore line in 1861 with a plan to generate lucrative mineral traffic between Tyneside, Tees-side and the Furness area of Lancashire. The London and North Western Railway had also set its sights on using the route as one stage of a project to reach Newcastle to challenge the North Eastern Railway's monopoly on Tyneside. In the event the plan was frustrated by the NER who eventually succeeded in absorbing the route in 1863.

By the mid-1950s, apart from local passenger traffic between Penrith and Darlington, the Stainmore line handled coke trains from County Durham to the iron and steel works of the Furness and up to 3000 tons of limestone per week from the Warcop and Merrygill quarries near Kirkby Stephen to the Dorman Long steel plants on Tees-side. The Kirkby Stephen-Tebay local service had expired in December 1952 but on summer Saturdays there were three holiday trains using the route each way between Newcastle, Darlington, South Shields and Blackpool. A notable train using the line on alternate Fridays was the 8.42am Ulverston-Durham returning at 2.49pm conveying Northumberland and Durham coal miners to and from their convalescent home at Conishead Priory near Ulverston. In addition, there were occasional special trains for Forces personnel from Broomielaw Camp and Barnard Castle to Preston and Manchester as well as regular day excursions from North East towns to the Lancashire coast and the Lake District. Together with the Standard Cl. 3 2-6-0s (77XXX) and Standard Cl. 3 2-6-2 tank engines (82XXX), the Standard Cl. 4 2-6-0s were in charge of much of the traffic on the Stainmore line, usually changing engines at Tebay. Observation at Kirkby Stephen for a short period on a typical summer Saturday, 4th August 1956, saw 76024 on one of the three holiday train workings from Blackpool and 76022 on a Penrith-Darlington local. Freight duties produced 76045/6 assisted by 76049 as banker on a westbound 31 wagon coke train whilst 76023 set off on the nine miles at 1 in 72/60/59 climb to Stainmore summit banked by 76048 with 20 mineral empties.

The Redhill engines, 76053-62 arrived between April and July 1955, releasing SR Maunsell Cl. U and U1 2-6-0s to London depots. Some of their first duties were on the Redhill-Reading passenger service; they were also noted on the 9.18am Margate-Birkenhead from Redhill as far as Reading General and the 7.35am return (1.14pm from Reading). Other rosters involved the 4.45am London Bridge-Eastbourne, 5.25pm (except Saturdays) London Bridge-Reading and the Sunday 8.58am Tonbridge-Hastings. During August 76061 was observed on the 10.56am Brighton-Victoria via Uckfield and the 3.52pm return and also kept time on the 9.05am Victoria-Newhaven boat train and

Fig. 183
76017 banks the down 'Bournemouth Belle' through Parkstone station up the 1 in 60/130 to Branksome on 27th March 1960, during diversion of main line trains through Wimborne due to engineering works.

(Courtney Haydon)

Fig. 184
Looking none the worse for its runaway derailment experience at Whitchurch a few weeks earlier, 76026 passes Woodfidley between Brocken-hurst and Beaulieu Road with a Sunday 8.45am West Moors-Eastleigh engineers' special on 10th April 1960.

(Courtney Haydon)

Fig. 185
76030 is in charge of a train from Redhill to Reading at Ash Junction on 31st October 1964. 76030 was one of five engines, 76030-4, initially allocated to the ER but transferred to the SR in November 1962. Note the recessed panel in the cabside to accommodate tablet exchange apparatus; this was applied to all five engines and was probably intended for single-line working on the ER's M&GN section from Bourne through South Lynn to Melton Constable and Yarmouth. The devices were never fitted as the engines were not regularly used on the M&GN but instead spent their time on the ER at either Stratford, Cambridge, Norwich or March. The large box on the running plate above the centre driving wheel accommodates the AWS apparatus.

(Rodney Lissenden)

Fig. 186
76032, with cabside recess, heads an up relief express 'under the wires' near Shenfield on 9th July 1955. Note the absence of electric warning flashes not introduced for several more years.

(Philip J. Kelley)

Fig. 187
76034, with cabside recess and electric warning flashes, pauses at Stamford Town with a Peterborough-Leicester London Road slow on 19th September 1961. The engine is fitted with BR AWS apparatus as confirmed by the presence of the protective plate behind the front coupling hook. *(P.H. Wells)*

Fig. 188
76035 hurries a down Saturdays Only holiday train for Scarborough through Pontefract Baghill on 18th June 1960. From 76035 onwards, the class was fitted with plain section coupling rods rather than the fluted type. *(Peter Cookson)*

5.48pm return, the latter with twelve coaches and two vans. The earlier concerns about indifferent steaming when 76005/6 were trialed in 1954 had clearly been overcome.

A further batch of seven engines 76063-9 was delivered to Eastleigh from Doncaster in July and August 1956 and five more, 76070-4 to the ScR from September to November; allocation was as shown:

SR	Eastleigh	(7)	76063-9
ScR	Motherwell	(2)	76070/1
	Dumfries	(2)	76072/3
	Eastfield	(1)	76074

The Motherwell engines joined 76000-4, sharing their duties which by now included some of the Cathcart Circle passenger workings. This was a frequent suburban service on an eight mile circuit with a journey time of around thirty five minutes from Glasgow Central via Mount Florida, Pollokshaws East and back to Central via Maxwell Park; the above, clockwise, route was known as the 'Outer Rail' and the anti-clockwise direction as the 'Inner Rail'. A considerable variety of motive power from several of the Glasgow area depots was regularly observed on these trains.

Dumfries received 76072/3 in October 1956. They were used mainly on passenger and freight work on the former Portpatrick and Wigtownshire Joint line to Stranraer displacing LMS Compound and Cl. 2P 4-4-0s. 76074 arrived at Eastfield in November and was noted on the local services from Glasgow Queen Street to Larbert and Helensburgh.

The next batch of twenty five engines, 76075-99, fifteen for the LMR and ten for the ScR was delivered from Horwich from December 1956 to November 1957:

LMR	Sutton Oak	(5)	76075-9
	Lower Darwen	(5)	76080-4
	Leicester Midland	(2)	76085/6
	Trafford Park	(3)	76087-9
ScR	Corkerhill	(10)	76090-9

By February 1957, 76075-9 were at work from Sutton Oak on local freights alongside LMS Cl. 4F 0-6-0s, having displaced Ivatt Cl. 4 2-6-0s (43XXX) to other depots. Longer distance freight work included trips to Mold Junction on mineral trains. The class was noted on passenger duties from Warrington Bank Quay to St Helens Shaw Street, Liverpool Lime Street to Wigan North Western via St Helens and Lime Street to Manchester Exchange via Earlestown.

The Lower Darwen engines, 76080-4, were used on local passenger and freight duties from the Blackburn area to Preston, Blackpool, Wigan Wallgate, Southport and Liverpool Exchange. They were also regulars on the numerous holiday extras and excursions to Blackpool, sharing the duties with Hughes-Fowler Crab Cl. 6P/5F 2-6-0s and Stanier Cl. 5 4-6-0s.

In June 1957, Leicester was using 76085/6 on local passenger services to Birmingham New Street, Nottingham, Chesterfield and Sheffield. Arriving at Leicester during the same period as the Standard Cl. 4 4-6-0s (75XXX), the new engines displaced the LMS Compound 4-4-0s on their last duty from London St Pancras, the 3.20pm semi-fast to Kettering.

Arriving at Trafford Park in time to power some of the Whitsuntide 1957 excursion traffic to Southport, 76087-9 were used on passenger services from Manchester Central to Chester Northgate and to Sheffield Midland via the Hope Valley line through Chinley. They could also be seen on regular trip freight workings in the Stockport area. By July, 76087 together with 76085 from Leicester had been re-assigned to Saltley. From here they appeared on a new fitted freight turn, the 2.15am (SuX) Water Orton-Southampton Docks over the WR via Bordesley Junction and Didcot. The duty was shared with Tyseley depot for a time, Saltley operating the Monday, Wednesday and Friday trips with Tyseley using GWR Cl. 43XX 2-6-0s on the alternate days. The return working was the 7.28pm Southampton-Water Orton; later Tyseley depot took over the whole of this duty. The Saltley engines were also noted on another fast freight, the 12.15pm Washwood Heath-Eastleigh as far as Oxford, returning on the 4.40pm Oxford Hinksey Yard to Water Orton. Passenger duties included Birmingham New Street-Worcester Shrub Hill, Redditch and Ashchurch line locals.

The Corkerhill group, 76090-9 was delivered between June and November 1957 and displaced LMS 2P 4-4-0s and Caledonian Railway 0-6-0s from local passenger duties to Paisley, Ayr, Ardrossan, Largs and Kilmarnock. They were also observed on both passenger and freight workings to Stranraer frequently acting as pilot to a Standard Cl. 5 4-6-0 (73XXX) on the heavy boat trains for the Northern Irish service to Larne. 76099 was the last steam engine to be built at Horwich thus ending an almost seventy year old tradition of steam engine building at the former Lancashire and Yorkshire Railway Works

The final batch of fifteen Standard Cl. 4 2-6-0s 76100-14 was delivered from Doncaster to the ScR over the period May to October 1957; allocation was as shown:

ScR	Dawsholm	(4)	76100-3
	Kittybrewster	(5)	76104-8
	Thornton Junction	(3)	76109-11
	Dumfries	(1)	76112
	St Rollox	(2)	76113/4

It was in May and June when 76100-3 arrived at Dawsholm, the former Caledonian Railway depot to the north west of Glasgow. The depot had the reputation locally of being 'a refuge for life-expired locomotives of distinction', so the new arrivals were something of a novelty. The engines began work on the Coatbridge-Balloch service via Glasgow Central Low Level, displacing Caledonian Railway 0-6-0s. They also appeared on Bridgeton Central-Helensburgh Central trains via Glasgow Queen Street Low Level. After less than a month 76102/3 were moved to Parkhead, the former North British Railway depot to the south east of Glasgow. From here they worked the Helensburgh line services sharing the duty with Parkhead's LNER Gresley Cl. V1 and V3 2-6-2 tank engines. An example of a regular roster for the Standard Cl. 4 2-6-0s is as shown:

6.12am	Shettleston-Helensburgh
8.25am	Helensburgh-Glasgow Queen Street
9.11am	Glasgow Queen Street-Helensburgh
10.57am	Helensburgh-Bridgeton Central

The Kittybrewster engines, 76104-8 were delivered in July and August 1957. They were put to work on passenger and freight services between Aberdeen, Keith, Elgin and Fraserburgh and along the Ballater branch. One of the class could usually be seen on pilot duty at the north end of Aberdeen Joint Station.

The Thornton Junction allocation, 76109-11 was put to work on passenger services from Thornton to Glasgow Buchanan Street, Edinburgh Waverley and Dunfermline, displacing LNER Director Cl. D11 4-4-0s. The original intention, as at Kittybrewster, had been to release Cl. 5 4-6-0 power for the increasing number of fast fitted freights timetabled in Scotland but the Moguls were regarded as having insufficient power in reserve for this role. By November, the class was being concentrated mainly on the Fife-Glasgow services.

76112 spent only three months at Dumfries, when in December 1957, it was moved to Stranraer for both Dumfries and Glasgow St Enoch line duties. Delivered in October 1957, the St Rollox pair, 76113/4 were used on the Glasgow Buchanan Street to Oban and Fife workings. 76114 was the last in an illustrious line of Doncaster-built steam engines, leaving the erecting shop on 16th October.

4.7.2 From 1958 to Withdrawal

Eastern Region

Following the transfer of responsibility for the former Great Central Marylebone line to the LMR in February 1958, the only Standard Cl. 4 2-6-0s remaining on the ER were 76030-4 at Stratford. The dieselisation of some of the Liverpool Street-Norwich services occurred in the spring of 1958 using Type 4 Cl. 40s and Type 2 Cl. 31s. The Britannia Cl. 7 Pacifics displaced from these duties were redeployed on the new Clacton interval service releasing B1 and B12 Cl. 4-6-0s for some of the secondary duties thus ousting the Standard Cl. 4 2-6-0s from much of their work on this route.

In June 1960, with gradual dieselisation in the Stratford area further reducing their workload, 76030/2/3 were moved to Cambridge. They appeared on local freight duties and the Kings Lynn-Hunstanton branch, taking excursions and holiday trains forward from Cambridge.

November 1960 saw the completion of the electrification programme for the Liverpool Street to Enfield Town, Chingford, Hertford East and Bishop's Stortford suburban routes. This caused a major change in the steam allocation at Stratford and the two remaining Standard Cl. 4 2-6-0s 76031/4 moved to March and Norwich (Thorpe) respectively. By then the Cambridge engines were also at March and were noted on locals from Peterborough East to both Northampton and Leicester as well as the Grimsby line services from Peterborough North. The class was also to be seen on freight and mineral workings as far as the Sheffield area. The Norwich engine, 76034 was used on Cambridge, Peterborough, Yarmouth and Lowestoft line duties; it joined the rest of the batch at March in September 1961. By the following summer, steam was a rare sight in East Anglia and 76030-4, having been stored at March from September 1962, were re-assigned to Brighton on the SR two months later. From that time there was no further allocation of the class to the ER.

Scottish Region

In March 1958, the Scottish allocation of thirty five engines 76000-4/70-4/90-114 was as follows, carrying out duties much as before:

Motherwell	(7)	76000-4/70/1
Dumfries	(2)	76072/3
Eastfield	(1)	76074
Corkerhill	(10)	76090-9
Dawsholm	(2)	76100/1
Parkhead	(2)	76102/3
Kittybrewster	(5)	76104-8
Thornton Junction	(3)	76109-11
Stranraer	(1)	76112
St Rollox	(2)	76113/4

The Motherwell engines tended to wander from their usual haunts. For example in June 1958, 76001 was noted on a Glasgow Buchanan Street-Stirling semi-fast whilst 76003 was in Fife on a Thornton Junction service; these workings were probably running-in turns from St Rollox Works. In August 1959, 76003 appeared on the West Highland line with the 3.00pm Glasgow Queen Street-Crianlarich. The following November Forfar depot, by then a sub-shed of Perth, still had a number of freight turns. For one of these to Stirling, Forfar usually borrowed a Motherwell Standard Cl. 4 2-6-0 for a week at a time, exchanging it for a fresh one at Stirling each Saturday. In June 1960, 76001 was transferred to Fort William and together with LNER B1 4-6-0s 61342/55 worked the West Highland line Mallaig extension. The regular turn for 76001 was the 3.15pm Fort William-Mallaig and the 5.40pm return. In the summer of 1962, dieselisation of the West Highland line with Type 2 Cl. 27s was complete and 76001 was back in the Glasgow area at Corkerhill by August. In January 1963, Motherwell's 76004/70/1 moved to Greenock Ladyburn depot and later to Polmadie where they shared the Glasgow Central-Gourock-Wemyss Bay passenger duties and local freight services with diesel and other steam power until June 1967 when the route was electrified. 76000/2/3 were retained at Motherwell, where they would remain for the whole of their working lives.

In August 1958, the local passenger service on the Dumfries-Stranraer route now regularly featured 76072/3 and 76112. They also shared the workings on the Castle Douglas-Kirkudbright branch with Cl. 4 2-6-4 tank engines of both LMS and BR variety until line closure in May 1965. The local service to Stranraer carried on for a few more weeks but was withdrawn on 14th June when the line from Maxwell Town near Dumfries to Dunragit Challoch Junction (where the Glasgow line joined) was closed completely. The 'Northern Irishman' boat trains, 7.30pm from Euston to Stranraer Harbour and 10.00pm return, run in connection with sailings to Larne, were re-routed via Ayr. The solitary Eastfield engine, 76074, was transferred in August 1961. After spending time at Parkhead, Grangemouth and Dawsholm, it eventually found a home at Dumfries in October 1964 as a replacement for the withdrawn 76072.

The Corkerhill engines 76090-9 were still regularly operating to Kilmarnock and Ayr. They also provided power for special workings, as for example on 19th April 1958 when 76090/7/9 powered football extras to Mount Florida, the station for Hampden Park football ground on the Cathcart

Fig. 189
76042 is involved in shunting duties south of Cricklewood on 6th September 1963; the engine later transferred to the West Midlands area and was withdrawn in June 1966.

(Peter Groom)

Fig. 190
76047 heads the 4.30pm Newcastle-Hawick near Thorneyburn on the Hexham-Riccarton Junction Border Counties line a few months before closure to passenger traffic in 1956. The train took around three hours for the 76 mile journey allowing through passengers on long summer evenings ample time to enjoy the rugged and beautiful scenery.

(Peter J. Robinson)

Fig. 191
76050 nears Appleby East with the 10.02am Darlington-Penrith on 13th August 1961. The passenger service was withdrawn following the closure of the Barnard Castle-Penrith section over Stainmore summit from 22nd January 1962.

(Courtney Haydon)

Fig. 192
76050 leaves Barnard Castle for Kirkby Stephen on a Stainmore line passenger service in the late 1950s/early 1960s period. 76050 was transferred to the ScR at Hawick in October 1963 and withdrawn in September 1965 after a life of less than ten years.

(N.E. Stead)

Fig. 193
The 10.10am Dorchester South–Millbrook freight passes Lyndhurst Road on 27th September 1960 behind 76056, fitted with high water capacity BR1B type tender, and Drummond 'Black Motor' 0-6-0 30695. 76056 had undergone a light intermediate overhaul at Eastleigh Works during the previous December, having completed over 160,000 miles in traffic.

(Courtney Haydon)

Fig. 194
Redhill-based 76058 is at the head of a Hastings-Ashford train approaching Ruckinge Crossing as it nears the top of the 1 in 100 climb from the levels of Romney Marsh on 5th August 1956; 76058 was probably the first of its class to visit the line. The coaching stock shows some variety; the lead vehicle appears to be from the 1920s Continental stock, followed by a Maunsell coach, and then a three coach ex-SECR set bringing up the rear.

(Dennis Ovenden)

Circle line. One of the Corkerhill engines was involved in a collision at Dalry early on the morning of 26th November 1960 when 76098 on a Kilmarnock-Elderslie freight ran into and derailed six wagons of a Paisley-Barassie freight. Early passenger trains serving Ayrshire were either cancelled, combined or diverted via Lochwinnoch.

Along with other depot's engines, Corkerhill's Standard Cl. 4 2-6-0s were called to the rescue when the new Glasgow suburban electric services, the 'Blue Trains', were suspended after only a few weeks on 19th December 1960. Problems with exploding transformers meant that the electric multiple units were returned to the makers AEI in Manchester for modification. 76090/1/3-5 and 76113 were sent to Parkhead to work alongside 76114, Gresley V1 and V3 2-6-2 tank engines and Ivatt Cl. 4 2-6-0s as substitutes until full resumption of the electric service on 1st October 1961. With the 'Blue Trains' re-established, Parkhead's Standard Cl. 4 2-6-0s which now included 76074, were re-assigned to Grangemouth, Motherwell, Corkerhill and St Rollox.

Dawsholm continued to operate 76100-2 on freight services after electrification. The engines were noted on passenger services from Glasgow Buchanan Street and also from Queen Street to Perth via the Devon Valley line through Alloa and Kinross Junction. After the depot closed in October 1964, the Standard Cl. 4 2-6-0 allocation was moved to Grangemouth.

In May 1962 Ayr Depot received its first Standard Cl. 4 Moguls when 76096/7/9 arrived from Corkerhill. From Ayr they were used on local freights, displacing Caledonian Cl. 3F 0-6-0s, and on passenger and freight work on the Stanraer and Glasgow lines.

The Kittybrewster group, 76104-8, continued their duties on the former Great North of Scotland Railway network north of Aberdeen. In the autumn of 1959, closure of Forres depot resulted in an increased number of the class's visits to Inverness. 76106/7 were moved to Keith depot in June 1960 for a twelve month stint and were noted on the Lossiemouth branch workings. In June 1961, Kittybrewster depot was dieselised, with multiple units and Type 2 Cl. 21s taking over from steam. 76104-8 moved to Aberdeen Ferryhill but were still regularly working north on freights to Elgin, Keith and the Speyside branch due to poor reliability of the Cl. 21s. In December 1961, 76105/6 were transferred to the former Caledonian Railway depot at Dalry Road, Edinburgh. They were noted on local passenger and freight duties to Glasgow Central, Carstairs, Stirling and Perth as well as on coal traffic from the West Calder, Breich and Fauldhouse areas. In the winter of 1963/4, 76104/7 still at Ferryhill were often used for train heating purposes at Aberdeen station; for a short period, they also supplied hot water to the station hotel after its boiler had failed.

In October 1958, the Thornton engines, 76109-11, one of which was based at Anstruther sub-shed, had virtually replaced the LNER Cl. D11 4-4-0s and the former North British Scott Cl. D30 and Glen Cl. D34 4-4-0s on the Edinburgh Waverley-Crail trains. In January and April 1960, the Thornton allocation was moved to Dunfermline where the engines were employed mainly on local freight duties although one was frequently seen on a late afternoon workman's train from Rosyth to Waverley. In the severe winter of 1962/63, 76109 was noted attached to a large snow plough, as a result of which its services were in great demand.

St Rollox continued to use 76113/4 on the Oban line and on passenger and freight duties to Perth, Aberdeen and the Fife coast. In October 1959, 76114 was observed as pilot on the 9.31am Fort William-Glasgow Queen Street, one of the earliest occasions when a member of the class was recorded on the West Highland line north of Crianlarich.

Hurlford depot at Kilmarnock received its first Standard Cl. 4 2-6-0, 76108 in January 1963. By October 76021/4 were also present, transferred from the NER in exchange for LMS Ivatt Cl. 4 2-6-0s 43133/4. This was part of a scheme to standardise spares at several depots and involved the transfer to the ScR of 76021/4/45/6/9/50 from the NER in exchange for Ivatt Cl. 4 2-6-0s 43132-8, 43140/1. Hurlford used 76021/4 on stopping trains to Ayr, Ardrossan and Glasgow both via Dalry and via Barrhead. The other transferees from the NER went to Grangemouth (76045), Dawsholm (76046) and Hawick (76049/50). Grangemouth's engines were noted on trip freights and local goods trains whilst the Hawick allocation was similarly employed also appearing on stopping trains to Edinburgh Waverley and Carlisle.

In July 1962, 76090 was at Beattock depot for trial on banking duties on the former Caledonian main line from Carlisle to Glasgow Central. The move was apparently successful as six other class members, 76070/94/8, 76100/3/14 were subsequently allocated to this duty at various times.

In June 1964, now supplemented by the NER transfers, a total of forty one Standard Cl. 4 2-6-0s were in Scotland, allocated as shown:

Motherwell	(3)	76000/2/3
Ardrossan	(3)	76001/98/9
Greenock Ladyburn	(2)	76004/71
Hurlford	(6)	76021/4/91/2/4/108
Grangemouth	(2)	76045, 76113
Dawsholm	(6)	76046/74, 76100-3
Hawick	(2)	76049/50
Beattock	(2)	76070/90
Dumfries	(2)	76072/3
Corkerhill	(3)	76093/5, 76114
Ayr	(2)	76096/7
Aberdeen Ferryhill	(2)	76104/7
Bathgate	(2)	76105/6
Dunfermline	(2)	76109/10
Thornton Junction	(1)	76111
Stranraer	(1)	76112

The main duties of the class at Motherwell, Ardrossan, Ayr, Hurlford, Grangemouth and Bathgate were now trip freights and coal trains, although these were increasingly being taken over by diesels. Dawsholm depot closed in October 1964, its remaining Standard Cl. 4 2-6-0s transferring to Dumfries and Grangemouth. The following December, 76004/71 from Greenock Ladyburn and 76070 from Beattock were acquired by Polmadie. From here the engines were still used on Clyde Coast line freights to Gourock and later took over from LMS Fairburn and BR Standard Cl. 4 2-6-4 tank engines on pilot duties at Glasgow Central.

The class could still be seen on passenger workings on the Ayrshire Coast line in the summer of 1965. The Saturday Heads of Ayr Holiday Camp special to Edinburgh was worked by Ayr depot and diagrammed for a Standard Cl. 4

2-6-0. At first the eight coaches were worked through to Edinburgh, leaving the engine just enough time for servicing before return. Later the Ayr engine came off at Polmadie and awaited the return train at that point. Ayr's 76096 was kept in particularly good condition for passenger workings at this time. In January 1966, for example, it was used as far as Carlisle on a special for fog-bound air travellers from Prestwick Airport to London.

On 21st March 1966, Hurlford's 76021 was involved in a collision at Annbank Junction on the Ayr-Mauchline line. The engine was unable to control a mineral train from Mauchline which ran away on the grade from Tarbolton and collided with an empty mineral train crossing on to the Drongan branch. The line was closed until the following day and the Euston boat trains were diverted via Kilmarnock and Barassie.

In addition to local and trip freights, the Dunfermline engines, 76109/10 performed pilot duties at Inverkeithing. The workings included paper mill traffic on the Rosyth branch, the Rosyth dockyard freights, coal trains to Townhill power station and the stores service to the Lathalmond Royal Naval depot. This duty also involved assisting freights and occasionally diesel multiple units up the two mile 1 in 70 gradient from Inverkeithing to the Forth Bridge. The Dunfermline engines also had their share of spills. On 24th August 76109, for example, on a haul of coal from Dollar mine to Kincardine collided with the rear of an Alloa-Kincardine coal train at the east end of Alloa station completely blocking the line until next morning.

By the end of 1966, the majority of Standard Cl. 4 2-6-0s remaining north of the border were in store at various locations including Ayr and Corkerhill. One of the class's last roles was the banking duty at Beattock. This came to an end when 76094/8 were replaced by Clayton Type 1 Cl. 17 diesels in May 1967 which date marked the withdrawal of all steam engines allocated to the Scottish Region.

Southern Region.
In April 1958, there were thirty seven Standard Cl. 4 2-6-0s allocated to the SR, distributed as shown:

Salisbury	(3)	76005/6/8
Eastleigh	(24)	76007/9-19/25-9/63-9
Redhill	(10)	76053-62

As before, the Salisbury allocation operated mainly to Bournemouth via the Fordingbridge line and on the South Wales-Portsmouth trains. An additional summer Saturday train in 1958 was a Bristol-Brighton service which a Salisbury engine worked through to the coast, returning on an empty stock train from Hove to Fratton. The engines were also employed on semi-fast workings to Waterloo. In May 1959, 76059/60 were acquired from Redhill and by spring 1960 ten examples, 76005/7/8/17/8/53-5/66/7 were on Salisbury's books, this group being a stable allocation for over four years.

The Redhill engines, 76053-62 continued work on the Reading-Redhill line including the inter-regionals to the Kent and Sussex coasts. They were also occasionally borrowed by Brighton for the through services to Plymouth and Cardiff as far as Salisbury and by Three Bridges for duties such as the 3.50pm Victoria-Brighton via Oxted. Altered arrangements in spring 1959 brought the Redhill allocation to

the Uckfield line at weekends. The Standard Cl. 4 2-6-0s shared with Maunsell Cl. N 2-6-0s the Saturday 7.55am, 11.55am, 4.55pm, and 5.55pm Brighton-Tonbridge and 9.10am, 1.12pm and 2.10pm returns; there was a similar pattern on Sundays. By April 1960, the Redhill Standard Cl. 4 2-6-0s had all been transferred to Salisbury, Bournemouth and Eastleigh; no further allocations of the class were made to Redhill.

The twenty four Standard Cl. 4 2-6-0s at Eastleigh, 76007/9-19/25-9/63-9 were operating widely over the Western Section. Apart from the Portsmouth through services to South Wales, they regularly worked to Bath Green Park, Reading and were also noted at Waterloo on the Saturday Lymington Pier boat trains. Local freight workings included the Bishop's Waltham branch, closed to passengers as far back as January 1933. When the passenger service on the Didcot, Newbury and Southampton line was withdrawn in March 1960, the Standard Cl. 4 2-6-0s continued on this route with regular freight workings. It was on this line that a derailment at Whitchurch Town took place under similar circumstances to the one in September 1954 noted earlier. On 12th February 1960 76026 was working the same goods service, the 9.50am Didcot-Eastleigh, when it failed to stop on the loop at Whitchurch and ran through the sand-drag ending up half way down the embankment. The day's remaining freights were cancelled and passenger trains terminated at Sutton Scotney, Newbury or Whitchurch Town with buses filling the gaps. 76026 was rerailed on 21st February using the Eastleigh and Salisbury cranes.

In another incident on 22nd May 1961, Eastleigh's 76019 was called to the rescue when Bulleid light Pacific 34057, working the 9.40am Brighton-Bournemouth caught fire and came to a stand between Hamble Halt and Netley. Fire brigades from Hamble and Botley were soon on the scene and the fire brought under control. 76019 arrived from the Southampton direction at about 12 noon and hauled train and engine to Netley where the Pacific was detached and, covered in foam, was left to cool off in the yard. 76019 continued with the train to Bournemouth West. In the first week of June 1961, the fruit specials to London and the North from Swanwick on the Netley line were again in the hands of the Standard Cl. 4 and Maunsell Cl. U 2-6-0s. In August main line duties included the 3.50pm Weymouth-Waterloo as far as Bournemouth and the 11.04am from Bournemouth Central to Sheffield Victoria as far as Basingstoke returning on the last leg of the 9.09am from Sheffield. Standard Cl. 4 2-6-0s shared the September Channel Islands tomato traffic with Weymouth's Standard Cl. 5 4-6-0s. Regular departures from Weymouth were 9.25am to York, 9.55am, 4.55pm and 8.00pm to Crewe, 10.20am to Chester Saltney and 3.00pm to Cardiff.

At the end of January 1963, the Southern Region allocation of forty two engines was distributed as follows:

Salisbury	(10)	76005/7/8/17/8
		76053-5/66/7
Eastleigh	(20)	76006/9-14/6/28/9
		76058-65/8/9
Bournemouth	(7)	76015/9/25-7/56/7
Brighton	(5)	76030-4

The Brighton engines had arrived from the ER in the previous November, made redundant from East Anglia by

187

Fig. 195
76060, with Engineers' Saloon D.S.1, runs into Southampton Central on 2nd March 1961 less than six months after its first general overhaul in Eastleigh Works at which time it had accrued nearly 190,000 miles.
(Courtney Haydon)

Fig. 196
76061 pilots 31781 Borsig 'German Engine' L Cl. 3P 4-4-0 near Lyghe Halt on a Tonbridge-Redhill local around 1956. 31781 was withdrawn in June 1959 after 45 years service and an accumulated mileage of nearly 1.4 million. 76061 lasted until January 1967 after less than twelve years of life with an estimated total mileage of 375,000, the two engines showing a remarkably similar overall annual mileage rate.
(K.W. Wightman)

Fig. 197
The last 10.10am Southampton Terminus-Cheltenham approaches Nursling behind 76066 on 28th June 1958. This train ran for many years and before World War II included through coaches for Liverpool. All the through Southampton-Cheltenham trains, except a solitary Saturday working, ceased in June 1958; the 10.10am was probably the most patronised service over the M&SWJR.
(Courtney Haydon)

Fig. 198
76069 winds its way towards Chilcompton Tunnel with the 4.15pm Templecombe-Bath Green Park on the S&DJR on 8th July 1961; 76069 is fresh from general overhaul at Eastleigh Works.

(Courtney Haydon)

Fig. 199
A few weeks after delivery new to Leicester Midland depot, 76085 leaves Stamford Town with a local from Peterborough to Leicester London Road on 18th May 1957. *(P.H. Wells)*

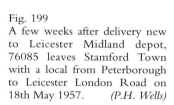

Fig. 200
Corkerhill-based 76093 shunts empty stock at Ardrossan on 4th August 1963. Apart from some months allocated to Parkhead in 1961, the engine spent the rest of its life at Corkerhill, operating mainly on the former G&SWR lines in Ayrshire.

(Courtney Haydon)

189

dieselisation. They were noted on Brighton-Lewes-Hastings freights and on summer Saturday inter-regional holiday trains. By September after a move to Guildford they appeared on Basingstoke-Waterloo semi-fasts and some passenger turns on the Reading-Redhill line.

The Bournemouth and Salisbury engines had by now taken over most of the workings on the Fordingbridge line displacing the LSWR T9 4-4-0s and making it a veritable Standard Cl. 4 2-6-0 stronghold. The line's days were numbered however and the last day of passenger traffic through Fordingbridge was the 2nd of May 1964. 76066 was on the 5.11pm Wimborne-Salisbury and the return 8.30pm to Bournemouth. At Fordingbridge the latter train encountered exploding detonators and a cheering crowd. The wake benefited from the presence of the local Carnival Queen accompanied by a brass band playing martial music including an emotional rendering of 'The Last Post'. Salisbury engines continued to reach Waterloo on semi-fasts whilst the Bournemouth allocation was still on the S&DJR line passenger and freight services to Bath Green Park until its closure in March 1966.

Line closures and dieselisation gradually encroached on to the Eastleigh Standard Cl. 4 2-6-0 duties. The Didcot, Newbury and Southampton route which had lost its passenger service in March 1960 was closed completely on 10th August 1964. From the end of October, the Portsmouth-Cardiff service was due to be taken over by Type 3 Cl. 33 diesels, after which the Standard Cl. 4 2-6-0s appeared occasionally as substitutes for failures. Christmas van traffic on the Brighton-Chichester-Portsmouth line was handled in part by Eastleigh's 76009/10/68/9 but by January 1965 three other Eastleigh engines, 76053/5/66 had moved to Feltham for a six month stint. From here they were used for trip freights and goods trains from Feltham to Nine Elms and Wimbledon to Raynes Park. They were also noted on shunting duties in Surbiton and Wimbledon yards, on the Morden South-Clapham Junction milk train, the Feltham-Cricklewood transfer freights and Waterloo-Basingstoke semi-fasts. Until October 1965, the 8.00pm Nine Elms-Southampton Docks freight was rostered for steam haulage and occasionally featured Standard Cl. 4 2-6-0s.

In the summer of 1966, the class still appeared on the Lymington Pier trains and the Swanage branch whilst 76061 worked the last steam train departure from Southampton Terminus, the 4.02pm Bournemouth stopper before it closed on 3rd September. In the run up to Christmas 1966, Standard Cl. 4 2-6-0s were still regularly powering two Waterloo line semi-fast services, the 6.09pm to Bournemouth and the 6.35pm from Salisbury, both frequently loading to ten coaches or more.

In early January 1967, withdrawals had reduced the Southern Region allocation to seventeen engines at four depots as shown; several survived only until the end of the month:

Bournemouth	(5)	76005/6/9/11/26
Salisbury	(3)	76007/8/67
Guildford	(5)	76031/3/53/8/69
astleigh	(4)	76061/3/4/6

The class was still used on a variety of duties including parcel trains, freight workings and semi-fasts on the Waterloo line.

The last steam operated branch in Southern England succumbed to the Type 3 Cl. 33 diesels when the Standard Cl. 4 2-6-0s and other types were finally displaced from the Lymington Pier workings in April 1967. The full Bournemouth line electrification timetable was scheduled for inauguration on 10th July 1967 and in the weeks before this date the remaining steam engines were not always in the best condition. For example on 1st July, 76064 made an unexpected appearance on a Waterloo-Southampton Docks boat train. The engine with an eleven coach load took ninety minutes to cover the forty eight miles to Basingstoke delaying several following trains including two more boat trains. 76064 caused considerable congestion beyond Worting Junction as the Birmingham Bromford Bridge-Southampton Fawley oil tank train was held in Basingstoke station for nearly twenty five minutes with its tail still extending on to the Reading line, completely blocking both up Waterloo lines. A week later, 76066 was noted on the 4.40am Waterloo-Woking but next day was at Salisbury depot officially withdrawn. In total, thirteen Standard Cl. 4 2-6-0s were at either Salisbury (76005-7/11/31/3/58/63/6/7) or Weymouth (76008/9/26) awaiting removal to the breaker's yard thus marking the end of steam on the Southern Region.

North Eastern Region

The Darlington-Penrith passenger service was dieselised in January 1958 and two months later, responsibility for the lines west of Kirkby Stephen was transferred to the LMR. This left only six Standard Cl. 4 2-6-0s remaining on the NER, 76021/4/45/6/9/50; all were allocated to West Auckland. The engines continued to operate on Stainmore line freights and passenger duties until through traffic was diverted via the Tyne Valley line (Newcastle-Carlisle) in July 1960. West Auckland depot also used the class on mineral workings to Tees-side, the Wear Valley, on the Shildon-Newport line and later to the new Tyne Yard near Lamesley between Newcastle and Chester-le-Street. Passenger workings included excursion traffic such as that associated with the annual Durham Miners' Gala Day; 76021 was noted there with a special on 20th July 1963. 76024 moved on to Gateshead in June 1959 and was often used on the 6.50am Newcastle-Carlisle parcels train during the summer. By November this turn had been taken over by Gateshead's new Type 4 Cl. 40 diesels for crew training before inauguration on the Kings Cross services. 76024 was then moved successively to Heaton, Sunderland, York and Thornaby before transferring with the rest of the West Auckland group to Scotland in October 1963. No further allocations of the class were made to the NER from that date.

London Midland Region

The LMR allocation of Standard Cl. 4 2-6-0s in March 1958 was thirty two allocated as shown:

Kirkby Stephen	(7)	76020/2/3/47/8/51/2
Neasden	(10)	76035-44
Sutton Oak	(5)	76075-9
Lower Darwen	(5)	76080-4
Saltley	(2)	76085/7
Leicester Midland	(1)	76086
Trafford Park	(2)	76088/9

The LMR had taken responsibility for the former NER depot at Kirkby Stephen in March 1958 as part of a general regional rationalisation move. With the dieselisation of the Darlington-Penrith passenger service, the Standard Cl. 4 2-6-0s were confined to freight work, excursions and the summer Saturday Blackpool trains. On 15th August 1959 for example, 76024/50 were on the 9.04am Newcastle-Blackpool Central whilst 76022/3 were on separate freights to the North East, assisted by Standard Cl. 2 2-6-0s 78013/7 respectively. By May 1960 the remaining Standard Cl. 4 2-6-0s at Kirkby Stephen, 76022/3/47/51/2 had been replaced by Ivatt Cl. 4 2-6-0s reportedly because of problems with loose tyres caused by the hilly nature of the line. It was clear at this time that moves were being made to close the route. Coke traffic to the Furness had dwindled over the previous two years after adoption of alternative sources from West Yorkshire. The remaining coke trains and the limestone traffic to Tees-side were now run via the Newcastle-Carlisle line with the summer Saturday Newcastle-Blackpool taking the same route. Darlington-Blackpool trains were re-routed via Harrogate and Skipton. The last train over Stainmore was the RCTS special of 20th January 1962 powered by 76049 with the assistance of Standard Cl. 3 2-6-0 77003. Two days later, the route was officially closed.

In the summer of 1958, the Neasden Standard Cl. 4 2-6-0s were still operating on semi-fasts to Leicester, goods services to Woodford Halse and the Marylebone suburban services including the so-called 'Aylesbury Flyer', the 6.12pm non-stop to Rickmansworth. From the beginning of 1960, the Great Central route daytime expresses from Marylebone to Sheffield Victoria and Manchester London Road were withdrawn and the service was reduced to a few semi-fasts between Marylebone and Nottingham. The new timings were originally planned for cross-country type diesel multiple units and some of the bookings were tight. In the event the service was steam operated with regular appearances by Standard Cl. 4 2-6-0s which were capable of fast running. For example on 17th July 1962, B1 4-6-0 61106 was short of steam whilst working the 12.25pm Nottingham Victoria-Marylebone. It was replaced at Woodford Halse by 76037 which easily kept time reaching a maximum of 81mph down the 1 in 105 gradient between Amersham and Chorleywood with the six coach load. Neasden depot was closed in June 1962, 76044 transferring to Woodford Halse whilst 76035-43 moved to Cricklewood on the Midland Division from where they continued to work on the Great Central line.

Cricklewood also received 76047/8/85/8/9 from the Manchester area in September plus 76086 in October and used the class together with Type 2 Cl. 27 diesels on the cross-London freight route from the Midland yard at Bow Junction on the former Great Eastern line to the Midland main line via South Tottenham. By mid-December 1964, the dieselisation of the Midland line south of Wellingborough was complete and Cricklewood depot closed. Ten engines, 76036/8/40/2/3/7/8/85/6/8 had already gone north to Saltley and Stoke-on-Trent whilst the remaining allocation 76035/7/9/41/89 moved to Willesden which was now responsible for supplying power for the Marylebone line. By October 1965 the Willesden group and 76044/87 from Woodford Halse left the area for Chester, Stoke-on-Trent, and the West Midlands, the Great Central line services now being operated by Britannia Cl.7 Pacifics, Stanier Cl. 5 and

Cl. 7P rebuilt Royal Scot 4-6-0s displaced from the West Coast and Midland main lines by diesels.

The Lower Darwen duties continued as before. For a short period from September 1958, 76084 was re-assigned to one of the last LMS Compound 4-4-0 strongholds, Lancaster Green Ayre, which still had five on its books, 41101/2/21/89/93. From here, 76084 took over some of the 4-4-0's duties on the Leeds City-Bradford Forster Square-Morecambe Promenade passenger service. Later, in June 1960, 76022/51, displaced from the Stainmore line by LMS Ivatt Cl. 4 2-6-0s, were at Green Ayre for almost two years on these duties. They were replaced in February 1962 by a much older design, LMS unrebuilt Patriot Cl. 4-6-0s 45505/7/10/8 made redundant from the West Coast main line by diesels. In March 1965 the Lower Darwen engines, 76080-4 joined 76075-9 at Sutton Oak but by the end of 1966 the amount of work left for steam at this depot was much reduced. The class had been used with Stanier Cl. 8F 2-8-0s on the Pilkington Glass freights which brought sand from the washing plant at Rainford to the sheet glass works at St Helens. This traffic ceased at the end of January 1967, the business going over to road haulage. By this time, dieselisation of the remaining local passenger services by multiple units and the use of Cl. 08 shunters on local freight, trip workings and shunting duties at St Helens Shaw Street goods yard was almost complete. The Sutton Oak engines were either withdrawn or had moved to Springs Branch by June 1967.

The Trafford Park engines, 76088/9 together with 76086 which arrived from Leicester in January 1959 were still used on the Chester Northgate service from Manchester Central until almost complete dieselisation by multiple units from September 1960. The class was still noted on the route on the one steam passenger working which remained until June 1962. The Hope Valley route to Sheffield Midland was also dieselised by this time but the Standard Cl. 4 2-6-0s continued to appear on the popular Rambler's Excursions to this line in the summer months.

In April 1965, allocation of the thirty four LMR engines was as shown:

Stoke-on-Trent	(8)	76020/3/44/51
		76075/85/9/99
Oxley	(1)	76022
Willesden	(4)	76035/7/9/41
Bescot	(6)	76036/42/7/86-8
Aston	(2)	76040/95
Saltley	(4)	76038/43/8/52
Sutton Oak	(9)	76076-84

76095/9 had been withdrawn by the ScR in July 1964 but reinstated by the LMR two months later.

The Stoke allocation was used mainly on local goods and colliery trip workings. Later 76051/75/85/9/99 moved to the former GNR depot at Colwick near Nottingham where they were noted working on the Belvoir ironstone branch from Bottesford when not in store.

By summer 1966, Oxley had six of the class on its books, 76022/37/9/41/87/8, 76022 being withdrawn in August. Apart from local freights, the engines were pressed into service working Paddington-Cambrian Coast passenger services forward from Wolverhampton at busy times. Chester and Machynlleth also had an allocation of the class during summer 1966. From Chester, 76036/47/52/95 worked to Birkenhead and Shrewsbury on both passenger and freight duties. In addition they could be seen on the Cambrian section frequently in double harness assisting the Machynlleth engines 76038/43. In September, Croes Newydd received 76040/8 for similar duties.

The Bescot engines 76036/42/7/86-8 replaced LMS Cl. 4F 0-6-0s which had been drafted in when the last surviving LNWR engines, four Super D Cl. 7F 0-8-0s 48895, 49361, 49407/30 were withdrawn from Bescot in December 1964. The Standard Cl. 4 2-6-0s, like the Bescot Super Ds, had enclosed cabs giving better protection to the enginemen whilst the 4Fs were well known to be rather spartan in that respect; the Moguls were used on local freights and parcels trains on the Wolverhampton-Birmingham-Coventry-Rugby line.

Aston had received its first allocation, 76020/2/3/51, from the North West in July 1962. The engines were tried out on freights to the Yorkshire area at first, including a Bescot-Healey Mills service returning the same day on the Mirfield-Bushbury goods. Later the engines were used on West Midlands area local freights but had moved to Stoke-on-Trent by the end of the year. 76040/95, arriving in January 1965 spent only a few months at Aston before the depot closed in October 1965, 76095 having moved to Chester Midland by the end of August.

The Saltley group, 76038/43/8/52 were used mainly on local freights. They had been displaced from most passenger duties by diesel multiple units but continued to appear on Birmingham New Street-Worcester and Gloucester locals for a period. The engines displaced LMS Cl. 4F 0-6-0s on banking duties for freights and summer Saturday holiday extras as required on the short stretch at 1 in 62/85 from Saltley up to Camp Hill on the Birmingham New Street avoiding line. By the summer of 1966, when their duties were taken over largely by Type 2 Cl. 24/25 diesels, the Saltley engines moved to Chester and the Cambrian section.

Other LMR depots which hosted the class for local freight and occasional passenger workings were Heaton Mersey, Crewe South, Stourbridge Junction and Uttoxeter. The latter depot received 76020/2/3 in October 1963 but had lost the allocation by the time it ceased operations in December 1964 as a result of the complete closure of the Uttoxeter to Leek and Buxton lines in January 1965.

In October 1967, only four Standard Cl. 4 2-6-0s, 76077/9/80/4, nominally remained in service, allocated to Springs Branch for local freight duties and the occasional enthusiasts' special; they had all been withdrawn by the end of the year with no fewer than three of them, 76077/9/84, destined for preservation.

Fig. 201   76113 lays a smokescreen over the countryside as it plods away from Grangemouth with an up mineral train on 16th August 1965. 76113 is in the typically unkempt condition which applied to many steam freight engines towards the end of their lives.

(Courtney Haydon)

4.7.3 Allocation Summary

76000   12.52 Motherwell; 5.67 Withdrawn.

76001   12.52 Motherwell; 4.55 Perth located Blair Atholl; 5.55 Motherwell; 5.60 Oban; 6.60 Fort William; 8.62 Corkerhill; 4.64 Ardrossan; 2.65 Ayr; 8.66 Withdrawn;

76002   12.52 Motherwell; 1.67 Withdrawn.

76003   12.52 Motherwell; 3.66 Withdrawn.

76004   12.52 Motherwell; 1.63 Greenock Ladyburn; 12.64 Polmadie; 10.66 Withdrawn.

76005   12.52 Eastleigh; 7.53 Bournemouth; 9.53 Eastleigh; 1.54 Brighton; 5.54 Dorchester; 2.55 Eastleigh; 6.55 Salisbury; 10.65 Bournemouth; 7.67 Withdrawn.

76006   1.53 Eastleigh; 7.53 Bournemouth; 9.53 Eastleigh; 1.54 Brighton; 5.54 Dorchester; 2.55 Eastleigh; 6.55 Salisbury; 3.60 Eastleigh; 10.65 Bournemouth; 7.67 Withdrawn.

76007   1.53 Eastleigh; 5.58 Salisbury; 4.67 Bournemouth; 7.67 Withdrawn.

76008   2.53 Eastleigh; 6.55 Salisbury; 4.67 Bournemouth; 5.67 Withdrawn.

76009   2.53 Eastleigh; 8.56 Redhill; 1.57 Eastleigh; 9.58 Yeovil Town; 1.59 Salisbury; 3.60 Eastleigh; 10.65 Bournemouth; 7.67 Withdrawn.

76010   3.52 Eastleigh; 9.58 Yeovil Town; 1.59 Eastleigh; 10.65 Bournemouth; 9.66 Withdrawn.

76011   3.53 Eastleigh; 9.58 Yeovil Town; 1.59 Eastleigh; 10.65 Bournemouth; 7.67 Withdrawn.

76012   4.53 Eastleigh; 6.66 Guildford; 9.66 Withdrawn.

76013   4.53 Eastleigh; 9.64 Bournemouth; 9.66 Withdrawn.

76014   5.53 Eastleigh; 8.56 Redhill; 1.57 Eastleigh; 9.64 Bournemouth; 9.66 Withdrawn.

76015   5.53 Eastleigh; 6.61 Bournemouth; 10.65 Withdrawn.

76016   5.53 Eastleigh; 6.66 Guildford; 10.66 Withdrawn.

76017   6.53 Eastleigh; 3.60 Salisbury; 7.65 Withdrawn. Preserved on the Mid-Hants Railway at Alresford.

76018   6.53 Eastleigh; 3.60 Salisbury; 8.64 Eastleigh; 7.66 Guildford; 10.66 Withdrawn.

76019   7.53 Eastleigh; 8.61 Bournemouth; 8.64 Eastleigh; 2.66 Withdrawn.

76020   12.52 Darlington; 7.56 Kirkby Stephen; 5.59 Nuneaton; 6.59 Sutton Oak; 7.62 Aston; 12.62 Stoke on Trent; 10.63 Uttoxeter; 12.64 Stoke on Trent; 7.65 Chester Midland; 4.66 Withdrawn.

76021   12.52 York; 2.53 Neville Hill; 3.53 Selby; 5.53 Malton; 1.54 Selby; 6.56 West Auckland; 10.63 Hurlford; 10.66 Withdrawn.

76022   12.52 Hull Dairycoates; 6.56 Kirkby Stephen; 4.60 Lancaster Green Ayre; 2.62 Springs Branch; 7.62 Aston; 12.62 Stoke on Trent; 10.63 Uttoxeter; 8.64 Stourbridge Junction; 11.64 Oxley; 8.66 Withdrawn.

76023   12.52 Sunderland; 6.55 West Hartlepool; 7.56 Kirkby Stephen; 4.60 Lancaster Green Ayre; 8.60 Sutton Oak; 7.62 Aston; 12.62 Stoke on Trent; 10.63 Uttoxeter; 6.64 Crewe South; 1.65 Stoke on Trent; 10.65 Withdrawn.

76024   1.53 Gateshead; 2.53 Blaydon; 3.53 Percy Main; 4.53 Tweedmouth located Alnmouth; 4.54 Blaydon located Alston; 12.55 Blaydon; 6.56 West Auckland; 6.59 Gateshead; 11.59 Heaton; 7.60 Sunderland; 9.61 York; 6.62 Thornaby; 10.63 Hurlford; 12.66 Withdrawn.

76025   10.53 Eastleigh; 5.61 Bournemouth; 10.65 Withdrawn.

76026   10.53 Eastleigh; 8.61 Bournemouth; 7.67 Withdrawn.

76027   10.53 Eastleigh; 6.55 Salisbury; 7.55 Eastleigh; 3.62 Bournemouth; 10.65 Withdrawn.

76028   10.53 Eastleigh; 6.55 Salisbury; 7.55 Eastleigh; 5.64 Withdrawn.

76029   11.53 Eastleigh; 6.55 Salisbury; 7.55 Eastleigh; 10.64 Withdrawn.

76030   11.53 Stratford; 6.60 Cambridge; 9.60 March; 11.62 Brighton; 9.63 Guildford; 1.65 Eastleigh; 4.65 Withdrawn.

76031   11.53 Stratford; 11.60 March; 11.62 Brighton; 9.63 Guildford; 1.65 Eastleigh; 6.66 Guildford; 7.67 Withdrawn.

76032   12.53 Stratford; 6.60 Cambridge; 9.60 March; 11.62 Brighton; 9.63 Guildford; 8.64 Withdrawn.

76033   12.53 Stratford; 6.60 Cambridge; 9.60 March; 11.62 Brighton; 9.63 Guildford; 1.65 Eastleigh; 6.66 Guildford;
2.67 Withdrawn.

76034   12.53 Stratford; 11.60 Norwich Thorpe; 9.61 March; 11.62 Brighton; 9.63 Guildford; 9.64 Withdrawn.

76035   5.54 Neasden; 3.55 Hitchin; 6.55 Woodford Halse; 7.56 Neasden; 6.62 Cricklewood; 12.64 Willesden;
7.65 Chester Midland; 5.66 Withdrawn.

76036   6.54 Neasden; 6.62 Cricklewood; 7.64 Saltley; 3.65 Bescot; 11.65 Stourbridge Junction; 4.66 Chester Midland;
1.67 Withdrawn.

76037   6.54 Neasden; 6.62 Cricklewood; 12.64 Willesden; 9.65 Oxley; 2.67 Chester Midland; 4.67 Croes Newydd;
6.67 Withdrawn.

76038   7.54 Neasden; 6.62 Cricklewood; 7.64 Saltley; 6.66 Machynlleth; 9.66 Withdrawn.

76039   7.54 Neasden; 6.62 Cricklewood; 12.64 Willesden; 9.65 Oxley; 3.67 Chester Midland; 4.67 Croes Newydd;
6.67 Withdrawn.

76040   7.54 Neasden; 6.62 Cricklewood; 7.64 Saltley; 1.65 Aston; 10.65 Saltley; 9.66 Croes Newydd; 4.67 Withdrawn.

76041   7.54 Neasden; 6.62 Cricklewood; 12.64 Willesden; 9.65 Oxley; 3.67 Chester Midland; 4.67 Withdrawn.

76042   8.54 Neasden; 7.62 Cricklewood; 7.64 Saltley; 3.65 Bescot; 11.65 Stourbridge Junction; 5.66 Oxley;
6.66 Withdrawn.

76043   8.54 Neasden; 7.62 Cricklewood; 7.64 Saltley; 6.66 Machynlleth; 9.66 Withdrawn.

76044   8.54 Neasden; 6.62 Woodford Halse; 6.64 Stoke on Trent; 3.66 Chester Midland; 10.66 Withdrawn.

76045   3.55 Gateshead; 10.55 Blaydon; 1.56 Gateshead; 6.56 West Auckland; 10.63 Grangemouth; 10.65 Carstairs;
1.66 Withdrawn.

76046   3.55 Gateshead; 7.55 Blaydon; 6.56 West Auckland; 10.63 Dawsholm; 10.64 Grangemouth; 10.65 Corkerhill;
5.67 Withdrawn.

76047   3.55 Gateshead; 10.55 Blaydon; 6.56 Kirkby Stephen; 6.60 Trafford Park; 9.62 Cricklewood; 9.63 Stoke on Trent;
10.63 Saltley; 3.65 Bescot; 3.66 Chester Midland; 12.66 Withdrawn.

76048   3.55 Gateshead; 10.55 Blaydon; 6.56 Kirkby Stephen; 10.58 Lancaster Green Ayre; 11.58 Skipton;
5.59 Heaton Mersey; 9.62 Cricklewood; 7.64 Saltley; 9.66 Croes Newydd; 2.67 Withdrawn;

76049   4.55 Gateshead; 6.55 Blaydon; 1.56 Gateshead; 6.56 West Auckland; 10.63 Hawick; 10.65 St Margarets;
1.66 Bathgate; 1.66 Withdrawn.

76050   8.56 Darlington; 10.56 West Auckland; 10.63 Hawick; 9.65 Withdrawn.

76051	8.56 York; 10.56 Kirkby Stephen; 4.60 Lancaster Green Ayre; 2.62 Springs Branch; 7.62 Aston; 12.62 Stoke on Trent; 2.66 Colwick; 11.66 Sutton Oak; 4.67 Withdrawn.
76052	9.56 York; 10.56 Kirkby Stephen; 5.60 Neasden; 7.62 Woodford Halse; 10.63 Saltley; 5.65 Oxley; 7.65 Saltley; 8.65 Chester Midland; 12.66 Withdrawn.
76053	4.55 Redhill; 4.60 Salisbury; 6.64 Guildford; 1.65 Feltham; 7.65 Eastleigh; 6.66 Guildford; 1.67 Withdrawn.
76054	4.55 Redhill; 4.60 Salisbury; 6.64 Guildford; 10.64 Withdrawn.
76055	4.55 Redhill; 4.60 Salisbury; 6.64 Guildford; 1.65 Feltham; 7.65 Salisbury; 10.65 Withdrawn.
76056	5.55 Redhill; 12.59 Bournemouth; 11.65 Withdrawn.
76057	5.55 Redhill; 12.59 Bournemouth; 10.66 Withdrawn.
76058	6.55 Redhill; 12.59 Bournemouth; 2.62 Eastleigh; 6.66 Guildford; 3.67 Withdrawn.
76059	6.55 Redhill; 5.59 Salisbury; 3.60 Eastleigh; 6.66 Guildford; 9.66 Withdrawn.
76060	7.55 Redhill; 5.59 Salisbury; 3.60 Eastleigh; 12.65 Withdrawn.
76061	7.55 Redhill; 5.59 Eastleigh; 1.67 Withdrawn.
76062	7.55 Redhill; 5.59 Eastleigh; 10.65 Withdrawn.
76063	7.56 Eastleigh; 4.67 Withdrawn.
76064	7.56 Eastleigh; 7.67 Withdrawn.
76065	7.56 Eastleigh; 10.65 Withdrawn.
76066	7.56 Eastleigh; 3.60 Salisbury; 8.64 Guildford; 1.65 Feltham; 7.65 Eastleigh; 7.67 Withdrawn.
76067	8.56 Eastleigh; 3.60 Salisbury; 4.67 Bournemouth; 7.67 Withdrawn.
76068	8.56 Eastleigh; 10.65 Withdrawn.
76069	8.56 Eastleigh; 10.66 Guildford; 6.67 Withdrawn.
76070	9.56 Motherwell; 1.63 Greenock Ladyburn; 4.64 Beattock; 12.64 Polmadie; 8.66 Withdrawn.
76071	10.56 Motherwell; 1.63 Greenock Ladyburn; 12.64 Polmadie; 1.66 Withdrawn.
76072	10.56 Dumfries; 10.64 Withdrawn.
76073	10.56 Dumfries; 4.66 Ayr; 6.66 Withdrawn.
76074	11.56 Eastfield; 8.61 Parkhead; 10.61 Grangemouth; 11.63 Dawsholm; 10.64 Dumfries; 3.66 Ayr; 10.66 Withdrawn.
76075	12.56 Sutton Oak; 10.62 Bescot; 1.63 Stoke on Trent; 2.66 Colwick; 11.66 Sutton Oak; 6.67 Springs Branch; 10.67 Withdrawn.
76076	12.56 Sutton Oak; 11.66 Withdrawn.
76077	12.56 Sutton Oak; 6.67 Springs Branch; 12.67 Withdrawn. Preserved on the Gloucestershire Warwickshire Railway at Toddington.
76078	12.56 Sutton Oak; 12.66 Withdrawn.
76079	2.57 Sutton Oak; 6.67 Springs Branch; 12.67 Withdrawn. Preserved on the East Lancashire Railway at Bury.

76080   2.57 Lower Darwen; 3.65 Sutton Oak; 6.67 Springs Branch; 12.67 Withdrawn.

76081   2.57 Lower Darwen; 3.65 Sutton Oak; 6.67 Springs Branch; 7.67 Withdrawn.

76082   3.57 Lower Darwen; 3.65 Sutton Oak; 10.66 Withdrawn.

76083   3.57 Lower Darwen; 3.65 Sutton Oak; 10.66 Withdrawn.

76084   4.57 Lower Darwen; 9.58 Lancaster Green Ayre; 11.58 Skipton; 2.59 Lancaster Green Ayre; 3.59 Lower Darwen;
         3.65 Sutton Oak; 6.67 Springs Branch; 12.67 Withdrawn.
         Preserved on a private site in North Leverton in Nottinghamshire.

76085   4.57 Leicester Midland; 7.57 Saltley; 1.59 Heaton Mersey; 9.62 Cricklewood; 9.63 Stoke on Trent; 10.63 Saltley;
         1.65 Stoke on Trent; 3.66 Colwick; 7.66 Withdrawn.

76086   5.57 Leicester Midland; 1.59 Trafford Park; 10.62 Cricklewood; 9.63 Stoke on Trent; 10.63 Saltley; 3.65 Bescot;
         3.66 Saltley; 6.66 Machynlleth; 9.66 Croes Newydd; 9.66 Withdrawn.

76087   5.57 Trafford Park; 7.57 Saltley; 1.59 Heaton Mersey; 9.62 Woodford Halse; 10.63 Saltley; 3.65 Bescot;
         3.66 Stourbridge Junction; 5.66 Oxley; 1.67 Withdrawn.

76088   5.57 Trafford Park; 9.60 Neasden; 12.60 Trafford Park; 9.62 Cricklewood; 9.63 Stoke on Trent; 10.63 Saltley;
         3.65 Bescot; 3.66 Oxley; 2.67 Chester Midland; 6.67 Withdrawn.

76089   6.57 Trafford Park; 9.62 Cricklewood; 12.64 Willesden; 1.65 Stoke on Trent; 2.66 Colwick; 9.66 Withdrawn.

76090   6.57 Corkerhill; 1.61 Parkhead; 10.61 Corkerhill; 10.61 Motherwell; 7.62 Beattock; 12.66 Withdrawn.

76091   6.57 Corkerhill; 1.61 Parkhead; 10.61 Corkerhill; 4.64 Hurlford; 12.66 Withdrawn.

76092   6.57 Corkerhill; 4.64 Hurlford; 8.66 Withdrawn.

76093   7.57 Corkerhill; 1.61 Parkhead; 10.61 Corkerhill; 2.67 Withdrawn.

76094   8.57 Corkerhill; 1.61 Parkhead; 10.61 Corkerhill; 6.64 Hurlford; 11.66 Beattock; 5.67 Withdrawn.

76095   8.57 Corkerhill; 1.61 Parkhead; 12.61 Corkerhill; 7.64 Withdrawn then Reinstated; 9.64 Saltley; 1.65 Aston;
         8.65 Chester Midland; 3.67 Withdrawn.

76096   9.57 Corkerhill; 5.62 Ayr; 12.66 Withdrawn.

76097   9.57 Corkerhill; 5.62 Ayr; 7.64 Withdrawn.

76098   10.57 Corkerhill; 4.64 Ardrossan; 2.65 Ayr; 12.65 Beattock; 5.67 Withdrawn.

76099   11.57 Corkerhill; 5.62 Ayr; 1.63 Corkerhill; 4.64 Ardrossan; 7.64 Withdrawn then Reinstated; 9.64 Saltley;
         1.65 Stoke on Trent; 3.66 Colwick; 8.66 Withdrawn.

76100   5.57 Dawsholm; 7.60 Parkhead; 1.61 Dawsholm; 10.64 Grangemouth; 10.65 Ayr; 12.65 Beattock; 6.66 Ayr;
         8.66 Withdrawn.

76101   6.57 Dawsholm; 10.64 Grangemouth; 10.65 Ayr; 11.65 Stranraer; 3.66 Ayr; 12.66 Withdrawn.
76102   6.57 Dawsholm; 6.57 Parkhead; 2.59 St Rollox; 7.60 Parkhead; 12.60 Dawsholm; 10.64 Grangemouth;
         10.65 Dumfries; 6.66 Hurlford; 12.66 Withdrawn.

76103   6.57 Dawsholm; 6.57 Parkhead; 3.59 St Rollox; 7.60 Parkhead; 1.61 St Rollox; 10.61 Grangemouth;
         10.63 Dawsholm; 10.64 Grangemouth; 10.65 Dumfries; 11.65 Polmadie; 4.66 Beattock; 6.66 Ayr; 7.66 Withdrawn.

76104   7.57 Kittybrewster; 6.61 Aberdeen Ferryhill; 11.64 Bathgate; 1.66 Polmadie; 5.67 Withdrawn.

76105   7.57 Kittybrewster; 6.61 Aberdeen Ferryhill; 12.61 Dalry Road; 3.64 Bathgate; 1.66 Polmadie; 1.66 Withdrawn.

76106   7.57 Kittybrewster; 5.60 Keith; 6.61 Aberdeen Ferryhill; 12.61 Dalry Road; 3.64 Bathgate; 8.65 Willesden; 9.65 Withdrawn.

76107   8.57 Kittybrewster; 5.60 Keith; 6.61 Aberdeen Ferryhill; 11.64 Bathgate; 10.65 Withdrawn.

76108   8.57 Kittybrewster; 6.61 Aberdeen Ferryhill; 1.63 Hurlford; 7.66 Withdrawn.

76109   8.57 Thornton Junction; 1.60 Dunfermline; 9.66 Withdrawn.

76110   8.57 Thornton Junction; 4.60 Dunfermline; 12.66 Withdrawn.

76111   8.57 Thornton Junction; 4.60 Dunfermline; 2.62 Thornton Junction; 11.64 Bathgate; 1.66 Withdrawn.

76112   9.57 Dumfries; 12.57 Stranraer; 10.65 Withdrawn.

76113   10.57 St Rollox; 1.61 Parkhead; 11.61 St Rollox; 5.62 Grangemouth; 10.65 Carstairs; 12.66 Withdrawn.

76114   10.57 St Rollox; 7.60 Parkhead; 10.61 St Rollox; 5.62 Corkerhill; 11.66 Beattock; 12.66 Withdrawn.

4.8 Maintenance

The official recommended minimum period for the class between Works visits for intermediate and general overhaul was 30 months and 60 months respectively. Table 47 gives actual repair costs and average mileage between overhauls for the Standard Cl. 4 2-6-0 compared with classes engaged in broadly similar work. Although works visits at 27 months for intermediate and 51 months for general overhaul on average were more frequent than intended, mileage accrued between each visit was significantly higher in the case of the Standard Cl. 4 2-6-0 compared with the other selected classes. Repair costs for the class also show considerable savings compared with the SR Cl. U and U1 2-6-0s. Record cards are incomplete but it is probable that each of the early SR allocation, 76005-19, would have achieved a final mileage of around half a million; for the later members of the class in Scotland, 76090-114, it is estimated that a figure of less than half of this would have been achieved. Cumulative mileage data for the original SR allocation of the class, 76005-19, 76025-9 and 76053-69 are listed in Table 47A.

Works responsibility for repairs is as shown:

Region	All repairs and overhauls
ScR	Doncaster (to early 1956)
	Cowlairs
	St. Rollox (to March 1964)
SR	Eastleigh
	Horwich (April 1963-April 1964)
ER/NER	Doncaster
	Stratford
LMR	Horwich (to April 1964)
	Derby (to November 1963)

From February 1964, the LMR allocation was overhauled at other Region's works; known examples are listed as follows:

Eastleigh	76022/39/44/77/9
	76082/8/9
Swindon	76037/41/75/6/81
Cowlairs	76052/83-5/9
Darlington	76020/40/51/80/1/95/9
Crewe	76040

4.9 Modifications in Service

The main modifications carried out on the Standard Cl. 5 4-6-0s and Cl. 4 4-6-0s were also applied to the Cl. 4 2-6-0s. These included changes to the rocking grate bars, the system of cylinder lubrication, the Downs pattern sanding gear and the cab-tender arrangements for those engines carrying Type 2 tenders; full details are given in section 2.9. In common with some of the other Standard designs, including the Cl. 5 4-6-0s, there were reports that the initial batches of engines suffered from the problem of the leading coupled wheels wearing a curved groove about a foot long on the frames at maximum height of the wheels above rail level. This was probably due to the insufficient clearance between the wheels and frames to allow for the locomotive 'rolling' or 'wagging its tail' at higher speeds. The problem was resolved by fitting extra strength cross-bracing to the frames.

4.9.1 Detail Modifications

Many Standard Cl. 4 2-6-0s had acquired the BR AWS apparatus by the early 1960s, including the whole of the SR allocation; the cost was quoted as £335 per locomotive. The original SR allocation, 76005-19, 76025-9, 76053-69, was also fitted with water softening apparatus, initially the French T.I.A system but later the standard BR briquette device. Many of the engines working on the S&DJR route from Bournemouth West to Bath Green Park were fitted with the Whitaker tablet exchange apparatus which was affixed to the tender on the driver's side adjacent to the cab. Most of the Bournemouth allocation and some of the Eastleigh engines acquired the device; known examples were 76012/3/4/5/9/61/6/7. The SR engines acquired the additional lamp bracket fittings as detailed in section 2.9.2 and there were other detail modifications made to this group also. The information is incomplete as changes were not always faithfully recorded, particularly from the early 1960s onward. The modification reference numbers are given below together with a brief description of the work involved: details are given in Table 47B.

Ref. No.	Work Involved
4983	Fitting of BR type AWS equipment Cost £335.

Table 47

Standard Cl. 4 2-6-0s 76000-76114
Comparison with Selected 2-6-0 Classes
Representative Repair Costs and Average Mileage to Overhaul

| Class | Data For Year | Cost per Mile (New Pence) | | | Average Mileage ('000s) to: | |
		Engine & Boiler	Tender	Total	Intermediate Overhaul	General Overhaul
BR Standard 4	1955-7	3.11	0.32	3.43	92.1	153.2
GWR 43XX	1955-7	-	-	-	65.6	138.0
SR U	1956	4.08	0.49	4.57	71.1	140.2
SR U1	1956	4.11	0.49	4.60	62.2	139.3
SR N	1956	-	-	-	64.8	139.0
SR N1	1956	-	-	-	69.0	133.0

Key: - Information not traced.

5900   Fitting of safety links between engine and tender. No cost quoted.

9089   Briquette tube feeder modification, part of the BR standard water softening system. No cost quoted.

9129   Fitting of continuous blowdown apparatus.

In addition to these modifications the SR made a number of other detail alterations to many of their allocation. These were associated with a specific Test Number but it has been possible to link only a few of the numbers to particular modifications; these are given where known. For the purposes of reference, arbitrary numbers for each alteration are assigned as shown; no cost information is available.

Ref. No.   Work Involved

SR01   Fitting of injector overflow pipes and brackets.

SR05   Piston head modification: SR Test Number 2272.

SR07   Fitting of safety chains to smokebox door.

SR09   Piston rod modified packing. SR Test Number 2263. Same as Ref. Mod. 8895.

SR10   Regulator valves and various boiler valves made of stainless steel. SR Test Number 2081.

SR11   Modification of tender coal hole door plates.

SR13   Isolating cocks and pipe gear.

SR14   Clack valve modification. SR Test Number 2237.

SR15   Pony truck axle guide. SR Test Number 2273.

SR16   Connecting and coupling rod bushes. SR Test Number 2283

SR17   Flexible steam brake connection.

SR18   Coupling rod joint pin arrangement.

SR Test Number 2317.

SR19   Provision of modified steam brake pipes. SR Test No. 2278

SR20   Modification of BR Standard firebars to permit improved steaming by reducing clinker build-up.

SR22   Modification of boiler fusible plug system. Front plug: SR type, back plug: BR type. SR Test No. 2338.

SR25   Modification of boiler fusible plug system. Both front and back plugs are of SR type.

SR29   Modification of cylinder release valve.

SR30   Modification of rocking grate firebars.

To amplify on SR18, dated June 1960, it has been confirmed that this was Staff Suggestion No. S.12958 and drew attention to the fact that open oil holes for the coupling rod joint pins on the Cl. 4 2-6-0s became blocked during service. The experiment made the provision for the fitting of standard grease nipples (type 21A BSS.1486 part 2). In order to ascertain whether steel bushes were better for this bearing than the existing Y.M.1 bushes the nine engines concerned were experimentally fitted as follows; in addition, three of the engines had a 'D' headed joint pin.

A: three engines fitted with existing Y.M.1. bushes to Item No. 1/SL/DN/S.571. Engines 76006/56/62

B: three engines fitted with BR.103/6F grade steel bushes but otherwise to the same Item No. as A. Engines 76009/54/5

C: three engines fitted with steel bushes and 'D' headed joint pins in accordance with Drawing No. W.12576. Engines 76005/26/53

SR Test No. modification 2276 was applied to engine 76016 but details of the nature of the experiment and date of testing are not known.

The SR Test Numbers were shown on the engine record

Standard Class 4 2-6-0s 76000-76114
Original SR Allocation: 76005-19, 76025-9, 76053-69
Cumulative Mileage at Various Dates

Engine Number	Cumulative Mileage	Date	Engine Number	Cumulative Mileage	Date
76005	359,186	1.63	76053	171,417	12.59
76006	328,454	11.62	76054	159,784	6.59
76007	363,637	7.63	76055	211,155	11.62
76008	365,782	4.63	76056	162,903	12.59
76009	305,986	4.62	76057	199,797	3.61
76010	321,496	9.63	76058	190,455	9.60
76011	346,938	12.63	76059	172,824	7.60
76012	325,323	10.63	76060	188,227	10.60
76013	320,712	7.63	76061	193,263	5.61
76014	345,788	5.63	76062	220,685	1.63
76015	359,530	2.63	76063	179,210	2.62
76016	304,570	1.63	76064	168,369	8.61
76017	229,034	5.59	76065	94,569	10.58
76018	345,790	5.63	76066	271,726	9.63
76019	216,990	6.59	76067	160,786	7.61
76025	172,217	11.58	76068	152,621	11.60
76026	315,800	12.62	76069	162,642	5.61
76027	328,125	3.61			
76028	171,519	10.58			
76029	172,946	12.58			

cards but several of these were subsequently crossed out. This could mean that the tests were either not carried out, were terminated or were regarded as successful and hence became adopted as a permanent feature of the locomotive. Engines subjected to the tests usually carried details of the test number on a small brass plate attached to the cabside under the numerals.

Other minor alterations recorded for three other members of the class operating on the SR are as follows.

76011:   (11.55) Everlasting blow-off cock fitted
76025:   (01.59) Modified blower pipe connection fitted.
76026:   (03.60) Tender 1045 lateral clearance to
              specification 3/SL/DE/20162.

On the ER, only one officially recorded modification to class members can be traced; details are as follows.

E/DA/L/71   Modification of cylinder cock activating
                  valve.
                  Engines: 76030 (08.57)   76033 (no date)

One other modification made to most if not all of the ER's Neasden based group, 76035-44, was the fitting of the trip cock apparatus to conform to the automatic train control requirements when operating on the London Transport Executive's Metropolitan lines; known examples were the first five of the group, 76035-9. No official records of specific modifications carried out on the LMR, NER and ScR allocations have been traced. A copy of The Railway Executive's protocol for dealing with experimental modifications to locomotives, entitled 'Proposals for Standard

Procedure for Dealing with Experiments', is reproduced as Appendix 5.

4.10 Names and Nicknames
None of the Standard Cl. 4 2-6-0s received names during their service with British Railways. In preservation, 76017 carries the name *Hermes* and 76079 was reported to have been named *Castell Dinas Bran* on 30th November 1994 at a special ceremony in one of the Boeing 747 'Jumbo' hangars at London Heathrow Airport. There does not appear to have been a network-wide nickname. On the SR, however, the term 'Standard U Boats' was occasionally heard. This referred to the fact that the class displaced some of the Maunsell Cl. U and U1 2-6-0s from their duties at certain depots; the latter two classes were widely known as 'U Boats'. The Maunsell Cl. N 2-6-0s were known as 'Mongolipers' or 'Woolworths'; there is no evidence that the Standard Cl. 4 2-6-0s picked up the 'Standard' version of these sobriquets.

4.11 Performance
The Standard Cl. 4 2-6-0s established themselves as excellent second line engines, mostly at home on secondary and main line passenger work. The SR had fifteen engines, 76005-19, of the first batch from Horwich and allocated them to Eastleigh. Here they gained a high reputation for their work on the heavy through services from the South Coast to Bristol and South Wales as far as Salisbury. Later 76053-69 at Redhill were also well thought of for their performance with the inter-regional expresses from the South Coast to the Midlands and North as far as Reading on the line from Tonbridge. The class was not universally welcomed on the SR however, depots such as Brighton on the Central Section and Yeovil

Table 47B
Standard Cl. 4 2-6-0s 76000-76114: Detail Modifications

Mod.★   Locomotive Modified and Modification Date

4983   The whole of the original SR allocation, 76005-19, 76025-9, 76053-69 was modified during the late 1950s; the only dates reported were: 76018/67, both in April 1959. Others known to have been modified were 76024/30-4/38/46/50/66/7/93/9, again with no dates.

Mod.★					
5900	76006: 11.57	76009: 03.58	76016: 01.58	76018: 12.57	76019: 04.58
	76028: 05.58	76029: 05.58	76059: 01.58		
9089	76005: 01.60	76006: 12.62	76007: 03.61	76010: 06.60	76011: 10.60
	76012: 12.60	76013: 01.58	76014: 02.61	76015: 11.60	76016: 09.60
	76017: 01.62	76018: 06.63	76019: 02.62	76025: 12.60	76026: 12.62
	76027: 04.61	76028: 01.58	76029: 09.61	76054: 12.57	76055: 11.57
	76056: 12.57	76057:no date	76058: 10.60	76059: 01.58	76060: 05.58
	76061: 03.58	76062:no date	76063: 03.62	76064: 09.61	76065: 03.61
	76066:no date	76067: 08.61	76068: 12.60	76069: 06.61	
9129	76059: 05.59				
SR01	76007: 09.60	76010: 06.60	76011: 10.60	76012: 12.60	76013: 01.56
	76015: 11.60	76016: 09.60	76018: 06.63	76025: 12.60	76058: 10.60
	76059: 08.60	76060: 11.60	76068: 12.60		
SR05	76006/7/10/1: no dates.				
SR07	76005: 02.58	76007: 03.58	76010: 05.58	76012: 05.58	76013: 01.58
	76014: 06.58	76015: 04.58	76054: 12.57	76055: 11.57	76056: 12.57
	76057: 06.58	76058:no date	76061: 03.58	76062: 02.58	76069: 06.61
SR09	76006:no date	76007:no date	76009: 10.59	76011:no date	76012:no date
	76013: 01.58	76015: 11.58	76017: 05.59	76018: 12.57	76019: 03.57
	76027: 11.58	76028: 11.58	76029: 01.59	76054: 07.59	76055: 09.59
	76061: 03.58	76062: 09.59	76064: 01.59	76067: 02.58	76069: 01.59
SR10	76067: 04.59				
SR11	76007: 03.61	76017: 01.62	76027: 04.61	76029: 09.61	76053: 09.62
	76054: 01.62	76056: 10.62	76057: 04.61	76061: 02.63	76062: 02.63
	76063: 03.62	76064: 09.61	76065: 03.61	76067: 08.61	76069: 06.61
SR13	76006: 07.59	76009: 10.59	76010: 05.58	76011: 07.58	76012: 05.58
	76014: 06.58	76015: 11.58	76017: 05.59	76025: 01.59	76027: 11.58
	76028: 11.58	76029: 01.59	76031:no date	76032: no date	76054: 07.59
	76055: 09.59	76057: 06.58	76059: 05.59	76060: 11.60	76062: 09.59
	76064: 01.59	76069: 06.61			
SR14	76005:no date				
SR15	76006/7/10/2/6/8/9/28: no dates				
SR16	76062: 08.57				
SR17	76017:no date				
SR18	76005: 01.60	76006:no date	76009:no date	76026: 03.60	76053: 01.60
	76054:no date	76055:no date	76056:no date	76062:no date	
SR19	76009: 10.59				
SR20	76018:no date				
SR22	76007/8/66/7:no dates				
SR25	76016: 03.62				
SR29	76011: 11.55	76012: 05.55	76013: 12.55	76014: 12.55	76015: 02.56
	76019: 05.55	76025: 03.56	76027: 03.56	76028: 04.56	76029: 06.56
SR30	76009/12/4:no dates.				

★ See text for key to work carried out under individual modification numbers.

200

Town on the Western Section initially finding them to be indifferent steamers incapable of keeping time.

On the S&DJR, the engines were warily received at first owing to their close resemblance to the double chimney 'Doodlebug' Ivatt Cl. 4 2-6-0s 43012/3/7/36 which had been allocated to Bath Green Park at various times over the period January 1949 to June 1953. The latter engines had not distinguished themselves on the route due to their poor steaming characteristics. It was soon apparent however that the Standard Cl. 4 2-6-0s were a considerable improvement over their forbears and the enginemen quickly accepted them as good, reliable locomotives. So much so that on busy summer Saturdays in the late 1950s, they were occasionally entrusted with the prestigious 'Pines Express', Bournemouth West-Manchester London Road/Liverpool Lime Street, usually piloted over the Mendips by an LMS Cl. 2P 4-4-0. In reality, however, it is likely that both engines would have been working to maximum capacity to maintain schedule with the typical load of twelve coaches weighing well in excess of 400 tons.

The class was also well received on the NER/LMR Stainmore route between Barnard Castle and Kirkby Stephen. Towards the end of steam the LMR used several members of the class on the Cambrian lines from Shrewsbury to the Cardigan Bay Coast. Here, however, they were not regarded as an adequate replacement for the Standard Cl. 4 4-6-0s on passenger work and were regularly used in tandem to ensure schedules were met. On the ER, ten of the class 76035-44, were at Neasden operating on the former GCR lines from Marylebone. Here the engines were regarded as free steamers, no matter what firing technique was used and capable of successfully working a wide variety of freight and passenger services on this route. Opinions at the other ER depot, Stratford, were mixed. 76030-4 were there for a period and were regarded as adequate for the normal tasks of cross-London freights and semi-fast passenger work but not as relief power for much of the heavy summer Saturday holiday traffic to the East Anglian coastal resorts. In Scotland probably the class's best work was done on the Ayrshire coast routes from Glasgow St. Enoch and on the former GNSR lines north of Aberdeen.

4.11.1 Performance in Day to Day Service
The log quoted in Table 48 compares the performance of Standard Cl. 4 2-6-0 76108 with that of NBL Type 2 Bo-Bo diesel D6148 on the up afternoon mail from Huntly to Aberdeen on the line from Inverness in 1958 and 1961 respectively; both runs were timed by Mr. R.I. Nelson. The line rises at an average of around 1 in 150/200 from Huntly to just beyond Kennethmont after which there is a generally falling gradient for the remaining 32 miles to Aberdeen. 76108 with its 10 coach load ran extremely well with a minimum speed of 38mph to the summit beyond Kennethmont and a maximum of 67mph down the 1 in 100 through Wardhouse. Between Insch and Inverurie the start to stop time of 13 min. 28 sec. over the distance of 10.7 miles was lively. Maxima of 68mph down through Oyne and Pitcaple with a further 65mph at Bucksburn allowed 76108 to be comfortably within schedule for the trip. The diesel D6148 had a fairly easy task with its 6 coach load although the schedule was tighter in 1961 compared with 76108's run in 1958.

4.12 Storage, Withdrawal and Disposal
On the ER, following dieselisation of virtually all the services in East Anglia in 1962, 76030-4 were stored at March between September and November of that year, prior to their reallocation to the SR. By the end of 1966, many of the remaining ScR allocation were in store at various locations including Ayr and Corkerhill. Table 49 gives dates of withdrawal and places of disposal; reported cutting-up dates appear to be unreliable and have been omitted. The first to be withdrawn was 76028 in May 1964 and all had left BR service by the end of 1967.

4.13 Preservation
Four Standard Cl. 4 2-6-0s have been preserved; all were retrieved from the Barry scrapyard of Woodham's Bros. in South Wales.

76017
Moved from Barry in January 1974, 76017 along with the tender of 76077, was first stored at the Quainton Railway Centre near Aylesbury before being moved to the Mid-Hants Railway at Ropley in March 1978. It entered service there in May 1984 in BR mixed traffic lined black livery. It is now owned by the Standard 4 Locomotive Group and carries the name *Hermes*.

76077
The engine was retrieved from Barry in May 1987 and is undergoing restoration at the Toddington site of the Gloucestershire Warwickshire Railway on the former GWR route from Cheltenham to Stratford-upon-Avon. 76077 is one of the assets of the P&O Locomotive Society which also owns SR Bulleid Merchant Navy Pacific 35006.

76079
Rescued from Barry in July 1974, 76079 was first kept at Steamport in Southport. The engine was purchased by Mr. Derek Foster in 1982 and restored at his works at Kirkby. In August 1989, 76079 was moved to the East Lancashire Railway at Bury which remains its home base. In May 2001, it was noted that the tender coupled to 76079 had acquired some extra coal rails to increase coal capacity.

76084
Removed from Barry in April 1983, 76084 awaited restoration on a private site at North Leverton with Habblesthorpe near Retford in Nottinghamshire. After the death of the owner Mr. Phillip Rollins, the locomotive was bought by the 76084 Locomotive Company Ltd. and in September 1997 transported to the Ian Storey engineering works near Morpeth, Northumberland for restoration. It is planned to use 76084 on the Eden Valley Railway between Kirkby Stephen and Appleby.

Table 48

Standard Cl. 4 2-6-0s 76000–76114
ScR Huntly–Aberdeen

Engine Number		76108 (Kittybrewster)			D6148 (Kittybrewster)		
Class		BR Standard 4 2-6-0			NBL Type 2 diesel		
Date		1958			1961		
Load, coaches		10			6		
Load, tons gross		365			225		

Distance Miles		Sch. Min.	Actual min.sec	Speeds mph	Sch. Min	Actual min.sec	Speeds mph
0.0	HUNTLY	0	0.00	–	0	0.00	–
5.0	Gartley		9.30	47		7.09	56/53
8.0	Kennethmont		13.47	38		10.32	57
9.7	Wardhouse		15.52	67		12.23	61
13.2	INSCH	20½	20.24	–	17½	16.25	–
16.2	Oyne		5.09	68		4.13	62¾
19.4	Pitcaple		8.07	64/68		7.26	67/61
20.4	INVERAMSAY		9.12	53/63		8.27	63¼
23.9	INVERURIE	15	13.28	–	13	12.28	–
–		–	–		sig.stop	–	
3.5	Kintore		6.27	54		7.30	–
6.3	Kinaldie		9.31	56½		11.02	55½
8.6	Pitmedden		11.46	63		13.21	62¼
10.7	DYCE JUNCTION		13.50	57	14	16.03	–
12.8	Bucksburn	pass	15.58	65		3.18	–
14.3	Woodside		17.26	–		4.44	64
15.5	KITTYBREWSTER	sigs. 21	– 19.59	–	– 7	– 6.39	–
1.0	Schoolhill		sigs. –	–		–	
1.4	ABERDEEN	4	4.32	–	4	3.17	–

First published in Railway Magazine, Vol 108, No. 733, May 1962.

Fig. 202   76018 is pictured on shed at Salisbury on 23rd May 1959. The engine spent its whole working life on the SR's Western Section and was withdrawn in October 1966.   *(Courtney Haydon)*

Fig. 203
76099 leaves Glasgow St Enoch with a local train on 27th March 1961. The former Caledonian Railway Glasgow Area Semaphore Route Indicator system, applied to some G&SWR departures for joint lines from St Enoch after the formation of the LMS in 1923, has been 'fingered' twice onto the smokebox door. It appears however to be erroneous as the configuration (No.16) refers to departures from Glasgow Central for Coatbridge; a full list of the semaphore codes is given in Appendix 7. 76099 is in lined black livery with the small second British Railways emblem on the tender. The latter has had the lining panel shortened at the rear to allow the emblem to appear at its centre, whilst at the same time avoiding as many rivet heads as possible! *(P.J. Cupper)*

Fig. 204
A smart-looking 76114 conducts an unidentified NBL Bo–Bo diesel and an ex-WD freight engine through Gleneagles towards Glasgow for Works visits on 2nd July 1964.

(Rodney Lissenden)

Fig. 205
76004, with missing dome cover, is seen on shed at Polmadie on 18th April 1965. The engine was the last of a group of five, 76000-4, delivered new to Motherwell from Horwich Works in December 1952. Until around mid-1956, the engines were maintained by the ER at Doncaster Works. This view suggests that 76004's last overhaul was at Cowlairs, judging by the large size cabside numerals, topped by the '4MT.' power classification mark.

(Courtney Haydon)

Table 49

Standard Cl. 4 2-6-0s 76000–76114
Construction, Withdrawal and Disposal Information

Engine	Built	With-drawn	Disposal	
76000	12.52	5.67	9.67	Motherwell Machinery and Scrap Co., Wishaw
76001	12.52	8.66	3.68	Arnott Young, Troon
76002	12.52	1.67	5.67	Motherwell Machinery and Scrap Co., Wishaw
76003	12.52	3.66	6.66	Motherwell Machinery and Scrap Co., Wishaw
76004	12.52	10.66	1.67	G. H. Campbell, Airdrie
76005	12.52	7.67	11.67	Birds Commercial Motors, Morriston
76006	1.53	7.67	11.67	Birds Commercial Motors, Morriston
76007	1.53	7.67	11.67	Birds Commercial Motors, Risca
76008	2.53	5.67	12.67	G. Cohen, Kettering
76009	2.53	7.67	1.68	J. Cashmore, Newport
76010	3.53	9.66	3.67	J. Buttigieg, Newport
76011	3.53	7.67	11.67	Birds Commercial Motors, Morriston
76012	4.53	9.66	3.67	J. Buttigieg, Newport
76013	4.53	9.66	3.67	J. Buttigieg, Newport
76014	5.53	9.66	1.67	J. Buttigieg, Newport
76015	5.53	10.65	1.66	G. Cohen, Morriston
76016	5.53	10.66	6.67	J. Cashmore, Newport
76017	6.53	7.65		Preserved on the Mid-Hants Railway, Ropley.
76018	6.53	10.66	6.67	J. Cashmore, Newport
76019	7.53	2.66	6.66	G. Cohen, Morriston
76020	12.52	4.66	7.66	Birds Commercial Motors, Long Marston
76021	12.52	10.66	2.67	G. H. Campbell, Airdrie
76022	12.52	8.66	12.66	J. Cashmore, Great Bridge
76023	12.52	10.65	1.66	J. Cashmore, Great Bridge
76024	1.53	12.66	4.67	Shipbreaking Industries, Faslane
76025	10.53	10.65	2.66	J. Cashmore, Newport
76026	10.53	7.67	9.67	G. Cohen, Morriston
76027	10.53	10.65	1.66	G. Cohen, Morriston
76028	10.53	5.64	8.64	R. A. King, Norwich
76029	11.53	10.64	3.65	G. Cohen, Morriston
76030	11.53	4.65	12.65	J. Cashmore, Newport
76031	11.53	7.67	12.67	Birds Commercial Motors, Morriston
76032	12.53	8.64	12.64	J. Cashmore, Newport
76033	12.53	2.67	11.67	J. Cashmore, Newport
76034	12.53	9.64	10.64	P. Wood, Queenborough, Kent
76035	5.54	5.66	8.66	J. Cashmore, Great Bridge
76036	6.54	1.67	7.67	G. Cohen, Morriston
76037	6.54	6.67	11.67	J. Cashmore, Newport
76038	7.54	9.66	12.66	J. Cashmore, Newport
76039	7.54	6.67	12.67	J. Buttigieg, Newport
76040	7.54	4.67	9.67	G. Cohen, Morriston
76041	7.54	4.67	2.68	G. Cohen, Kettering
76042	8.54	6.66	11.66	G. Cohen, Kettering
76043	8.54	9.66	12.66	J. Cashmore, Newport
76044	8.54	10.66	3.67	G. Cohen, Morriston
76045	3.55	1.66	6.66	Motherwell Machinery and Scrap Co., Wishaw
76046	3.55	5.67	9.67	G. H. Campbell, Airdrie
76047	3.55	12.66	2.68	J. Cashmore, Newport
76048	3.55	2.67	7.67	J. Cashmore, Newport
76049	4.55	1.66	5.66	Motherwell Machinery and Scrap Co., Wishaw
76050	8.56	9.65	11.66	Shipbreaking Industries, Faslane
76051	8.56	4.67	12.67	J. Cashmore, Great Bridge
76052	9.56	12.66	2.68	J. Cashmore, Newport
76053	4.55	1.67	8.67	J. Cashmore, Newport
76054	4.55	10.64	3.65	R. & S. Hayes, Bridgend
76055	4.55	10.65	1.66	J. Buttigieg, Newport

Engine	Built	Withdrawn	Disposal	
76056	5.55	11.65	3.66	J. Cashmore, Newport
76057	5.55	10.66	7.67	J. Cashmore, Newport
76058	6.55	3.67	12.67	J. Buttigieg, Newport
76059	6.55	9.66	3.67	J. Cashmore, Newport
76060	7.55	12.65	5.66	G. Cohen, Morriston
76061	7.55	1.67	6.67	J. Cashmore, Newport
76062	7.55	10.65	2.66	J. Cashmore, Newport
76063	7.56	4.67	12.67	J. Buttigieg, Newport
76064	7.56	7.67	11.67	Birds Commercial Motors, Morriston
76065	7.56	10.65	6.66	G. Cohen, Morriston
76066	7.56	7.67	11.67	G. Cohen, Morriston
76067	8.56	7.67	11.67	G. Cohen, Morriston
76068	8.56	10.65	2.66	J. Buttigieg, Newport
76069	8.56	6.67	3.68	J. Cashmore, Newport
76070	9.56	8.66	1.67	Motherwell Machinery and Scrap Co., Wishaw
76071	10.56	1.66	6.66	Motherwell Machinery and Scrap Co., Wishaw
76072	10.56	10.64	1.65	Shipbreaking Industries, Faslane
76073	10.56	6.66	11.66	Arnott Young, Troon
76074	11.56	10.66	1.67	G. H. Campbell, Airdrie
76075	12.56	10.67	4.68	J. Buttigieg, Newport
76076	12.56	11.66	4.67	T. W. Ward, Killamarsh
76077	12.56	12.67		Preserved at Gloucestershire Warwickshire Rly, Toddington
76078	12.56	12.66	4.67	T. W. Ward, Beighton, Sheffield
76079	2.57	12.67		Preserved on East Lancashire Railway, Bury
76080	2.57	12.67	4.72	Woodham Bros. Barry
76081	2.57	7.67	12.67	J. Cashmore, Newport
76082	3.57	10.66	4.67	A. Draper, Kingston upon Hull
76083	3.57	10.66	3.67	J. Cashmore, Great Bridge
76084	4.57	12.67		Undergoing restoration by the the 76084 Locomotive Co. Ltd. at Morpeth, Northumbria for use on the Eden Valley Railway.
76085	4.57	7.66	11.66	J. Cashmore, Great Bridge
76086	5.57	9.66	5.67	G. Cohen, Morriston
76087	5.57	1.67	9.67	J. Cashmore, Newport
76088	5.57	6.67	12.67	J. Buttigieg, Newport
76089	6.57	9.66	12.66	A. Draper, Kingston upon Hull
76090	6.57	12.66	4.67	Shipbreaking Industries, Faslane
76091	6.57	12.66	4.67	Shipbreaking Industries, Faslane
76092	6.57	8.66	11.66	G. H. Campbell, Airdrie
76093	7.57	2.67	4.67	G. H. Campbell, Airdrie
76094	8.57	5.67	9.67	G. H. Campbell, Airdrie
76095	8.57	3.67	5.68	G. Cohen, Kettering
76096	9.57	12.66	7.67	Shipbreaking Industries, Faslane
76097	9.57	7.64	1.65	Motherwell Machinery and Scrap Co., Wishaw
76098	10.57	5.67	3.68	T. W. Ward, Inverkeithing
76099	11.57	8.66	11.66	J. Cashmore, Great Bridge
76100	5.57	8.66	4.68	Arnott Young, Troon
76101	6.57	12.66	5.67	Shipbreaking Industries, Faslane
76102	6.57	12.66	5.67	Shipbreaking Industries, Faslane
76103	6.57	7.66	11.66	Arnott Young, Troon
76104	7.57	5.67	9.67	G. H. Campbell, Airdrie
76105	7.57	1.66	4.66	Motherwell Machinery and Scrap Co., Wishaw
76106	7.57	9.65	11.65	J. Cashmore, Great Bridge
76107	8.57	10.65	6.66	J. McWilliam, Shettleston
76108	8.57	7.66	11.66	Arnott Young, Troon
76109	8.57	9.66	1.67	Motherwell Machinery and Scrap Co., Wishaw
76110	8.57	12.66	4.67	Shipbreaking Industries, Faslane
76111	8.57	1.66	4.66	Motherwell Machinery and Scrap Co., Wishaw
76112	9.57	10.65	2.66	Shipbreaking Industries, Faslane
76113	10.57	12.66	4.67	Shipbreaking Industries, Faslane
76114	10.57	12.66	4.67	Shipbreaking Industries, Faslane

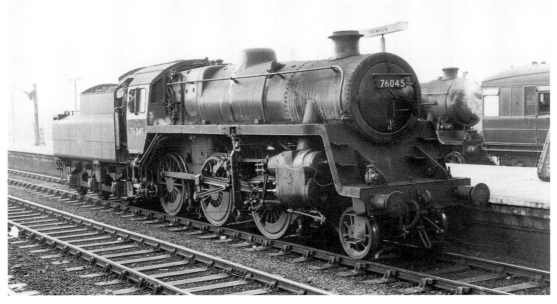

Fig. 209   76062, equipped with the high water capacity (4725 gal.) BR1B type tender, is ex-Works at Doncaster on 17th July 1955 awaiting transfer to the SR where it will be allocated initially to Redhill. The ER Route Availability code 'RA4' continues to be routinely applied by Doncaster despite the fact that 76062 will see no service, apart from the odd running-in turn, on either the ER or the NER.

(G. Wheeler)

Fig. 210   76064 is pictured at Eastleigh on 7th October 1961 shortly after its first general overhaul. The engine had completed around 170,000 miles by this date. Note the imposing BR1B type tender and the '4P 4F' power classification mark above the cabside numerals.

(P.H. Wells)

Fig. 211
76085 of Saltley depot is at rest on Eastleigh shed in June 1957. The engine had arrived on the 2.15am Water Orton-Southampton Docks freight, a short-lived through working rostered for Saltley engines via Bordesley Junction and Didcot; the balancing turn was the 7.28pm Southampton-Water Orton freight. This duty, initially shared with the WR's Tyseley depot, was taken over completely by the WR after a short period. *(L. Elsey)*

Fig. 212
Horwich-built 76088 is on shed at its home depot, Cricklewood, on 19th May 1963; also on view are stablemates 76043 and 76089. The depot had some fifteen of the class on its books at the time, nine of which, 76035-43 had arrived from Neasden when the GC line London depot had closed on 18th June 1962. From that date, Cricklewood took over responsibility for servicing steam power at the southern end of the GC line.
(Peter Groom)

Fig. 213
Ancient and Modern at Ardrossan shed on 4th August 1963; 76099 was built in November 1957 whilst Caledonian Cl. 3F 0-6-0 57566 first saw the light of day in August 1899. The 0-6-0 was withdrawn a few days after the picture was taken whereas 76099, condemned by the ScR in July 1964, was re-instated and transferred to the LMR for service at Saltley two months later; the engine was finally withdrawn in August 1966.

(Courtney Haydon)

Fig. 214   76020 is pictured at Bolton MPD on 7th April 1962. The engine was probably fresh from overhaul at Horwich Works which usually despatched its finished jobs to Bolton for onward transfer. Note the draught screens on the BR2 type tender and also the shortened panel liner to allow the BR logo to be positioned at its centre.   *(D.R. Forsyth)*

Fig. 215   76021 is at York station shortly after delivery in early 1953. Note the Doncaster Works trademarks: the power classification mark on the buffer beam, the Route Availability code beneath the cabside numerals and the panel lining applied close to the tender's edges.   *(Lance Brown)*

Fig. 216
76025 reposes at Eastleigh shed in September 1954. Although the 76025-9 batch was destined for the SR, Doncaster Works applied the ER cabside Route Classification code 'RA4' which is still in evidence on 76025 almost a year later. From 76025 onwards, the class was delivered with the Smith-Stone speedo-meter fitted from new; the earlier SR allocation, 76005-19, acquired speedometers soon after entering into SR service.
(L.Elsey)

Fig. 217
76026 is depicted on 20th February 1960 at Whitchurch Town following its derailment eight days earlier when working the 9.50am Didcot-Eastleigh goods. 76026 was re-railed the following day. Note the 4P 4F power classification mark and the absence of the Doncaster-applied Route Availability code 'RA4' probably erased from the cabside at the engine's first Eastleigh Works visit. Despite this adventure, 76026 survived until July 1967, the last month of steam operation on the SR.
(Courtney Haydon)

Fig. 218
76030, with recessed cabside panel, receives attention to the cylinders at its home depot, Stratford on 20th March 1955. In common with class members 76031-4, also based at Stratford at this time, 76030 was used on cross-London freights to the LMR and on Saturday holiday extras to the Essex coast.

(Frank Hornby)

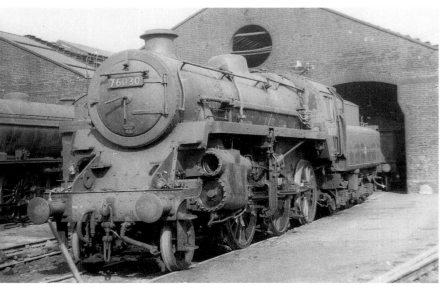

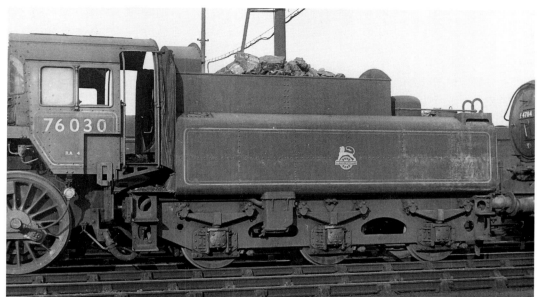

Fig. 219
A close-up of 76030 on Stratford shed on 27th January 1957 shows the recessed panel in the cabside, designed to accommodate tablet exchange apparatus which was never fitted. 76030 carries the draught screens on the BR2 tender and the Smith-Stone speedometer, activated by the rear driving wheel.
(A.R. Goult)

Fig. 220
76032, with recessed cab panel, waits at Northampton Castle with a Peterborough East local on 27th May 1961. In September 1962, the engine was put into store at March together with class members 76030/1/3/4; all five were transferred to the SR's Central Section Brighton depot in November. *(L.Hanson)*

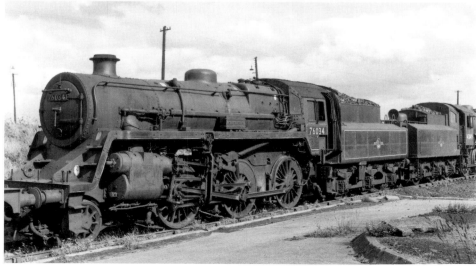

Fig. 221
76034 rests next to an example of the LMS class on which it was based, Ivatt Cl. 4 2-6-0 43149, at March depot in June 1958. On its tender, 43149 carries tablet exchange apparatus for working on the single track M&GN line whilst 76034, incorporating the cabside recessed panel specifically to accommodate such a device, does not carry one. The engine's power classification mark '4' is placed immediately under the numerals which have been applied high up on the cabside to clear the recessed panel. 76034 is by now liberally sprinkled with electric warning flashes and has also been fitted with AWS apparatus as confirmed by the large box on the running plate. *(G. Wheeler)*

5. Class 3 2-6-0 77000-19

5.1 Purpose

This small class of only twenty engines was delivered to the NER and ScR from Swindon over the eight month period from February 1954. The design was the tender version of the Cl. 3 2-6-2 tank engine (82XXX) having the same tractive effort and approximately doubling the latter's working range. The engines had a 16 ton axle load allowing them to be used on certain branch lines over which Cl. 4 locomotives were barred for weight reasons and where train loadings were such that they could not be handled by Cl. 2 types. Almost from the start however, the role which the Cl. 3 2-6-0 was to have fulfilled was being eroded by several developments. By the time the last of the class had been delivered in late 1954 it was clear that many branch lines were becoming hopelessly uneconomic due to the loss of both passenger and freight revenue to road competition offering a more convenient service; also the gradual but accelerating trend toward private car ownership was beginning to take its toll on passenger numbers. Many of these branch lines would soon close and the diminishing traffic on the survivors would prove to be easily within the scope of a Cl. 2 type. At the same time, other secondary lines deemed to have a viable future were being upgraded to allow the use of Cl. 4 types with 17 ton axle loads. A final factor was the coming of the diesel multiple unit introduced as an attempt to stem the loss of passenger revenue by providing a novel alternative for the branch line traveller at a lower operating cost. As a consequence of this disappearing role, production of a further batch of engines, 77020-4, for the NER was held in abeyance from the end of 1954 and eventually cancelled in September 1956.

The class was probably most at home on the Stainmore route between Barnard Castle and Kirkby Stephen and on the Border Counties line, also known as the North Tyne line, from Hexham to Riccarton Junction. Other routes where the class could perhaps have made a contribution were the WR's Cambrian lines from Machynlleth to the Welsh coast, the SR's 'Withered Arm' from Exeter to the coasts of Devon and North Cornwall and possibly the S&DJR route from Bath to Bournemouth or the M&SWJR line from Cheltenham to Southampton.

5.1.1 Design Development

The Standard Cl. 3 2-6-0 was a departure from normal British railway practice in that none of the pre-Nationalisation or pre-Grouping companies had produced such a type. The nearest equivalent was from the LNER which had a scaled-down version of the K1 2-6-0 on the drawing board in 1947. This could be described as a 'Class 2½' but was abandoned in favour of further batches of the Ivatt Cl. 4 2-6-0s (43XXX) already in production. A comparison of the leading dimensions of this proposed design with that of the Standard Cl. 3 2-6-0 is given in Table 50. Although the BR7 boiler carried by the Standard Cl. 4 2-6-0 (76XXX) was suitable dimensionally, it was considered too heavy to enable a 16 ton axle load to be achieved. Hence a modified version of the GWR Swindon No. 2 boiler as fitted to tank engines of the 0-6-2 Cl. 56XX and the 2-6-2 Cl. 51XX and 81XX was adopted using the same flanging plates during manufacture; it was designated BR6. In practice, the BR6 boiler weighed much the same as the BR7 type in full working order, weight savings to achieve the specified axle load being made on other parts of the design. A summary of the annual building programme for the class is given in Table 51; Appendix 1 details year end totals from 1954-1967.

5.2 Dimensions and Data

The parent design office was Swindon with certain details being undertaken at Brighton, Derby and Doncaster; principle dimensions and axle loads are given in Diagram 6. Details of the BR6 boiler fitted to the class are given in section 5.3; firebox dimensions appear in Appendices 2 and 2A. The firebox steel outer wrapper plate and the copper inner wrapper plate were both $9/16$" thick. The throat and backplates were vertical, the former $5/8$" thick and the latter $1/2$" thick. All firebox water space stays were made of Monel metal fitted with nuts inside the firebox while the roof, longitudinal and transverse stays were of steel. The lagging of both the boiler and the firebox consisted of asbestos mattresses. Rocking grate, self emptying ashpan, self cleaning smokebox, frame design, piston, crosshead, slidebars, axleboxes and axlebox guides, method of lubrication, cylinder

Table 50

Standard Class 3 2-6-0s 77000-77019
Comparison of Leading Dimensions of two Class 3 Mixed Traffic 2-6-0s

Class	Date of Introduction	Cylinders Diameter x Stroke	Coupled Wheel Diameter	Boiler Pressure p.s.i.	Total Heating Surfaces sq.ft.	Super heater sq. ft.	Grate Area sq. ft.	Tractive Effort at 85% boiler pressure lb.	Engine Weight in Working Order
BR Standard 3	1954	17½" x 26"	5' 3"	200	1226	184	20.35	21,490	57 tons 9wt
LNER Proposed design (1)	1947	17" x 26"	5' 2"	200	1155	160	19.40	20,603	50 tons 5wt

(1) Scaled down version of LNER K1 Class 2-6-0

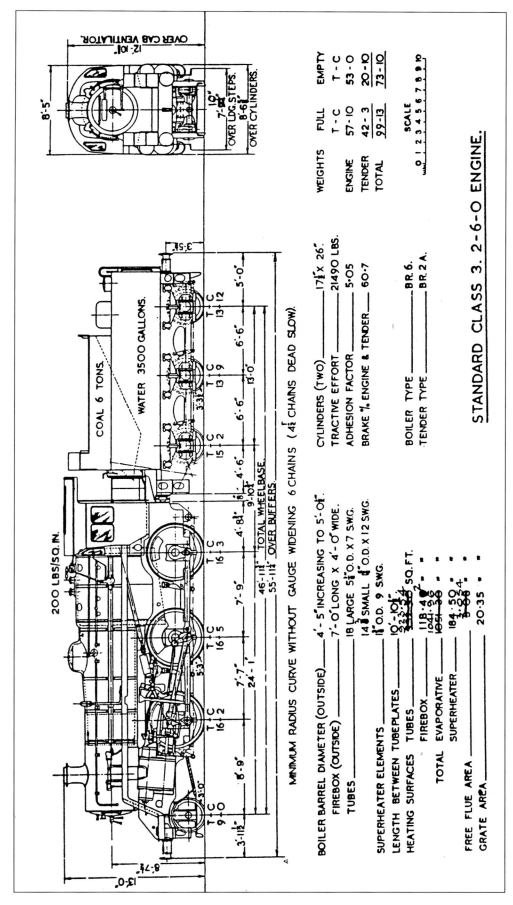

Diagram 6. Standard Cl.3 2-6-0s: Locomotive diagram.

213

Table 51

Standard Cl. 3 2-6-0s 77000-77019: Annual Building Programme

Programme Year	Works	Lot Numbers	Engine Numbers	Total	Delivery Date	Initial Allocated Region
1953	Swindon	406	77000-04	5	02.54-03.54	North Eastern
			77010-14	5	06.54-07.54	North Eastern
	Swindon	407	77005-09	5	03.54-06.54	Scottish
			77015-19	5	07.54-09.54	Scottish
	Swindon	414	77020-24	5	Cancelled 09.56	Intended for North Eastern

cock and sanding arrangements, reversing gear, bogie and cab design details were standard with the other classes and are described in section 2.2.

Valve gear was of the conventional Walschaerts type; cylinder and valve gear dimensions appear in Appendices 3 and 3A. The cylinders were of cast steel with cast iron liners, the same as for the Cl. 3 2-6-2 tank engines (82XXX). Nominal 10" diameter valves were provided, the rear heads being $1/8$" smaller in diameter for ease of insertion and removal. The leading pony truck was also of standard design, side play being controlled by helical springs. Steam brakes were provided for both engine and tender. Various improvements, made as a result of experience with the other Standard classes introduced earlier, were incorporated in the Cl. 3 2-6-0 design from new. These included the provision of the Smith-Stone speedometer, rectangular section coupling rods in place of the fluted type, and footsteps on the rear of the tender to provide a stable platform for the fireman during the water filling operation.

The two batches of Standard Cl. 3 2-6-0s were built over the short period of eight months to the same specification; no significant detail alterations were made.

5.3 Boilers

The BR6 boiler fitted to the Standard Cl. 3 2-6-0s was also that developed earlier for the Standard Cl. 3 2-6-2 tank engines (82XXX); details are given in Appendices 2 and 2A. The modifications to the 51XX Swindon No. 2 boiler included shortening the length by $5^{13}/_{16}$" to give a between tubeplates length of 10' $10^1/_2$" and to reduce weight even further high tensile steel plates of $1/_2$" thickness were used instead of $5/_8$" mild steel plate. An 18 element superheater was incorporated in place of the original 7 element version; additionally a dome was introduced to accommodate the regulator. Boiler mountings, manifold, safety valves and clack valves were also as specified in the other Standard designs. All boilers were constructed at Swindon; details of initial allocation are given in Table 52. The record of the boilers carried later by individual class members after major overhaul is incomplete and appears to be unreliable.

5.4 Tenders

The Standard Cl. 3 2-6-0s were furnished with the BR2A type tender, with serial numbers 1064-1083 believed to have been allocated in sequence. The inset tender with its 6 tons coal, 3,500 gallon water capacity and weight in working order of 42.15 tons was exactly the same design as the BR2 type except that it incorporated the fitting of gangway doors and a fall plate to reduce the footplate draughtiness problem discussed in section 2.4. Tender nos. 1256-1260 allocated to the cancelled lot no. 414 (77020-4) were not built, neither were the serial numbers used for other tender types.

5.5 Construction Costs

The representative departmental first cost for the Standard Cl. 3 2-6-0s in 1954 was £16,054 each. No final cost information is available but comparable figures for other Standard classes built at the same time suggest the representative cost would probably be an underestimate of up to 20%.

5.6 Liveries

The Standard Cl. 3 2-6-0s were turned out in the BR lined mixed traffic lined black livery as detailed in section 2.6. Swindon applied the power classification mark '3' above the cabside numerals on delivery but this was routinely omitted on engines given overhauls at Darlington Works. None of the class was either allocated to the WR or made visits to any WR works for repairs and hence did not appear in any form of BR green livery, lined or otherwise. Engines visiting St. Rollox and Cowlairs on the ScR received the usual treatment of large size cabside numerals and in the latter case the name of their home depot applied to the buffer beam. Photographic evidence suggests St Rollox applied the power classification mark '3MT' whilst Cowlairs used '3MT.'. As an economy measure towards the end of steam, several of the class received

Table 52

Standard Cl. 3 2-6-0s 77000-77019: Initial Boiler Allocation

Locomotive Number	Boiler Number Nominal Allocation	Date of Boiler Construction	Boiler Built at
77000-19	1243-1262	11.53-04.54	Swindon
77020-24	1547-1551	Cancelled 09.56	
Spare Boilers	1375-1379	10.55-01.56	Swindon
	1873	01.60	Swindon
	1948	03.61	Swindon

unlined black livery after overhauls, 77000 for example, being noted in this state in June 1966.

5.7 Allocation and Duties

5.7.1 From Delivery to Withdrawal, 1954–1967

This small class of only twenty engines was delivered to the NER and the ScR from Swindon over the eight month period beginning early February 1954. Many of the duties for which it was designed were either soon to be dieselised or were able to be worked by larger engines following track strengthening and permanent way improvements. As a consequence, a further batch from Swindon, 77020-4 for the NER, was cancelled in September 1956.

Allocation was evenly divided between the ScR and NER; 77005 was originally allocated to Dawsholm in March 1954 but was re-assigned to Hamilton by the end of the month:

NER	Darlington	(10)	77000-4, 77010-4
ScR	Dawsholm	(1)	77005
	Hamilton	(2)	77006/7
	Perth (Blair Atholl)	(2)	77008/9
	Hurlford	(5)	77015-9

Some of the class experienced delays of at least one month from being put into traffic to arriving at their home depot as a result of excessive time spent running-in from Swindon. They were regularly noted on the usual turns, the Swindon-Ludgershall-Tidworth branch pick-up goods service on the M&SWJR and the 7.15am Swindon-Bristol stopping passenger service. The engines ranged much further afield however, 77006 being observed at Exeter on Good Friday 1954, for instance, on the previous night's 10.50pm Marston Sidings-Plymouth Millbay fish. The class was also noted on the rostered return for this working, the 3.55pm (FX) Plymouth Millbay-Swindon parcels and empty stock train; on Fridays, return was with the 3.35pm Plymouth North Road-Cardiff relief passenger service as far as Bristol. Delivery of engines allocated north of the border was via both the East Coast and West Coast main lines; examples noted were 77015 at York in August and 77019 at Crewe in September, both on route to Hurlford. 77011, released to traffic in mid-June 1954, was found in early July at Dalry Road depot in Edinburgh, apparently wrongly delivered.

North Eastern Region
The Darlington allocation was run in on local goods turns and later graduated to the Darlington Croft-Heaton (Newcastle) and Dringhouses (York) freights as well as occasional passenger duties on the York line. The engines were intended to replace LNER Cl. J21 and J25 0-6-0 types and assist the LMS Cl. 2 2-6-0s (464XX) and the newly delivered Standard Cl. 2 2-6-0s (78XXX) on the line over Stainmore summit (1370 feet above sea level) from Barnard Castle to Kirkby Stephen, Tebay and Penrith. Apart from the Darlington-Penrith local passenger service, the main workings over the route were mineral trains and the summer Saturday passenger trains from North East towns to Blackpool.

Fig. 222   77001 departs from Knottingley with the 12.32pm Wakefield Kirkgate-Goole in June 1957. The engine is in the Darlington Works version of lined black livery which omitted the power classification '3' over the cabside numerals.   *(Peter Cookson)*

Table 53

Allocation of Standard Cl. 3 2-6-0s 77000-77019, May 1956–November 1966

Region/Depot	May 1956	May 1958	May 1960	June 1961	January 1963	June 1964	April 1965	November 1966
North Eastern Region								
Hull Botanic Gardens	77000/1/10	77001/10	-	-	-	-	-	-
Hull Springhead	-	77000	-	-	-	-	-	-
Hull Dairycoates	-	-	77000/1/10	77000/1/10	77002	-	-	77002/12
York	-	-	77012/3	77012	77012	-	-	-
Scarborough	-	-	77004	77004/13	77004/13	-	-	-
West Auckland	77002/3	77002/3	77002/3	77002/3	77003	-	-	-
Gateshead	-	-	77011/4	-	-	-	-	-
Darlington	77004	77004	-	-	77000	-	-	-
Thornaby	-	-	-	-	77001/10/1/4	-	-	-
South Blyth	-	-	-	77011/4	-	-	-	-
Stourton	-	-	-	-	-	77000/2-4 77010/1/3/4	77000/3/10/3	77000/3/4
Farnley Junction	-	-	-	-	-	77001/12	-	-
Blaydon	77011	77011/4	-	-	-	-	-	-
Whitby	77012-4	77012/3	-	-	-	-	-	-
Bradford Manningham	-	-	-	-	-	-	77001/12	-
Tweedmouth	-	-	-	-	-	-	77002/4	-
Scottish Region								
Hamilton	77005-7	77005-7	77006	77006	77007-9	-	-	-
Polmadie	77008/9	77008/9	77007-9	77007-9	-	-	-	-
Hurlford	77015-9	77015-9	77015-9	77015-9	77015-9	77007/15-9	77007/15-9	77007/17-9
Carstairs	-	-	77005	77005	77005/6	-	-	-
Motherwell	-	-	-	-	-	77005/8	77005/8	77005
Grangemouth	-	-	-	-	-	77006/9	77006/9	-
London Midland Region and Southern Region								
Northwich (LMR)	-	-	-	-	-	-	77011/4	-
Guildford (SR)	-	-	-	-	-	-	-	77014

The Standard Cl. 3 2-6-0s were not immediately authorised on the route as they were erroneously classified as equivalent in axle load to the LMS Ivatt and Standard Cl. 4 2-6-0s (43XXX and 76XXX repectively) considered too heavy for safe transit over two viaducts on the line. The viaducts in question were Belah, one mile south of Barras on the descent to Kirkby Stephen and Deepdale, one mile west of Lartington. Both structures, 196 feet and 161 feet in height respectively, were of iron girder construction rather than stone. Built nearly a century previously to a design of Thomas Bouch, a local engineer also responsible for the design of the Tay Bridge blown down in a gale in 1879, they were now subject to a rigorous safety re-appraisal.

Whilst the situation was being resolved, the Darlington engines were used elsewhere. In May, 77000 was loaned to Saltburn to work an LNER Cl. A8 4-6-2 tank engine roster to Darlington and Richmond, whilst 77001 was at Northallerton on an LNER Cl. D20 4-4-0 turn to West Hartlepool which included the 7.20am and 3.45pm Northallerton-West Hartlepool and the 11.15am and 6.45pm returns from Saltburn and West Hartlepool respectively.

By July the Standard Cl. 3 2-6-0s had taken up regular work on the Saltburn and Scarborough passenger services from Darlington. Here they proved popular with crews, especially on the Scarborough line where their excellent water consumption figures and accurate tender water-level gauges made intermediate water stops optional. This was in contrast to the LNER Cl. A8 4-6-2 tank engines and B1 Class 4-6-0s which usually took water at Whitby and sometimes also at Loftus. The daily 8.00am from Darlington to Scarborough returning at 7.10pm was almost exclusively worked by the class over the summer of 1954. The Darlington engines were popular for excursion duties, for example during Redcar Race Week in 1954 when 77012

worked an eleven coach Stockton-Redcar shuttle service on 14th August.

By the early summer of 1954, permission had been granted for the class to work the Stainmore route. Initially two trains were not allowed to cross on the viaducts at the same time and passenger trains were limited to 165 tons in weight equating to a five-coach load but this restriction was soon rescinded. The result was the transfer of seven engines, 77000-4/10/1 to West Auckland in July and August. The first to work through to Tebay was 77011 on the 9.20am (SO) Darlington-Blackpool North on 10th July with a load of five coaches unassisted. A mineral test train was run on 14th July from St Helen's Yard, West Auckland to Tebay, consisting of 22 x 21 ton loaded coke hoppers hauled by 77001/2 whilst two days later 77002 worked 14 similar wagons unassisted. The tests resulted in a new load schedule introduced on 20th September for the coke workings using longer trains with three engines per train, two at the head plus a banker. For the latter purpose, at least two of the class, 77004/12 were observed fitted with a cable-worked front slip-coupling device operated remotely from the cab for detaching the engine without stopping the train it was banking. Some details of the new load schedule are noted below:

No. of loaded 21 ton hoppers	Power Combination: Double-header plus banker
35:	3 x Cl. J21 0-6-0 or 3 x Cl. 2 2-6-0 (78XXX)
38:	2 x Cl. J21 0-6-0 plus 1 x Cl. 3 2-6-0 (77XXX)
40:	1 x Cl. J21 0-6-0 plus 2 x Cl. 3 2-6-0 (77XXX)
42:	3 x Cl. 3 2-6-0 (77XXX)

Fig. 223   77003, complete with small snowplough and decorative wreath, pilots Standard Cl. 4 2-6-0 76049 away from Kirkby Stephen East with the RCTS 'Stainmore Limited' rail tour on 20th January 1962, the last weekend of services before closure of the Barnard Castle-Penrith section over Stainmore summit. Note the vacuum pipe extended above the buffer beam to accommodate a medium size snowplough if required.

(N.E. Stead)

The Standard Cl. 3 2-6-0s regularly worked the Blackpool trains as far as Tebay where the turntable in the former North Eastern Railway yard was used to prepare for the return trip. The popular Sunday excursions from Saltburn to Keswick via Stainmore and Penrith were also often in their charge. Later, in November 1954, 77013/4 were further afield at Barrow-in-Furness with an FA Cup Tie special from Darlington.

In May 1955 following strengthening work, the viaduct restrictions were lifted, allowing the allocation of LMS Ivatt Cl. 4 2-6-0s (43XXX) to West Auckland and Kirkby Stephen for duty on the route. The Ivatts lasted for a year, after which they were displaced by Standard Cl. 4 2-6-0s (76XXX). A Blackpool train at this time would consist of eight coaches, typically double-headed to provide sufficient power for negotiating the line's fierce gradients.

In May 1956, following the influx of the higher powered engines, there remained only three Standard Cl. 3 2-6-0s regularly operating on the Stainmore route, 77002/3 at West Auckland and 77004 at Darlington. The rest of the NER based class was at either Hull Botanic Gardens, Blaydon or Whitby (see Table 53). It was 77003 piloting Standard Cl. 4 2-6-0 76049 which worked the last train over Stainmore on 20th January 1962. This was an RCTS farewell tour consisting of nine coaches including buffet car from Darlington, taking in Tebay and Carlisle before returning to Darlington in the wake of the last diesel multiple unit working from Penrith (8.30pm). 77003 remained at West Auckland for two more years where it was often used on local, pick-up and branch goods trains to Tow Law, St John's Chapel, Cornsay and Butterknowle.

Botanic Gardens, situated close to Hull Paragon terminus, was the main passenger engine depot of the former North Eastern Railway in the Hull area. 77000/1/10 arrived in June 1955 and began working alongside LNER B1 4-6-0s, D49 4-4-0s and tank engines of the V1 and V3 2-6-2 and A5 and A8 4-6-2 classes. The new Standard Cl. 3s were noted on the 4.25pm Hull-Bridlington and 6.25pm return. They also worked freight and passenger services on the Hornsea and Withernsea branches and the Brough and Goole lines. The class was largely displaced from these duties from the spring of 1957 by the introduction of diesel multiple units into the area. 77000/1/10 also appeared on passenger services on the former Lancashire and Yorkshire Railway route from Goole to Wakefield Kirkgate via Knottingley with through trains from Hull. Later the engines were noted on a Scarborough-Hull parcels working introduced with the winter timetable in September 1957 when diesel multiple units took over a number of services on the line.

77000/10 moved to Hull Springhead in January and September 1958 respectively. A feature of the Hull railway scene was the operation of many transfer freights linking the various dock complexes with the concentration yards adjacent to Springhead and Dairycoates, the other main freight engine depot in the Hull area and the largest shed on the former North Eastern Railway. Some of the transfer freights were run on a regular timetable basis whilst other services were operated as required in connection with the arrival and departure of cargo vessels. Springhead, the headquarters of the former Hull and Barnsley Railway (H&BR), employed 77000/10 on trip freight and shunting duties for the coal depots at Ella Street and Sculcoates. The engines were also used for transfer work to the Eastern docks area which covered the Drypool, Victoria, Alexandra and King George docks as well as the nearby extensive timber storage yards. By this time, dieselisation and line closures had reduced the Standard Cl. 3 2-6-0s' scope for passenger workings. The former H&BR passenger service from Paragon to South Howden had been withdrawn at the end of July 1955 but occasional special trains continued to run from South Howden to Bridlington until the summer of 1958 when 77010 worked the last public excursion over the line on 30th August. Although remaining open until July 1961 for diesel servicing, Springhead closed to steam in December 1958. The engines transferred to Hull Dairycoates, where they were joined six months later by 77001. Dairycoates also operated transfer freights to the Eastern docks area but its main responsibility was freight and shunting duties for the Western docks, consisting of St Andrews fish dock, Sir William Wright and Albert docks. 77000/1/10 continued to be used on these transfer freights as well as on trip, mineral freight and shunting turns. Cl. 08 350hp diesel shunting locomotives had begun to take over these duties from 1958 and had displaced the Standard Cl. 3 2-6-0s by the end of 1963.

Hull Dairycoates had one or two passenger diagrams apart from summer Saturday holiday trains to and from the coast. The Standard Cl. 3 2-6-0s shared these duties with several other classes including K3 Cl. 2-6-0s and the occasional B1 Cl. 4-6-0. They were also used for the special workings on the Springhead line from Paragon to Boothferry Park Halt, the station serving the adjacent Hull City football ground.

Most of the former Hull and Barnsley Railway was closed in April 1959 when the section between Little Weighton and Wrangbrook Junction near South Elmsall was closed to all traffic. 77000/1/10 were used on the daily pick-up goods service which still operated for a period between Hull and Little Weighton.

Blaydon was host to 77011 in June 1955 from where it was employed on the Haltwhistle-Alston branch. 77011 also worked alongside Standard Cl. 4 2-6-0s (76XXX), LNER Cl. D49 4-4-0s, V1 and V3 2-6-2 tank engines and J39 0-6-0s on the Border Counties line, the former North British Railway branch linking Hexham with Riccarton Junction on the Waverley route from Carlisle to Edinburgh. This steeply graded line proved more suited to the Standard Cl. 3 2-6-0s than to the D49 4-4-0s and the engines were well received. Later, the extensive repairs required to the Border Counties bridge west of Hexham were not deemed justifiable in the light of poor traffic receipts and the line was closed in October 1956.

77014 transferred to Blaydon in June 1956 and, together with 77011, was employed on the Haltwhistle-Alston line on passenger, local freight and the Lambley colliery coal train duties. This branch, the last steam operated one in the area, finally succumbed to two-car diesel multiple unit operation in September 1959; the local freight service was taken over by a Carlisle Canal-based engine, the Lambley coal trains having ceased when the colliery closed in 1959.

77011/4 moved to Gateshead from where they found work on trip and local freights before transferring a year later to Tyne Dock for use on the Washington pilot duty and on local goods and mineral workings in the South Shields area. After only a few months they were moved to South Blyth for trip coal train working and then in October 1962 to Thornaby where they joined 77001/10 ousted by diesels from

Fig. 224
77003 and 77012 pound past Bleathgill up the 1 in 72/60/59 to Stainmore summit with a summer Saturday holiday special from Blackpool to the North East area in the mid–1950s.
(J.W. Armstrong)

Fig. 225
77007, sporting a Caledonian Railway semaphore route indicator, leaves Glasgow Central at the head of the 3.35pm Cathcart Inner Circle suburban service on 16th June 1955.
(Ben Stone)

Fig. 226
77011 traverses Belah Viaduct with a twelve coach summer Saturday working from Blackpool to the North East in the summer of 1954. With such a heavy train, 77011 would need assistance on the climb to Stainmore which is provided on this occasion by a banker, probably an Ivatt Cl. 4 2-6-0.
(E.E. Smith)

Hull Dairycoates. Thornaby used the class on local freight turns on Teeside, to Darlington and Shildon as well as ballast workings in connection with the building of Tees Yard. The engines were also tried out on some of the lighter trip freights from the collieries of south and west Durham to the Newport coal reception sidings between Thornaby and Middlesbrough but were regarded as insufficently powerful. Thornaby was a modern facility opened in June 1958 to replace the four neighbouring depots at Newport, Middlesbrough, Stockton-on-Tees and Haverton Hill. It had ample space for engine storage to which the remaining allocation consisting of 77001/11/4 was assigned by September 1963 when there was found to be little other suitable work for them in the area. The other member of the Thornaby quartet, 77010, had been sent to West Auckland in April 1963 where it was used with 77003 mainly on local and trip freights. 77010 worked the last steam-hauled 6.35am Shildon-Stanhope pick-up goods on 1st February 1964, the last day of operations at West Auckland depot.

Earlier, in October and November 1955, Whitby had received 77004/12-4 for work on the Malton, Middlesbrough and Scarborough lines. The engines were used on both passenger and freight workings including the Scarborough-Whitby pick-up goods. 77004/13 were at Whitby in April 1959 when the depot was closed after the last steam-operated local passenger line in the area, the Whitby-Pickering-Malton service, was given over to diesel multiple units. The engines transferred to Neville Hill for a few weeks where they were noted on Leeds Central pilot duties and local freights. A few months later in November, 77004 was back on the coast line at Scarborough having been at Selby and York since leaving Neville Hill. 77004, fitted with a small snowplough, was used on shunting duties in Scarborough goods yard, mineral freights to York and ballast trains on the Whitby line. 77013 rejoined its former Whitby partner at Scarborough in October 1960 and during the following summer they were employed at both Scarborough Central station and the Londesborough Road excursion platforms on pilot duties for the still heavy summer Saturday holiday traffic to this resort. By November 1962, Scarborough had no regular rosters for its two remaining steam engines, 77004/13, although they were still available for ballast and snowplough duties as required. They were regularly called on as substitutes for failed engines, reaching York on either the 5.45pm fitted freight or the 7.49pm mail train on several ocasions. In the severe winter weather of January 1963, 77004 was noted on both the Whitby and Hull lines deputising for diesel multiple units prone to wheel slipping problems. Scarborough depot closed in April 1963 after which 77004/13 returned to York. From here on the last day of the same month, 77004 found itself in illustrious company. LNER A4 Pacific 60017 had worked a special train for Ampleforth College from Kings Cross to Malton where 77004, still fitted with small snowplough, acted as banker for the train on the 1 in 55 gradient from the station to Scarborough Road Junction. The roles were then reversed and 77004 set off up the branch towards Pilmoor as far as Gilling, the station for the College, assisted by 60017 still attached to the rear of the train. On arrival, the Pacific was uncoupled and headed light engine for York.

September 1963 saw the beginning of a mass transfer of the whole of the NER-based class to the Leeds area where they replaced former MR and LMS Cl. 4 0-6-0s; by June 1964, 77001/12 were at the former LNWR depot at Farnley Junction and the rest at the ex-MR shed at Stourton. The latter depot's engines were employed on trip freights and mineral workings in the Leeds area, together with longer distance goods trains and occasional passenger and parcels workings on the Carnforth and Morecambe lines. For a period, they were noted on what appeared to be a triangular working consisting of the 6.05am trip freight from Hunslet to Ilkley and Skipton, the 8.40am Skipton-Rose Grove near Burnley, returning to Yorkshire on the 12.15pm Rose Grove-Hunslet goods.

In addition to undertaking trip and local freight work, the Farnley Junction engines, 77001/12 together with Standard Cl. 2 2-6-0s 78010/1/4 also at Farnley for a few months, displaced LMS 'Jinty' Cl. 3F 0-6-0 tank engines from their long-standing shunting duties at the former LNWR/L&YR goods depot at Leeds Wellington Street adjacent to Leeds Central passenger station. The steam engines were themselves displaced by Cl. 08 350hp diesel shunters at the end of 1964. Passenger duties included the Leeds Central-Bradford Exchange locals via Pudsey Greenside. Both Stourton and Farnley engines were loaned to Huddersfield depot for parcels workings from time to time during 1964. In December 77001/12 moved from Farnley Junction to the former MR depot at Manningham. Here they were mainly used on station pilot, trip freight and shunting duties. They were also noted on the occasional passenger working such as a troop special from West Yorkshire to the Midlands via Rotherham and Chesterfield on 22nd May 1965. In reality what little work there was for the engines was rapidly being given over to diesel operation and within a year both were briefly at Hull Dairycoates before transferring to Goole in December 1965 for trip working and shunting duties in the docks area; 77001 was withdrawn one month later whilst 77012 went to South Blyth for a short spell in March 1966.

Two other depots which had the class on their books for a period were Selby and Tweedmouth. Selby had 77004/13 for a four month stint in May 1959 from where they were used on local freight work and passenger turns on the Leeds and Bridlington lines until the depot closed in September 1959. Tweedmouth received 77002/4 from Stourton in November 1964. The engines were used on local freight turns. One such working was the Mondays, Wednesdays and Fridays 7.30am Tweedmouth-Reston-Duns pick-up goods returning at 11.10 am. On Tuesdays, Thursdays and Saturdays the engine took a permanent-way special on to the closed Kelso branch whose double track was being singled at this time. Following the eventual closure of its local branch lines and the established through working for both engines and crews on the now dieselised passenger and freight services on the East Coast main line between Newcastle and Edinburgh, Tweedmouth depot became redundant and was closed in June 1966; 77002/4 returned to Stourton.

York had an allocation of Standard Cl. 3 2-6-0s on several occasions from 1958, usually of short duration although 77012 was there from December 1958 to September 1963 when it was used mostly on Scarborough line passenger and freight workings. After its short spell at South Blyth in March 1966, 77012 was again moved to York where it appeared to become the engine of choice for officers' specials and inspection saloon work. 77002 was also at York from October

1966, but again there was little regular work for the pair. 77002/12 lingered on until withdrawal in June 1967, the last of their class to survive on the NER by a margin of six months.

London Midland Region

In November 1964, 77011/4 transferred from Stourton to the former Cheshire Lines Committee (CLC) depot at Northwich. The engines appeared on passenger workings on the former CLC lines deputising for diesel multiple units. On 12th April 1965, for example 77014, fresh from overhaul at Crewe, was on the 7.10am Manchester Central-Liverpool Central and later the same week hauled the 4.57pm Irlam & Cadishead-Liverpool. The engines were used on local freight and parcels trains and also on trip freights on the number of small branches serving the ICI chemical company's Alkali Division salt workings near Northwich. In March 1966 they were replaced by LMS Ivatt Cl. 2 2-6-0s 46405/14; 77011 was withdrawn whilst its companion 77014 began yet another lease of life, this time on the SR.

Southern Region

Allocated to Guildford, reportedly for a short period in connection with working an enthusiasts' special, 77014 was noted en route at Basingstoke on 17th March 1966. Later the same month it was observed at Woking on an up ballast train and then at Nine Elms depot on 26th March. This daily ballast spoil train to Feltham was 77014's only regular duty but because of its novelty value as the only member of the class to be allocated to the SR, the engine was increasingly in demand for enthusiasts' rail tours, working at least five during its time in the Region. It took part in the RCTS Longmoor Railway tour on 16th April 1966. Later in the year on 16th October, by now sporting a substitute front numberplate reported to be made from wood, the engine was involved in the Locomotive Club of Great Britain (LCGB) Dorset and Hampshire Rail Tour from Waterloo taking in Totton, Blandford Forum and Ringwood; 77014 was in charge from Totton to Blandford and back to Broadstone. Again, on 5th February 1967, it powered the Twickenham-Windsor leg of another LCGB special, the South Western Suburban Tour of the London network, the 100th special train run by the club since 1953. Meanwhile the engine was regularly used for parcels, freight and engineering trains as well as the occasional passenger working. For example, during the weekend engineering works re-started at the end of the summer 1965 timetable in connection with the Bournemouth line electrification, 77014 took a prominent part in pilot duties on 18th September. On that day, most Waterloo-Bournemouth line trains were diverted via Alton and the mid-Hants line leaving and re-joining the main line via the junctions at Pirbright and Winchester. 77014 was observed piloting Bulleid Light Pacific 34102 over this hilly line on the down 'Bournemouth Belle' Pullman service amongst others. The engine was still in service right up until the last days of steam operation on the Southern Region. After working a Salisbury-Northam van train on 7th July 1967, 77014 was on the 10.43am Southampton-Bournemouth local next day and for a 'positively final appearance' on 9th July, found itself on the last steam arrival at Weymouth, a parcels train from Bournemouth. Next day it was on Weymouth depot awaiting disposal, the last of its class to be withdrawn from service by one month.

Scottish Region

The Scottish allocation was in place in September 1954 distributed as shown:

Hamilton	(3)	77005-7
Perth (Blair Atholl)	(2)	77008/9
Hurlford	(5)	77015-9

The Hamilton engines joined the roster of LMS Cl. 3 2-6-2 and Cl. 4 2-6-4 tank engines on the frequent and tightly timed service from Hamilton to Glasgow Central. They were also used on the Cathcart Circle trains from Glasgow Central and could be seen on outer suburban duties serving Coatbridge, Motherwell, Strathaven, Carstairs, Coalburn, Holytown, Lesmahagow, East Kilbride, Uplawmoor, Kirkhill and Lanark. Freight turns included colliery yard shunting duties, local trip workings and visits to the Bonnybridge area on coal trains.

From July 1959, a start was made on the dieselisation of the local passenger services in the area. As a result by September 77005/7 had moved to Polmadie to leave 77006 remaining mainly on freight duties until it transferred to Carstairs in November 1962 when Hamilton depot was completely dieselised.

The Perth allocation 77008/9 went to the sub-shed at Blair Atholl. 77009's arrival was delayed until June whilst, along with several other engines, it was exhibited, resplendent with polished rods, tyres and cylinder covers at the International Railway Congress held in the roundhouse at the LMR's Willesden depot towards the end of May. The engines were used for Druimuachdar banking duties on the 16 mile 1 in 70 climb to Dalnaspidal on the former Highland Railway main line to Inverness. With their 'all-in' cabs they provided improved cover for crews when running downhill in reverse. They were also noted on the Blair Atholl-Perth passenger service and colliery trip freights south of Perth. Whether they were regarded as unsuitable for the banking tasks or the fact that they were generating very low annual mileage rates for such new engines, 77008/9 had been moved to Polmadie by December 1954.

From Polmadie the engines were noted on night freights on the Clyde Coast line from Glasgow Central to Greenock and Wemyss Bay as well as the inevitable Cathcart Circle line passenger work. They could regularly be seen on football excursions to Mount Florida for Hampden Park and were used on the Orange Walk specials to Glasgow St Enoch from Greenock Princes Pier in July 1955. The local service on the latter route was withdrawn between Kilmacolm and Greenock in February 1959 but the engines continued to appear occasionally on services connected with the ocean liner traffic from Princes Pier.

In September 1959, 77005/7 arrived at Polmadie having been displaced from their passenger duties at Hamilton by diesel multiple units. They joined their stable-mates on Cathcart Circle and other suburban line work although these services were now also being given over to diesel operation. The first stage of the Glasgow suburban electrification from Helensburgh and Balloch to Airdrie was inaugurated in November 1960. Problems with transformer units on the new electric multiple units led to their temporary withdrawal and 77007-9 still at Polmadie were retained on some of these suburban workings until full re-introduction of the electrics in

Fig. 227
77012 drifts by on a train of empty coaching stock which appears to include diesel multiple units in the rear; the view was taken at Clifton Sidings, York in October 1966. 77012 in unlined black livery is adorned with electric warning flashes on the boiler and firebox.
(Peter Cookson)

Fig. 228
77012 sets off from Eaglescliffe with a Saltburn-Darlington local on 4th September 1955. The engine was allocated to no fewer than ten different NER depots during its thirteen years of life.
(D. Trevor Rowe)

Fig. 229
77014 meanders through Totton with an enthusiast's special for Blandford Forum on 21st May 1966. The engine has a non-standard front numberplate, possibly fashioned out of wood.
(L.Elsey)

October 1961. After this, despite the difficulty in finding other suitable work for the class, 77007-9 remained at the depot mainly on local freight duties until August 1963 when they moved to Hurlford, Motherwell and Carstairs respectively. The latter depot had received 77005 from Polmadie in May 1960 and 77006 from Hamilton in November 1962. It used the engines on local and trip freights with occasional visits to Carlisle Kingmoor on fitted freight work. Although Carstairs was a stronghold of steam in Scotland almost until the end in May 1967, it had lost its Standard Cl. 3 2-6-0s by December 1963.

Motherwell played host to 77005/8 from June and August 1963 respectively; later, in October 1965, 77006 arrived for the last few months of its life, all three being withdrawn from the depot during 1966. Now displaced from passenger work by diesels and electrification, the engines were used on the usual trip freights, colliery yard shunting duties and other mineral train working. Grangemouth had 77006/9 for almost two years from the end of 1963 until the depot was given over to diesels in October 1965. Again the engines' main duties were trip workings and mineral goods traffic.

Hurlford depot near Kilmarnock received 77015-9 between July and September 1954. 77018 first appeared in Scotland on 9th September on the 9.45pm class D fitted freight from Heaton to Edinburgh Niddrie yard whilst 77019 worked through Carlisle on 14th September with a Leyburn-Ayr horsebox special. Apart from 77019, which went to Polmadie in February 1963 before returning in October, 77015-9 remained allocated to Hurlford for the whole of their brief lives, withdrawal taking place during 1966. The engines appeared on station pilot duties at Kilmarnock and displaced some of the LMS 2P 4-4-0s from local passenger services to the Ayrshire coast and to Glasgow St Enoch both via Barrhead and via Dalry, the latter duties shared with Glasgow Corkerhill depot. One of the class at Hurlford was usually kept on standby for working the breakdown train, filling in its time on shunting duties at some of the local industrial sidings. By early 1955, they were regularly working the former Glasgow and South Western Railway's Nith Valley route to Dumfries on the 9.25am from Glasgow St Enoch which called at virtually all stations from Kilmarnock onward; the return working was the 3.08pm slow to St Enoch.

It was on this route that one of Hurlford's engines was involved in a notable rescue operation in 1961. 77018 was on an early morning colliery trip freight near New Cumnock on 9th September when Coronation Pacific 46249 was observed gingerly approaching from the south leaving the lineside burning in its wake after discharging most of its fire through disintegrating fire bars on the climb from Kirkconnel. The Pacific was working the previous night's 11.40pm Euston-Glasgow St Enoch sleeping car express loading to thirteen vehicles weighing well in excess of 500 tons. After the

Fig. 230   77017 performs pilot duties at Kilmarnock on 17th April 1965. Note the stone-built former Kilmarnock shed on the left, closed as early as 1877 on the opening of the nearby Hurlford depot. The shed was used as a locomotive servicing point well into BR days; later the track was removed and the premises leased to a local business. 77015-8 spent the whole of their working lives of twelve years or so at Hurlford depot.

(Courtney Haydon)

Fig. 231   77000 is pictured at Darlington in the mid–1950s. The engine spent over seven years allocated to depots in the Hull area before returning to Darlington in January 1963. Note the rear driving wheel activated Smith-Stone speedometer with which the class was fitted from new.

(N.E. Stead)

Fig. 232   Newly completed 77002 awaits its life-long tender partner at Swindon Works on St Valentine's Day, 14th February 1954. Note the power classification mark above the cabside numerals; this was routinely omitted in later years by Darlington Works where the NER allocation of ten engines, 77000-4/10-4 was maintained.

(E.W. Fry)

removal of 46249 to a siding, 77018 was conscripted to work the train forward to Kilmarnock. Although the line between New Cumnock and the three miles to Polquhap summit is virtually level, 77018 did well to start the train unaided at the first attempt. After Polquhap the twenty miles or so to Kilmarnock are almost all downhill so it was perhaps the engine's braking power at least as much as its horsepower which was put to the test on this occasion.

Other passenger work included the Ardrossan-Kilmarnock service and the Ayr-Dalmellington branch. Diesel railbuses took over most of the Dalmellington branch service in April 1959, although a weekly steam working, the Saturdays Only 12.25pm from Kilmarnock and 1.35pm return operated until closure on 6th April 1964. The Ardrossan-Kilmarnock service was withdrawn on the same day with 77016 busy working the last steam service on both lines.

Hurlford's Standard Cl. 3 2-6-0s also replaced LMS Cl. 2P 4-4-0s and Caledonian Railway Cl. 2P 0-4-4 tank engines in January 1959 on the Muirkirk-Lanark branch. A few weeks later they were themselves displaced by LMS Cl. 3 2-6-2 tank engine 40049, a refugee from Dundee Tay Bridge. This engine did not prove a success owing to insufficient water capacity and the Standard Cl. 3 2-6-0s returned, one being sub-shedded at Muirkirk for this service until displaced by diesel multiple units in May 1962. A daily goods train for Kennox colliery continued to run until 1965 when the pit closed and the whole of the Muirkirk-Lanark section of track was lifted. The years 1964-66 saw virtually all of the Ayrshire branch passenger services withdrawn and dieselisation of the remaining services in the area. The only passenger role left for the Standard Cl. 3 2-6-0s was as standby for diesel failure and it was not uncommon to see the class still operating on the Ayr-Kilmarnock local service for a time.

Freight turns for the Standard Cl. 3 2-6-0s at Hurlford included a few colliery trip duties around the extensive Ayrshire coalfield. These trains were worked to the large Falkland Junction concentration yard at Ayr and after re-marshalling were forwarded to the steel plants and power stations in the Clyde valley and Glasgow areas. One option had been to use the class as a replacement for the life-expiring Caledonian Railway Cl. 3F 0-6-0s on those mineral branches where weight restrictions were applicable and loads were considered too heavy for lighter engine classes such as the Standard Cl. 2 2-6-0s (78XXX). In reality this type of work in the area was fast disappearing. The engines could not be used on the coalfield's heavier mineral workings as they were clearly no match for the LMS Hughes Fowler Crab Cl. 6P/5F 2-6-0s, Stanier Cl. 5 4-6-0s and Standard Cl. 4 2-6-0s (76XXX) which remained the mainstay of these duties until the end of steam in the area in October 1966.

By the mid 1960s, the closure of the smaller, uneconomic mines in the Ayrshire coalfield meant that the requirement for trip coal workings had virtually ceased. Full length trains from the remaining large collieries such as Barony near Auchinleck, Killoch on the Drongan branch and Waterside on the Dalmellington branch, were operated direct either to Falkland Junction Yard or to the harbour at Ayr which still had a significant coal export trade; by this time motive power was mainly diesels of Type 1 Cl. 20 and Type 2 Cl. 25 based in the Glasgow area. Thus the Standard Cl. 3 2-6-0s were redundant from both their passenger and freight duties. Hurlford depot, itself equally redundant, was closed in October 1966. Prior to closure, the locomotive yard at Hurlford had slowly been taken over by the adjacent 'Johnny Walker' whisky bottling plant. The locomotives and their associated facilities were being confined to a smaller and smaller area outside the shed buildings. With this reduction in available space, stored and withdrawn engines were despatched to the former Kilmarnock locomotive Works site for storage. The four remaining Standard Cl. 3 2-6-0s at Hurlford, 77007/17-9 were withdrawn at the end of November thus marking the end of the class in Scotland.

Fig. 233   77004 shunts the yard at Alnwick on 19th August 1965. Graffiti artists appear to have left their palm prints in white paint on the side of the tender, making it easier for the fingerprint experts at the local constabulary to identify the culprits, should they be so inclined!

(Courtney Haydon)

5.7.2 Allocation Summary

77000   2.54 Darlington; 7.54 West Auckland; 6.55 Darlington; 7.55 Hull Botanic Gardens; 1.58 Hull Springhead; 12.58 Hull Dairycoates; 1.63 Darlington; 5.64 Stourton; 12.66 Withdrawn.

77001   2.54 Darlington; 7.54 West Auckland; 6.55 Darlington; 7.55 Hull Botanic Gardens; 6.59 Hull Dairycoates; 4.62 Thornaby; 9.63 Stourton; 12.63 Farnley Junction; 12.64 Manningham; 11.65 Hull Dairycoates; 12.65 Goole; 1.66 Withdrawn.

77002   2.54 Darlington; 7.54 West Auckland; 12.62 Darlington; 1.63 Hull Dairycoates; 9.63 Stourton; 11.64 Tweedmouth; 6.66 Stourton; 10.66 York; 6.67 Withdrawn.

77003   2.54 Darlington; 7.54 West Auckland; 2.64 Stourton; 12.66 Withdrawn.

77004   3.54 Darlington; 8.54 West Auckland; 1.55 Darlington; 10.55 Whitby; 11.55 Darlington; 8.58 York; 9.58 Whitby; 4.59 Neville Hill; 5.59 Selby; 9.59 York; 11.59 Scarborough; 4.63 York; 9.63 Stourton; 11.64 Tweedmouth; 6.66 Stourton; 12.66 Withdrawn.

77005   3.54 Dawsholm; 3.54 Hamilton; 9.59 Polmadie; 5.60 Carstairs; 6.63 Motherwell; 11.66 Withdrawn.

77006   3.54 Hamilton; 11.62 Carstairs; 12.63 Grangemouth; 10.65 Motherwell; 3.66 Withdrawn.

77007   3.54 Hamilton; 9.59 Polmadie; 8.63 Hurlford; 11.66 Withdrawn.

77008   4.54 Perth located Blair Atholl; 11.54 Polmadie; 8.63 Motherwell; 6.66 Withdrawn.

77009   6.54 Perth located Blair Atholl; 12.54 Polmadie; 8.63 Carstairs; 10.63 Grangemouth; 10.65 Motherwell; 5.66 Withdrawn.

77010   6.54 Darlington; 8.54 West Auckland; 6.55 Darlington; 7.55 Hull Botanic Gardens; 9.58 Hull Springhead; 12.58 Hull Dairycoates; 4.62 Thornaby; 4.63 West Auckland; 2.64 Stourton; 11.65 Withdrawn.

77011   6.54 Darlington; 8.54 West Auckland; 6.55 Blaydon; 12.55 Blaydon located Alston; 9.59 Gateshead; 9.60 Tyne Dock; 4.61 South Blyth; 10.62 Thornaby; 9.63 Stourton; 11.64 Northwich; 2.66 Withdrawn.

77012   6.54 Darlington; 1.55 West Auckland; 11.55 Whitby; 12.58 York; 9.63 Stourton; 12.63 Farnley Junction; 12.64 Manningham; 11.65 Hull Dairycoates; 12.65 Goole; 3.66 South Blyth; 4.66 York; 6.67 Withdrawn.

77013   7.54 Darlington; 11.55 Whitby; 4.59 Neville Hill; 5.59 Selby; 9.59 York; 10.60 Scarborough; 4.63 York; 9.63 Stourton; 3.66 Withdrawn.

77014   7.54 Darlington; 11.55 Whitby; 6.56 Blaydon; 9.59 Gateshead; 9.60 Tyne Dock; 4.61 South Blyth; 10.62 Thornaby; 9.63 Stourton; 11.64 Northwich; 3.66 Guildford; 7.67 Withdrawn.

77015   7.54 Hurlford; 7.66 Withdrawn.

77016   8.54 Hurlford; 3.66 Withdrawn.

77017   8.54 Hurlford; 11.66 Withdrawn.

77018   8.54 Hurlford; 11.66 Withdrawn.

77019   9.54 Hurlford; 2.63 Polmadie; 10.63 Hurlford; 11.66 Withdrawn.

Fig. 234
77005 reposes at Motherwell MPD on 29th May 1966. The engine uniquely acquired a Standard Cl. 4 chimney, shorter and wider than the original, during a visit to Cowlairs Works in the early 1960s. Note the '3MT.' power classification mark above the cabside numerals and the tender lining applied close to the panel edges. *(Mike Burnett)*

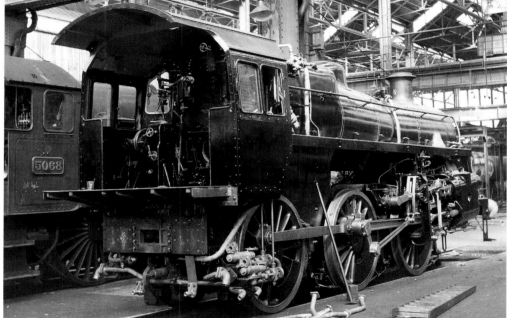

Fig. 235
77007 is under construction at Swindon Works 'A' Shop in April 1954. The class was run-in on Swindon–Bristol locals and M&SWJR line workings to Cheltenham and Andoversford as well as occasionally on freights as far as Exeter and Plymouth.

(G. Wheeler)

Fig. 236
77007 contemplates a Scottish future in Swindon Works yard after completion on 28th March 1954. Allocated to Hamilton, Polmadie and Hurlford at various times, the engine was withdrawn in November 1966. *(W. Potter)*

5.8 Maintenance

Works responsibility for major overhauls and repairs is given in Table 54. The official recommended period between works visits was 33 months for intermediate and 66 months for general overhauls. A comparison of repair costs per mile (in new pence) for the Standard Class 3 2-6-0s with the Class 3 2-6-2 tank engines for the year 1957 is given as follows.

Repair Costs per Mile
(new pence)

	Engine & Boiler	Tender	Total
Class 3 2-6-0	3.24	0.15	3.39
Class 3 2-6-2 Tank	3.22	-	3.22

Annual mileage figures on both the ScR and NER were not recorded on a regular basis but in the case of the Standard Class 3 2-6-0s may be assumed to be in the range of 20,000-25,000 per locomotive on average.

Table 54

Standard Cl. 3 2-6-0s 77000-77019 Works Repairs

Region	All Repairs including Intermediate and General Overhauls	Light Casual and Non-classified Repairs Only
ScR	Cowlairs★ St. Rollox (to March 1964)	Inverurie Kilmarnock
NER	Darlington (to mid-1964) Crewe (from mid-1964)	Gateshead
LMR	Crewe	
SR	Eastleigh	

★ NER based 77003 visited Cowlairs Works in August 1964 and was noted 'running-in' from Corkerhill in September.

5.9 Modifications in Service

Experience with the earlier Standard locomotives introduced from 1951 onwards enabled many improvements to be incorporated into the design of the Standard Class 3-6-0s from new, see section 5.2 No significant modifications were made to the class once in service.

5.9.1 Detail Modifications

Several of the ScR allocation, 77005-7 working out of Glasgow Central were fitted with the former Caledonian Railway route indicators attached to the top lamp bracket. On the former Caledonian lines, engines working passenger trains carried a small white two arm semaphore, usually in front of the chimney but sometimes above the buffer beam, the position of the arms indicating the route to be traversed by the train (see Appendix 7). In the early 1960s, 77005 emerged from an overhaul at Cowlairs with a Standard Class 4 2-6-0 chimney, a shorter but wider version of the class' normal chimney. (See Fig. 234) There is no information as to whether the engine's steaming characteristics were either compromised or significantly improved by this change.

On the NER, some of the class working over Stainmore were fitted with a cable-worked front slip coupling operated from the cab. This device enabled the engine to be uncoupled remotely when on banking duties thus reducing delays by eliminating the need to stop the train. Other NER engines carried snowploughs during the winter months, particularly on the Stainmore route and the exposed lines serving Scarborough; at least three of the class, 77003/4/13, were noted with cowcatcher-type snowploughs at various times. 77003/4 were fitted with vacuum pipes extended above the front buffer beam to accommodate the larger snowploughs if required. Finally, most if not all of the class had been fitted with BR AWS apparatus by the early 1960s.

5.10 Names and Nicknames

None of the class ever carried official names in BR service. Local nicknames in Scotland included the 'Wee Standards' and the 'Doodlebugs', making it possible to see two types of 'Doodlebug' in the Glasgow area. The other class so named was the Ivatt Class 4 2-6-0, six of which, 43132-7 were at the former NB depot at Eastfield in the mid 1950s; by then however, the latter engines were perhaps becoming better known as the 'Flying Pigs'.

5.11 Performance

In Scotland, the Standard Class 3 2-6-0s were afflicted by the usual problem associated with classes containing very few locomotives. Individual engine men were not assigned to the engines often enough to become familiar with them and thus establish optimum working techniques. The fact that many of the engines were frequently moved from depot to depot did not help in this regard and confirmed to some extent that the operating authorities were for ever casting around for suitable roles for the class. The Polmadie engines in particular, appear to have spent a considerable time 'on shed' due to the lack of suitable work. In contrast, 77015-9 spent all their working lives at Hurlford, with the exception of 77019 which had a few months at Polmadie in 1963. The Hurlford continent was busily employed on both freight and passenger traffic on the Ayrshire lines. As a result of their lengthy allocation there, enginemen came to know them well and to appreciate their free steaming characteristics and excellent fuel economy.

On the NER, the class performed well enough on the Stainmore route, although enginemen preferred the Standard and Ivatt Class 4 2-6-0s with their extra reserve of boiler capacity when tackling the stiff grades under adverse weather conditions. The Standard Class 3 2-6-0s were generally regarded as having good riding characteristics but required careful firing on account of their long narrow fireboxes.

5.12 Storage, Withdrawal and Disposal

Several of the class were put in store at various times towards the end of steam operation on BR. 77001/11/4 were noted at Thornaby in the late summer of 1963 and some of the Hurlford contingent, 77017-9 were also out of action in the autumn of 1966 prior to withdrawal. Table 55 gives dates of withdrawal and places of disposal. The first to be withdrawn was 77010 in November 1965 whilst the last to succumb in July 1967 was 77014 in exile on the SR.

5.13 Preservation

Although perhaps the ideal engine for today's steam

preservation lines, none of the class was preserved. Probably, the nearest approach was with 77012. This engine, allocated to York from December 1958 to September 1963, was frequently used on officers' specials to all parts of the NER and kept in very good condition. After a visit to Crewe works in 1965, where it was withdrawn and subsequently re-instated, there were hopes that 77012 would have been bought for preservation but the plans fell through and the engine was withdrawn in June 1967.

Table 55

Standard Cl. 3 2-6-0s 77000-77019
Construction, Withdrawal and Disposal Information

Engine	Built	Withdrawn	Disposal	
77000	2.54	12.66	3.67	T. W. Ward, Beighton, Sheffield
77001	2.54	1.66	2.66	T. W. Ward, Killamarsh
77002	2.54	6.67	2.68	Garnham, Harris & Elton, Chesterfield
77003	2.54	12.66	3.67	T. W. Ward, Beighton, Sheffield
77004	3.54	12.66	3.67	T. W. Ward, Beighton, Sheffield
77005	3.54	11.66	4.67	Motherwell Machinery and Scrap Co., Wishaw
77006	3.54	3.66	6.66	J. McWilliam, Shettleston
77007	3.54	11.66	4.67	T. W. Ward, Wishaw
77008	4.54	6.66	10.66	Motherwell Machinery and Scrap Co., Wishaw
77009	6.54	5.66	10.66	Motherwell Machinery and Scrap Co., Wishaw
77010	6.54	11.65	2.66	Arnott Young, Parkgate
77011	6.54	2.66	5.66	Central Wagon Co., Wigan
77012	6.54	6.67	2.68	Garnham, Harris & Elton, Chesterfield
77013	7.54	3.66	6.66	T. W. Ward, Beighton, Sheffield
77014	7.54	7.67	2.68	Birds Commercial Motors, Risca
77015	7.54	7.66	11.66	G. H. Campbell, Airdrie
77016	8.54	3.66	6.66	Motherwell Machinery and Scrap Co., Wishaw
77017	8.54	11.66	4.67	T. W. Ward, Wishaw
77018	8.54	11.66	4.67	T. W. Ward, Wishaw
77019	9.54	11.66	4.67	T. W. Ward, Wishaw

Fig. 237   77007 rests in Polmadie shed yard on 16th August 1960; here the engines were known as the 'Wee Standards'. The class was equipped with the BR2A type tender as also fitted to some Standard Cl. 4 4-6-0s and 2-6-0s.

(Peter Groom)

Fig. 238   77010 is at Darlington MPD on 25th July 1954 having recently arrived from Swindon. In the enginemen's park to the right, note the motor cycle and sidecar combination, a popular mode of transport for the family in the 1950s.

(Alan Bowman, John S. Phillips Collection)

Fig. 239   77012 awaits attention at Crewe Works on 11th April 1965. There were hopes that the engine would be preserved after its visit to Crewe, where it was at first condemned and later re-instated; but the plans came to nought and 77012 was withdrawn in June 1967.

(Courtney Haydon)

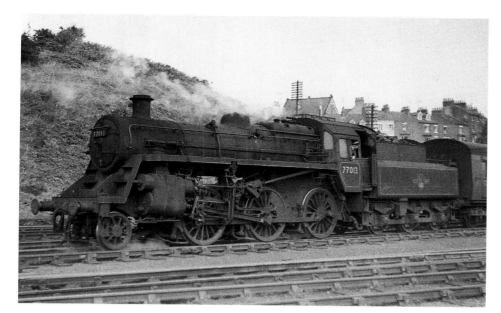

Fig. 240
77013 shunts the yard at Boghall Junction, Whitby in August 1958. 77013 was allocated to Whitby from November 1955 to April 1959 for work on the Malton, Middlesbrough and Scarborough lines. *(Peter Cookson)*

Fig. 241
77014 is pictured at Tyne Dock MPD on 19th August 1960. The engine was officially allocated to the depot one month later but was soon on the move again, this time to South Blyth in April 1961. *(Peter Groom)*

Fig. 242
77019, seen here at Crewe on 11th September 1954 en route from Swindon to Hurlford depot; Crewe held on to the engine for a short period presumably to put it through its paces on typical running-in turns.
(David Tyreman Collection)

6. Class 2 2-6-0 78000-64

6.1 Purpose

The design of the Standard Cl. 2 2-6-0s followed very closely that of the Ivatt Cl. 2 2-6-0s (BR 464XX-465XX) introduced by the LMS in 1946 for use mainly on secondary and branch line work, both passenger and freight. The new Standards were similarly employed but were also allocated to all other BR regions with the exception of the SR. The latter Region rarely saw the class on regular duties apart from occasional appearances by Willesden-based engines in the 1960s on transfer freights in the West London area. The tank engine equivalent of the LMS Ivatt class was the mechanically identical Cl. 2 2-6-2 tank engine (BR 412XX-413XX) introduced at the same time and perpetuated by BR as a standard design in the form of the 84XXX class. A comparison of the leading dimensions of the Standard Cl. 2 2-6-0s with their Ivatt predecessors is given in Table 56.

6.1.1 Design Development

The Standard Cl. 2 2-6-0s benefitted from the work carried out to improve the steaming characteristics of one of the Ivatt Cl. 2 2-6-0s, 46413, in 1949/50. An initial road trial of the Ivatt engine compared with a GWR Dean Goods 0-6-0 was made between Stoke Gifford and Didcot in November 1949 and showed little if any advantage for the Mogul. In the summer of 1950, 46413 was taken into the Swindon Works Testing Station for modification before further trials. Here improvements were made to the draughting arrangements by fitting a taller, much narrower chimney; alterations were also made to the choke and blastpipe dimensions. The net result was an increase in maximum water evaporation from 9,850 lbs per hour to 14,000 lbs per hour using Blidworth grade 2B coal. 46413 was then subject to further road trials in August 1950, again on the Bristol main line, from Stoke Gifford to Swindon. The engine managed to work up a 15 coach test train weighing 455 tons to over 60mph at Little Somerford. This was achieved after a minimum of 40mph on the 10½ mile climb at 1 in 300 from just west of Winterbourne to Badminton, whilst simultaneously maintaining both boiler pressure and water levels. The modified draughting arrangements together with slightly larger cylinders (16½" x 24") were applied to the rest of the Ivatt Cl. 2 2-6-0 batches

when construction recommenced with 46465 in June 1951 and were also adopted for the new Standard Cl. 2 2-6-0s. A further modification was made to the Ivatts after the completion of 46490. This involved yet a third style of chimney which was essentially a taller but only slightly narrower version of the first type; this final version of the Ivatts' chimney was virtually identical to the one fitted to the Standard Cl. 2 2-6-0s.

The other visual difference between the LMS Ivatt Cl. 2 2-6-0s and the BR Standard version concerned mainly the cab. On the new Standard engines the cabs were slightly modified so that the upper side sheets sloped inwards compared with those on the Ivatts thus increasing route availability even further to allow almost universal access to the BR network. The Standard locomotives also had smaller windows on the cab spectacle plate. The LMS top-feed water delivery system in the boiler was replaced by the Standard BR clack valve arrangement and the BR regulator in the dome was a vertical grid type operated by an external rod at the side of the firebox instead of the original LMS internal design. Following the Ivatt design as faithfully as they did, the Standard Cl. 2 2-6-0s did not display the BR Standard 'family marque' of high running plate and deep valance. Also the Type BR3 tender with which the class was fitted was virtually the same as that carried by the Ivatts and hence did not conform to the Standard BR cab layout.

All members of the Standard Cl. 2 2-6-0s were built at Darlington which was already familiar with the type, having built 38 of their Ivatt predecessors, 46465-46502 between June 1951 and March 1952. The first ten Standard types, 78000-9 for the WR, were completed to Swindon lot number 402 between December 1952 and April 1953; over the same period Swindon itself was turning out the last of the Ivatt types, 46503-27 also for the WR. The class continued on the secondary and branch line work for which it had been designed until the early 1960s. After about 1963, the steady closure of branch lines and the dieselisation of the remaining services under the BR modernisation plan saw the class increasingly employed on freight, pilot and other shunting duties. Even this type of work was quickly disappearing from the BR scene and by the end of May 1967, the last of the class

---

Table 56

Standard Cl. 2 2-6-0s 78000-78064

Comparison of Leading Dimensions of BR Standard and LMS Ivatt Cl. 2 Mixed Traffic 2-6-0s

Class	Date of Introduction	Cylinders Diameter x Stroke	Coupled Wheel Diameter	Boiler Pressure p.s.i.	Total Heating Surfaces sq. ft.	Superheater sq. ft.	Grate Area sq. ft.	Tractive Effort at 85% boiler pressure lb.	Engine Weight Working Order
BR Standard 2	1952	16½" x 24"	5' 0"	200	1149.0	124	17.5	18,515	49 tons 5 cwt
LMS Ivatt 2 (46400-46464)	1946	16" x 24"	5' 0"	200	1159.5	134	17.5	17,410	47 tons 2 cwt
LMS Ivatt 2 (46465-46527)	1951	16½" x 24"	5' 0"	200	1159.5	134	17.5	18,515	47 tons 2 cwt

Fig. 243   78000 pilots GWR Manor Cl. 4-6-0 7818, Granville Manor, on an Aberystwyth-Manchester extra at Llanymynech on 1st September 1962; 78000 is in unlined green livery. The Cambrian lines were still busy on summer Saturdays in the early 1960s with through holiday services from London, the West Midlands and the North West.   *(P.H. Wells)*

Fig. 244   Machynlleth-based 78003 leaves Towyn on 8th August 1959 with a holiday train of LMR stock. The engine later spent time at Bangor, Willesden, Nuneaton and Shrewsbury depots before withdrawal in December 1966.   *(P.H. Wells)*

Fig. 245   78000 pilots GWR 43XX Cl. 2-6-0 6378 on the ascent to Talerddig summit with a Paddington train on 1st September 1962. 78000 appears to have spent the day piloting heavy holiday trains over Talerddig, a typical summer Saturday duty for the class.

(P.H. Wells)

Fig. 246   78006, in lined green livery, heads a stopping passenger train away from Barmouth on 30th July 1958. The engine was the first of the class to receive green livery, at Swindon in March 1957. GWR 43XX Cl. 2-6-0 5399 waits for a clear road in the adjacent bay platform.

(P.H. Wells)

Table 57

Standard Cl. 2 2-6-0s 78000-78064: Annual Building Programme

Programme Year.	Works	Lot Numbers	Engine Numbers	Total	Delivery Date	Initial Allocated Region
1952	Darlington	Swindon Lot 402	78000-09	10	12.52-04.53	Western
1953	Darlington	-	78010-19	10	12.53-03.54	North Eastern
	Darlington	-	78020-44	25	04.54-12.54	London Midland
1954	Darlington	-	78045-54	10	10.55-12.55	Scottish
1956	Darlington	-	78055-64	10	08.56-11.56	London Midland

Key: - It was Darlington Works policy not to assign Lot Numbers for new locomotive construction.

had been withdrawn. A summary of the annual building programme for the class is given in Table 57. Appendix 1 details year end class totals from 1952-67.

6.2 Dimensions and Data

The main design office for the Standard Cl. 2 2-6-0s was Derby with certain components designed at Swindon, Brighton and Doncaster. Principal dimensions and axle loads are given in Diagram 7; details of the BR8 boiler carried by the class appear in section 6.3.

Firebox data appear in Appendices 2 and 2A. The steel wrapper plate was $^{17}/_{32}$" thick and the inner copper firebox wrapper $^9/_{16}$" thick. The throat and back plate were both vertical and were $^5/_8$" and $^{17}/_{32}$" thick respectively. All firebox stays were of Monel metal, fitted with steel nuts inside the firebox; fibreglass insulation was used for both the boiler and firebox.

Frames were of carbon steel 1" thick and stayed both horizontally and vertically in a similar manner to the other BR Standard classes as described in section 2.2. Axlebox horns and liners, coupled axleboxes and bearings and also their method of lubrication were also similar to those used in the other Standard designs except those fitted with roller bearings to coupled axles; the pony truck was also of Standard design.

Valve gear was of the conventional Walschaerts type; cylinder and valve dimensions are given Appendices 3 and 3A. The 8" valves were lubricated by atomised oil delivered through atomisers from the mechnical lubricator situated on the running plate above the cylinders. Pins on the valve gear were grease lubricated, except the expansion link, radius rod and die paths which were oil lubricated. The bearing of the return crank big end was of the self-aligning ball bearing type. The cylinder drain cocks were steam operated and of Standard design. The crossheads were of the two-bar type; the top bar was mechanically lubricated, being the load carrying bar when the engine was working forward. The connecting rod big end and coupling rod bearings were lined with white metal and the oil distributed over the bearing by felt pad which was lubricated by splash feed from an oil box integral with the rod above the bearing. Steam and vacuum brake equipment was identical to that carried on the other BR Standard locomotives.

Apart from the provision of Smith-Stone speedometers on all new engines beginning with 78010, the only significant variation in production batches was the substitution of rectangular coupling rods in place of the original fluted type from 78035 onwards.

6.3 Boilers

The principal dimensions of the BR8 boiler fitted to the Standard Cl. 2 2-6-0s were identical to those of the LMS Ivatt Cl. 2 2-6-0s with the same working pressure of 200 p.s.i.; the same boiler was adopted for the Standard Cl. 2 2-6-2 tank engines (84XXX). The barrel consisted of two rings made of carbon steel plate, the second of which was tapered equally at top and bottom; dimensional details are given in Appendices 2 and 2A. A relatively large dome was provided and contained a vertical grid-type regulator operated by an external pull-rod connected to a transverse shaft which entered the second barrel through a stuffing box. Two separate feeds were provided from two live steam injectors situated below the cab on the right hand side, the water entering the boiler through two clack valves placed at 30 degrees on each side of the vertical centre line of the first barrel and passing over deflecting trays. The boiler fittings were of the type used on other BR Standard designs; they included a manifold, separate shut-off cocks and a manually operated blowdown valve on the front of the firebox. The boilers for the Standard Cl. 2 2-6-0s together with one spare were all built at Darlington; four more spare BR8 boilers were constructed at Crewe. The BR8 boilers for the Standard Cl. 2 2-6-2 tank engines (84XXX) were built at Darlington and Crewe, which also built three more spares. The boilers of the tank engine and tender engine classes were interchangeable but there is no evidence that this was a widespread practice and may not have occurred at all. Details of original boiler allocations are given in Table 58: boiler numbers were not necessarily allocated in serial number sequence. The record of which boilers were carried by individual class members after general overhaul is incomplete and may be unreliable.

6.4 Tenders

The Standard Cl. 2 2-6-0s were fitted with the Type BR3 tender having a coal capacity of four tons and 3,000 gallons of

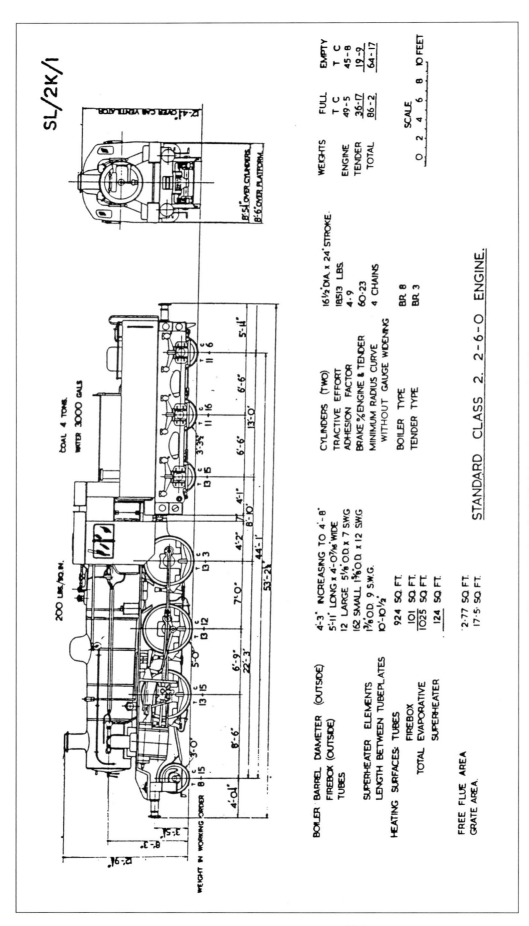

SL/2K/1

COAL 4 TONS.
WATER 3000 GALS

200 LBS./SQ.IN.

12'-4" OVER CAB VENTILATOR

8'-5" OVER CYLINDERS
8'-6" OVER PLATFORM.

WEIGHT IN WORKING ORDER

BOILER · BARREL DIAMETER (OUTSIDE)	4'-3" INCREASING TO 4'-8"		
FIREBOX (OUTSIDE)	5'-11" LONG x 4'-0⁷⁄₁₆" WIDE		
TUBES	12 LARGE 5¼"OD x 7 SWG		
	162 SMALL 1¾"OD x 12 SWG		
SUPERHEATER ELEMENTS	1⅛"OD. 9 S.W.G.		
LENGTH BETWEEN TUBEPLATES	10'-10½"		
HEATING SURFACES: TUBES	924 SQ. FT.		
FIREBOX	101 SQ. FT.		
TOTAL EVAPORATIVE	1025 SQ. FT.		
SUPERHEATER	124 SQ. FT.		
FREE FLUE AREA	·2·77 SQ. FT.		
GRATE AREA.	17·5 SQ. FT.		

CYLINDERS (TWO)	16½"DIA x 24" STROKE.	
TRACTIVE EFFORT	18513 LBS	
ADHESION FACTOR	4·9	
BRAKE % ENGINE & TENDER	60·23	
MINIMUM RADIUS CURVE	4 CHAINS	
WITHOUT GAUGE WIDENING		
BOILER TYPE	BR 8	
TENDER TYPE	BR 3	

WEIGHTS	FULL	EMPTY
	T C	T C
ENGINE	49·5	45-8
TENDER	36-17	19-9
TOTAL	86-2	64-17

SCALE
0 2 4 6 8 10 FEET

STANDARD CLASS 2. 2-6-0 ENGINE.

Diagram 7. Standard Cl. 2 2-6-0s: Locomotive Diagram.

236

Table 58

Standard Cl. 2 2-6-0s 78000-78064: Initial Boiler Allocation

Locomotive Number	Boiler Number Nominal Allocation	Date of Boiler Construction	Boiler Built at
78000-09	1068-1077	12.52-04.53	Darlington
78010-44	1263-1297	12.53-12.54	Darlington
78045-54	1552-1561	10.55-12.55	Darlington
78055-64	1837-1846	02.56-06.56	Darlington
Spare Boilers	1369	09.56	Crewe
	1601-2	01.58-09.58	Crewe
	1875	09.56	Darlington
	1949	12.60	Crewe

Table 59

Standard Cl. 2 2-6-0s 78000-78064 Locomotives Acquiring BR Green Livery

Loco No.	Date	Lined (L) Unlined (U)	Works
78000	4.61	U	Swindon
	10.64	(note 1)	Crewe
78001	5.62	U	Swindon
78002	??.??	(note 2)	
78003	10.63	U	Crewe
78004	4.62	U	Crewe
78005	4.60	L	Caerphilly
	7.62	L	Caerphilly
78006	3.57	L	Swindon
	2.58	L	Swindon
	7.62	L	Swindon
78007	5.60	U	Swindon
	12.62	U	Swindon
	6.64	U (note 3)	Crewe
78008	6.58	L	Swindon
	1.62	U	Swindon
78009	3.58	L	Swindon

Notes:
(1) Reported reversion to lined black livery.
(2) Application of green livery not confirmed.
(3) Tender lined green but engine unlined green.

water, weighing 36.85 tons in full working order. The tender was virtually the same as that carried by the Ivatt Cl. 2 2-6-0s modified only by the fitting of roller bearings and smaller windows; hence the layout did not conform to the Standard BR cab pattern. The conventional fall plate was retained and the cabs were hence not subject to the problem of draughtiness experienced with some types of BR tender as described in section 2.4. Provision was also made for the fitting of water pick-up apparatus and this was carried by some of the class. Allocation of tenders to individual batches of engines is given as follows; in the case of 78000-9, they were not fitted in serial number sequence.

Engine No.	Tender Number Allocation
78000-09	939-948
78010-19	1084-1093
78020-44	1094-1118
78045-54	1261-1270
78055-64	1500-1509

In common with all Standard tenders, the BR3 type was equipped with water sieves developed to filter out impurities and prevent injectors becoming blocked.

6.5 Construction Costs

Departmental representative costs per locomotive for the Standard Cl. 2 2-6-0s increased 17.4% from £14,377 for the first batch in 1951/2 to £16,871 for the final batch turned out in 1956. The 1951/2 figure was around 4.5% more than the £13,754 cost of each of the final batch of Ivatt Cl. 2 2-6-0s, 46503-27 produced at Swindon over the same period. Final cost information is not available but could well be of the order of 20% more than the representative first cost based on comparable figures for the other Standard classes built over the same period.

6.6 Liveries

On delivery, the Standard Cl. 2 2-6-0s appeared in BR mixed traffic lined black livery, details of which are given in section 2.6. The first batch, 78000-9, for the WR were apparently the

only members of the class to receive the larger 10" size numerals when new, the rest of the class being turned out with the 8" type. From early 1957, the WR began applying the lined Brunswick Green livery to their allocation as they passed through works for overhaul. Details of the green livery style are given in section 2.6 whilst dates and Works of application for the Standard Cl. 2 2-6-0s appear in Table 59. Although some of the class spent relatively long periods of several months in Swindon Works during overhaul in the late 1950s, probably due to non-availability of spare boilers, the opportunity to apply the green livery does not appear to have been taken in all cases. A curious feature of the Standard locomotives repainted at Swindon was the use of thicker 8" numerals without the usual black edging, often mixed with 9" numerals on the same engine. As an economy measure, the lining on some of the green repaints for the class was omitted from about February 1960 onwards; adoption of thinner transfer numerals, albeit still without the black edging, also dated from early 1960.

For the ScR allocation, Cowlairs produced some livery variations on 78045-54 from time to time with the usual 10" cabside numerals being replaced by the 8" type. In 1958, 78050 was observed with a red backed front numberplate; this feature may have been applied to other members of the class.

On the LMR, standard mixed traffic lined black livery was applied until early 1964 when as an economy measure several of the class were turned out in unlined black. Examples noted were: 78000/10/44 (1964), 78028/55 (1965), 78013/23 (1967).

Photographic evidence suggests that the class was delivered with the power classification mark 'CLASS 2' on

Fig. 247
78006 pilots GWR 43XX Cl. 2-6-0 5344 out of Barmouth towards Portmadoc and Pwllheli with a through holiday service on 26th July 1958. Note 5344's spartan cab facilities, (with rudimentary tarpaulin protection attached to the cab roof), compared with the enclosed cab comfort of 78006. 5344 appears to be carrying a spare set of lamps on the running plate. *(P.H. Wells)*

Fig. 248
78007 heads toward Swindon near Red Post Junction with the 2.30pm freight from Andover Junction on 28th May 1960. The engine has emerged from Swindon Works painted in unlined green and is on one of the regular M&SWJR line running-in turns. *(Courtney Haydon)*

Fig. 249
78019 pilots Standard Cl. 4 2-6-0 76052 through Coal Road between Barnard Castle and Bishop Auckland on a mineral train in the late 1950s.

(Cecil Ord Collection)

Fig. 250
78020 sets off for Raunds with the mid-day Cambridge-Kettering local on 27th December 1957. The service was down to three per day in each direction by this date. Through services ceased in June 1959 with the withdrawal of passenger facilities from the St Ives-Kettering sector of the line. *(Peter Groom)*

Fig. 251
78023 leaves Pontefract Baghill with an 11.00am York-Sheffield Midland stopping service in 1958; note the second style BR emblem on the tender. The absence of the power classification mark '2', normally to be seen above the cabside numerals, suggests this ER-based engine's last Works visit was to either Doncaster or Darlington. *(Peter Cookson)*

Fig. 252
78025 pilots LNER J39 0-6-0 64860 on an up goods train at Ripon; 78025 was probably on its delivery journey from Darlington Works to Sheffield Grimesthorpe depot in June 1954. *(G.W. Sharpe & Co.)*

the buffer beam rather than the figure '2' on the cabside. This was normal practice for Darlington which also applied the scheme to engines passing through for overhaul; on the newly delivered group for the WR, 78000-9, the buffer beam legend was reported to have been painted out. From LMR and WR Works, the engines usually emerged with the figure '2' above the cabside numerals whilst Cowlairs, which maintained the ScR allocation, applied their cabside trademark '2MT.' as well as the engine's depot on the buffer beam during Works visits.

The tender lining panel applied by LMR Works was smaller in area compared with the original Darlington finish, whereas Cowlairs routinely turned the class out with the largest area tender panels, applying the lining very close to the top and bottom edges and virtually flush with the rear handrail; the WR Works' tender livery was similar to the original Darlington style.

6.7 Allocation and Duties

6.7.1 Delivery Period 1952-1956

The first batch of Standard Cl. 2 2-6-0s, 78000-9, was delivered from Darlington over a five month period from December 1952. All were allocated to the WR's Oswestry depot for work on the former Cambrian Railway's lines in mid-Wales. 78004/8/9 had been in store at Swindon works for a short time before allocation. During the same period, Oswestry was taking delivery from Swindon Works of twenty-two LMS designed Ivatt Cl. 2 2-6-0s, 46503-24 of which the Standard version was a virtual copy. The new 2-6-0s displaced GWR Dean Goods and former Cambrian Railways 0-6-0s from both passenger and freight work.

Initially the new engines were noted on Ellesmere and Whitchurch local passenger workings and the Llanfyllin branch goods. On 18th February 1953 78001 appeared on the 8.00am Oswestry-Aberystwyth, spending the next few days on trials over the Aberystwyth-Carmarthen line. Within a few weeks, the Ivatt 2-6-0s were earmarked mainly for duties on the line from Moat Lane through Builth Wells and Three Cocks Junction to Brecon; 46516-8/21-4 were transferred to Brecon whilst 46503-15/9/20 operated from Moat Lane and Llanidloes, both sub-depots of Oswestry. During April and May 1953, in exchange for GWR Cl. 2251 0-6-0s, 78000-5 transferred to Machynlleth for work between Shrewsbury, Oswestry and the Cambrian Coast resorts of Aberystwyth, Barmouth, Pwllheli and Portmadoc; 78006/7 followed in September. Meanwhile 78008/9, apparently surplus to requirements, were moved to Worcester in July. The new 2-6-0s were well received by the Cambrian line crews on account of the much increased protection from the Welsh mountain weather afforded by the modern cab design compared with that of the ageing Cambrian Railways 0-6-0s they replaced; for reasons never fully explained, the Swindon-built Ivatts were more popular with crews than the Darlington-built Standards.

In addition to the passenger and freight workings on the coast line, the Standard Cl. 2 2-6-0s regularly worked through to Shrewsbury. One diagram, previously the province of a GWR Dukedog Cl. 90XX 4-4-0 or 2251 Cl. 0-6-0, involved the mid-day stopping train from Aberystwyth to Shrewsbury as far as Welshpool. The engine then took the 4.15pm Welshpool-Llanymynech school train, returning light to Welshpool to pick up the 6.30pm goods to Shrewsbury. After performing several shunting tasks there, return to Aberystwyth was on a goods train arriving about 1.00am next day. The Machynlleth engines were also employed on banking duties on one of the most formidable climbs on the WR, the fourteen mile ascent from Machynlleth to Talerddig summit which steepens to 1 in 52 for the last three and a half miles from Llanbrynmair.

The engines were regularly noted between the coast and Dovey Junction on the Aberystwyth and Pwllheli portions of the 'Cambrian Coast Express' to and from Paddington. In the 1954 summer timetable, they were diagrammed to take this train through to Shrewsbury. The service often loaded to more than seven coaches from Dovey Junction and despite banking assistance up to Talerddig, timekeeping suffered. By the start of the winter schedule GWR Manor Cl. 4-6-0s and 43XX Cl. 2-6-0s had been brought in as substitutes; the Standard Cl. 2 2-6-0s continued to work the Aberystwyth-Shrewsbury stoppers and the Llanfyllin branch.

From July 1953, Worcester played host to 78008/9 until the early 1960s. They were joined during 1954 by 78001 (May) and 78004 (October), the latter having spent a few months at Swindon where it had appeared on freight workings on the former Midland and South West Junction (M&SWJ) line to Andoversford and Savernake. The Worcester engines were noted on Gloucester-Swindon goods turns and later displaced the GWR Dean Goods Cl. 0-6-0s from their stronghold at Kingham sub-shed on the line to Oxford. Here the engines were used on the Chipping Norton branch passenger and freight duties, the two daily goods services from Moreton-in-Marsh to Shipston on Stour and a Sunday morning pick-up goods working to Charlbury eight miles further toward Oxford. The other sub-shed to which they were allocated was Evesham. From here they worked the all-stations passenger service between Worcester, Honeybourne Junction, Stratford on Avon and Leamington Spa. The engines generally remained at each sub-shed for a three or four week stint, change-over usually occurring on Monday mornings. Other duties involved visits to Kidderminster, Wooferton, Tenbury Wells and Malvern Wells when substituting for the occasional failure of a GWR diesel railcar of which Worcester had six (W5-7/10/9/32W) and Leamington had two (W17/26W) in May 1955.

The second batch, consisting of thirty five engines 78010-44 delivered over twelve months from December 1953, was destined for the NER and the LMR; initial allocation was as shown:

NER	West Auckland	(9) 78010-8
	Kirkby Stephen	(1) 78019
LMR	Kettering	(2) 78020/1
	Millhouses	(3) 78022-4
	Grimesthorpe	(1) 78025
	Canklow	(2) 78026/7
	Leicester Midland	(2) 78028/9
	Preston	(3) 78030/6/7
	Tebay	(1) 78031
	Rhyl	(5) 78032-5/9
	Bescot	(1) 78038
	Bank Hall	(5) 78040-4

Fig. 253
78028 of Leicester Midland depot whisks an inspection saloon through an unidentified location on 24th April 1957. The class was often used on this type of work, 78030 for example being the regular engine for such duties at Crewe from April 1956 until its withdrawal in October 1965.
(P.H. Wells)

The NER allocation 78010-9 joined a batch of thirteen Darlington-built LMS Ivatt Cl. 2 2-6-0s, 46470-82, which had been delivered to West Auckland, Kirkby Stephen and Darlington depots between July and October 1951. West Auckland used the new Standard Cl. 2-6-0s on NER Cl. A8 4-6-2 tank engine passenger turns to Saltburn as well as the usual Tebay mineral workings over Stainmore summit. 78016-8 moved to Kirkby Stephen within a few weeks and together with 78019 were used on the mineral traffic and on passenger services from Penrith to Darlington and Richmond. Several of the class were reported to have been fitted with the cable-worked front slip-coupling device similar to that fitted to the Standard Cl. 3 2-6-0s (77XXX) for banking work over Stainmore. In March 1954, 78018 featured in a British Transport Film Unit production which depicted its rescue from a snow drift in blizzard prone Bleathgill cutting. The class was also popular for excursion work, 78015 being noted at Relly Mill on a Durham Miners' Gala special in the following July and 78014 on a Bishop Auckland-Redcar excursion on August Bank Holiday.

In March 1955, 78010-4 transferred to the small depot at Northallerton replacing J21 and J25 Cl. 0-6-0s and G5 Cl. 0-4-4 tank engines The new engines were used on pick-up freight workings to Newport, Cowton and Melmerby; one of the class also covered the Northallerton Low Yard pilot turn, formerly the domain of J73 0-6-0 tank engine 68359 which returned to West Hartlepool. The 10.00 (SX) and 8.00 (SO) Low Yard-Thirsk Town pick-up freight was also a regular turn until taken over by the York pick-up goods duty on 7th May 1962. Following the withdrawal of the Wensleydale branch passenger service between Northallerton and Hawes in April 1954, two new parcels services, the 7.35am and 4.00pm Northallerton-Leyburn and return had been introduced; these were now diagrammed for a Standard Cl. 2 2-6-0. It was whilst involved in working the 4.00pm parcels on 15th November 1956 that 78013 was derailed at the south end of platform 5 at Northallerton. On the morning working, the engine was booked to shunt Leyburn goods yard, the Express Dairy, Horse and Cattle docks and Ord and Maddison's Quarry which had been the duties of resident Y3 Sentinel locomotive 68159 until Leyburn sub depot closed in April 1954. The class was also used on the branch for the numerous troop specials to Leyburn (for Bellerby Camp) as well as the pick-up freights and the occasional horse box special from Leyburn. Other special duties included permanent way maintenance specials and the delivery of oil and coke to Wiske Moor pump house on Sunday mornings. This installation pumped water from the local river to serve the water troughs on the East Coast main line just south of Danby Wiske.

Kettering had received 78020/1 by May 1954 from where they were used alongside six Ivatt Cl. 2 2-6-0s 46402-4/44/95/6 already operating from the depot on the Cambridge line passenger and freight services. During Cambridge stopovers, the engines occasionally worked to Hitchin on an evening goods train returning on the 9.35pm Hitchin-Cambridge local passenger service. They were also employed on the only Kettering duty to Nottingham at that time, a stopping train arriving at 8.45pm; the return working was the 6.00am service next day to Leicester, often double-heading with a Nottingham LMS Cl. 4 2-6-4 tank engine. At the start of the winter 1955 timetable, the engines featured on a new roster which included the 4.32pm Leicester Midland-Birmingham New Street and the 9.30pm return. The workings were part of a two-day round trip from Kettering which also included visits to Cambridge and Bletchley.

Millhouses, the main LMR depot for passenger engines in the Sheffield area, received 78022-4 in May 1954. The trio worked alongside LMS Cl. 2P and Compound 4-4-0s on passenger services to Leeds City, Nottingham Midland via the Erewash Valley main line and to Manchester Central via the Hope Valley line. Freight duties included trip workings serving the many steelworks and metal foundries in the area; 78022-4 displaced ex-MR Cl. 2F and 3F 0-6-0s from some of these turns. Station pilot work at Sheffield Midland included trips to the main carriage sidings at Nunnery and Heeley plus the occasional visit to the overflow sidings at Dore and Unstone. The engines also shunted the Queens Road and Wicker goods yards as well as the former LNWR goods depot at Wharf Street. In April 1956, 78023 was regularly observed on Sheffield Midland-Barnsley Court House passenger duties.

Fig. 254
78033 is engaged on empty stock workings at Euston in 1965. Willesden MPD was responsible for these duties and some fifteen members of the class were operating from the depot on this and other tasks at various times in 1965.

(Peter Hay)

Fig. 255
78038 is pictured off its beaten track at Beckenham Junction with the LCGB 'Surrey Wanderer' rail tour on 5th July 1964. The adjacent yard to the left is now the site of a Waitrose supermarket.

(Rodney Lissenden)

Fig. 256
78039 of Willesden depot returns empty stock from Euston to Wembley carriage sidings on 1st August 1963. The cylinder positioned on the running plate confirms the engine was fitted with AWS equipment as were the other class members based at Willesden at that time. *(Peter Groom)*

Fig. 257   78045 is ready to leave Banff with the 4.25pm to Tillynaught on 3rd July 1963. This was the only passenger service on the former GNSR to remain regularly steam-hauled by this date; the passenger service was withdrawn in July 1964.

(Courtney Haydon)

Fig. 258   Steam in the Scottish Highlands was becoming something of a rarity by the early 1960s but on 22nd August 1961, Aberdeen Ferryhill shed turned out grimy 78045, lately of Keith shed, to work an Engineers' special from Boat of Garten to Craigellachie. The train is seen heading eastwards through Cromdale. The men appear to have opted for the hopper wagons rather than the coach provided for the journey.

(Courtney Haydon)

Grimesthorpe was host to 78025 for five months from June 1954. Here the engine was used on local freight and pick-up work until transfer to Millhouses in November. The Canklow engines 78026/7, also delivered in June 1954 were similarly employed, remaining at the depot until 1962.

Leicester Midland took delivery of 78028/9 in July 1954. The engines worked on most of the local passenger services including the branch to Burton-on-Trent via Coalville, Ashby-de-la-Zouch and Moira. Regular rosters included excursions to East Anglia and through workings on summer Saturday holiday trains to Clacton-on-Sea. Both engines were noted on an excursion duty on 8th September 1956 when they double-headed a train through Kettering as far as Huntingdon East where the pilot was detached for servicing whilst its companion carried on with the train to Cambridge; the pilot rejoined at Huntingdon for the return journey.

78030 arrived at Preston in September 1954 to be followed in November by 78036/7. The latter two displaced Ivatt Cl. 2 2-6-0s 46429/30 to Stoke-on-Trent. The engines were employed on station pilot duties, Longridge branch pick-up freights and local passenger work including services to Accrington from which they displaced LMS Cl. 2P 4-4-0s; 78030 transferred to Crewe North in April 1956.

78031 was first allocated to Tebay in September 1954 reportedly for trials on banking duties to Shap summit This initiative was probably unsuccessful as one month later, 78031 joined Ivatt Cl. 2 2-6-0 46441 at Lancaster Green Ayre. From here 78031 was used on parcels trains to Leeds City and transfer freights between the former MR and LNWR yards. Although the Glasson Dock branch was closed to passengers in July 1930, 78031 was noted on the remaining freight services on the line; transfer to Chester Northgate was made in October 1956.

Rhyl depot had received several Ivatt Cl. 2 2-6-0s temporarily transferred each summer from 1952-4 for the holiday season workings. In September 1954, the first allocation of the Standard variety was made in the form of 78032/3 to be supplemented with 78034/5/9 by the end of November. The engines found work on the stopping passenger services from Rhyl to Chester General, Bangor and Denbigh displacing LMS Cl. 2P 4-4-0s and Ivatt Cl. 2 2-6-2 tank engines. During the following summer, the class was used on the North Wales Land Cruise circular service to Portmadoc outward via Corwen returning along the coast line through Bangor. This popular service ran on several weekdays during the holiday season; on Sundays, the Land Cruise stock was used for the afternoon Rhyl-Menai Bridge and Llanfair PG buffet car specials. In May 1956, the Rhyl engines were transferred to Widnes in exchange for Ivatt Cl. 2 2-6-0s 46423/6/32/3/45 from other LMR Western Division depots.

Bescot depot took delivery of 78038 in November 1954 where it joined Ivatt Cl. 2 2-6-0s 46425/6/90. The engine was mainly employed on local freight and trip workings in the 'Black Country' area. Occasional passenger work included appearances on services from Birmingham New Street to Rugeley and Coventry. 78038 left Bescot for Chester Northgate in October 1956 in exchange for Ivatt mogul 46459 from Chester Midland.

The final engines in the second batch, 78040-4 were allocated to Bank Hall from where they displaced Ivatt Moguls 46406/13/4/6/7/35/83 to other former L&YR depots at Bury and Wakefield. The new engines were prominent on local passenger workings from Liverpool Exchange to Preston and to Rochdale via Wigan Wallgate, Bolton Trinity Street and Bury Knowsley Street. Speeds of 60mph and above were common down the three mile gradient at 1 in 131/167 from Aughton Park to Maghull on the Preston line but frequently resulted in a rather uncomfortable 'fore and aft' motion for the luckless front coach passengers.

The third batch, consisting of ten engines 78045-54, was delivered to the Scottish Region from October to December 1955; allocation was as follows:

Kittybrewster	(1)	78045
Hawick	(2)	78046/7
St Margarets	(2)	78048/9
Motherwell	(5)	78050-4

Kittybrewster, already operating Ivatt Moguls 46460/4, received 78045 in October 1955. The engine was sub-shedded at Fraserburgh where it displaced the last of the former GER F4 2-4-2 tank engines 67157 from its duties on the five mile St Combs branch. The service consisted of eight trains per day in each direction (nine on Saturdays) with a journey time of twenty minutes; the F4 saw out its days as the pilot at Kittybrewster carriage sidings.

78046/7 arrived at Hawick, on the Waverley route from Carlisle to Edinburgh, in October 1955. The engines were used on Riccarton Junction pilot work and banking duties to Whitrope summit. Much of the eleven mile southbound climb was at 1 in 75/80; the ten mile northbound gradient from Newcastleton was even steeper, virtually all at 1 in 70; LNER Cl. J36 0-6-0s were displaced from the banking duties. In summer 1956, the Lauder branch from Fountainhall Junction north of Hawick was upgraded to allow axle-loads of 14 tons enabling Standard and Ivatt Cl. 2 2-6-0s to be used. Although the passenger service had been withdrawn in September 1932, the line still saw regular pick-up freights. The previous rostered power for the branch had been the former GER Cl. J67 0-6-0 tank engine 68492 which was withdrawn. The tank engine had run coupled to an ex-HBR tender to provide the water supply, the locomotive tanks having been run 'dry' to conform with the axle loading requirement for the branch. The Standard Cl. 2 2-6-0s also appeared from time to time on the Border Counties line, 78047 being noted in charge of the 4.32pm passenger service from Hawick to Newcastle on 23rd June 1956.

By the end of November 1955, 78048/9 were at St Margarets where Ivatt Moguls 46461/2 had been at work since June 1950. The new engines were used on the Gifford branch freight services, regular passenger trains having been withdrawn from the line in April 1933. Other turns included St Margarets' workshops pilot duties and appearances at Edinburgh Waverley on the suburban circular service, known as 'The Sub', via Portobello, Morningside Road and Haymarket Central Junction. 78048/9 were also regular power for inspection saloon work, one being noted, for example, on the Bo'ness branch in December 1955 and again at Innerwick on the East Coast main line to Newcastle, the following March.

Motherwell depot received 78050-4 in November and December 1955, using them on local freights and coal workings to industrial complexes such as the Ravenscraig steel works. A year later 78052 was first transferred to Inverness and then to Helmsdale, on the line to Wick and Thurso. From Helmsdale the engine was used on both passenger and pick-up freight work on the Dornoch branch. At the same time 78053/4 were on the move to Aberdeen Ferryhill but were soon transferred to Keith. From here they were employed on the Craigellachie-Boat of Garten passenger service displacing former GNSR D40 Cl. 4-4-0s, the last four 62264/5/71/7 all being at Keith at that time. As the new engines were too long to be turned at Craigellachie, they returned tender-first from Boat of Garten. The class was well liked by the crews and kept in spotless condition. Other work included turns on the Lossiemouth branch and the Elgin-Buckie line.

The fourth and final batch of Standard Cl. 2 2-6-0s consisting of ten engines 78055-64 was delivered to the LMR from August to November 1956; allocation was to two depots only, the former CLC depot at Chester Northgate and the ex-L&YR shed at Wigan Central:

Chester Northgate	(5)	78055-9
Wigan Central	(5)	78060-4

78055-9 arrived at Northgate in August and September 1956; one month later they were joined by 78031/8 from Lancaster and Bescot. The new arrivals were put to work on the passenger service to Manchester Central, displacing former GCR Cl. C13 4-4-2 tank engines from these duties. The ex-GCR Director Cl. D11 4-4-0s diagrams to Manchester were not affected, Northwich depot's 62661/2/4/5/9 remaining active on their usual turns. The new engines also found employment on freight duties displacing GCR Cl. J10 0-6-0s which were put into store at Trafford Park.

By the end of November 1956, the Wigan Central

engines 78060-4 were working alongside LMS Cl. 4 2-6-4 tank engines on local passenger services including those to Manchester Victoria; local and trip freight duties for the new engines involved replacing the last of the former LYR Cl. 3F 0-6-0s at the depot.

6.7.2 From 1957 to Withdrawal

Western Region

In April 1957, the ten Standard Cl. 2 2-6-0s allocated to the Western Region, 78000-9, were at two depots, Machynlleth and Worcester:

Machynlleth	(6)	78000/2/3/5-7
Worcester	(4)	78001/4/8/9

The Machynlleth sextet continued to appear on the Cambrian Coast lines to Aberystwyth and Pwllheli. By the summer of 1957, following bridge strengthening, the coastal section from Dovey Junction to Barmouth Junction and Portmadoc was cleared for larger engines. GWR Manor 4-6-0s, 43XX Cl. 2-6-0s and Standard Cl. 4 4-6-0s (75XXX) were permitted on the heavier trains which now regularly loaded to eleven or twelve coaches on summer Saturdays. The Standard Cl. 2 2-6-0s worked the route on lighter traffic sometimes double-heading with either the remaining Dukedog 90XX Cl. 4-4-0s, almost all of which were then either at Machynlleth or Oswestry, 55XX Cl. 2-6-2 tank engines or 2251 Cl. 0-6-0s. Two Standard Cl. 2 Moguls were regularly sub-shedded at Pwllheli with another at Penmaenpool for working Dolgellau-Barmouth trains and shunting Dolgellau yard; the sub-shed allocations were changed every few days.

By summer 1963, now under the control of the LMR, the Cambrian lines had received a number of the higher powered Standard Cl. 4 4-6-0s (75XXX). This move resulted in the dispersal of 78000/2/3/7 to LMR depots at Nottingham,

Fig. 259
78052 heads an up coal train through Bathgate Upper on 26th March 1964. As a result of a recent overhaul, probably at Cowlairs judging by the large numerals and '2MT.' power classification mark on the cabside, 78052 is looking unusually smart for the period.

(Courtney Haydon)

Fig. 260
The date is 10th April 1961 and 78000 is running-in ex-Swindon Works at Andover Junction on the M&SWJR line. The engine is in unlined green livery but was later reported as having reverted to lined black livery after an overhaul at Crewe in October 1964.

(G. Wheeler)

Fig. 261
78003 pauses between duties in the company of several other class members and Stanier Cl.8F 2-8-0 48518 at Willesden MPD on 22nd August 1965; souvenir hunters may have been responsible for the absence of 78003's front numberplate. The engine was reported as having received unlined green livery from Crewe Works in October 1963 but in this view it is clear that the tender is lined.

(Rodney Lissenden)

Fig. 262
78003 stands in Swindon MPD yard in lined black livery, but without the power classification mark on either the cabside or the front buffer beam, after delivery from Darlington Works in early 1953. *(G.W. Sharp & Co.)*

Fig. 263   78004, immaculate in lined green livery, basks in the spring sunshine at Hay on the Hereford-Brecon line on 24th April 1962. In the late 1950s/early 1960s period, the engine was something of a fixture on this route, its regular role being the 9.35am Moorfields-Three Cocks Junction freight and 11.35am return.
(Ken Cooper)

Wigan Central, Bangor and Crewe North; 78005/6 had already moved in late 1962 displacing Ivatt Moguls 46526/7 at the former MR depot at Gloucester Barnwood which had been under the control of the WR since early 1958.

The spring 1957 Worcester allocation, 78001/4/8/9 continued to work on the Evesham local freights, the Shipston-on-Stour branch goods and Kingham-Chipping Norton passenger services. In June 1957, 78004 transferred to Hereford. It was used on freight workings over the former MR line to Brecon. For several years, the engine's regular job was the 9.35am Moorfields-Three Cocks Junction pick-up goods returning on the 11.35am service. 78004 was noted on other duties including Hereford-Gloucester Central local passenger trains and pick-up freights to Ross-on-Wye and Gloucester. 78004 then had a spell at Llanelly from January 1964 where it was employed on local freight work until transfer to Gloucester Horton Road six months later. The Kingham-Chipping Norton passenger service was finally withdrawn in December 1962, Worcester's 78001 being in charge of the last trains. 78009 was involved in an unusual working on 23rd January 1963 when it was noted at Derby coupled inside a Type 4 Cl. 46 diesel on the 7.55am Swansea-Newcastle passenger service. Apparently the diesel's train heating boiler had failed in the severe weather and 78009 provided warmth as far as York; it departed light engine for the south two days later. During the next twelve months, Worcester lost its allocation of Standard Cl. 2 2-6-0s to Wolverhampton Stafford Road, by then under the control of the LMR and to Gloucester Barnwood. 78008 went to Stafford Road in March 1962 where it was noted on the daily parcels service to Stourbridge Junction and on transfer freights from Stourbridge to the Dudley and Wednesbury areas. 78008 moved to Oxley when Stafford Road closed in September 1963 but continued on similar duties until withdrawal in October 1966. 78009 was transferred to Barnwood in March 1963 and 78001 followed in January 1964.

In March 1963, 78005/6/9 at Gloucester Barnwood were noted on the Gloucester-Bristol stopping passenger service and local freights on the Ledbury branch. Motive power depot rationalisation led to the closure of Barnwood in May 1964 but the Standard Cl. 2 Mogul allocation, by now consisting of 78001/5/6, had moved to the former GWR depot at Gloucester Horton Road the previous month. From here, the engines were used on goods work on the Nailsworth branch, the passenger service on this line having been withdrawn in June 1949; the branch closed completely in February 1966. The class was also employed on the Sharpness docks branch freights and pick-up goods trains to Ross-on-Wye, Lydbrook Junction and the Dursley branch including the Stroud Goods spur. In July 1964, 78001 was observed at Andoversford on a permanent way special removing track lifted from the former M&SWJ line closed in September 1961. Other turns included station pilot duties at Gloucester and occasional passenger work on the line to Hereford. Displaced by diesels, the two remaining Horton Road engines 78001/6 were condemned at the end of 1965; these withdrawals marked the end of the class allocation to the WR.

North Eastern Region

In May 1957, the NER allocation of ten engines 78010-9 was as follows:

Northallerton	(6)	78010-5
Kirkby Stephen	(4)	78016-9

The Northallerton engines continued to appear on local passenger and freight work. In the severe weather of 26th February 1958, although the passenger service on the Wensleydale branch to Hawes had been withdrawn in April 1954, passenger accommodation was included in the two daily parcels trains, all roads to the town having been blocked by snow. 78010 was on the 7.20am all stations, returning mid-morning and also took the 3.50pm returning at 8.03pm. 78013 moved to Kirkby Stephen in January 1958, its place being taken at Northallerton by 78016 with this locomotive being exchanged in March 1958 for West Auckland's Ivatt Mogul 46471, the only LMS design locomotive to be allocated to Northallerton. In February 1959, 78015 failed at Thirsk with a cracked firebox and was put in store, first at Northallerton and later at Darlington depot's dead-line. The engine was not noted in revenue service again and was the first of the class to be withdrawn in November 1963. When any of Northallerton's Standard Cl. 2 2-6-0s were in Works for overhaul, an Ivatt Cl. 2 2-6-0, usually from the Darlington allocated 46473-7/9 group, would be sent as replacement. After the closure of Starbeck depot at Harrogate in September 1959, Northallerton gained an extra duty, the 11.00pm Northallerton Low Yard to Newport sidings, (later Tees Yard) and return working which were diagrammed for the Standard Cl. 2 2-6-0s. Until early 1960, the class was still employed on the Leyburn parcels duty which also included trips to the limestone quarries at Wensley and Redmire. Increased output from the quarries eventually led to the replacement of the class on these duties by the more powerful LNER Cl. K1 2-6-0s of which 62003/59 were allocated to Northallerton in March 1960. The depot closed on 3rd March 1963 resulting in the transfer of 78011/2/4/5 to Darlington; their duties were taken over by Thornaby-based Type 2 diesels complete with brake tenders. It is interesting to note that 78010 was the last locomotive 'dumped' at Northallerton and on closure of the depot was towed to Darlington depot by that shed's only LMS Fowler 2-6-4 tank engine, 42405, the first and last visit of the type to Northallerton depot. 78010, not in good condition, had brief spells at Polmadie and Motherwell before it too returned to the NER at Darlington, unmourned by the ScR. Darlington depot had also received two other members of the class, 78024/5, from the ER storage yard at March in December 1962. With dieselisation of many services well underway, there was little suitable work at Darlington and by the end of 1963, its allocation had either been withdrawn or dispersed to West Auckland, Farnley Junction and Tweedmouth.

The Kirkby Stephen engines 78013/6-9 continued operating on Stainmore line duties. In November 1958, 78019 was noted in place of the usual Ivatt Mogul shunting the former LNWR goods yard at Carlisle Crown Street and working trip freights to the Upperby St Nicholas Yard from where southbound freights were formed and despatched. Kirkby Stephen depot was transferred to the LMR in early 1958, 78016 being retained on the NER by moving to

Northallerton and then on to West Auckland. The latter depot was also called on to provide emergency passenger services during adverse winter weather. On 9th January 1959, for example, 78016 was noted double-heading one such service with Standard Cl. 3 2-6-0 77003, offering an alternative to snow blocked roads on the Crook-Tow Law line from which regular passenger trains had been withdrawn in June 1956. The pair was also engaged on snow clearing duties on other branches in the Bishop Auckland area. By May 1960 with the continuing run-down of freight services in preparation for the closure of the Stainmore route, the remaining members of the class at Kirkby Stephen, 78013/7-9 were transferred to other LMR depots at Kirkby-in-Ashfield, Springs Branch and Chester Midland.

The other depots on the NER from which Standard Cl. 2 2-6-0s operated were Tweedmouth, Farnley Junction and Manningham. Tweedmouth had received 78012/24/5 from Darlington by November 1963, displacing Ivatt Moguls 46474/5/9 to Dumfries and Stranraer on the Scottish Region. The engines were noted on the daily freight to Coldstream, Wooler and Alnwick. They were reallocated to the LMR at the former GCR's Manchester depot at Gorton in December 1964 and replaced by Standard Cl. 3 2-6-0s 77002/4 at Tweedmouth.

78010/1/4 arrived at Farnley Junction from Darlington in November 1963, remaining there until the following April when 78010 moved to Crewe South and 78011/4 to Manningham. At Farnley Junction, together with Standard Cl. 3 2-6-0 77001/12, the engines displaced the LMS 'Jinty' Cl. 3F 0-6-0 tank engines from their shunting duties at the former LNWR goods depot at Leeds Wellington Street, moving to Bradford when Cl. 08 diesel shunters took over. Based at Manningham 78011/4 carried out station pilot work at Bradford Forster Square and were observed on local and trip freights until displaced by Standard Cl. 3 2-6-0s 77001/12 to Gorton in December 1964. The transfer of the Tweedmouth and Manningham engines to the LMR brought to an end the class allocation to the NER.

Scottish Region

In April 1957, the ten engines in Scotland 78045-54 were allocated as shown:

Kittybrewster	(1)	78045
Hawick	(2)	78046/7
St Margarets	(2)	78048/9
Motherwell	(2)	78050/1
Helmsdale	(1)	78052
Keith	(2)	78053/4

Kittybrewster's 78045 was still in use on St Combs branch line work but also appeared on the Maud Junction-Peterhead line from time to time. In June 1960 the engine was transferred to Keith.

From February 1958, diesel multiple units were introduced on the majority of the Edinburgh suburban services, displacing 78048/9 at St Margarets from any remaining passenger work in the city area. One of the class was sub-shedded at St Boswells for working the branch to Berwick-upon-Tweed. The service required a reversal at Tweedmouth accomplished by the engine running round the usual one coach load. When St Boswells sub-shed closed in

Fig. 264
78006 stands in the yard at Swindon on 2nd February 1958 following overhaul at the Works. The engine is in fully lined green livery with the early 'cycling lion' BR tender crest, but without the cabside power classification mark normally applied by Swindon.
(G. Wheeler)

Fig. 265
78008, in unlined green livery, reposes at Wolverhampton Stafford Road shed next to stored King Cl. 4-6-0, 6022, King Edward III, on 29th September 1962. On closure of Stafford Road one year later, 78008 moved to nearby Oxley and was withdrawn in October 1966. (Peter Groom)

Fig. 266
78009 is in Swindon works on 7th June 1953. The engine has been assigned to Oswestry depot after spending a short time in the Works store following delivery from Darlington in April. Castle Cl. 4-6-0 5072, Hurricane, on the adjacent track awaits entry to the Works. (J.B. Arnold)

Fig. 267
78014 rests on Northallerton Low Yard in March 1959. The engine spent the last few months of its life in the Manchester area based at Gorton and Trafford Park depots working trip freights and p.w. trains before withdrawal in September 1965.

(David Tyreman Collection)

Fig. 268
78017 is pictured at Kirkby Stephen on 26th April 1954, a month after delivery new to West Auckland MPD from Darlington Works. Alongside is the virtually identical Ivatt Cl. 2 2-6-0 46474, built in August 1951, also a product of Darlington. Note the upper side sheets on 78017's cab slope inwards compared with those on 46474, one of the few differences between the classes.   *(H.C. Casserley)*

Fig. 269
78018 is depicted stuck in a snowdrift in the blizzard-prone Bleathgill Cutting on the Stainmore line near Kirkby Stephen in February 1954. On withdrawal in November 1966, 78018 was sold to Woodham Bros. and consigned to their famous scrapyard at Barry in south Wales. 78018 was rescued from Barry in November 1978 and after a spell in storage on the 'Battlefield Line' near Market Bosworth in Leicestershire is now undergoing restoration by the Darlington Railway Preservation Society.

(David Tyreman Collection)

Fig. 270   78019's tender takes on rather too much water at Willesden shed on 22nd August 1965. The box situated on the running plate next to the cab confirms the engine is equipped with AWS apparatus. Alongside, nemesis looms in the shape of English Electric Cl. 20 Bo-Bo diesel locomotive D8001. Fate had other ideas however as both locomotives are now preserved, D8001 at the Midland Railway Centre at Butterley near Ripley in Derbyshire and 78019 on the GCR at Loughborough in Leicestershire.

(Rodney Lissenden)

June 1959, Hawick was made responsible for the duty and 78049 was transferred there; 78048 followed from St Margarets a year later.

The April 1957 Hawick allocation 78046/7 continued their Riccarton Junction pilot and Whitrope banking work, occasionally straying on to other duties such as when 78047 was noted on a new Sunday passenger service from Corstorphine to North Berwick in July 1957. The Lauder branch freight service was withdrawn in October 1958, the last train being a Branch Line Society special with two coaches from Edinburgh in charge of St Margarets' 78049 on 15th November.

By July 1960, Hawick now had four of the class on its books, 78046-9. Their regular workings included the St Boswells-Berwick branch until services were withdrawn in June 1964 and local passenger trains to Carlisle and Galashiels on the Waverley route. By the end of 1961, Type 2 Cl. 27 and both Cl. 40 and Cl. 45 Type 4 diesels had taken on the majority of the Edinburgh-Carlisle through trains. One of Hawick's roles was to provide substitutes for failures and the Standard Cl. 2 2-6-0s were regularly called on for this type of duty acquitting themselves well. On 9th December 1961 for example, a Type 2 Cl. 27 failed at Hawick on the 12 noon Waverley-Carlisle passenger service; station pilot 78047 took over and despite its own problems raising sufficient steam reached Carlisle without assistance. By September 1966, with local passenger and freight services discontinued or given over to diesels, Hawick's allocation of Standard Cl. 2 2-6-0s had either been withdrawn or transferred to Bathgate and St Margarets.

In spring 1957, the engines remaining at Motherwell, 78050/1, continued to work on local and trip freights until transfer to Dawsholm in October 1963. Here they took over the freight duties of former North British Railway Cl. J36 0-6-0s 65285/325 which went for scrapping one month later. The following July, three months before the depot closed, 78050/1 moved to Bathgate and Dumfries respectively.

For two months from February 1957 Helmsdale's 78052 was in use on the Dornoch branch as a 'stop-gap' following the withdrawal of the previous power for the branch, the last former Highland Railway locomotive, Cl. 1P 0-4-4 tank engine 55053. In April a rather unusual permanent replacement for 55053 arrived in the shape of GWR 0-6-0 pannier tank engine 1646 from Croes Newydd (WR). This engine became the main passenger power for the branch whilst 78052 was retained as a spare and for freight duties. Later, in July 1958, a second pannier tank engine appeared, 1649, from St Philip's Marsh (WR). 78052 was now effectively redundant and after a few weeks at St Margarets from September 1958, moved to Aviemore in November. Here the engine shared station pilot duties with a former Caledonian Railway Cl. 3F 0-6-0 displacing another Caledonian engine, Cl. 2P 0-4-4 tank engine 55173 into store, the latter having been almost a fixture on this duty for over a year. 78052 officially transferred to Perth in July 1962 but was noted working from Oban in June on the Ballachulish branch just before services were taken over by Type 2 Cl. 27 diesels; 78052 operated the freight turns alongside Ivatt Moguls 46460/8 which had the passenger duties. At Perth the engine was used on pilot work but spent some time in store before transfer to Bathgate in November 1963.

The 1957 Keith allocation, 78053/4 was still performing on the Craigellachie-Boat of Garten service. In October,

251

78053 had a five week stint working from Fraserburgh on the St Combs branch deputising for the regular branch engine 46460 away at Crewe for overhaul. The engine was fitted with a cowcatcher, officially required for work on this line.

In February 1958, it was announced that the Boat of Garten-Craigellachie passenger service was to be handed over to diesel railbus operation. The first example began work in the following November with an ambitious daily roster of 300 miles linking Aviemore, Boat of Garten, Craigellachie and Elgin. 78053/4, joined by 78045 in June 1960 were then regularly observed on the Banff-Tillynaught branch. Most trains were of 'mixed' configuration carrying both passenger and freight vehicles and were hence not suitable for diesel multiple unit operation. By the summer of 1961, the branch had the only passenger service on the former GNSR to remain regularly steam-hauled. 78045 continued to appear frequently on the branch until passenger services were withdrawn in July 1964, although it had been nominally transferred along with 78053/4 to Ferryhill in June 1961.

In January 1963, the Scottish allocation of the class was now eleven engines and included 78026 acquired from the ER one year earlier; allocation was:

Dumfries	(1)	78026
Aberdeen Ferryhill	(2)	78045/54
Hawick	(4)	78046-9
Motherwell	(2)	78050/1
Perth	(1)	78052
Stirling	(1)	78053

78026 had spent a year at Ayr mainly on local goods trips to Kilmarnock and Irvine as well as the Catrine branch freights before moving to Dumfries. The engine was joined at the latter depot by 78016 from the NER via Motherwell in October 1963. Together with Ivatt Mogul 46474, the engines took over the duties of the remaining former Caledonian Railway Cl. 2F 0-6-0s 57296/302 and Cl. 3F 0-6-0s 57600/88 which were withdrawn. On 7th December 1963 for example, 78016 was working the ex-GSWR goods yard, with 78026 shunting the ex-CR yard at St. Mary's whilst 46474 acted as station pilot. Other work included the local pick-up goods services to Maxwelltown, Gretna Green and Carlisle as well as the Whithorn branch freights from Newton Stewart; the latter duty included a weekly trip down the increasingly weed-overgrown spur from Millisle to Garlieston. In February 1964, 78016/26 moved to Stranraer in exchange for Ivatt Moguls 46467/79; 78051 took the place of 46467 at Dumfries a few months later when the Ivatt was withdrawn, and remained at the depot until transfer to Ayr in June 1966.

At Stranraer, 78016/26 were used on harbour and goods yard pilot work. 78016 lasted at the depot until withdrawal in August 1966 whilst 78026 transferred to Corkerhill in November 1964. From here 78026 was regularly used on pilot work at Glasgow St Enoch terminus which was given over mainly to parcels traffic before closure to passengers in June 1966; 78026 was withdrawn two months later.

Three other depots to operate the class were Polmadie, Stirling and Bathgate. Polmadie received 78010 from the NER in March 1963 but the engine was in poor condition and after transfer to Motherwell for a few weeks was quickly returned to Darlington in the following June. From January 1963 until its withdrawal in July 1964 Stirling used 78053 on trip freight and shunting work on the Bridge of Allan,

Dunblane and Callander lines. Bathgate was host to several of the class toward the end of their days. Six engines, 78045-7/50/2/4 were allocated at various times from November 1963. They were used on mineral trip freights from local collieries and the occasional enthusiasts' special. Apart from 78051 at Ayr, the surviving members of the class in Scotland, 78046/7/9 were concentrated at St Margarets from August 1966, although by this time there was little suitable work available. Withdrawal of 78046/51 in November 1966 denoted the end of the Standard Cl. 2 2-6-0s on the ScR.

London Midland Region & Eastern Region

In April 1957, the LMR still had the lion's share of the class; thirty five engines 78020-44/55-64 were allocated over eleven depots:

Kettering	(2)	78020/1
Millhouses	(4)	78022-5
Canklow	(2)	78026/7
Leicester Midland	(2)	78028/9
Crewe North	(1)	78030
Chester Northgate	(6)	78031/8/55/6/8/9
Widnes	(5)	78032-5/9
Preston	(2)	78036/7
Wigan Central	(6)	78040/60-4
Bank Hall	(4)	78041-4
Rhyl	(1)	78057

The Kettering engines 78020/1 continued regular passenger and freight workings through to St Ives and Cambridge sharing the duties with Ivatt Moguls 46403/4/44/95/6. During the summer months, they also took charge of a perishables special from Histon to Kettering which cleared fruit and flower traffic for the Midlands from intermediate stations. 78028 arrived from Leicester in January 1959 but the St Ives passenger service was withdrawn in the following June and by November 78020/1/8 had transferred to Nottingham relinquishing their remaining duties to the Ivatt Moguls.

In February 1958 regional boundary reorganisation resulted in the ER taking over responsibility for the LMR depots in the Sheffield area. The Millhouses engines, 78022-5, now joined by Ivatt Moguls 46400/94 continued working as before on local passenger, shunting and pilot work. In June 1960, they also occasionally appeared on the new 8.44am Halifax-London St Pancras through service as far as Sheffield Midland, returning from Sheffield at 8.46pm (5.10pm from St Pancras). By November 1961 a Standard Cl. 2 2-6-0 was regularly noted on the 9.38am(SO) Sheffield Midland to York returning at 1.00pm. In January 1962, when Millhouses depot was closed 78022-5 moved to Doncaster where they took up station pilot duties. There appeared to be insufficient work for the class there as by August, they had been nominally transferred to the former GER depot at Stratford along with 78027 from Canklow. At least one of the class was noted in the area when 78023 appeared on the Chingford branch with a special goods on 2nd August. Within a month, 78022-5/7 were on the move again, this time to March where they were observed on freight workings in the Cambridge area. By November 1962, all five engines were in store, 78023/4 at Cambridge and 78022/5/7 at March. One month later 78022/3/7 were reallocated to Barrow-in-Furness and 78024/5 to Darlington. The other Canklow engine, 78026

Fig. 271
78019 is pictured in the company of LMS forerunner Ivatt Cl. 2 2-6-0 46512 at the celebrated Barry scrapyard of Woodham Bros. in South Wales. Both are seen here reserved for the East Anglian Locomotive Preservation Society but were eventually moved to the Severn Valley Railway for restoration. 46512 is now preserved on the Strathspey Railway at Aviemore and 78019 is undergoing restoration on the GCR at Loughborough in Leicestershire.

(Courtney Haydon)

had been moved to Ayr on the Scottish Region in January 1962. No further allocations of Standard Cl. 2 2-6-0s were made to the ER from the end of 1962.

The Leicester Midland pair 78028/9 were still engaged on local freights and passenger workings including regular visits to Cambridge on summer Saturday holiday trains to the Essex coast. In January 1959, 78028 moved on to Kettering with 78029 going to Nottingham in the following November. At this time Nottingham was operating four of the class, 78020/1/8/9. They took over from ex-MR Cl. 3F 0-6-0s on freight workings and Cl. 2P 4-4-0s on local passenger services until displaced from the latter by diesel multiple units in the early 1960s.

The lone example of the class at Crewe North 78030 was used on station pilot and shunting duties mainly confined to the immediate Crewe area. 78030 was usually kept in very clean condition for regular use on officers' specials and inspection saloon work. It was noted at Harlech for example on such duties in June 1963. Other turns included occasional passenger workings on the Crewe-Wellington branch. The Chester Northgate allocation 78031/8/55/6/8/9 had all moved to North Wales by June 1959 displaced from the Manchester services by LMS Cl. 4 2-6-4 tank engines.

78032-5/9 at Widnes had arrived from Rhyl in May 1956 displacing Ivatt Moguls 46420-4 from shunting work and local goods turns, the Ivatts moving to other LMR Western Division depots. The allocation was gradually whittled down by dieselisation and reduced traffic requirements until the last remaining allocation 78035/9 left for the London area in May 1963. Preston used 78036/7 on station pilot duties and local goods turns. When banana boats at Preston docks were being unloaded, the class was authorised to work down the Ribble branch to heat the vans as the Ribble Navigation and Docks Company's tank engines were not fitted with steam heating apparatus. Preston depot closed in September 1961, its demise hastened by a serious fire in June 1960. 78036/7 were

transferred to the nearby former L&YR depot at Lostock Hall from where they continued on the same duties.

78060-4 at Wigan Central now joined by 78040 from Bank Hall were still working to Liverpool and Manchester on passenger and freight duties as before. The depot was responsible for providing pilot assistance from Wigan for specials run in connection with the annual Grand National Steeplechase at Aintree. On 25th March 1961, for example, 78061/3 were noted double-heading two LMS Cl. 7P 4-6-0s, rebuilt Patriot 45530 and rebuilt Royal Scot 46146 respectively, on excursions from south of Crewe. The trains took the connection from the ex-LNWR main line to the ex-L&YR line immediately south of Wigan requiring a three mile climb at 1 in 108/92 to Orrell tunnel. Occasionally the Wigan engines were noted much further afield. On 13th March 1962 for example, the 3.30pm Manchester Piccadilly-Plymouth arrived at Pontypool Road without the two through coaches from Glasgow Central; these appeared an hour later hauled by 78060. The engine continued with the short train through to Bristol, returning north the following day.

78041-4 at Bank Hall, usually kept in immaculate external condition continued to be used on passenger services from Liverpool Exchange to Preston as well as on the Preston-Southport line. The class also worked a high proportion of the Liverpool-Rochdale semi-fasts via Bolton and Bury. The sole example at Rhyl, 78057 was displaced from the summer Land Cruise work by Standard Cl. 4 4-6-0s (75XXX) and transferred to Chester Midland in July 1957.

During the period from 1957 to the beginning of 1963, other depots operating the class were Aintree, Bangor, Barrow in Furness, Bescot, Kirkby in Ashfield, Llandudno Junction, Northwich, Skipton, Stoke on Trent, Wigan Springs Branch and Workington. At various times, Aintree was host to 78040/3/4/60 and used them together with Ivatt Moguls 46405/12/39 mainly on transfer freights between the extensive sorting sidings near the depot and North Mersey

Fig. 272
Millhouses-based 78025 performs pilot duties at Sheffield Midland station on 25th March 1961. Responsibility for Millhouses depot was transferred from the LMR to the ER in February 1958. The depot's four Standard Cl. 2 2-6-0s, 78022-5, were then maintained by Doncaster which resulted in the application of larger cabside numerals during Works visits as noted on 78025.

(Courtney Haydon)

Goods Yard, Bankfield Yard and the yard at Bootle Oriel Road, all part of the adjacent Liverpool Docks complex.

In November 1957, Bangor received 78057 for a two year stay; after it departed for Northwich, 78058/9 arrived from Llandudno Junction followed by 78034 in September 1961. The engines were used for shunting the freight and permanent way yards as well as for pilot work in the up yard at Bangor, mainly used for the marshalling of passenger and parcels vehicles. The class was also noted on the Caernarvon trip freight which required the engine to spend most of the morning working the quay yard there. Other regular turns were passenger and freight workings between Bangor and Amlwch and the Menai Bridge yard shunting duty, requiring marshalling of the Menai Bridge-Mold Junction goods service.

78022/3/7 were transferred to Barrow in Furness in December 1962 from store at March on the ER; Ivatt Mogul 46400 was already present for working the Lakeside-Haverthwaite branch. The new arrivals were used to replace the ageing ex-MR Johnson Cl. 2F 0-6-0s, 58120/60/77/82 on the Plumpton Junction-Canal Bridge freight workings which required low axle load engines to satisfy weight restrictions over Ulverston Canal Bridge. The class also had trip workings into other dock complexes including the Buccleuch Junction-Ramsden dock branch. There was not really enough suitable work for the engines and by June 1963, they had transferred to Aintree (78022/3) and Wigan Central (78027).

Although Bescot lost its only class member 78038 in October 1956 to Chester Northgate, the latter depot loaned 78055 to Bescot for a month in the following summer. This was the occasion of the International Scout Jamboree held at Sutton Coldfield in July and resulted in an extensive programme of special workings. The normal eight trains per day each way between Birmingham New Street and Walsall via the venue at Sutton Park were replaced by an interval auto-train service worked by Ivatt Cl. 2 2-6-2 tank engines 41212/20/4 and 41320. 78055 was used to supplement other local passenger services in the area. Chester Midland operated 78018/32/3/57 at various times in the 1957-1963 period. Their main duties involved local passenger workings along the coast to Rhyl, Colwyn Bay and Llandudno. The latter depot had an allocation of three engines in the summer of 1959; 78055/8/9 were used on local passenger and freight services. Kirkby in Ashfield received 78013 in June 1960. The engine's main duty was the return daily four coach workmen's train, unadvertised in the public timetable, from Mansfield to Chilwell ordnance depot near Nottingham. Mansfield depot had relinquished the duty to Kirkby when it closed in April 1960. 78013 displaced Ivatt Mogul 46501 to Skipton, the latter engine having had virtual monopoly of the service from 1953. Northwich used 78038/57 on the CLC Manchester Central passenger services until displaced by diesel multiple units in May 1960. Later 78019/55 arrived at Northwich and all four shared trip and local freight duties including the ICI salt workings. Skipton received 78036/7 from Lostock Hall in exchange for Ivatt Moguls 46452/501 in September 1962. The engines found work on parcels and local freights to the Leeds, Bradford and Burnley areas. At Stoke on Trent, 78017/56, reallocated from Rhyl in April 1962, took over the usual shunting turns, trip and local freight workings from Ivatt Moguls 46429/30 which left for Bescot.

Springs Branch was mainly a mineral and freight traffic depot providing engines for shunting the nearby Bamfurlong sorting sidings and trip freights from the many local collieries. 78017/9 arrived in April 1960 and worked alongside several Ivatt Moguls on some of the lighter duties. They were also noted on local passenger work to Manchester Central and Liverpool Exchange until reallocated to Rhyl and Northwich in June 1961. Workington operated 78018 between June and September 1962 mainly on passenger and parcels trains as far as Penrith on the picturesque former Cockermouth, Keswick and Penrith (CK&P) line. The engine was noted on the 'Lakes Express' (9.05am to Euston, 8.40am SO) returning at 6.20pm from Penrith (11.35am from Euston).

Fig. 273
BR3 type tender No. 1100 is seen here attached to 78026 at Canklow MPD on 15th June 1958. Compared with the original Darlington Works livery style, the tender lining panel is smaller in area in this view; photographic evidence suggests this was a characteristic of the LMR's Works, in particular of the Derby paint shop. The Scottish Works routinely produced the largest area tender panels, pushing the lining much nearer the top and bottom edges and almost flush with the rear handrail.

(A.R. Goult)

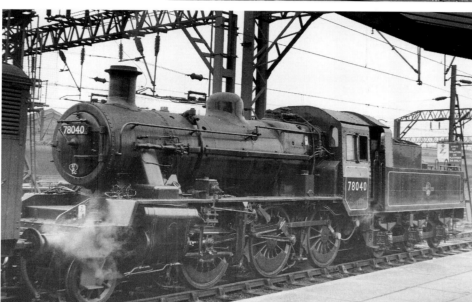

Fig. 274
78040 is in use as station pilot on 29th August 1960 at Crewe after a visit to the Works. The engine has received the Crewe paint shop full treatment, ie. mixed traffic black with complete lining including boiler and cylinder casings. 78040 is equipped with electric warning flashes on the firebox and buffer frame in readiness for the introduction of the 25kV overhead wire service to Manchester London Road two weeks later, the first stage of the LMR West Coast Main Line electrification project eventually linking London with Glasgow. *(Courtney Haydon)*

Fig. 275
Hawick-based 78049 is on shed at St Margarets MPD, Edinburgh on 16th April 1965. The engine was allocated to one or other of these two depots for the whole of its working life. 78049 has the typical Cowlairs finish, large cabside numerals topped by the '2MT.' power classification mark, depot name painted on the buffer beam and large area panel lining on the tender.

(Courtney Haydon)

In January 1963, the LMR allocation was thirty six engines distributed as shown:

Kirkby in Ashfield	(1)	78013
Stoke on Trent	(2)	78017/56
Chester Midland	(3)	78018/32/3
Northwich	(3)	78019/38/57
Nottingham	(4)	78020/1/8/9
Barrow In Furness	(3)	78022/3/7
Crewe North	(1)	78030
Crewe South	(2)	78031/55
Bangor	(3)	78034/58/9
Widnes	(2)	78035/9
Skipton	(2)	78036/7
Aintree	(4)	78040/3/4/60
Bank Hall	(2)	78041/2
Wigan Central	(4)	78061-4

Kirkby's 78013 was soon moved to Nottingham which also operated 78000/20/1/3/8/9/42/4/55/62 for various periods mainly on freight workings until it closed in April 1965. The depot's steam turns were taken on by the ex-GNR shed at nearby Colwick but the class members still at Nottingham, 78042/4/55/62, were reallocated to Toton either into store or to be used on local freights. 78017/56 remained at Stoke on Trent on trip and local freights until 1966 when 78059 arrived to replace the withdrawn 78056 in July; both 78017/59 left Stoke in the following October.

During 1963 several depots including Barrow in Furness, Chester Midland, Northwich and Widnes lost their allocation of the class. The main beneficiary was the London area with Willesden receiving seven engines 78018/9/33/8/9/60/3 in May whilst by June, Watford also had 78029/34/5. The new arrivals displaced a similar number of Ivatt Moguls some of which were a direct exchange for the Standards at their previous depots. The reason reported for the move was the decision that, as far as possible, all engines in the London area should be fitted with the Automatic Warning System installed in the cab for enhanced train control. Displacing 46401/24/72/503-6/17, the Willesden engines were used on empty stock workings between Euston and Wembley carriage sidings, as well as for permanent way ballast trains and shed and yard pilot duties. They were also noted on the Euston-Bletchley suburban passenger service and on freight workings over the West London Extension Line to Clapham Junction, the only time Standard Cl. 2 2-6-0s appeared regularly on the SR. On 5th July 1964, 78038 was in charge of the Locomotive Club of Great Britain's 'Surrey Wanderer' enthusiasts' tour around some long-electrified suburban lines which rarely saw steam power, taking in Crystal Palace Low Level, Tulse Hill and Beckenham Junction. The Watford allocation, 78029/34/5 was used in place of Ivatt Moguls 46423/31/70 chiefly on local freight or yard shunting work and local passenger services until these were either dieselised, electrified or withdrawn. Watford depot closed at the end of March 1965 and 78029/34/5 transferred to Willesden.

Fig. 276   78061 performs station pilot duties at Derby Midland on 11th July 1964. Although nominally a Leicester Midland engine at this date, 78061 retains its Derby shedplate. The engine was not withdrawn until November 1966 and, judging by its external appearance, would probably be scheduled for an overhaul at Crewe within a few weeks.   *(Courtney Haydon)*

With the dieselisation and ultimately electrification of the West Coast main line, Crewe North depot was gradually being run down during the 1960s, closing in May 1965; 78030 now joined by 78007 had transferred to Crewe South by October 1964 where both engines spent their days on shunting and local freight duties. 78003/32 had joined 78058/9 at Bangor by September 1963, although 78034 had departed for the London area the previous May. 78059 spent a few months at Holyhead from April 1964 mainly on station pilot duties before returning to Bangor. In the spring of 1964, Skipton, Aintree and Bank Hall lost their allocation of the class. Wigan Central depot closed in April 1964, 78020/7/57/61/2 transferring to nearby Springs Branch before moving to the Midlands the following month.

In December 1963, Coalville depot acquired its first Standard Cl. 2 2-6-0, 78013 for duty on the single track Leicester West Bridge-Glenfield branch. The line had been worked until then by the last of the ex-MR Johnson Cl. 2F 0-6-0s, 58143/8/82 as they were of sufficiently small dimension to pass through the narrow horseshoe-shaped Glenfield tunnel. This structure, just over one mile in length was built as part of the very early Leicester-Swannington line opened in July 1830. The route had been closed to passengers since September 1928 but retained a trip freight service. The line was reputed to be the one on which the train whistle was invented as the tunnel had very little clearance between train and walls and no manhole recesses; hence permanent way gangs had to be vigilant. 78013 had been modified at Crewe with cut-down corners to the roof and cab; 58182 was retained as spare until 78028, similarly modified, arrived in January 1964. 78013/28 were transferred to Leicester Midland in September 1964 but continued operating the branch until closure in May 1966. Other duties for the class at Leicester, whose allocation now included 78027/61 augmented by 78021 a few months later, were station pilot work, deputising for failed diesel multiple units and occasional appearances on

the Stamford-Seaton push-pull service. The modified 78013/28 were often in demand for enthusiasts' tours, as for example on 3rd July 1965 when 78028 headed an LCGB brake van special to Market Harborough, Wellingborough and on to the Loddington branch at Kettering.

Other depots with allocations of the class in 1964 were Derby and Lostock Hall. Derby received 78000/21 in January 1964. They were used on the Shirland Colliery branch, a spur off the North Midland line between Ambergate and Clay Cross. Three of the few remaining MR Johnson Cl. 3F 0-6-0s 43342/620/58, were displaced from this duty, the last one (43620) being withdrawn by the end of February. 78000/21 also appeared on parcels and local passenger services often substituting when diesel multiple units were unavailable. In May 1964 Derby received 78020/7/37/57/61 from Springs Branch displacing Ivatt Moguls 46402/40/7/500/2 in return to Springs Branch and Aintree. By June 1964, Lostock Hall had an allocation of three of the class, 78002/22/40, which was used on Preston station pilot duties, local freights and parcels work.

In April 1965, the LMR allocation had grown to forty-five engines allocated over ten depots as shown:

Derby	(3)	78000/20/64
Lostock Hall	(6)	78002/22/37
		78040/1/57
Bangor	(4)	78003/32/58/9
Gorton	(6)	78007/11/2/4
		78023/62
Oxley	(1)	78008
Crewe South	(4)	78010/30/1/6
Leicester Midland	(5)	78013/21/7/8/61
Stoke on Trent	(2)	78017/56
Willesden	(11)	78018/9/29/33-5
		78038/9/43/60/3
Toton	(3)	78042/4/55

Fig. 277   On 5th August 1957, 78052 is pictured at its home shed, Helmsdale, the most northerly allocation of any of the BR Standard steam fleet. Helmsdale, situated on the former Highland railway route from Inverness to Thurso and Wick supplied power for the Dornoch branch on which 78052 was used; the engine is still in original Darlington Works finish with power classification mark 'Class 2' on the buffer beam.

(J.B. Arnold)

By the end of October 1966, the engines at Oxley, Stoke and Derby had been either reallocated, put into store at Toton or withdrawn. Bangor lost its allocation to Willesden in June 1965 whilst the engines at Lostock Hall continued on local freights and Preston station pilot turns. The Gorton allocation was noted on various duties including trip freights and station pilot work at Guide Bridge before transfer to nearby Trafford Park on the closure of Gorton in June 1965. From Trafford Park, the engines were still employed on the usual trip freights and shunting duties but could also be seen further afield as in April 1966 when 78062 was noted working from Machynlleth on permanent way trains on the Cambrian lines. The survivors at Trafford Park 78007/12/23/62 were all at Bolton by November 1966.

Leicester Midland depot closed to steam in June 1966 and the remaining class members there, 78013/21/8/61 went for store at Toton. The latter depot, although officially closed to steam in the same month continued to house several of the class in and around the old steam shed. From April 1965 to November 1966, ten engines 78013/20/1/8/42/4/55/61/ 2/4 were allocated to the depot at various times. Seven of these, 78013/20/1/8/44/55/62 survived to be transferred to the north west ending their days at either Bolton or Lostock Hall.

Willesden continued to use its allocation on freights, engineers' trains, empty stock workings and shunting turns until it closed in September 1965. Eleven of the class still at the depot, 78003/18/9/34/5/8/9/58-60/3 were despatched light engine, mostly in pairs to Nuneaton which kept six engines, the remainder being taken by Crewe South and Shrewsbury. Nuneaton used its allocation, 78003/18/9/39/59/63 when not in store, on the three times daily parcels service to Leamington Spa. The class also took over from Ivatt Cl. 4 2-6-0s (43XXX) on the local goods yard shunting turns and the remaining trip freight workings to Coventry. By April 1966, steam workings in the area were few and in June 78059 was in store at Nuneaton, the rest having moved to Crewe South and Shrewsbury; later in the month 78059 was transferred to Stoke then to Crewe South. By October 1966 the latter depot had four of the class on its books, 78019/31/6/59 although there was little suitable work. Earlier, on 23rd April 1966, 78036 had been used on one leg of the RCTS 'St George' Railtour from Nuneaton. The special was a typical example of the many enthusiasts' workings arranged toward the end of steam. It ran via Wolverhampton High Level to Stafford and Shrewsbury. 78036 took over at Wellington for the run to Nantwich via the Market Drayton line through Crewe to Winsford Junction. From here the train was propelled over the mile long branch to Over and Wharton after which 78036 continued north as far as Hartford Junction where LMS Hughes Fowler Crab Cl. 6P/5F 2-6-0 42727 took over for the return to Nuneaton via Crewe, Stoke, Uttoxeter, Burton-on-Trent and the former LNWR/MR joint line through Shackerstone Junction.

At the beginning of December 1966, the seventeen remaining members of the class were concentrated on the LMR at three depots; allocation was as shown:

Shrewsbury	(5)	78003/17/36/58/63
Bolton	(8)	78007/12/3/23/8/44/55/62
Lostock Hall	(4)	78020/1/37/41

The first members of the class at Shrewsbury had been 78035/8/58/60 allocated in September 1965 when Willesden depot closed; others arrived during 1966. When not in store, the engines were employed on the daily duties to Nantmawr quarries beyond Oswestry and the thrice weekly goods trains to Minsterley. The quarry trains were often doubled up to reduce line occupancy resulting in the frequent sight of a pair of Standard Cl. 2 2-6-0s tackling these heavy trains. Shunting work included the goods yard at Coton Hill, the permanent-way yard at Hookagate and pilot duty at the Abbey station. By the end of December 1966, the remaining engines were withdrawn and their duties given over to Type 2 Cl. 25 diesels and Cl. 08 diesel shunters.

Lostock Hall and Bolton were two of the depots in the North West where steam was concentrated in its final years. The engines continued working until significant repairs were required at which point they were withdrawn. The Bolton engines could be observed on pilot work at Trinity Street station. When not in store, the Lostock Hall engines were similarly used at Preston station together with the occasional parcels turn to Skipton and Colne. In January 1967, a Cl. 05 diesel shunter was trialed on day-time station pilot work at Preston but was not considered powerful enough; a Cl. 08 shunter was already in use on the all-night turn. In May 1967 the remaining class members at both Bolton, 78007/12/3/23/44/62, and Lostock Hall 78020/1/37/41, were withdrawn; 78037, the only serviceable one at the latter depot was noted on the Preston late evening pilot duty during its final week of life. These withdrawals signified the end of the line on BR for the Standard Cl. 2 2-6-0s, many of which had completed little more than ten years' active service.

6.7.3 Allocation Summary

78000   12.52 Oswestry; 4.53 Machynlleth; 5.63 Nottingham; 1.64 Derby; 6.65 Withdrawn.

78001   12.52 Oswestry; 4.53 Machynlleth; 5.54 Worcester; 1.64 Gloucester Barnwood; 4.64 Gloucester Horton Road; 12.65 Withdrawn;

78002   12.52 Oswestry; 5.53 Machynlleth; 8.63 Wigan Central; 10.63 Bank Hall; 6.64 Lostock Hall; 6.66 Withdrawn.

78003   12.52 Oswestry; 4.53 Machynlleth; 3.58 Worcester; 5.58 Machynlleth; 5.63 Bangor; 6.65 Willesden; 9.65 Nuneaton; 1.66 Shrewsbury; 12.66 Withdrawn.

78004   1.53 Swindon store; 3.53 Oswestry; 5.53 Machynlleth; 1.54 Swindon; 10.54 Worcester; 6.57 Hereford; 1.64 Llanelly; 7.64 Gloucester Horton Road; 11.65 Withdrawn.

78005   2.53 Oswestry; 5.53 Machynlleth; 10.62 Gloucester Barnwood; 4.64 Gloucester Horton Road; 9.64 Withdrawn.

78006   3.53 Oswestry; 9.53 Machynlleth; 9.62 Gloucester Barnwood; 4.64 Gloucester Horton Road; 12.65 Withdrawn.

78007   3.53 Oswestry; 9.53 Machynlleth; 6.63 Crewe North; 6.64 Crewe South; 3.65 Gorton; 6.65 Trafford Park; 8.66 Bolton; 5.67 Withdrawn.

78008   3.53 Swindon store; 5.53 Oswestry; 7.53 Worcester; 3.62 Wolverhampton Stafford Road; 9.63 Oxley; 10.66 Withdrawn.

78009   4.53 Swindon store; 5.53 Oswestry; 7.53 Worcester; 3.63 Gloucester Barnwood; 2.64 Withdrawn.

78010   12.53 West Auckland; 3.55 Northallerton; 3.63 Polmadie; 5.63 Motherwell; 6.63 Darlington; 11.63 Farnley Junction; 4.64 Crewe South; 9.66 Withdrawn.

78011   12.53 West Auckland; 3.55 Northallerton; 3.63 Darlington; 11.63 Farnley Junction; 4.64 Manningham; 12.64 Gorton; 6.65 Trafford Park; 9.65 Withdrawn.

78012   1.54 West Auckland; 3.55 Northallerton; 3.63 Darlington; 11.63 Tweedmouth; 12.64 Gorton; 6.65 Trafford Park; 8.66 Bolton; 5.67 Withdrawn.

78013   1.54 West Auckland; 3.55 Northallerton; 1.58 Kirkby Stephen; 6.60 Kirkby in Ashfield; 3.63 Nottingham; 12.63 Coalville; 9.64 Leicester Midland; 7.66 Toton; 11.66 Bolton; 5.67 Withdrawn.

78014   2.54 West Auckland; 3.55 Northallerton; 3.63 Darlington; 11.63 Farnley Junction; 4.64 Manningham; 12.64 Gorton; 6.65 Trafford Park; 9.65 Withdrawn.

78015   2.54 West Auckland; 12.56 Northallerton; 3.63 Darlington; 11.63 Withdrawn.

78016   3.54 West Auckland; 4.54 Kirkby Stephen; 1.58 Northallerton 3.58 West Auckland; 8.63 Motherwell; 10.63 Dumfries; 2.64 Stranraer; 8.66 Withdrawn.

78017   3.54 West Auckland; 4.54 Kirkby Stephen; 4.60 Springs Branch; 6.61 Rhyl; 10.61 Widnes; 3.62 Rhyl; 4.62 Stoke on Trent; 10.66 Shrewsbury; 12.66 Withdrawn.

78018   3.54 West Auckland; 4.54 Kirkby Stephen; 4.60 Chester Midland; 6.62 Workington; 9.62 Chester Midland; 5.63 Willesden; 9.65 Nuneaton; 4.66 Shrewsbury; 11.66 Withdrawn.
Undergoing restoration by the Darlington Railway Preservation Society.

78019   3.54 Kirkby Stephen; 4.60 Springs Branch; 6.61 Northwich; 5.63 Willesden; 9.65 Nuneaton; 1.66 Crewe South; 11.66 Withdrawn. Undergoing restoration on the Great Central Railway at Loughborough.

78020   4.54 Kettering; 11.59 Nottingham; 12.63 Wigan Central; 4.64 Springs Branch; 5.64 Derby; 10.66 Toton; 11.66 Lostock Hall; 5.67 Withdrawn.

78021   5.54 Kettering; 11.59 Nottingham; 1.64 Derby; 2.65 Leicester Midland; 7.66 Toton; 11.66 Lostock Hall; 5.67 Withdrawn.

78022   5.54 Millhouses; 1.62 Doncaster; 8.62 Stratford; 9.62 March; 12.62 Barrow in Furness; 5.63 Aintree; 12.63 Lostock Hall; 9.66 Withdrawn. Preserved on the Keighley & Worth Valley Railway at Haworth.

78023   5.54 Millhouses; 1.62 Doncaster; 8.62 Stratford; 9.62 March; 12.62 Barrow in Furness; 5.63 Aintree; 5.64 Nottingham; 3.65 Gorton; 6.65 Trafford Park; 8.66 Bolton; 5.67 Withdrawn.

78024   5.54 Millhouses; 1.62 Doncaster; 8.62 Stratford; 9.62 March; 12.62 Darlington;10.63 Tweedmouth; 12.64 Gorton; 2.65 Withdrawn.

78025   6.54 Grimesthorpe; 11.54 Millhouses; 1.62 Doncaster; 8.62 Stratford; 9.62 March; 12.62 Darlington; 1.63 West Auckland; 10.63 Tweedmouth; 12.64 Gorton; 2.65 Withdrawn.

78026   6.54 Canklow; 1.62 Ayr; 1.63 Dumfries; 2.64 Stranraer; 11.64 Corkerhill; 8.66 Withdrawn.

78027   6.54 Canklow; 8.62 Stratford; 9.62 March; 12.62 Barrow in Furness; 5.63 Bank Hall; 6.63 Wigan Central; 4.64 Springs Branch; 5.64 Derby; 9.64 Leicester Midland; 9.65 Withdrawn.

78028   7.54 Leicester Midland; 1.59 Kettering; 11.59 Nottingham; 1.64 Coalville; 9.64 Leicester Midland; 7.66 Toton; 11.66 Bolton; 2.67 Withdrawn;

78029   7.54 Leicester Midland; 11.59 Nottingham; 5.63 Oswestry; 6.63 Watford; 4.65 Willesden; 10.65 Withdrawn.

78030   9.54 Preston; 4.56 Crewe North; 10.64 Crewe South; 10.65 Withdrawn

78031   9.54 Tebay; 10.54 Lancaster Green Ayre; 10.56 Chester Northgate; 6.59 Rhyl; 4.62 Crewe South; 10.66 Withdrawn.

78032   9.54 Rhyl; 5.56 Widnes; 2.60 Chester Midland; 4.60 Kirkby Stephen; 5.60 Chester Midland; 9.63 Bangor; 6.65 Willesden; 10.65 Withdrawn.

78033   9.54 Rhyl; 2.55 Crewe North; 3.55 Rhyl; 5.56 Widnes; 2.60 Chester Midland. 5.63 Willesden; 10.65 Withdrawn.

78034   10.54 Rhyl; 5.56 Widnes; 9.61 Nuneaton; 9.61 Bangor; 5.63 Watford; 4.65 Willesden; 9.65 Crewe South; 1.66 Withdrawn.

78035   10.54 Rhyl; 5.56 Widnes; 4.58 Preston; 5.58 Widnes; 5.63 Watford; 4.65 Willesden; 9.65 Shrewsbury; 12.65 Withdrawn.

78036   11.54 Preston; 9.61 Lostock Hall; 9.62 Skipton; 5.63 Crewe South; 11.66 Shrewsbury; 12.66 Withdrawn.

78037   11.54 Preston; 9.61 Lostock Hall; 9.62 Skipton; 3.64 Springs Branch; 5.64 Derby; 3.65 Lostock Hall; 5.67 Withdrawn.

78038   11.54 Bescot; 10.56 Chester Northgate; 3.58 Rhyl; 11.59 Northwich; 5.63 Willesden; 9.65 Shrewsbury; 8.66 Withdrawn.

78039   11.54 Rhyl; 5.56 Widnes; 5.63 Willesden; 9.65 Nuneaton; 4.66 Shrewsbury; 9.66 Withdrawn.

78040   12.54 Bank Hall; 2.57 Wigan Central; 1.61 Aintree; 4.64 Lostock Hall; 1.66 Withdawn.

78041   12.54 Bank Hall; 6.64 Lostock Hall; 5.67 Withdrawn.

78042   12.54 Bank Hall; 5.64 Nottingham; 4.65 Toton; 9.65 Withdrawn.

78043   12.54 Bank Hall; 11.56 Aintree; 3.57 Bank Hall; 9.62 Aintree; 5.63 Willesden; 10.65 Withdrawn.

78044   12.54 Bank Hall; 9.62 Aintree; 12.63 Lostock Hall; 4.64 Aintree; 5.64 Nottingham; 4.65 Toton; 11.66 Bolton; 5.67 Withdrawn.

78045   10.55 Kittybrewster; 6.60 Keith; 6.61 Aberdeen Ferryhill; 6.64 Bathgate; 1.66 Withdrawn.

78046   10.55 Hawick; 1.64 Bathgate; 9.66 St Margarets; 11.66 Withdrawn.

78047   10.55 Hawick; 10.65 St Margarets; 1.66 Bathgate; 9.66 St Margarets; 9.66 Withdrawn.

78048   10.55 St Margarets; 7.60 Hawick; 7.64 Withdrawn.

78049   11.55 St Margarets; 6.59 Hawick; 1.66 St Margarets; 8.66 Withdrawn.

78050   11.55 Motherwell; 10.63 Dawsholm; 7.64 Bathgate; 1.66 Withdrawn.

78051   11.55 Motherwell; 10.63 Dawsholm; 7.64 Dumfries; 6.66 Ayr; 11.66 Withdrawn.

78052   11.55 Motherwell; 11.56 Inverness; 2.57 Helmsdale; 9.58 St Margarets; 11.58 Aviemore; 7.62 Perth; 11.63 Bathgate; 1.66 Withdrawn.

78053   11.55 Motherwell; 10.56 Aberdeen Ferryhill; 11.56 Keith; 6.61 Aberdeen Ferryhill; 1.63 Stirling; 7.64 Withdrawn.

78054   12.55 Motherwell; 10.56 Aberdeen Ferryhill; 11.56 Keith; 6.61 Aberdeen Ferryhill; 6.64 Bathgate; 12.65 Withdrawn.

78055   8.56 Chester Northgate; 7.57 Bescot; 8.57 Chester Northgate; 6.59 Llandudno Junction; 11.59 Rhyl; 9.60 Northwich; 11.62 Crewe South; 5.63 Skipton; 3.64 Aintree; 5.64 Nottingham; 4.65 Toton; 11.66 Bolton; 2.67 Withdrawn.

78056   8.56 Chester Northgate; 4.59 Rhyl; 4.62 Stoke on Trent; 7.66 Withdrawn.

78057   9.56 Chester Northgate; 1.57 Rhyl; 7.57 Chester Midland; 11.57 Bangor; 11.59 Northwich; 5.63 Wigan Central; 4.64 Springs Branch; 5.64 Derby; 3.65 Lostock Hall; 5.66 Withdrawn.

78058   9.56 Chester Northgate; 6.59 Llandudno Junction; 11.59 Bangor; 6.65 Willesden; 9.65 Shrewsbury; 12.66 Withdrawn.

78059   9.56 Chester Northgate; 4.59 Llandudno Junction; 11.59 Bangor; 4.64 Holyhead; 10.64 Bangor; 6.65 Willesden; 9.65 Nuneaton; 6.66 Stoke on Trent; 10.66 Crewe South; 11.66 Withdrawn.
         Undergoing conversion on the Bluebell Railway to a Standard Cl. 2 2-6-2T, to be numbered 84030.

78060   10.56 Wigan Central; 9.62 Aintree; 5.63 Willesden; 9.65 Shrewsbury; 10.66 Withdrawn.

78061   10.56 Wigan Central; 4.64 Springs Branch; 5.64 Derby; 6.64 Leicester Midland; 7.66 Toton; 11.66 Withdrawn.

78062   10.56 Wigan Central; 4.64 Springs Branch; 5.64 Nottingham; 4.65 Toton; 4.65 Gorton; 6.65 Trafford Park; 11.66 Bolton; 5.67 Withdrawn.

78063   11.56 Wigan Central; 5.63 Willesden; 9.65 Nuneaton; 4.66 Shrewsbury; 12.66 Withdrawn.

78064   11.56 Wigan Central; 2.64 Derby; 10.66 Toton; 11.66 Withdrawn.

6.8 Maintenance

The official recommended period between works visits was 36 months for intermediate and 72 months for general overhauls. For the WR allocation, 78000-9, average mileage to intermediate overhaul in the early 1960s was 83,100 whilst for general overhaul, the comparable figure was 168,700; this represented an annual average mileage of around 28,000. During 1963, several of the WR allocation were reassigned to the LMR; the annual mileage figure for the transferees then fell to less than half this figure indicating the significant reduction in the amount of suitable work available. In the case of 78003 for example, which moved from Machynlleth to Bangor in May 1963, a figure of only 9,000 miles was recorded for the whole year. Annual mileage figures for locomotives operating on the ScR and NER were not systematically recorded but may be expected to be in the 20,000-25,000 range during the first ten years of their lives. A comparison of repair costs per mile (in new pence) for the Standard Class 2 2-6-0s and the Class 2 2-6-2 tank engines (84XXX) for the year 1957 is given as follows:

Class	Repair Costs per Mile (new pence)		
	Engine & Boiler	Tender	Total
BR 2 2-6-0	2.87	0.25	3.12
BR 2 2-6-2 tank	3.70	–	3.70

Works responsibility for major overhauls and repairs is given as follows:

Region	Works
WR	Swindon (to March 1962)
	Wolverhampton (to March 1962)
	Caerphilly (to March 1962)
	*Oswestry (to March 1962)
	Crewe (from March 1962)
NER	Darlington
ER	Doncaster
	Darlington
	Stratford
LMR	Crewe
	Derby (until November 1963)
ScR	Cowlairs
	*Inverurie
	Darlington (from March 1960)

*Light and non-classified repairs only

6.9 Modifications in Service

There were very few changes made to the Standard Class 2 2-6-0s after they entered service. The WR allocation, 78000-9, was fitted with both GWR-style lamp brackets as detailed in section 2.9.2 and standard GWR ATC apparatus. Several of the class operating on other regions acquired BR AWS equipment during the early 1960s. The majority of the class was equipped with Smith Stone speedometers powered off the rear driving wheel, either fitted from new or acquired later.

The only other significant modification was that made to two members of the class operating on the Leicester West Bridge-Glenfield branch. Originally this authorisation, covered by job number 5968, called for the alteration of the cab profile by cutting down the corners of the roof and cab on five Standard Class 2 2-6-0s for use on both the Shirland Colliery branch (near Wingfield on the Derby-Chesterfield line) and the West Bridge branch. These engines were earmarked to replace several life-expired MR Class 2F and 3F 0-6-0s due for withdrawal. The reason for the modification was to accommodate the tight clearances encountered in the 189 yard Shirland Tunnel No. 1 and in Glenfield Tunnel No. 3, just over one mile in length. Modification drawing nos. DRS 8834 (tender cab roof) and DRS 8835 (locomotive cab roof) were completed and authorisation given for Crewe Works to proceed. In the event, only two locomotives, 78013/28, were modified, in December 1963 and January 1964 at a cost of £300 each, for use on the West Bridge branch. It was presumably considered that clearances in the Shirland tunnel were sufficient not to require the modifications after all, as the unmodified 78000/21 duly took on the branch duties in January 1964.

6.10 Names and Nicknames

None of the Standard Class 2 2-6-0s was officially named during BR service. A widely observed nickname was that of 'Mickey Mouse', a reference to Walt Disney's hilariously puny cartoon character. This name was said to have been bestowed by WR crews who regarded the 'pulling power' of the class as weak. Rarely heard but probably from the same stable was the term 'Ricers' alluding to the claim that the engines 'couldn't pull the skin off a rice pudding'. The locomotives also picked up the sobriquet 'Go-anywhere'

engines, as a result of their low axle weight and external dimensions which allowed them to operate on almost any line on the BR network. A name the class did not pick up was the one said to have been applied to their Ivatt Class 2 2-6-0 forebears, ie. 'Penrith Lizzies'. This stemmed from the strong performances of the Ivatts over the route of the former Cockermouth, Keswick and Penrith lines between Penrith and the Cumbrian coast. The term 'Lizzie' was widely used in LMS days to refer to the powerful and free-running Stanier Pacifics.

6.11 Performance

The Standard Class 2 2-6-0s were generally well received by the footplate crews. The increased protection from the elements afforded by the enclosed cabs was a significant improvement on the spartan facilities offered by some of the ageing Class 0-6-0s they replaced, many of which had been introduced in pre-grouping days. This applied particularly to the GWR Dean Goods 0-6-0s on the WR's Cambrian lines and the LNER J21 and J25 0-6-0s over the bleak Stainmore route. No complex firing techniques were necessary to achieve a free-steaming performance as the firebox was fairly deep with little slope on the grate. The class was equally at home on a wide variety of tasks, from station pilot to general freight and secondary passenger work. The engines were capable of a fair turn of speed on the latter duties, as for example on the Preston-Liverpool Exchange locals where speeds of up to 60mph or more were common down the 1 in 131 from Aughton Green to Maghull. Moreover in January 1963, one of the class, 78009, must have reached speeds of up to 80mph when coupled inside a Type 4 diesel to provide carriage heating on a Swansea-Newcastle express between Worcester and York following failure of the diesel's train heating boiler.

6.12 Storage, Withdrawal and Disposal

A few of the Standard Class 2 2-6-0s were placed in store at various times for want of suitable work. On the ER, 78022-5/7 were stored at March depot for a month in November 1962, whilst on the NER 78011/2/4/5/24 were in store at Darlington in August 1963. Several of the LMR allocation were stored serviceable for short periods from time to time including 78042/4/56/62 at Toton in April 1965 and 78003/18/9/39/59/63 at Nuneaton in the following November. Table 60 gives dates of withdrawal and places of disposal for the whole class. The first to be condemned was 78015 in November 1963; all had been withdrawn by the end of May 1967.

6.13 Preservation

Four Standard Class 2 2-6-0s are preserved, all having been rescued from Woodham's scrapyard at Barry in South Wales.

78018

This engine arrived at Shackerstone on the Market Bosworth Light Railway, now known as The Battlefield Line, in November 1978. 78018 is now undergoing restoration by the Darlington Railway Preservation Society in the former goods yard adjacent to the Darlington North Road Railway Museum.

78019

Moved from Barry in March 1973, 78019 was stored for a

period at the Severn Valley Railway at Bridgnorth. The locomotive is now undergoing restoration on the Great Central Railway at Loughborough in Leicestershire. The boiler earmarked for 78019 is BR8/1119, the one originally fitted to Standard Cl. 2 2-6-2 tank engine 84007.

78022

The engine was rescued from Barry in June 1975 and moved to the Keighley and Worth Valley Railway; after restoration it was resteamed in October 1992. 78022 was the subject of experimentation with the Giesl Ejector to enhance steaming performance in 1995 but re-entered service with its old chimney restored. The larger blastpipe area of the Giesl Ejector had the effect of reducing the amount of horsepower absorbed in driving out the exhaust steam from cylinders and, at the same time, was more effective in entraining and expelling the exhaust gases from the grate, with a reduced level of smokebox vacuum. These features combined to yield savings in coal and water and increased the power available for work; reduced fuel costs of the order of 4% were reported.

78059

Purchased from Barry in May 1983 without a tender, 78059 is now based on the Bluebell Railway at Horsted Keynes in East Sussex. Work is in hand to convert it to one of its Standard Class 2 2-6-2 tank engine equivalents, to be renumbered 84030.

Ivatt Class 2 2-6-0s

Seven of the Ivatt Class 2 2-6-0 antecedents to the Standard Class 2 2-6-0s have also been preserved. They are:

46428:	East Lancashire Railway, Bury
46441:	Steamtown, Carnforth
46443:	Severn Valley Railway, Bridgnorth.
46447:	Buckinghamshire Railway Centre. Quainton Road near Aylesbury.
46464:	Brechin Caledonian Railway. Awaiting restoration at Bridge of Dun.
46512:	Strathspey Railway, Aviemore
46521:	Severn Valley Railway, Bridgnorth

Table 60

Standard Cl. 2 2-6-0s 78000-78064
Construction, Withdrawal and Disposal Information

Engine	Built	With-drawn	Disposal	
78000	12.52	6.65	1.66	J. Cashmore, Great Bridge
78001	12.52	12.65	3.66	Birds Commercial Motors, Morriston
78002	12.52	6.66	10.66	Central Wagon Co., Wigan
78003	12.52	12.66	9.67	J. Cashmore, Newport
78004	1.53	11.65	2.66	J. Cashmore, Newport
78005	2.53	9.64	3.65	J. Cashmore, Newport
78006	3.53	12.65	3.66	Birds Commercial Motors, Morriston
78007	3.53	5.67	12.67	A. Draper, Kingston upon Hull
78008	3.53	10.66	1.67	J. Cashmore, Great Bridge
78009	4.53	2.64	12.64	Swindon Works
78010	12.53	9.66	12.66	J. Cashmore, Newport
78011	12.53	9.65	12.65	T. W. Ward, Killamarsh
78012	1.54	5.67	10.67	A. Draper, Kingston upon Hull
78013	1.54	5.67	10.67	A. Draper, Kingston upon Hull
78014	2.54	9.65	12.65	T. W. Ward, Killamarsh
78015	2.54	11.63	1.64	Darlington Works
78016	3.54	8.66	5.67	Arnott Young, Troon
78017	3.54	12.66	10.67	J. Cashmore, Newport
78018	3.54	11.66		Undergoing restoration by the Darlington Railway Preservation Society in premises adjacent to Darlington Railway Museum
78019	3.54	11.66		Undergoing restoration on the Great Central Railway at Loughborough
78020	4.54	5.67	11.67	Motherwell Machinery and Scrap Co., Wishaw
78021	5.54	5.67	11.67	Motherwell Machinery and Scrap Co., Wishaw
78022	5.54	9.66		Preserved on the Keighley & Worth Valley Railway, Haworth
78023	5.54	5.67	10.67	A. Draper, Kingston upon Hull
78024	5.54	2.65	1.66	Birds Commercial Motors, Long Marston
78025	6.54	2.65	11.65	Birds Commercial Motors, Long Marston
78026	6.54	8.66	12.66	Arnott Young, Old Kilpatrick
78027	6.54	9.65	2.66	J. Cashmore, Great Bridge
78028	7.54	2.67	6.67	J. Cashmore, Great Bridge
78029	7.54	10.65	1.66	J. Cashmore, Great Bridge
78030	9.54	10.65	12.65	J. Cashmore, Great Bridge

Engine	Built	With-drawn	Disposal	
78031	9.54	10.66	3.67	J. Cashmore, Newport
78032	9.54	10.65	1.66	J. Cashmore, Great Bridge
78033	9.54	10.65	11.65	J. Cashmore, Great Bridge
78034	10.54	1.66	4.66	T. W. Ward, Killamarsh
78035	10.54	12.65	4.66	J. Cashmore, Great Bridge
78036	11.54	12.66	8.67	J. Cashmore, Newport
78037	11.54	5.67	11.67	Motherwell Machinery and Scrap Co., Wishaw
78038	11.54	8.66	12.66	J. Cashmore, Great Bridge
78039	11.54	9.66	3.67	J. Cashmore, Newport
78040	12.54	1.66	5.66	T. W. Ward, Beighton, Sheffield
78041	12.54	5.67	11.67	Motherwell Machinery and Scrap Co., Wishaw
78042	12.54	9.65	12.65	T. W. Ward, Killamarsh
78043	12.54	10.65	1.66	J. Cashmore, Great Bridge
78044	12.54	5.67	10.67	A. Draper, Kingston upon Hull
78045	10.55	1.66	4.66	Motherwell Machinery and Scrap Co., Wishaw
78046	10.55	11.66	6.67	Arnott Young, Old Kilpatrick
78047	10.55	9.66	1.67	Shipbreaking Industries, Faslane
78048	10.55	7.64	4.65	Motherwell Machinery and Scrap Co., Wishaw
78049	11.55	8.66	12.66	Motherwell Machinery and Scrap Co., Wishaw
78050	11.55	1.66	4.66	Motherwell Machinery and Scrap Co., Wishaw
78051	11.55	11.66	3.67	Motherwell Machinery and Scrap Co., Wishaw
78052	11.55	1.66	4.66	Motherwell Machinery and Scrap Co., Wishaw
78053	11.55	7.64	4.65	P. & W. McLellan, Bo'ness, Linlithgow
78054	12.55	12.65	3.66	Shipbreaking Industries, Faslane
78055	8.56	2.67	6.67	J. Cashmore, Great Bridge
78056	8.56	7.66	11.66	Birds Commercial Motors, Long Marston
78057	9.56	5.66	8.66	Motherwell Machinery and Scrap Co., Wishaw
78058	9.56	12.66	9.67	J. Cashmore, Newport
78059	9.56	11.66		To be rebuilt on Bluebell Railway as Class 2 2-6-2 tank, 84030
78060	10.56	10.66	3.67	J. Cashmore, Newport
78061	10.56	11.66	3.67	T. W. Ward, Killamarsh
78062	10.56	5.67	10.67	A. Draper, Kingston upon Hull
78063	11.56	12.66	12.67	J. Cashmore, Newport
78064	11.56	11.66	3.67	T. W. Ward, Killamarsh

Fig. 278   78028 with cut down cab for use on the Leicester West Bridge–Glenfield branch line pauses at Leicester Belgrave Road with the LRS 25th Anniversary brake van special on the 7th November 1964.

(John Edgington)

Glossary of Technical Terms

Ashpan
A container below the firegrate to collect the ash and cinders from the fire. It is also fitted with doors, known as dampers, to control the air admitted to the firebed.

Atomiser
A device that emulsifies lubricating oil by mixing it with steam before it is fed to the cylinders.

Axlebox
The container of the bearing in which the axle journal rotates. The axlebox moves vertically in guides known as horn guides, the movement controlled by springs.

Balance Weights
Weights fitted to the driving wheels of locomotives to counterbalance the weight of all the revolving and a proportion (50% in the case of the Standard Classes) of the reciprocating weights.

Blastpipe
The pipe in the smokebox through which spent steam from the cylinders is directed upwards to exhaust through the chimney. In so doing, a partial vacuum is induced in the smokebox resulting in a draught which draws air through the firebed and hot gasses through the boiler tubes to the chimney.

Blower
A steam operated device fitted to the top of the blastpipe to compensate for the lack of exhaust steam when the regulator is shut and the smoke box vacuum thereby diminished, so preventing a dangerous blowback of fumes into the cab from the firebox. Also of use when raising steam and in instances of poor steaming.

Brick Arch
An arch of refractory bricks fitted into the front of the firebox on the tubeplate, protecting the tubeplate from flame damage and assisting the combustion of gases in the firebox.

Clack Valves
Self-acting non-return valves mounted on the boiler at the feed water intake allowing water to be admitted from the injector against boiler pressure without any loss of steam.

Continuous Blowdown Valve
A device designed to rid the boiler periodically of sludge deposits by allowing a definite but limited amount of water to be blown out of the boiler continuously from the lower part of the firebox as long as the regulator is open. It thus prevents an otherwise harmful build-up of scale and sludge.

Cylinder Drain Cocks
Cocks fitted to front and rear, at the lowest point of the cylinders which are opened by rods operated by the driver usually when the engine is at rest and starting away, to clear condensate from the cylinders and prevent the cylinder ends

from being knocked out. Also used should the boiler prime and carry over water to the cylinders.

Dome
A raised feature positioned on the boiler top at the best position for collecting dry steam; it sometimes contains the regulator valves.

Drag Box
The component fitted at the rear of the engine and front of the tender in which the ends of the drawbar connecting engine and tender are housed.

Flue Tubes
Large diameter boiler tubes containing superheater elements fitted above the small smoke tubes.

Fusible Plug
A protective device in the form of a plug screwed into the crown sheet of the inner firebox. The plug has a central core filled with a lead alloy so constituted that, should the water level fall to a dangerous level, the alloy melts and water escapes to the firebox thus relieving pressure and alerting the crew.

Horn Guides
Pairs of polished steel guides fitted very accurately to the main frames of the locomotive, between which the axleboxes fit and are guided in their vertical movement controlled by the spring gear.

Injector
A device which combines either live or exhausted steam with the feed water to the boiler in such a way that its pressure overcomes that of the boiler and so passes the clack valves.

Lap
The amount by which the valve overlaps the steam ports when the valve is in mid-stroke.

Lead
The amount by which the valve uncovers the steam port to admit steam as a 'cushion' before the piston reaches the end of its stroke measured with the crank on its dead centre.

Manifold
A large casting mounted on the rear of the firebox in the cab and from which steam is distributed via valves to the injectors, brake apparatus, carriage warming system and other steam operated auxiliaries such as coal pushers and sanding equipment.

Priming
This occurs when water inadvertently passes from the boiler to the cylinders as a result of the water level being too high in the boiler or agitation/foaming of the water results from excess impurities in it.

Stays and Crown Stays

Threaded metal rods fitted to the firebox to separate and secure the boiler plates round the firebox sides. They are riveted over on their outer ends and secured with nuts on their inner ends to protect them from flame damage. Crown stays are fitted to the firebox roof to secure the crown sheet to the outer wrapper plate.

T.I.A System (Traitement Intégral Armand)

A French system of water treatment fitted by the SR to several of its locomotive classes in order to soften boiler feed water to reduce boiler damage and the frequency of boiler washouts required in hard water areas.

Tractive Effort

A calculation giving an indication of any locomotive's ability to haul or start loads rather than of its output. Usually calculated by the following formula for non-compound locomotives denoting their actual power.

$$\frac{0.85 \, d^2 \, s \, n \, p}{2 \, w}$$

where
d = cylinder diameter in inches
s = piston stroke in inches
n = number of cylinders
p = boiler pressure in p.s.i.
w = driving wheel diameter in inches

The factor 0.85 is used to reduce the design boiler pressure in the calculation to allow for the drop in pressure which takes place between boiler and cylinders.

Washing Out

As the water in the boiler is converted into steam, it releases dissolved salts that form a sludge which accumulates in the water spaces above the firebox foundation ring and also deposits scale on the internal surfaces. These areas need to be washed out and rodded to reduce the causes of priming and poor steaming.

Fig. 279   78022, temporarily fitted with a Giesl ejector, is depicted under repair in Haworth Yard on the Keighley and Worth Valley Railway on 18th August 1976. The 10D shedplate refers to the last BR allocation for the engine, Lostock Hall near Preston, from where it was withdrawn in September 1966.   *(John Edgington)*

266

Appendix 1

BRITISH RAILWAYS STANDARD 4-6-0 and 2-6-0 CLASSES: SUMMARY OF YEAR END TOTALS

End Year Class	1951	1952	1953	1954	1955	1956	1957	1958	1959	1960	1961	1962	1963	1964	1965	1966	1967	1968
4-6-0																		
73000	29	30	50	75	119	149	172	172	172	172	172	172	172	156	115	76	23	0
75000	16	20	45	50	63	68	80	80	80	80	80	80	80	78	67	46	10	0
4-6-0 Total	45	50	95	125	182	217	252	252	252	252	252	252	252	234	182	122	33	0
2-6-0																		
76000	–	10	35	45	60	79	115	115	115	115	115	115	115	108	92	40	0	0
77000	–	–	–	20	20	20	20	20	20	20	20	20	20	20	19	3	0	0
78000	–	4	12	45	55	65	65	65	65	65	65	65	64	60	43	12	0	0
2-6-0 Total	–	14	47	110	135	164	200	200	200	200	200	200	199	188	154	55	0	0
Grand Total	45	64	142	235	317	381	452	452	452	452	452	452	451	422	336	177	33	0

Appendix 2

BR Standard 4-6-0 and 2-6-0 Classes: Boiler Dimensions

Class			73000	75000	76000	77000	78000
BR Designation			BR3	BR4	BR7	BR6	BR8
Boiler Diameter Outside	maximum		5' 8½"	5' 3"	5' 3"	5' 0½"	4' 8"
	minimum		4' 11¹¹⁄₁₆"	4' 9"	4' 9"	4' 5"	4' 3"
Firebox Outside	length		9' 2¹³⁄₁₆"	8' 6"	7' 6"	7' 0"	5' 11"
	maximum width		3' 11⁷⁄₈"	4' 0½"	4' 0½"	4' 0"	4' 0⁷⁄₁₆"
Tubes small	Outside diameter		1⁷⁄₈"	1³⁄₄"	1⁵⁄₈"	1⁵⁄₈"	1⁵⁄₈"
	Number		151	157	156	143	162
large	Outside diameter		5¹⁄₈"	5¹⁄₈"	5¹⁄₈"	5¹⁄₈"	5¹⁄₈"
	Number		28	21	24	18	12
Superheater Elements	Outside diameter		1³⁄₈"	1³⁄₈"	1³⁄₈"	1³⁄₈"	1³⁄₈"
Length between Tubeplates			13' 2⁷⁄₈"	13' 0"	10' 10½"	10' 10½"	10' 10½"
Heating Surface Tubes	sq. ft.		1479	1301	1075	924	924
Firebox	sq. ft.		171	143	131	118	101
Total	sq. ft.		1650	1444	1206	1042	1025
Superheater	sq. ft.		358	258	247	184	124
Grate Area	sq. ft.		28.7	26.7	23.0	20.35	17.5
Working Pressure	p.s.i.		225	225	225	200	200
Firebox Volume	cu. ft.		170	131	115	107	83
Water Surface at half-glass	sq. ft.		103	87	77	72	63
Volume of Steam above half-glass	cu. ft.		96	82	70	76	53

Appendix 2A
BR Standard 4-6-0 and 2-6-0 Classes: Boiler Proportions

Class		73000	75000	76000	77000	78000
Free area through Tubes	large sq. ft.	2.33	1.74	1.96	1.49	0.98
	small sq. ft.	2.22	2.04	1.70	1.59	1.76
	Total sq. ft.	4.55	3.78	3.66	3.08	2.74
Area through large Tubes as % of total		51.1	46.0	53.6	48.4	36.5
Total free area as % of Grate Area		15.9	14.2	16.5	15.2	15.9
Area/Surface ratio large tubes		$1/383$	$1/368$	$1/334$	$1/302$	$1/343$
small tubes		$1/392$	$1/405$	$1/368$	$1/374$	$1/369$
Steam Pipe in Boiler Bore		6"	$5\frac{1}{2}$"	$5\frac{1}{2}$"	$5\frac{1}{2}$"	5"
Cross sectional area sq. in.		28.3	23.8	23.8	23.8	19.6
Regulator Full Open Area sq. in.		26.3	24.3	22.2	24.3	21.5
Superheater Elements Total area sq. in.		27.5	20.6	22.3	17.7	11.1
Steam Pipes to Cylinders Total area sq. in.		39.3	31.8	31.8	31.8	22.1
Blast Pipe Cap Diameter		$5\frac{1}{8}$"	$4\frac{3}{4}$"	$4\frac{3}{8}$"	$4\frac{1}{2}$"	$4\frac{1}{8}$"
Area sq. in.		20.6	17.7	15.0	15.9	13.4
Chimney Throat Diameter		1' $2\frac{1}{4}$"	1' $1\frac{1}{2}$"	1' $0\frac{11}{16}$"	1' $0\frac{3}{4}$"	1' 0"
Area sq. ft.		1.11	1.00	0.88	0.89	0.79
Throat area as % of Grate Area		3.88	3.75	3.82	4.35	4.40
Height between Blast Pipe Cap and Chimney Throat		2' $9\frac{5}{8}$"	2' 7"	2' $7\frac{3}{4}$"	2' 7"	2' $5\frac{1}{2}$"
Taper of Chimney		1 in 14	1 in 14	1 in 14	1 in 14	1 in 14

Appendix 3

BR Standard 4-6-0 and 2-6-0 Classes: Cylinder and Valve Gear Dimensions

Class		73000	75000	76000	77000	78000
Cylinders: Diameter x Stroke		19" x 28"	18" x 28"	17½" x 26"	17½" x 26"	16½" x 24"
Piston Swept Volume (One Cylinder)	cu. in.	7939	7125	6254	6254	5134
Clearance Volume as % of Piston Swept Volume		11.3	10.8	11.6	11.6	N/A
Maximum Piston Thrust	lb.	63,794	57,256	54,119	48,106	42,765
Steam Chests						
Volume between Valve Heads	cu. in.	4056	3895	3037	3037	N/A
Volume as % of Piston Swept Volume		51.1	54.6	48.5	48.5	N/A
Piston Valves	Diameter	11"	10"	10"	10"	8"
Steam Lap		1¹¹/₁₆"	1¹¹/₁₆"	1½"	1½"	¹⁵/₁₆"
Lead		¼"	¼"	¼"	¼"	¼"
Exhaust Clearance		Nil	Nil	Nil	Nil	Nil
Maximum Travel of Valves		7.73"	7.34"	6.25"	6.25"	5.92"
Maximum Cut-off %		78.0	75.0	75.0	75.0	78.0
Travel at 20% Cut-off		4.05"	4.05"	3.62"	3.62"	3.23"

Note: N/A indicates information Not Available

Appendix 3A

BR Standard 4-6-0 and 2-6-0 Classes: Balancing Data

Class		73000	75000	76000	77000	78000
Revolving Masses: Weight per Cylinder	lb.	1419	1415	1316	1189	1172
Reciprocating Masses:						
Total Weight per Cylinder	lb.	826	760	737	737	564
Percentage Balanced		50	50	50	50	50
Unbalanced Weight per Cylinder	lb.	413	380	369	368	282
Ratio of Unbalanced Reciprocating Weight per Cylinder to Total Weight of Locomotive		$^1/_{422}$	$^1/_{400}$	$^1/_{363}$	$^1/_{350}$	$^1/_{391}$
Hammer Blow at 5 Wheel Revolutions per second:						
Per Wheel	tons	2.61	2.40	2.17	2.17	1.53
Per Axle	tons	3.11	2.86	2.58	2.58	1.82
Per Rail	tons	6.95	6.49	5.93	5.93	4.29
Whole Locomotive	tons	8.28	7.73	7.05	7.05	5.11

Appendix 4

Memo from R.C.Bond (5th January 1949)

Notes on the Design of the Proposed New Standards

I am doubtful of the wisdom of building two new designs of 4-6-2 mixed traffic locomotive which differ relatively little in their power characteristics. A proposed Class 5 engine weighing 84.15 tons will be 11.4 tons (equal to 15.7%) heavier than the average of the existing Class 5s. It cannot be said in general that the present Class 5s on all regions are not up to their job. The interchange trials (1948 Locomotive Exchanges) have shown the mixed traffic engines to be economical and well able to do the work required of them with plenty of reserve. Rates of combustion are not excessive and coal consumption both per drawbar horsepower hour and per mile were economical. The increased weight of the proposed new Class 5 Pacific will involve an increased 'first cost' of, say £140 per ton equivalent to £1,600, plus interest and renewal charges of, say 6% per annum, or £96.

Class 5s on the LMR and B1s on the ER&NER run approximately 39,000 and 45,000 miles per year respectively. Average coal consumption during the interchange trials was 46.4 lb per mile. Assuming Class 5 mixed traffic locomotives throughout the country average 42,000 miles per year and burn 50 lbs coal per mile, each will burn 940 tons of coal per year. Suppose the increased grate area of the proposed new design will ensure an increased boiler efficiency and reduced coal consumption to the extent of 5%, then the new engine should for an equal amount of work burn 47 tons of coal less each year. At £2 per ton, this will save £94 per year. Saving on coal is thus balanced by increased annual charges.

There are three further points to consider.
(1) a larger grate area will entail higher standby losses.
(2) footplate staff will demand longer preparation time compared with the existing Class 5s.
(3) repair costs of the trailing truck will not be negligible.

Hence the new Class 5 Pacific, if built as a '5' will cost the Railway Executive more to do a given amount of work compared with the existing Class 5s and will have even more power in hand. Arguments put forward for the wide firebox are sound but to some extent mutually incompatible. If the larger boiler is used to provide maximum steam production, the advantage obtainable from the lower rate of combustion due to large grate is to some extent lost. A scrutiny of the boiler properties of the new Class 5 and existing Class 6s show that the proposed new Class 5 could easily encompass work at present carried out by Class 6s. There is in my view little doubt that in practice the proposed new Class 5s would very soon find themselves on Class 6 work as a regular thing. Hence I propose with some slight increase in weight occasioned by the boiler perhaps being greater by 1" to 1½" in diameter to improve free area characteristics, the proposed Class 5 should be built but put on the road as a Class 6. If found possible to do so, I would suggest
(1) increasing the diameter of the boiler slightly as referred to above and increasing the coupled wheel axle loading to 18 tons which would still give a wide route availability

(2) reducing the factor of adhesion to say 4.5 by making the cylinders slightly larger to an extent which would be determined by whether 6' 0" or 6' 3" coupled wheels are adopted.

Such an engine, as a Class 6, would:
(1) avoid the criticism of being heavier and more costly than existing Class 5s.
(2) go where existing Class 6s with their relatively heavier axle loadings cannot go today.
(3) be only slightly heavier than existing Class 6 engines whereas the new Class 6 at present proposed weighing 92.95 tons would be 7.74 tons equal to 9.1% heavier than the average existing Class 6 engines.

It is in the Class 6 power range much more than in the Class 5 that the disabilities of 4-6-0 engines have made themselves evident in our experience and I think we should be well advised from every point of view to limit ourselves to one design of mixed traffic locomotive which should be a Class 6 as referred to above. I suggest that we should seriously consider the advisability of getting out a Class 5 4-6-0 combining the best points of all existing Class 5 mixed traffic locomotives but which at the same time could be expected to do Class 5 work at less and not greater overall cost which I am afraid would be the case if we went forward with the proposed new Class 5 4-6-2. Existing Class 5 engines are relatively well endowed with grate area in relation to the work they do, which is not the case to the same extent with the Class 6s, except the ER&NER V2 2-6-2s and the SR West Country locomotives.

If however it is decided that both the proposed designs of Pacific shall be built, the following points appear to merit attention.
(a) Why have two different coupled wheel diameters varying only by 3"? There would be considerable advantage from the maintenance point of view in having one diameter each for the coupled wheels and their axles. The difference in axle loading is probably not so great as to demand differences in axle diameters and by using one coupled wheel diameter we could have coupled wheels completely interchangeable between the two classes of locomotive.
(b) If the Class 6 engine were provided with 6' 0" diameter coupled wheels with the tractive effort remaining the same at 30,166 lbs the cylinder diameter at present proposed at 19½" could be reduced to 19". It would then probably be possible to use 19" diameter cylinders, identical between the two classes, on the Class 5 engine. The tractive effort of the Class 5 engine would be increased slightly to 28,255 lbs and its factor of adhesion would be reduced to 4.2. This would probably however not be too low, bearing in mind the sensitive control that will be given by the multiple-valve regulator. It may be stated in reply that the 18½" and 19½" diameter cylinders at present

272

proposed for the Class 5 and Class 6 engines respectively will be cast from the same patterns with a thicker cylinder barrel liner used for the smaller diameter. Be this as it may, there would be the further advantage of interchangeable piston heads between the two classes of engine if the cylinder diameter could, by relatively minor adjustments be made the same. Alternatively, if the Class 5 engine were provided with 6' 3" diameter coupled wheels and the tractive effort maintained at its present value, the cylinders would require to be increased to 19" and if this diameter of cylinder were used on the Class 6 engine in the interests of standardisation, its tractive effort of 30,166 lbs could be maintained by a small increase in the boiler pressure.

(c) Why should the spacing between the coupled wheels be different on the two designs of engine? It would surely be advantageous to increase the spacing of the Class 5 engines to seven feet, the distance between the driving axle and the centre line of the cylinders would thus be identical on both engines. We could expect to have completely interchangeable motion and it might even be reasonable to expect interchangeable coupling and connecting rods. The bar frames of both engines would thus be identical if slight adjustments were made in the dimensions from the leading bogie axle to the front buffer and from the centre line of the trailing trucks to the drag box which differ slightly in the two designs at present. The increase in weight entailed by widening the spacing of the coupled wheels of the Class 5 engine would be negligible and there is the further point that it would probably not be difficult, in working out the detailed design, to ensure the interchangeability of boilers between the two classes of locomotive.

signed, RCB

Appendix 5

Proposals for Standard Procedure for Dealing with Experiments

These proposals are to cover experiments in the Mechanical and Electrical Engineers' and Carriage & Wagon Engineers' Departments.

1. Definition of an Experiment

Trial of :

New detail design (including proprietary fittings).

New materials.

New repair methods (in certain cases).

It does not include:

Engine or vehicle performance testing.

Alterations to rolling stock as a result of an experiment successfully concluded.

2. Initiation and Control

Any Divisional or Regional Officer may request an experiment to be opened on rolling stock or equipment under the control of the Member for Mechanical and Electrical Engineering. This request should be sent through the usual departmental channels to the Regional head of the Mechnical and Electrical Engineers' Department who will act as Controller and whose office will act as central clearing house for all experiments on his Region. There will thus be five central registrys and control points for experiments.

3. Supervision

One or more experimental draughtsmen in each Region to control documentation.

Draughtsmen or inspectors, (as required), for:

(a) records

(b) examinations and spot checks of experimental fiitings in works, sheds, etc., in suitable cases or where early decision or information is required.

4. Procedure

By use of forms rather than correspondence suggested as follows:

Form A: Initiation form will be issued by Controlling Officer, giving nature, origin, object, scope, approximate cost, etc., of proposed experiment. This form to be filled in by applicant for experiment. Controlling Officer's authorisation etc. will be subsequently given on a footnote to this form.

Form B: Notification form for Motive Power and Carriage & Wagon Depots. One issued for each locomotive or vehicle fitted, giving details of experiment and when reports required.

Form C: Periodical Report form for use by Works, Depots and Experimental Section.

Form D: Conclusion form giving details of final results and future action.

5. Periodical Reports

(a) From Works: Yearly (for other than rolling stock experiments).

When vehicle shopped.

On completion.

(b) From Motive Power Depots and Carriage & Wagon Departments:

Yearly, via regional Motive Power Superintendent or Carriage & Wagon engineer.

In addition and in certain cases, experimental staff will submit separate reports.

6. Contact with Motive Power Department and Carriage & Wagon Department.

(a) Motive Power Superintendent or Carriage & Wagon Engineer may ask for experiments to be initiated.

(b) Even where Motive Power Superintendent may not ask for such experiments, they are frequently based on information given by Motive Power Superintendent. In such cases, Motive Power Superintendent would be informed of Controlling Officer's proposals.

(c) Shed reports forwarded annually through Motive Power Superintendent to Controlling Officer.

7. Advice to Railway Executive.

Railway Executive to be given:

(a) list of all current experiments.

(b) advice of all new experiments opened which cost more than £200 in total.

(c) annual report covering:

(1) revisions to list of experiments.

(2) reports on experiments concluded (Form D).

(3) progress with a limited number of experiments in which the Railway Executive is especially interested.

8. Identification

Each locomotive or vehicle which is the subject of an experiment to carry a suitable disc giving experiment number and title. Position of disc and wording to be decided after investigation.

9. Financial Control

Following Railway Executive instructions or in absence of these, according to Regional practice.

The Railway Executive
6th December 1948

Appendix 6

Location of Selected Motive Power Depots

Depot	Area Location	Depot	Area Location
Agecroft	Manchester	Landore	Swansea
Aintree	Liverpool	Lostock Hall	Preston
Aston	Birmingham	Manningham	Bradford
Bank Hall	Liverpool	Millhouses	Sheffield
Bescot	Walsall	Mold Junction	Chester
Botanic Gardens	Hull	Nine Elms	London SR
Bricklayers Arms	London SR	Neasden	London ER/LMR
Bushbury	Wolverhampton	Neville Hill	Leeds
Canklow	Rotherham	New England	Peterborough
Canton	Cardiff	Norwood Junction	London SR
Colwick	Nottingham	Old Oak Common	London WR
Corkerhill	Glasgow	Oxley	Wolverhampton
Cricklewood	London LMR	Parkhead	Glasgow
Croes Newydd	Wrexham	Patricroft	Manchester
Dairycoates	Hull	Percy Main	Newcastle upon Tyne
Dalry Road	Edinburgh	Polmadie	Glasgow
Darnall	Sheffield	Rose Grove	Burnley
Dawsholm	Glasgow	Rowsley	Matlock
Eastfield	Glasgow	St Philip's Marsh	Bristol
Edge Hill	Liverpool	St Rollox	Glasgow
Exmouth Junction	Exeter	St Margarets	Edinburgh
Farnley Junction	Leeds	Saltley	Birmingham
Feltham	London SR	Speke Junction	Liverpool
Ferryhill	Aberdeen	Springs Branch	Wigan
Gorton	Manchester	Springhead	Hull
Grimesthorpe	Sheffield	Stafford Road	Wolverhampton
Haymarket	Edinburgh	Starbeck	Harrogate
Heaton	Newcastle upon Tyne	Stewarts Lane	London SR
Heaton Mersey	Stockport	Stourton	Leeds
Hither Green	London SR	Stratford	London ER
Holbeck	Leeds	Sutton Oak	St Helens
Hurlford	Kilmarnock	Thornton Junction	Glenrothes
Kentish Town	London LMR	Toton	Nottingham
Kings Cross	London ER	Trafford Park	Manchester
Kingmoor	Carlisle	Tyseley	Birmingham
Kittybrewster	Aberdeen	Walton on the Hill	Liverpool
Laira	Plymouth	Willesden	London LMR
		Woodford Halse	Woodford, Northants

Appendix 7

Caledonian Railway Glasgow Area Semaphore Route Indicators

Semaphore Configuration and Code

The Caledonian Railway's Glasgow area semaphore route indicator system was introduced to help signalmen at busy junctions identify trains to and from Glasgow Central. Engines working passenger trains carried a small white two arm semaphore above the top lamp bracket or on the buffer beam, the position of the arms indicating the route to be taken by the train.

Certain lines were jointly operated with the GSWR which had had an equally intensive outer suburban service from Glasgow St Enoch to Kilmarnock on the Barrhead Joint Line and to Ayrshire via Paisley. Before Grouping, the two company's trains had been easily distinguished by their respective liveries but on the formation of the LMS in 1923, this was no longer possible. The situation was further complicated when former Caledonian engines regularly began to appear on ex-GSWR line services.

To avoid confusion, a carefully selected set of indicators was adopted for the Glasgow St Enoch trains; it was not considered necessary to extend the system to other GSWR routes such as the Kilmarnock-Ardrossan and Muirkirk-Ayr lines. By early BR days, the practice had all but lapsed for the St Enoch services apart from those to Greenock Princes Pier. It should be noted that on the Glasgow Central Low Level line, the indicators applied only to outbound services.

The configurations are displayed below with the code given in the adjacent columns.

Note that for Nos. 20 and 21, the position of the arms indicated the direction that westbound Low Level trains took at Stobcross Junction; the configuration was altered at Partick Central to one which would indicate the train's terminus.

Codes 1 and 2 on the Caledonian Railway Route were also referred to as 'Main Line' and were carried by trains serving Edinburgh where appropriate.

Code	Caledonian Railway Routes
1	Glasgow Central and Carlisle via Motherwell.
2	Glasgow Central and Carlisle via Holytown.
3	Glasgow Central and Kirkhill and Burnside.
4	Glasgow Central and Hamilton, Strathaven and Lesmahagow. Also to and from Leith
5	Glasgow Central and Edinburgh direct.
6	Glasgow Central & Low Level trains to Newton; also High Level trains to and from Newton.
7	Glasgow Central to Tollcross.
8	Glasgow Central empty stock trains.
9	Glasgow Central and Gourock, also to Dumbarton or Balloch.
10	Glasgow Central to and from East Kilbride and Low Level trains terminating at Rutherglen. Also Barnton Line.
11	Glasgow Central to and from Renfrew.
12	Glasgow Central to and from Paisley, also to Kilbowie or Clydebank.
13	Glasgow Central to and from Ardrossan or Kilmarnock, via the Cathcart route.
14	Glasgow Central to and from Kilmarnock, via the Barrhead route.
15	Trial running of carriages from St Rollox Works for either Denny West Junction or Stirling (usually between 10.00am and 12noon).
16	Glasgow Central to Coatbridge. Also to and from Balerno.
17	Glasgow Central to Airdrie.
18	Glasgow Central to Maryhill via Kelvin Bridge.
19	Glasgow Central to Maryhill via Partick; also to and from Wemyss Bay.
20	Glasgow Central Low Level Circle trains outbound via Kelvin Bridge and inbound via Partick; also Cathcart Inner Circle ordinary trains.
21	Glasgow Central Low Level Circle trains outbound via Partick and inbound via Kelvin Bridge; also Cathcart Outer Circle ordinary trains
22	–
23	Cathcart Inner Circle relief or special trains.
24	Cathcart Outer Circle relief or special trains.
25	Glasgow Central and Bothwell. Also to and from the North.

Code	Glasgow and South Western Railway Routes
1	Glasgow St Enoch and Ayr.
2	–
3	–
4	Glasgow St Enoch and Stranraer.
5	Glasgow St Enoch and Girvan.
6	Glasgow St Enoch and Largs.
7	–
8	Glasgow St Enoch station pilot.
9	–
10	–
11	Glasgow St Enoch and Renfrew.
12	Glasgow St Enoch and Paisley West, including Corkerhill.
13	Glasgow St Enoch and Ardrossan.
14	–
15	–
16	Glasgow St Enoch and Greenock Princes Pier.
17	Glasgow St Enoch and Kilmarnock via Dalry.
18	–
19	–
20	–
21	–
22	Glasgow St Enoch and Kilmarnock, Dumfries and Carlisle via Barrhead.
23	–
24	–
25	Glasgow St Enoch and Dalry, including Johnstone and Milliken Park.

'The information in Appendix 7 was supplied from several sources including the ScR publications officer and the well - known local Glasgow enthusiast Mr. G.H. Robin. The bulk of the data was first published in Trains Illustrated, Vol. 7, No12, December 1954, page 506. Supplementary information appeared in Modelling Railways Illustrated, November 1995, pp146-7'.

J. Walford
AM030311

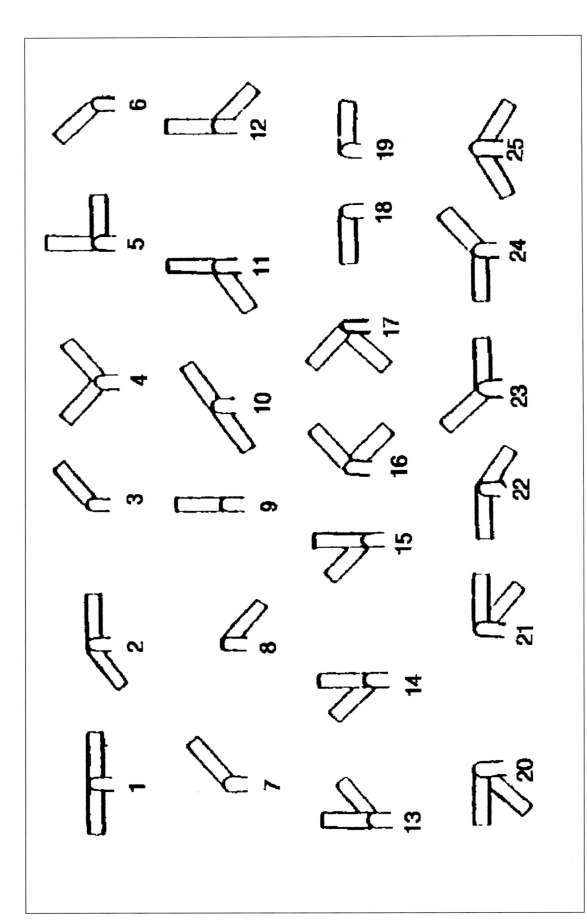

CALEDONIAN RAILWAY GLASGOW AREA SEMAPHORE ROUTE INDICATORS
KEY TO CONFIGURATION CODE

Acknowledgements

Mr. P.J. Atkins

Mr. R. Bond

Mr. D.C.Bradley

Mr. M.J. Burnett

Mr. A.C. Clothier

Mr. P.J. Cupper

Mr. F.K. Davies

Mr. R.H. Deer

Mr. P. Doggett

Mr. G. Evans

Mr. K. Gregory

Mr. P.K. Jones

Mr. A.J. Lait

Mr. E. Langridge

Mr. G. Morris

Mr. K.R. Phillips

Mr. W.B. Price

Mr. B. Radford

Mr. R. Strange

Mr. A.R. Sainty

Mr. G.B. Sullivan

Mr. D. Tee

Mr. J. True

Mr. D.W. Tyreman

Mr. D. Upton

Mr. A. Wild

A Select Bibliography

A Pictorial Record of British Railways Standard Steam Locomotives,
E. Talbot, Oxford Publishing Co. 1982.

The Standard Steam Locomotives of British Railways,
Rodger P. Bradley, David & Charles Ltd. 1984.

British Railways Standard Steam Locomotives,
E. S. Cox, Ian Allan, 1966, 1973.

BR Standard Steam Album,
Alan Williams, Ian Allan 1980.

The Book of the BR Standards,
Richard Derry, Irwell Press 1997.

The Stanier Black Fives,
John F. Clay, Ian Allan 1972.

The Stanier 4-6-0s of the LMS,
J. W. P. Rowledge and Brian Reed, David & Charles 1977

Living with London Midland Locomotives,
A. J. Powell, Ian Allan 1977.

The Last Steam Locomotive Engineer: R. A. Riddles
H. C. B. Rogers, George Allen & Unwin 1970.

Steam Locomotives 1955, 70000-90774. Standards and Austerities
Eric Sawford, Sutton Publishing 1998

The Locomotive Exchanges 1870-1948 and New Light on the Locomotive Exchanges,
Cecil J. Allen, Ian Allan 1949 and 1950 respectively.

British Railways Steam Locomotive Shed Allocations 1950-1968, Part Four, Eastern Region and British Railways Standard
and Austerity Locomotives.
Midland Railway Society 1972

The XPress Locomotive Register, Volume 4, Western Region (ex-GWR) and BR Standard Locomotives (All Regions) 1950-
1960
XPress Publishing 2000

Reference has been made to various issues of the following journals; Railway Observer, Stephenson Locomotive Society
Journal, Railway Magazine, Railway World, Trains Illustrated, Modern Railways, Steam Days, Steam World, Railways South
East, British Railways Illustrated, Railway Locomotives, Locomotives Illustrated.

Some other RCTS Books

BRITISH RAILWAYS STANDARD STEAM LOCOMOTIVES
Volume 1 Background to Standardisation and the Pacific Classes

Immediately British Railways was formed in January 1948, the railway Executive instructed Robert Riddles to design a series of standard locomotive designs. The intention was to gain material savings in running and maintenance costs by adopting as standard the best practices of the four independent companies. In this major new series, the Society presents for the first time the complete story of British locomotive standardisation from the days of the Robinson ROD 2-8-0s to the twelve BR Standard designs totalling 999 locomotives. This book, by Paul Chancellor and Peter Gilbert, presents the Standards' design history and for each of the 66 locomotives in the popular Britannia, Duke and Clan classes its complete construction, modification, allocation and operating history.

Page size 212 x 272mm, Casebound, 184 pages, 151 illustrations including 17 in colour.

Volume 3 The Tank Engine Classes

From Penzance to Wick, the Standard tank classes were designed to modernise secondary route power. Railway enthusiasts throughout the land became familiar with their high running plates which gave the 230 engines of three types their "family" appearance. Author Paul Chancellor presents their full story, from their design origins, construction, modifications, allocation, use and liveries. Whether these engines hauled you reluctantly to school – your reviewer's experience – or you only came across them in preservation, the Class 4's handsome curved tank sides will evoke many a nostalgic memory. With their construction at all six main workshops, local livery variations and national use, there is something for everyone to savour in this book, the second in the Society's BR Standard series. Diagrams of each design are included.

Page size 212 x 272mm, Casebound, 189 photographs including sixteen in colour.

RAISING STEAM ON THE LMS
The Evolution of LMS Locomotive Boilers

This absorbing read opens at Grouping with an LMS locomotive fleet of poor steaming designs unsuited to the heavy and growing traffic levels. The Board's historic decision to hire Stanier from the rival Great Western and his revolutionary work to equip the LMS with a more suitable locomotive fleet revolved around more effective raising and use of steam. The complete story is presented here, from early LMS practice based on pre-Grouping designs, through Stanier's importation of GWR practices, early results and comprehensive details of his design improvements culminating in the largest British pacifics, the Coronation class. The necessary technical content is presented concisely by author Arthur Cook in useful tables and an Appendix, allowing the text to be presented in an infectious, readable style. Readers can almost imagine themselves in the mutual improvement classes at the running shed.

Casebound, page size 180 x 235mm, 233 pages, 138 photographs and drawings, one in colour,

LMS LOCOMOTIVE NAMES
The Named Locomotives of the LMS and its Constituent Companies

The LNWR had a vigorous naming policy and the Midland Railway an equally determined anti-naming stance. The 1923 grouping set the stage for an absorbing battle within the management teams over naming policy with Derby's early policy success followed by Crewe's ultimate victory. Author John Goodman's absorbing read presents the full story of the LMS and its constituent companies' naming policies and the history of each named engine owned by the LMS, a total of 812. The LNWR contributed 668 of these and a complete presentation of its complex re-naming system is an invaluable inclusion.

Casebound, 211 pages, 124 photographs, 25 drawings.
WE OFFER FOR JUST £10.00 WHEN BOUGHT WITH L&NW LOCO NAMES